VAUGHAN WILLIAMS ESSAYS

To William Llewellyn, MBE
and
to the Carthusian Trust

Vaughan Williams Essays

Edited by

BYRON ADAMS

and

ROBIN WELLS

ASHGATE

Published by
Ashgate Publishing Limited
Gower House
Croft Road
Aldershot
Hants GU11 3HR
England

Ashgate Publishing Company
Suite 420
101 Cherry Street
Burlington, VT 05401-4405 USA

Ashgate website: http://www.ashgate.com

British Library Cataloguing in Publication Data
Vaughan Williams essays
   1. Vaughan Williams, Ralph, 1872–1958 - Criticism and interpretation
   I. Adams, Byron, 1955- II. Wells, Robin, 1943-
   780.9'2

Library of Congress Cataloging-in-Publication Data
Vaughan Williams essays / edited by Byron Adams and Robin Wells.
       p. cm.
   Includes bibliographical references and index.
   ISBN 1-85928-387-X (alk. paper)
      1. Vaughan Williams, Ralph, 1872-1958--Criticism and interpretation. I. Adams, Byron, 1955- II. Wells, Robin, 1943-

ML410. V3 V44 2002
780'.92--dc21

                                         2002023201

ISBN 1 85928 387 X

Typeset in 10/11pt Times New Roman by Q3 Bookwork, Loughborough, Leicestershire and printed in Great Britain by MPG Books Ltd, Bodmin, Cornwall.

Contents

List of Music Examples

List of Plates

All reproduced with permission.

List of Tables

Acknowledgements

The profound gratitude of the editors and contributors is offered first to William Llewellyn, MBE, whose foresight and energy made the Ralph Vaughan Williams Research Fellowship a reality, and to the Carthusian Trust, especially to Harry Foot and the Vaughan Williams Fellowship Committee, for their unfailing support, counsel and generosity. The Fellows are indebted to the helpful staff of the Music School at Charterhouse, especially Geoffrey Ford and David Wright, whose hospitality has warmed and encouraged many of them. Many of the Fellows have been grateful for the thoughtfullness and the kindness of Stephanie Wells.

All musicologists who study this composer's life and work are indebted to Ursula Vaughan Williams, without whose unflagging assistance, graciousness, and devotion to her husband's memory this volume would not exist. A gifted poet, her biography of Vaughan Williams remains the *fons et origo* for students of his long and productive life. Her wise and noble stewardship of her husband's legacy is exemplified by her gifts of manuscripts, letters and other primary sources to the British Library, a rare and precious benefice to the British nation.

Special thanks must be rendered to Michael Kennedy, whose indefatigable work as a devoted scholar of Vaughan Williams's music has proved invaluable to the scholarly generations that have followed his inspiring example.

For sharing their insights and expertise, we thank the following individuals: Felix Aprahamian, William Austin, Stephen Banfield, Chris Banks, Philip Brett, Hugh Cobbe, Stephen Connock and the Ralph Vaughan Williams Society, Lenore Coral, Jennifer Doctor, Roy Douglas, Ruth Dyson, Sir Keith Falkner, Robert Fink, Lewis Foreman, Alain Frogley, Sophie Fuller, Andrew Herbert, Deirdre Hicks, Duncan Hinnells, Charles Hoag, Peter Horton, John Huntley, Rolf Jordan, Mai Kawabata, Susan Knowles, Mitchell Morris, Glenn Morrow, Mary Mullinar, Graham Muncy, Sir Roger Norrington, Simona Packenham, Lionel Pike, Anthony Pople, Oliver Neighbour, Sarah Randall, Arthur Searle, Renee Stewart, Peter Ward Jones and John Wilson.

The editors especially wish to express their indebtedness to Louis Niebur for his expert and efficient editorial assistance in the preparation of this volume.

We are also grateful to the following collections, archives and libraries, especially those that have granted us permission to reproduce manuscripts, photographs and other materials from their collections: The British Library (especially the Music Division); The National Sound Archive; The Leith Hill Music Festival; The English Folk Song and Dance Society (Cecil Sharpe House); The Library and librarian of Charterhouse School; The Royal College of Organists; The Harvard Theatre Collection, The Houghton Library, Frederic Woodbridge Wilson, Curator; Huntley Film Archives; The Sidney T. Cox Library of Music and Dance, Cornell University; The Surrey Performing Arts Library; The John Rylands Library (Manchester

University); Royal Opera House; The British Broadcasting Corporation; The British Film Institute; The Library of The Royal College of Music; The Archive of the Arts Council of Great Britain; The National Gallery; The Bodleian Library (Oxford University); Fitzwilliam Museum (Cambridge University) and the Library of the Royal Academy of Music.

We thank Ursula Vaughan Williams for permission to quote from documents in her possession, as well as both Vaughan Williams Ltd and the Vaughan Williams Trust. Oxford University Press, Faber Music, Novello Publishing Ltd., Stainer and Bell Ltd. London, Boosey and Hawkes Publishers Ltd. and *The Spectator* magazine have granted us permission to reproduce musical examples, and both *The Musical Quarterly* and the *International Journal of Musicology* have graciously allowed for the reprinting of articles that originally appeared in their pages.

The editors, contributors and publisher have made every effort to contact copyright holders; any that have been inadvertently omitted here are requested to notify the publisher for prompt amendment to future editions.

Finally, the editors are united in thanking Rachel Lynch of Ashgate Publishing, whose patience, persistence, encouragement and professionalism have been of incalculable value in the creation and production of this volume.

Byron Adams
Robin Wells

List of Ralph Vaughan Williams Fellows, 1985–2002

1985	Byron Adams
1986	Anthony Barone
1987	Murray Dineen
1988	William Spencer
1989	David Conte
1990	Alison Sanders McFarland
1991	Randy Neighbarger
1992	Walter Aaron Clark
1993	Stephen Town
1994	Julian Onderdonk
1995	Rufus Hallmark
1996	Renée Chérie Clark
1997	Nathaniel Geoffrey Lew
1998	Daniel Goldmark
1999	Charles Edward McGuire
2000	Deborah Heckert
2001	Louis Niebur
2002	Eric Saylor

Introduction

Byron Adams

E.M. Forster, who was scarcely prone to hyperbole, once wrote in a letter that Ralph Vaughan Williams was a 'noble' man, high praise indeed coming from such a finely ethical and discriminating sensibility. Characteristically, Forster modified this pronouncement with a caveat,[1] but the word 'noble' continues to echo brightly through this passage, despite the author's equivocation. Vaughan Williams's dignity, his humanity and his fundamental honesty doubtless impressed Forster. The author of *Howard's End* collaborated with the composer in 1934 on the *Abinger Pageant*, which was a prophetic protest against the misuse of England's precious natural resources. Many others besides Forster were charmed by Vaughan Williams's humor and modesty, including countless attractive young women. Still, members of the Leith Hill Festival Choirs, where Vaughan Williams was festival conductor for over fifty years, learned to respect and fear his sudden titanic rages. Vaughan Williams's stubborn indifference to fashion, whether musical, social or political, irritated more than a few of those critics and colleagues who practised a facile adaptability in art and ethics.

Forster, who possessed uncanny powers of discernment, may have recognized the ambiguities that lie at the heart of the composer's richly layered, sophisticated and essentially intellectual personality. Vaughan Williams celebrated the English countryside and worked hard to preserve the heritage of English folk music (although his methods of doing so were as inimitable, conflicted and inconsistent as the man himself), but he composed a tough, urban and socialist symphony titled after the city that he loved so deeply, the *London*. (Vaughan Williams may have enjoyed periodic tramps through lanes and over downs, but he preferred to live in the heart of London.) Although he wrote a substantial body of music using biblical texts, he was an agnostic for most of his life. As Ursula Vaughan Williams writes, 'He was an atheist during his later years at Charterhouse and Cambridge, though he later drifted into a cheerful agnosticism: he was never a professing Christian.'[2] The composer who created vast mystical frescoes based on Christian texts, such as the *Sancta Civitas* and *The Pilgrim's Progress* was the same man who bluntly declared, 'There is no reason why an atheist could not write a good Mass.'[3]

Most controversially, Vaughan Williams was a composer who used folk-song and hymnody to advance a distinctly nationalist agenda. Some have claimed that Vaughan Williams's agenda was at best insular and at worst xenophobic. But these critics forget that this was the man who, after harrowing service as an ambulance orderly and artillery officer in the First World War, worked tirelessly for the creation of a federated Europe. Vaughan Williams's passionate cultural nationalism was at variance with his yearning to erase the national boundaries and petty rivalries that wantonly destroyed millions of lives in the ghastly wars that raged throughout much of the last century. Try as he might, and he did try earnestly, he could not fully reconcile the conflict between his love of his country and what he perceived of as its traditions with his internationalist concern for humanity. And it should be noted that Vaughan Williams did not embrace all British traditions, for, as a left-leaning Radical, he declined knighthood in order to preserve his political independence.

In fact, Vaughan Williams was musically less insular and reactionary than is generally supposed by admirers and detractors alike. In the course of an article on Musorgsky's *Khovanshchina*, Roland John Wiley pointedly observes,

> Surely we should not accept at face value composers' statements about composers, including themselves. They are not always the best sources of information about creative process, and when pride and polemics are involved ... we should not be inclined to agree with them but rather be suspicious of their motives if one disclaims the influence of another.'[4]

In later years, Vaughan Williams understated the profound influence that his erstwhile teacher Maurice Ravel had exercised upon his stylistic development. In a letter to his pupil Elizabeth Maconchy, Vaughan Williams referred to Stravinsky as 'that Russian Monkey-brain',[5] but elements of Stravinsky's brilliant orchestration and rhythmic élan are found in both the 'London' Symphony and the *Concerto accademico*. Paul Hindemith's *Sinfonia Serena* of 1946 may well have had a potent influence upon the structure and instrumentation of the English composer's Eighth Symphony. A partial list of other composers who had a discernible and lasting impact upon Vaughan Williams's music might include Debussy, Bartók, Musorgsky, Dvořák, Rimsky-Korsakov and Puccini, as well as such early loves as J.S. Bach, Wagner, Verdi, Brahms and Gounod. Such a cosmopolitan roster is a testament to the catholic nature of Vaughan Williams's musical predilections and hints at his astonishing ability, shared by all first-rate composers, to absorb a variety of influences while sustaining an authentic and individual style.

Unfortunately, the earlier generations of those who wrote about Vaughan Williams, such as Frank Howes, Hubert Foss and Percy Young, were less likely to investigate the composer's stylistic richness than to collude with him in the creation of a downright, British and homespun persona behind which lurked a sensitive and ambivalent perfectionist. After the composer's death in 1958, Michael Kennedy and Ursula Vaughan Williams loyally accomplished the heroic task of presenting the man and his work as he wished to be viewed by posterity. Their dual task was made more challenging by the adverse critical reaction against Vaughan Williams that had already begun to assert itself during the final years of the composer's long life.

Critical and academic disparagement of Vaughan Williams's music deepened and accelerated throughout the next two decades. With the exception of James Day, Hugh Ottaway and a few other sympathetic authors, little substantial scholarly attention was paid to Vaughan Williams during this period; his music, though savored and performed by thousands in England and America, had become utterly unfashionable. The scholarly neglect of Vaughan Williams reached its nadir during the years surrounding the composer's centenary in 1972; astonishingly, hardly any substantial biographical or musical studies were published to mark this important anniversary.

This sad state of affairs continued into the 1980s, broken only occasionally, such as by the publication of Roy Douglas's charming and informative book of reminiscences. In his preface to *Vaughan Williams Studies*, published in 1996 by Cambridge University Press, Alain Frogley wrote that 'when I first began Vaughan Williams research some ten years ago, the possibility of bringing together a book of this kind seemed to belong strictly to the realms of futuristic fantasy'.[6] Commenting upon the quickening of interest in the composer's work since that time, Frogley notes that: 'One important practical stimulus was the establishment in 1985 of a fellowship, offered by the Carthusian Trust and the Charterhouse School, which enables American and Canadian scholars to spend time in Britain working on Vaughan Williams.'[7]

This volume is a collection of essays written by eleven of those musicologists from North America who have been awarded the Ralph Vaughan Williams Fellowship, created and supported by the Carthusian Trust.

The Fellowship was the inspired idea of William Llewellyn, MBE, who was the Director of Music at Charterhouse from 1965 to 1987. In this post at Vaughan Williams's own school, Llewellyn was fully cognizant of the pressing need for new and fresh research concerning the composer's life and music. He convinced the Carthusian Trust that the historic connections between Vaughan Williams and North America, as well as the continuing and loyal affection of American audiences for Vaughan Williams's work, would provide a stable basis for such a fellowship. On the advice of Ursula Vaughan Williams, Llewellyn then wrote to the chair of the music department at Cornell University, where the composer had been in residence for several months in 1954. The faculty of the Cornell University Department of Music, encouraged by the great scholar of twentieth-century music William Austin, nominated Byron Adams as the first fellow in 1985. Since then a series of fellows, often graduate students or young academics, have journeyed to Charterhouse each summer for an intensive period of research. This tradition continues under the supervision of Robin Wells, William Llewellyn's successor as Director of Music at Charterhouse.

As evinced by the selection of essays published here, the fellows have created an impressive, wide and detailed body of scholarship dealing with Vaughan Williams's protean achievement as a composer. Many of these essays were read as papers during a week-long Vaughan Williams Symposium, sponsored by the Carthusian Trust, that was held at Charterhouse in July of 2000. The essays collected in this volume range over a wide variety of topics and genres, including symphony, opera, dance, song, hymnody and film music. Byron Adams's manuscript study of the Sixth Symphony reveals Vaughan Williams's compulsive perfectionism, while Murray Dineen offers a searching meditation upon the intersection between aesthetics and formal procedures in the Fifth Symphony. Stephen Town investigates the origins and initial sketches of *A Sea Symphony* as well as examining the varied and sundry contemporary British influences upon that massive score. Charles Edward McGuire touches upon the 1910 première of *A Sea Symphony* in the course of a fascinating investigation of Vaughan Williams's relationship to prominent English music festivals during the first decade of the twentieth century.

Several essays have as their topic Vaughan Williams's engagement with both stage and screen. Nathaniel Lew's study of Vaughan Williams's operatic morality *The Pilgrim's Progress* traces its development from incidental music for an amateur theatrical held in Reigate in 1906 to its première at Covent Garden in 1951. Walter Clark demonstrates how Vaughan Williams employs octatonicism to symbolize the minatory forces of nature in his opera *Riders to the Sea*. In her essay on Vaughan Williams's 'masque for dancing', *Job*, Alison McFarland illuminates Vaughan Williams's complex interaction with the visual art of William Blake. In a different context, Daniel Goldmark elucidates Vaughan Williams's musical response to visual images through a survey of the composer's music for films.

Both Rufus Hallmark and Renée Chérie Clark make important contributions to the relatively slim body of scholarship concerning Vaughan Williams's songs. On one hand, Hallmark's essay contains an investigation of the origins of Vaughan Williams's early cycle using texts by Robert Louis Stevenson, *Songs of Travel*. Clark, on the other hand, provides a penetrating examination of the circumstances behind the creation of the *Four Last Songs*, music that Vaughan Williams composed in his mid-eighties. Finally, Julian Onderdonk reveals the intimate and fascinating connections between Vaughan Williams's activities as a collector of folk-song and as an editor of hymnals.

In what Alain Frogley has felicitously referred to as a 'curious synchronicity',[8] interest in Vaughan Williams has increased exponentially since the fellowship was founded in 1985. In addition to his consummate editing of *Vaughan Williams Studies*, Alain Frogley has produced an invaluable monograph, *Vaughan Williams's Ninth Symphony*, published in 2001 by Oxford University Press. In 1998, Lewis Foreman edited an intriguing volume of essays, *Vaughan Williams in Perspective*, published under the aegis of Albion Press Ltd, which featured the work of a younger generation of scholars based in England, such as Jennifer Doctor, Duncan Hinnells and Andrew Herbert. The same press recently reissued Wilfrid Mellers's problematic but provocative study, *Vaughan Williams and the Vision of Albion*. Oxford University Press published an extensively revised edition of James Day's useful short biography in 1998; several bibliographies have appeared in print, including a helpful discography complied by Stephen Connock. Imaginative theorists such as Lionel Pike and Anthony Pople have begun to forge an analytical vocabulary flexible enough to elucidate the composer's subtle use of tonality. At this writing, all scholars of the composer's life and music are eagerly awaiting the publication of Hugh Cobbe's monumental edition of Vaughan Williams's collected correspondence. The founding and flourishing of the Vaughan Williams Society, along with its lively and varied *Journal*, has provided a forum for those scholars, performers and listeners who love the music and seek to learn more about the man and his milieu.

Much remains to be accomplished, of course. Despite the musicological activity outlined above, and represented by this volume, scholars are just beginning to plumb the depths of Vaughan Williams's oceanic achievement. Only imaginative analysis and meticulous manuscript study can illuminate fully Vaughan Williams's technical assurance and formal inventiveness. In addition to such research, biographical studies must be undertaken to place Vaughan Williams firmly within an informed and specific cultural and historical context. And, finally, there is Vaughan

Williams's music itself, which must continue to be studied and listened to with unflagging care and attentiveness, for this music contains within it the essence of what Forster identified so aptly as its composer's nobility.

Notes

1   P.N. Furbank, *E.M. Forster: A Life.* vol. 2, *Polycrates' Ring (1914–1970)* (London: Secker and Warburg, 1978), 226. Furbank notes that Forster liked and admired Vaughan Williams although he thought that the composer could be 'chuckle-headed – a "goose" – in matters of judgement'.
2   Ursula Vaughan Williams, *R.V.W.: A Biography of Ralph Vaughan Williams* (Oxford: Oxford University Press, 1964), 29.
3   Ibid., 138.
4   Roland John Wiley, 'The Tribulations of Nationalist Composers: A Speculation Concerning Borrowed Music in *Khovanshchina*', in *Musorgsky: In Memoriam 1881–1981*, ed. Malcolm Brown (Ann Arbor: UMI Research Press, 1982), 168.
5   Quoted in Jennifer Doctor, '"Working for her own Salvation": Vaughan Williams as teacher of Elizabeth Maconchy, Grace Williams and Ina Boyle', in *Vaughan Williams in Perspective*, ed. Lewis Foreman (London: Albion Music Ltd, 1998), 197.
6   Alain Frogley, 'Preface', *Vaughan Williams Studies*, ed. Alain Frogley (Cambridge: Cambridge University Press, 1996), xi.
7   Ibid., xii.
8   Ibid., xii.

Chapter 1

The Stages of Revision of Vaughan Williams's Sixth Symphony

Byron Adams

For William Llewellyn

The appearance in 1948 of Ralph Vaughan Williams's Sixth Symphony created both an overwhelmingly favorable impression and a certain degree of incomprehension. Following the serene and diatonically modal Fifth Symphony (1943), the violent, chromatic and octatonic modality of the Sixth Symphony was especially startling to the work's first listeners and led critics and commentators to seek a programmatic basis for the score's restless intensity of expression. Frank Howes rightly maintained that the Sixth Symphony was a 'war symphony',[1] while others wrote of the mysterious Epilogue as a representation of a landscape devastated by atomic bombardment.[2]

As was his wont in such situations, the composer vehemently rejected such speculation. As he remarked to his musical assistant Roy Douglas: 'It never seems to occur to people that a man might just want to write a piece of music.' However, Vaughan Williams would later hint of a possible inner programme for the Sixth Symphony. In a letter written 22 January 1956 to Michael Kennedy, he states: 'With regard to the last movement of my No. 6, I do NOT BELIEVE IN meanings and mottoes, as you know, but I think we can get in words nearest to the substance of my last movement in "We are such stuff as dreams are made on, and our little life is rounded by a sleep." '[3]

According to the composer's programme note, the Sixth Symphony 'was begun probably about 1944 and finished in 1947'.[4] Although his recollections of the chronology of his works are sometimes less than exact, Vaughan Williams's own testimony regarding the origins of the Sixth Symphony is the best information presently available. The symphony was sufficiently complete by 14 July 1946 for the composer to hear it played through at the piano by Michael Mullinar, his friend and former student, to whom the symphony is dedicated. The first mention of the work in the correspondence between the composer and his musical assistant, Roy Douglas, occurs in a letter dated 13 February 1947 that Vaughan Williams begins, 'I have been foolish enough to write another symphony.' It was nearly seven months later, however, that Douglas actually received scores of the work from which to copy a fair full score.[5]

There are no holograph sketches or sketchbooks presently available in the British Library collection of Vaughan Williams's manuscripts that could illuminate the origins of the Sixth Symphony. Vaughan Williams placed little value on his

1

sketchbooks and manuscripts, sometimes giving manuscripts to friends or simply discarding them. Enough sketch pages and sketchbooks of other symphonic works do survive to provide insight into Vaughan Williams's process when beginning an orchestral score.

Vaughan Williams often begins by noting down basic ideas and then gradually expands those ideas into larger units, concentrating especially on the development of small motivic and rhythmic cells into thematic material. He organises this thematic material into paragraphs, concentrating on the melodic continuity of entire sections while occasionally adding a bass line, a harmonic progression, or a rhythmic alteration or addition as he proceeds. At this stage the music is notated on two, occasionally four, and rarely three, staves of music paper, suggesting an embryonic piano reduction.

Vaughan Williams then further expands and refines these sections. Each section becomes longer, and the musical paragraphs are arranged into entire pages and chapters. Several variants of a given passage may be made, such as the holograph sketches made for the opening of the last movement of the Third Symphony (*Pastoral*, 1922, BL Add. MS 50369). At this point the harmonic successions begin to be established, and instrumental indications may also appear, although these may be found in earlier sketches – as is the opening horn call of the Fifth Symphony (BL Add. MS 50371). Invariably Vaughan Williams uses his final draft rather than an earlier version of a sketched passage, as Beethoven occasionally did.

Three manuscript sources for the Sixth Symphony are in the British Library: an incomplete holograph short score, a complete fair copy of the short score prepared by Michael Mullinar[6] with additions and revisions in Vaughan Williams's hand; and a holograph full score containing extensive revisions. A fourth manuscript source is in the library of the Royal College of Music. This consists of a fragmentary piano solo reduction of a section of the slow movement and the Scherzo; the handwriting of this fragmentary piano solo reduction is also that of Michael Mullinar, with additions, deletions and corrections by Vaughan Williams.

The earliest manuscript source, the holograph short score, represents the organization of the sketch materials into a cogent and continuous form. The first three movements in this holograph short score are cast in a two-piano format using four staves, while the Epilogue exists in both a solo piano and two-piano format. This holograph short score is missing two passages from the first movement and the Scherzo; these passages will be discussed later in relation to revisions made in those sections of the symphony.

Owing to confusion caused by the disparity in the kinds of manuscript paper used, the holograph short score is not a single entity but is bound in four separate volumes. The first movement and a 166-measure section that roughly corresponds to the first 160 measures of the Scherzo in its final form (with 17 canceled or rewritten measures, including those found on addition sheets) are bound in a large volume also containing a fair copy of the short score prepared by Mullinar (BL Add. MS 50374). The second movement, the continuation of the Scherzo, and the piano solo and two-piano versions of the last movement are each bound in a small volume (BL Add. MS 50373 A, B, C). The incomplete first movement and the section corresponding to the opening 160 measures of the Scherzo (BL Add. MS 50374) are written predominantly in black ink, with some use of blue ink (the addition sheets are also in blue ink); alterations and cancellations are made in pencil. Vaughan Williams uses both recto and verso of folios of irregular stave size, but each consistently has 20 staves. This manuscript contains 11 folios written recto and verso, one folio written only on one side, and five smaller insertion sheets.

The second movement (Book A), the Scherzo continuation (Book B), and the Epilogue (Book C) are written in quarto manuscript books; each book originally contained 24 pages of 12 staves each. Book A consists of a title page, 19 pages written recto and verso, and one blank page. Book B has a title page with 'Symphony, Scherzo continuation' written on it at the top and contains 16 pages, 14 of which are written recto and verso, and one blank page. A curious feature of Book B is that fragments of old orchestral, choral and dance-band parts, clearly not by Vaughan Williams, are found on sides of four pages, perhaps the result of wartime paper shortages. In addition to these old choral and orchestral parts, page 14 of Book B is a sketch for a passage of Vaughan Williams's opera *The Pilgrim's Progress*, beginning at measure 34 of Scene II (at the words 'Cast thy burden upon the Lord') and continuing until rehearsal 2 in the published vocal score. Book C contains a title page and 12 pages written recto and verso in black ink and dark blue pencil with some revisions in light blue ink and cancellations made in pencil.

The fragmentary piano solo reduction in the Royal College (RCM. MS 5360d.) consists of part of the second movement, from five bars before rehearsal 6 to the end (three pages, recto and verso), and the complete Scherzo (ten pages, recto and verso). The music is notated on 12-stave manuscript paper, with black ink predominating. Mullinar used blue ink for certain revisions in the Scherzo. Vaughan Williams's additions and changes are made in graphite pencil and green pencil. Red pencil is used only for marking rehearsal numbers, which do not match those of the published score. There are also additions by Vaughan Williams affixed on the manuscript with brown postal tape.

This fragmentary piano solo reduction has an interesting and involved history. On 10 June 1947, Vaughan Williams arranged for a series of four private auditions of the symphony at the Royal College.[7] These performances were given for an invited audience of about forty colleagues and conductors in order to seek their advice concerning technical and formal details of the new work. The pianist on this occasion was Michael Mullinar. Mary Mullinar remembered that her husband copied out the score he used for the Royal College performances directly from Vaughan Williams's holograph short score.[8] Roy Douglas, who was Vaughan Williams's musical assistant from 1944 until the composer's death in 1958, was present for these performances. Douglas recalled that Mullinar performed from a complete solo piano version of the score.[9] Douglas remembered that the piano reduction of the symphony sent to him on 10 July 1947 was cast on two staves. Douglas further speculated that Vaughan Williams may have returned this score to Mullinar as a gift along with the holograph full score. Upon Mullinar's death in 1973, his widow donated the holograph full score of the Sixth Symphony, given to him by the composer, to the British Library. At that time a piano solo score of the symphony was not discovered in Mullinar's library; only in 1976 did the fragmentary piano solo reduction come to light at the Royal College. This score – which surely represents the surviving portion of a complete piano solo reduction by Mullinar of the symphony – was given to the library of the Royal College and catalogued there in the late 1980s.

Mullinar also made a fair short score of the symphony that is consistently in two-piano format (BL Add. MS 50374). As there are fingerings written into this score from time to time, this fair short score must have been used for a private performance at some point. (Perhaps this fair short score was made for Vally Lasker and Helen Bidder, who often assisted Vaughan Williams by playing over new works for him on two pianos.[10]) Mary Mullinar speculated that this fair short score was the one used by her husband for the Royal College performances, for she recalled that her husband may have relied on his formidable skill as a score reader to make the necessary reduction from four staves in performance.[11] The discovery of the fragmentary piano solo reduction casts doubt upon this hypothesis, however; the complexities of the Sixth Symphony evidently defeated even Mullinar's remarkable expertise.

This fair short score in two-piano format consists of 22 16-stave folios (43 numbered pages), with 11 insertion sheets in Vaughan Williams's hand, all but one of which are written on both sides. The same size of paper is used by the copyist throughout, using both recto and verso of each folio except for the last page of the first movement. Black ink predominates except for one passage in the Scherzo corresponding to one measure before rehearsal 29 to the end of the published edition, where blue ink is used. (Mullinar obviously ran out of ink at this point.) There are cancellations and revisions made in both green and graphite pencil by Vaughan Williams, just as there are in the fragmentary piano solo reduction. Red ink occasionally appears in the Scherzo. Among the several additions made by the composer is a new opening page for the Scherzo.

The final and latest manuscript source for the Sixth Symphony is the holograph full score dating from 1947 (BL Add. MS 58072). This consists of 82 folios numbered recto/verso (163 numbered pages), with some confusion in the ordering of the folio sides numbered 140 to 145. Revisions have obviously caused the irregular pagination here; there are two folio sides numbered 140, including a blank folio with that number as well as an empty verso of the folio numbered 143. An unnumbered blank folio is bound between pages 30 and 31, as well as a title page for the Epilogue numbered 149 a/b with the music proper beginning on the following folio, numbered 149. The verso of the final folio of this holograph full score is blank.

As in the holograph short score, Vaughan Williams uses different sizes of manuscript paper for the holograph full score. A wide variety of orchestral-sized paper is used, with the paper of the first movement distinctly larger than that used for the other movements. The holograph full score is written in black and dark blue ink with additions made in varying shades of blue ink, as well as graphite pencil, red pencil and, less frequently, blue pencil. For revisions Vaughan Williams attaches new manuscript pages over the original, often using brown postal tape, with occasional use of transparent tape. These revision pages are fitted above the originals with great ingenuity, sometimes resulting in a mosaic-like pattern.

Vaughan Williams's musical handwriting warrants a brief description. Although naturally left-handed, Vaughan Williams was trained to write with his right hand in childhood, and this difficulty, combined with the nervous rapidity with which he notated his music, contributed to the creation of a striking, unwieldy, and occasionally obscure musical handwriting. Although his handwriting at the later stages of his career could scarcely be considered tidy, Vaughan Williams is nevertheless obviously concerned with the clarity of his notation, especially in the clear indications for revisions.

The 1947 holograph full score, along with a piano reduction, served as the sources of Roy Douglas's fair copy of the full score. Douglas's fair copy was in turn the basis for the 1948 Oxford University Press edition. Unfortunately, the Douglas fair score was used as a working rental score, with subsequent revisions pasted over the original pages and with conductor's markings all but obliterating some passages. This makes the Douglas fair score virtually useless as a manuscript source. Thus it is not clear that Vaughan Williams used the Douglas fair score to revise the symphony for the 1950 revised edition published by Oxford University Press, although he used all three primary sources found in the British Library to sketch in the 1950 revisions.

The most recent and accurate edition of the Sixth Symphony was published in 1983 by Edition Eulenberg (No. 1507). This re-engraving of the score, prepared with scrupulous care as the result of Roy Douglas's participation, is the most reliable edition of the symphony, with many corrections made for the first time. It cannot be stressed too strongly that an approach to Vaughan Williams's late scores based solely on manuscripts in his hand would be both harmful and misleading, as the composer relied on the published score as most fully representing his final intentions.

The process of revision was not necessarily complete when a score was published, however. Vaughan Williams revised the Second Symphony (*London*, premièred 1914) no less than three times (1918, 1920 and 1934), ultimately reducing the duration of the score by more than ten minutes. In the early 1950s a projected series of recordings led Vaughan Williams to revise the *Pastoral*, Fifth, and Sixth Symphonies. The alterations in the scores of the *Pastoral* and Fifth symphonies were made to clarify the instrumental balance and were comparatively modest in scope, while the changes made in the Scherzo of the Sixth Symphony were more substantive.

It is significant that the revisions of this symphony, made in stages, occurred after performances. Revisions were made as a result of the 14 July 1946 private audition when Michael Mullinar played the score for Vaughan Williams at the composer's home in Dorking.[12] Further revisions were made between the 10 June 1947 performance given by Mullinar at the Royal College of Music and 10 July when Roy Douglas received the holograph full score and a piano arrangement from which he copied the fair full score.[13] An alteration in the orchestration of the Scherzo was made after the private orchestral run-through on 16 December 1947 by the BBC Symphony Orchestra conducted by Sir Adrian Boult at BBC Maida Vale Studios.[14] The final revisions, including clarifications of the orchestration and thematic additions to the Scherzo, were made in 1950. These revisions came not only after the première given on 21 April 1948 by Boult and the BBC Symphony Orchestra,[15] but after over one hundred subsequent performances, publication of an engraved score and two recordings as well.

Vaughan Williams paid meticulous attention to detail. The manuscript sources of the Sixth Symphony are covered with hundreds of small corrections, additions and clarifications that affect the musical substance of the work, as well as numerous alterations in dynamics and articulation. These smaller revisions fall into three basic categories: concern for melodic direction and motivic consistency, phrase length and repetition, and clarity and convenience of orchestration.

An example of a melodic alteration is found five measures after rehearsal 3 in the second movement. As altered in the holograph full score, the B flat on the second beat is altered to a C natural, giving the thematic line greater directional thrust while reinforcing the important motivic contour of alternating major and minor thirds found throughout the score (Example 1.1).

Example 1.1   Rehearsal 3 in the second movement

Allied to this concern for thematic coherency and consistency is a desire for maximum concision within phrases. While there are only two expansions of material in the revisions of the symphony, there are several deletions of repetition. An omission made to tighten the musical argument is the excision of two measures (½ measure, 1 measure, ½ measure), six measures after rehearsal 10 in the fair score of the first movement. This change was made before this passage was orchestrated in the holograph full score. While this excision predates the performance at the Royal College, several omissions were made after this date, such as the deletion of two repeated measures (initially a four-measure unit) two measures before rehearsal 10 in the second movement. This deletion is found both in the fair short score and in the fragmentary piano solo reduction.

Vaughan Williams was particularly careful to adjust his orchestration in order to obtain the optimum clarity, especially to assure the projection of the basic melody. Often he revised the orchestration to reinforce a melodic line; an example of this is the 1950 addition of the xylophone to the melodic line four measures before rehearsal 6 in the Scherzo. Selected measures within tutti passages are rescored in the holograph full score in order to clarify the orchestral layout and improve the instrumental part-writing. Such a passage is found on the folio side numbered 130 of the holograph full score, where two measures, corresponding to two measures before rehearsal 24 in the Scherzo, have been taped over for purposes of orchestral realignment.

Vaughan Williams was also concerned with the effect of his scoring upon the orchestra personnel, striving to avoid making awkward demands upon the instrumentalists. One such alteration is in the first movement, second measure, in the oboe part. In order to give the oboes a chance to breathe and spare them what was originally an uncomfortable leap from a low B on the second sixteenth of the last beat to a C sharp on the following sixteenth, the C sharp was omitted. This sort of improvement abounds throughout the holograph full score.

The metronome markings change considerably in the process of revision. According to Roy Douglas, Vaughan Williams evidently did not own a metronome,[16] and he may have felt uncomfortable assigning numerical tempo indications to his scores. He generally errs on the fast side in his initial metronomic approximations, which is certainly the case for the Sixth Symphony. The holograph full score has an impossibly fast ♩ = 140 for the first movement, which is then modified to a still very rapid ♩ = 128, with the final indication in the published scores of ♩ = 100. The second movement was initially marked ♩ = 78 in the holograph full score, with a subsequent change to the present ♩ = 72. The metronome markings for the Scherzo in the fair short score are ♩ = 150 and 𝆗 = 75; these incredible directions are altered in the holograph full score to ♩ = 150, which is crossed out in turn with ♩ = 132 added in pencil. All published editions, including both the 1948 and 1950 editions, carry the indication ♩ = 120–128 for the Scherzo, which makes it difficult to verify Sir John Barbirolli's claim that the composer altered the metronome marking of the Scherzo after a 2 June 1949 performance by Barbirolli and the Hallé Orchestra.[17] The Epilogue is marked ♩ = 60 in the fair short score, but the holograph full score and the published scores all bear the indication ♩ = 56.

The most illuminating revisions of the Sixth Symphony are those that reveal the composer searching for new solutions to major creative challenges. Certain of these challenges necessitated the reconsideration of earlier attempts, significantly changing thematic content, tightening formal cogency, and improving orchestral clarity. From the myriad changes made on the symphony, the larger ones particularly exemplify Vaughan Williams's process of revision.

Two of the earliest revisions made in the first movement are of unusual interest. Both are found in the holograph short score; the final versions agree in the fair short score and the holograph full score. These revisions were made between the private performance of 14 July 1946 and the Royal College performance 10 June 1947.

The first of the two early revisions is an alteration of the second measure of the first movement. The original measure has been crossed out and a second draft written in above. This second variant is also rejected, and a third and final version is written below the initial idea (Example 1.2).

Example 1.2   Drafts of second bar, Movement One

The second of the earlier revisions, dealing with the conclusion of the first movement, is more extensive. After a large gap in the holograph short score (corresponding to nine measures before rehearsal 14 to three measures after rehearsal 16, 27 measures in all, see Example 1.3), the initial draft of this conclusion is markedly different from the final version of this passage. The conclusion was

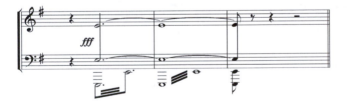

Example 1.3   First draft, conclusion of Movement One

originally longer, harmonized differently, and included a final nine-measure variation on material from the movement's first five measures. The same paper and ink are used before and after the gap in the manuscript.

Vaughan Williams further modified this section, writing the new material in the same ink on smaller-sized manuscript paper, inserting the new sheets into the holograph short score. This second version, including small alterations made in the course of orchestration, was copied into the fair full score and is essentially the same in the holograph full score and the published editions.

The only two expansions of material made in the symphony are both found in the first movement. The first is a three-measure transition beginning three measures before rehearsal 8. This was appended to both the fair short score and the holograph full score after the performance at the Royal College and before to the Roy Douglas fair full score. The original page contained the four measures beginning in the published score at rehearsal 8. An addition sheet with the new transition has been loosely attached to the front of the original; another addition sheet, corresponding to three measures after rehearsal 8, has been added to the verso of the original folio side.

The second expansion consists of two measures added four measures after rehearsal 9. These measures are not found in any of the manuscript sources or in the 1948 edition. Vaughan Williams probably inserted a new sheet into either a copy of the 1948 edition or a hire score.

The title page in Book A of the holograph short score, which contains the second movement, has the words 'theme for Flemish Farm' written at the top and subsequently canceled. This would suggest that material from this movement was intended for the score of the 1943 wartime propaganda film of that name. Although the opening music of the second movement may have been initially composed for the film score, an examination of Vaughan Williams's scores for *Flemish Farm* (BL Add. MS 50429 and 50430) fails to disclose any such connection.

A vague programmatic basis for the second movement is suggested by the word 'Processional' written at the head of the first folio of the second movement in the holograph full score. Vaughan Williams – as if to forestall any programmatic speculation – crossed this out, substituting the more prosaic direction of 'Moderato'.

One of the few harmonic adjustments made in the symphony is found in the second movement, four measures before rehearsal 2. In the original version of this passage, which exists in both the holograph and fair short scores, the upper strings move in parallel open-position triads in second inversion. In the holograph full score and all published editions the violins move in parallel sixths, doubled an octave lower by violas and cellos. This effective alteration evidently occurred to the composer in the course of orchestration.

Two other early revisions in the holograph short score of the second movement are concerned with rhythm and melodic line. Between rehearsals 12 and 13, Vaughan Williams alters the original irregular spacing of the trumpet figure to a regular, terrifyingly insistent pattern. The composer writes the final version of the trumpet figure on single staves that are cut into long strips and taped directly above the original irregular patterns.

The melody assigned to the English horn at rehearsal 14 was initially longer by three measures (Example 1.4). (This English horn solo is found in its final form in

Example 1.4   Movement Two

the fragmentary piano solo reduction, suggesting that this was an early revision.) The length of the melodic line and the placing of the accompanying triplet pattern gave Vaughan Williams considerable trouble. He experimented with ways to score this accompaniment, making a tentative first assignment of this figure to three solo cellos.

Two revisions of this movement, involving transitional passages, were made after the Royal College performance. The first is found four measures before rehearsal 5 and appears in all the manuscript sources in the British Library. This transition, originally six measure of ascending cello line, is now telescoped into four measures.

The second revised transition, located between rehearsals 6 and 7, was also longer in its original form and is changed in all the manuscript sources in the British Library. The compression of this transition is more radical than the first, however, reduced from 20 measures to five measures in the final version – the original form of this passage is visible beneath the taped-on correction sheet in the fair short score. While the second version of this passage in the holograph full score is written on orchestral paper obviously different in size from the paper used throughout this manuscript, the light blue ink matches the ink used to revise the transition three measures before rehearsal 8 in the first movement. This shade of ink is found only in these two sections, suggesting that both passages were revised at the same time, before Roy Douglas copied the fair full score.

The Scherzo of the symphony was the most difficult movement for the composer to cast in its final form. Important changes are made at every stage of the revision process. Unlike revisions to the other movements, those made to the Scherzo in 1950 are important additions that significantly enhance the movement's impact.

Unfortunately, a large gap exists in the holograph short score of the Scherzo, corresponding to the passage between rehearsals 39 and 47. Only two fragments survive for this section: two drafts of the same 12 measures beginning at rehearsal 39. Of these two fragments, one is clearly a later version of the other, possessing a melodic line much closer to the final form. As mentioned above, the holograph short score of the Scherzo was started on large orchestral paper and continued into a quarto manuscript book; this may account for the missing pages.

An important early revision of the Scherzo alters the opening section up to rehearsal 2. The first eight measures remain constant in both the holograph and fair short scores. The following section, however (which corresponds to three measures before rehearsal 1 to rehearsal 2), has a melodic contour quite different from the final version (Example 1.5).

Example 1.5   Early draft, Scherzo

Vaughan Williams expands this section from seven to eleven measures by adding new material from three measures before rehearsal 1 to four measures after rehearsal 1. The descending rushing scales four measures before rehearsal 2 remain the same in both versions. The change is written on an addition sheet inserted into the holograph short score, and Vaughan Williams provides an unusually neat revision sheet for insertion into the fair short score. The holograph full score contains the revised passage, suggesting that this alteration was made during orchestration before the Royal College performance, but either during or after the short score was copied.

One of the most extensive revisions of the symphony, between rehearsals 14 and 16 in the Scherzo, concerns the trio theme scored for saxophone solo. The first form of this theme, in the holograph short score, is 13 measures long and is blandly modal and rhythmically square in comparison to the more chromatic music of the preceding section. The original accompaniment reflected this square rhythm, with regular running semiquavers above a bass line cast in regular quavers placed consistently after the beat (Example 1.6).

Example 1.6   Early draft, Saxophone theme, Scherzo

This passage, with a slightly more chromatic upbeat, was initially the same in the fragmentary piano solo reduction, the fair short and holograph full scores as in the holograph short score. Vaughan Williams then substantially revised the saxophone theme, its accompaniment, and all the other music of the Scherzo connected with it. The theme is recast rhythmically, through the introduction of more syncopation and two measures of triple time, and melodically, becoming more chromatic, with an emphasis on the interval of a tritone, a prominent melodic feature throughout the movement. The accompaniment is rewritten to suit the new form of the theme. (In its revised form this saxophone theme sounds suspiciously like a grotesque jazz improvisation on Stephen Foster's 'Swanee River', which, under the title 'Old Folks At Home', Vaughan Williams had earlier arranged for male chorus.[18]) The running semiquavers have been adjusted, and the bass, which has the distinctive timbre of pizzicato parallel fifths, is given the new rhythmic and contrapuntal interest. The overall effect of these changes is to heighten the jazzy and diabolical aspects of this passage, which is fitting in a movement that was initially inspired by the deaths of members of a jazz band in the bombing of the Café de Paris during the Blitz.[19]

The tutti reprise of the saxophone theme between rehearsals 16 and 18 was accordingly altered after the theme itself was rewritten. All alterations were first made into the fragmentary piano solo reduction and the fair short score; it was then orchestrated on to addition sheets attached to the holograph full score. Measures in the holograph full score that have been changed by erasure, such as the measure at rehearsal 14 that has been altered from duple to triple meter, indicate that the original version of this passage is the same in the fragmentary piano solo reduction, the fair short score and the holograph full score.

The manuscript paper used for the revision of the saxophone theme of the Scherzo matches the paper used for the second addition sheet attached to the holograph full score for the revision made three measures after rehearsal 8 in the first movement. This clearly suggests that these revisions to the holograph full score were made at roughly the same time, after Mullinar's performance at the Royal College. As Douglas did not recall having to recopy any of the revisions later, and as they are not mentioned in the correspondence between Douglas and Vaughan Williams, these alterations may well have been made before the copying of the fair full score. This further suggests that the four primary manuscript sources were complete in their original forms before 10 June 1947.

Therefore, many of the revisions made in all manuscript sources or in the fair short and holograph full scores were probably made either during the course of the Royal College performances or in the month between that event and the posting of the scores to Roy Douglas.[20]

Another striking change made in the Scherzo that may also date from this period is the complete recasting of the transitional passage between rehearsals 38 and 39. In its original form, found in the fragmentary piano solo reduction as well as the fair short and holograph full scores, this section offers a marked contrast to the final version, with a different thematic contour and a quiet conclusion (Example 1.7). The present dramatic version was added to the fragmentary piano solo arrangement and fair short score, and then altered in the holograph full score.

The last large revision of material in the Scherzo, previous to the Douglas fair score, is located between rehearsals 39 and 42. This passage is a tutti recall of the

Example 1.7   Early draft, Scherzo

saxophone theme in augmentation and therefore needed to be changed after the revision of the earlier music.

When Vaughan Williams returned to this movement in 1950, he added significant new thematic material. This took the form of fanfare-like themes constructed with an emphasis on the tritone, which, as has been noted, is a pervasive feature throughout the Scherzo.[21] These fanfare themes are invariably scored for brass with occasional woodwind doublings.

These themes have been inserted into the Scherzo at seven points in the 1950 edition. To make these insertions, Vaughan Williams first turned to the fair short score, using red ink to sketch in the new material. The composer did not use the holograph full score to fix the final form and placement of the themes – he may have already given it to Michael Mullinar – but probably used a hire score (perhaps the Douglas fair score) or a copy of the 1948 edition instead. Not all the fanfare themes sketched into the fair short score were included in the final additions, as two themes from the fair short score fail to appear in the 1950 edition. (There are two recordings made before the 1950 edition that do not have the fanfare themes: Sir Adrian Boult conducting the the London Symphony on HMV C3875 with the matrix numbers 2EA13627-1 and 13628-1 on the Scherzo, and Leopold Stokowski conducting the New York Philharmonic on Columbia ML 4212.)

The muted epilogue was the subject of much speculation after the symphony's première, prompting Vaughan Williams in 1956 to provide Michael Kennedy with a clue to the movement's unique atmosphere by a quotation from *The Tempest* (IV, i, 171–77). Vaughan Williams had already made this connection musically by setting this text from *The Tempest* as the second of his 1951 *Three Shakespeare Songs* for a cappella mixed chorus. The musical connections between this partsong, entitled 'The Cloud-Capp'd Towers', and certain passages of the symphony are readily apparent. Although 'The Cloud Capp'd Towers' begins in F sharp minor in the published score, the composer's holograph copy (BL Add. MS 50481) begins in E minor, also the key of the Sixth Symphony. The contour of the partsong's first thematic idea is similar to the second phrase of the second movement, and the vacillation between E minor and E flat major triads that forms the conclusion of the

Epilogue is found at several important points of the part-song, transposed but with identical spacing (Example 1.8).

Example 1.8   'The Cloud-Capp'd Towers'

While the Epilogue is an example of a daring conception fully realized in musical terms, it presented Vaughan Williams far fewer problems requiring revision than the more conventionally conceived Scherzo. The most important revision is an early one, a recasting of the oboe solo at rehearsal 11. The solo is altered because its initial range descended into a register too low to play softly (Example 1.9). This change is first made in the two-piano version of the Epilogue found in Book C.

Example 1.9   Revision in the Epilogue

The only revision of the Epilogue that postdates the Royal College performance is found five measures after rehearsal 10. The composer omits the return of two further statements of the sighing chord progressions at rehearsal 10, and he elides the bass clarinet solo by introducing a meter change. No alterations of orchestration were needed for this movement; all of the first orchestral indications present in the holograph short score correspond to the scoring of those passages in the published editions.

Discussion of Vaughan Williams's music has often been characterized by language more applicable to a narrow aspect of the man's public personality than to his work. Cecil Gray's description of Vaughan Williams as one who 'flounders about in a sea of his ideas like a vast and ungainly porpoise' is typical of the superficial terms all too often applied to the music by detractors and admirers alike. Gray, a trenchant critic who was also a spectacularly unsuccessful composer, writes further in this vein that Vaughan Williams 'is apt to present us with what is after all only the raw material of a work of art, and not the work itself'.[22]

Such commentary, along with the composer's characteristic candor and modesty, has contributed to a distorted and sometimes dismissive estimation of Vaughan Williams's technical expertise. The composer of the Sixth Symphony was no mere gentleman amateur, and the artist who painstakingly revised this score stands revealed as an anxious, even restless, perfectionist ever striving for greater clarity and concision. Following the process of revision of the Sixth Symphony illuminates Vaughan Williams's artistic integrity and complete professionalism, but beyond this, shows a composer unable to rest until his vision was completely realized.

Acknowledgements

This essay was written in 1986 and first published in *The Musical Quarterly* in 1989 (vol. 73, no. 3). The discovery of the fragmentary piano arrangement of the Sixth Symphony by Michael Mullinar at the Royal College and other interesting new information has since come to light and necessitated a revision of the article itself. In addition, this essay assumes that the reader has access to a post-1950 edition of the score of the Sixth Symphony for ready reference. The author acknowledges the cooperation of Mrs Ursula Vaughan Williams, Mr Roy Douglas and Mrs Mary Mullinar in providing information crucial to this investigation, as well as his thanks to both the Carthusian Trust and Oxford University Press for their support of this research.

Notes

1   Frank Howes, *The Music of Ralph Vaughan Williams* (London: Oxford University Press, 1954), 53. For further confirmation of Howes's intuition, see Oliver Neighbour's essay, 'The Place of the Eighth among Vaughan Williams's symphonies', in *Vaughan Williams Studies*, ed. Alain Frogley (Cambridge: Cambridge University Press, 1998), 224.
2   Michael Kennedy, *The Works of Ralph Vaughan Williams*, 2nd edn (London: Oxford University Press, 1980), 301.
3   Ibid., 302.
4   Reprinted in Michael Kennedy, *A Catalogue of the Works of Ralph Vaughan Williams*, rev. edn. (London: Oxford University Press, 1996), 180.
5   Roy Douglas, *Working with Vaughan Williams* (London: The British Library, 1988), 9.
6   I am able to identify Michael Mullinar's musical script through information contained in a letter sent by Thomas B. Pitfield to Michael Kennedy on 19 November 1962. Pitfield wrote that 'I have kept a letter from V.W. of the middle war years (undated) about a very unusual carol tune I had taken down ... I had to get his, then, amanuensis, Michael Mullinar, to decypher it for me! The latter was a close friend, & I was staying with him when he was making a 2-piano version of the 5th Symphony from a very sketchy score so that the composer could hear it played' (John Rylands University Library of Manchester, The Michael Kennedy Collection 1925–1975, KEN/3/1/24). By comparing the fair two-piano score of the Fifth Symphony mentioned in this letter with the relevant manuscript sources of the Sixth Symphony, I was able to identify Mullinar as the copyist for the piano reductions, both for solo piano and in two-piano format, of both symphonies.
7   Douglas, *Working with Vaughan Williams*, 10.

8   Mary Mullinar, telephone conversation with the author, 21 May 1986.
9   Roy Douglas, interview with the author, Tunbridge Wells, Kent, 2 July 1985.
10   Ursula Vaughan Williams, *R.V.W.: A Biography of Ralph Vaughan Williams* (Oxford: Oxford University Press, 1984), 182.
11   Mary Mullinar, telephone conversation with the author, 21 May 1986.
12   Kennedy, *Works*, 290.
13   Douglas, *Working with Vaughan Williams*, 11.
14   Ibid., 13.
15   Kennedy, *Works*, 290.
16   Roy Douglas, *Working with R.V.W.* (London, 1972), 66.
17   Quoted in Kennedy, *Works*, 304.
18   Vaughan Williams's arrangement of 'Old Folks at Home' was published by Stainer and Bell in 1921, but may have been completed while the composer was on active service during the First World War.
19   Ursula Vaughan Williams, interviewed by Simon Heffer in the *Sunday Telegraph*, 4 November 1998.
20   This chronology seems to cast doubt upon Stephen Banfield's contention that, like Gerald Finzi, Vaughan Williams solicited advice from colleagues only to disregard completely their suggestions. See Stephen Banfield, *Gerald Finzi: An English Composer* (London: Faber and Faber, 1997), 63.
21   These new fanfare themes, and several other passages in the Scherzo, are strongly reminiscent of the music Vaughan Williams created to delineate the German bombers in the wartime propaganda film *Coastal Command* (1942).
22   Cecil Gray, *A Survey of Contemporary Music* (London, 1924), 252–3.

Chapter 2

Vaughan Williams's Fifth Symphony: Ideology and Aural Tradition[1]

Murray Dineen

Vaughan Williams's first sketches for the opening of his Fifth Symphony (see Example 2.1) may well be contained on the recto of the manuscript British Library 50371 A, folio 2. As sketches they are remarkably prescient. But for one detail, all the thematic material of the opening to the first movement is represented – the rhythm and approximate melodic shape of the opening horn motto [1], a theme in rising quarter notes [2], another theme, with its characteristic dotted-note rhythm registered in the space above the system [3].

**Example 2.1   A diplomatic facsimile of the sketch BM 50371A, folio 2r,
Ralph Vaughan Williams, Fifth Symphony, first movement**

Example 2.2   BM 50371A, folio 2v

The verso to folio 2, however, captures a moment of inspiration when an essential aspect of the symphony's identity took shape (see Example 2.2). There lies the horn motto that appeared on the recto page, but now with a pedal C striking an unstable tritone against the horn's F sharp. The symphony is about instability, in the sense of something mutable, given to flux and change – expressed compactly by the opening tritone, which has lead commentators to find the tonality unstable. (Indeed the composer himself had trouble settling on G or D to designate the key.) No one, however, has observed that some of the themes in the symphony appear quite as unfixed too.

The usual consequent to the procedure of sketching is a firming or settling of sketched materials into definitive form. In the case of the first and second movements of Vaughan Williams's Fifth Symphony, however, no firm statement of theme emerges in subsequent sketches or indeed in the score itself. Instead, if there is a definitive theme, it would seem to underlie the movement, as a source of melodic material. The absence of definitive themes in the first two movements poses questions not simply about this symphony and the nature of thematic material in Vaughan Williams's symphonies, but indeed about the very function of theme in his work. For elucidation, one might turn to the composer's thoughts, specifically those on the aural tradition in folk music.

One of Vaughan Williams's constant inspirations was the folk-song; hence it seems natural that his treatment of theme in the Fifth Symphony's first and second movements should recall the instability – the flux and change – that he took to be characteristic of folk traditions where songs pass aurally from singer to singer.[2] In these aural traditions, without written records, the original version of a song is lost in antiquity, along with any record of its development or evolution. In similar terms, Vaughan Williams presents various passages that share common motivic content, seemingly the offspring of some original theme antedating the symphony proper (and indeed its sketches), a theme never presented definitively.

In this chapter, I shall discuss the treatment of themes in the symphony in light of the aural folk-song tradition as Vaughan Williams conceived of it. I shall examine the thematic material of the first movement, turn to Vaughan Williams's writings on folk-song for explication, and conclude by examining themes in the second movement. Throughout I shall consider two interrelated issues: the problem of a folk-music aesthetic transferred to the symphonic tradition, and the effect of an ideology underlying much of Vaughan Williams's thought – that music must be expressly 'national'.[3]

Tables 2.1 and 2.2 centonize – list in successive formulations – two principal themes as they appear in the exposition to the first movement of the Fifth Symphony in its published form.[4] In these tables, thematic fragments have been classified by vertical arrangement into lettered columns – for example, columns *a* through *h* in Table 2.1. Entries missing in columns do not signify rests, but rather fragments omitted in a given instance. So, for example, the violins in m. 12 of Example 2.3 present the characteristic dotted rhythm of the theme – labeled

Table 2.1   First movement, theme group A

Table 2.2   First movement, theme group B

Example 2.3   First movement, mm. 12–18

Example 2.4   First movement, mm. 3–10

fragment b in Table 2.1 – as well as fragments c and g. The appearance of a theme in m. 15, on the other hand, combines fragments b, c, d, e, and f of Table 2.2 (compare Example 2.3, mm. 15ft).

There is only one fragment common to all the versions of the theme in Table 2.1 (fragment b, the dotted rhythm) and no element in common in Table 2.2. Nonetheless, all instances of a theme in either table belong together through their common content and association in the movement. It would be incorrect, however, to draft an *Urthema* or ancestral version combining all the fragments of Table 2.1, a through h, for example. In the symphony, the common identity of this family of themes is not demonstrated by relationship to one original and thus referential theme; no such theme is ever stated. (It should be noted that Tables 2.1 and 2.2 do not exhaust all the statements of these themes to be found in the first movement. As well, there are other themes to be discovered that would require separate tables.)

The influence of a folk aesthetic is felt not only in the themes themselves, but also in the larger, formal design of certain movements. In broad formal terms, the first movement of the Fifth Symphony is cast in the sonata-movement design as Vaughan Williams knew it, with exposition, development and recapitulation. The themes of the exposition and recapitulation, however, are treated in an unusual manner according to the textbook conception of sonata – not so much contrasted as they are continually intertwined. The measure numbers indicated on Tables 2.1 and 2.2 show that the two themes are not placed in two distinct parts of the exposition, as a sonata's contrasting main and subordinate or secondary themes are customarily thought to be. The influence of the folk-song, we might say, effected not only a loosening of thematic conception but also of the formal function of themes.

That Vaughan Williams knew and appreciated the aural tradition is attested to constantly by his writings. He understood its necessarily 'oral' mode of transmission: 'The folk-song lives only by oral transmission, ... if it fails to be passed from mouth to mouth it ceases to exist.'[5] Since it lacks a definitive written form, the folk-song – unlike its counterpart, the art-song – is in a constant state of flux, as Cecil Sharp, the mentor to a generation of folk-song collectors, noted:[6]

Art-music is the work of the individual: it is composed in, comparatively speaking, a short period of time and being committed to paper it is forever fixed in one unalterable form. Folk-music is the product of a race and reflects feelings and tastes that are communal rather than personal; it is always in solution; its creation is never completed, while at every moment of its history it exists not in one form but in many.

For Vaughan Williams there was no definitive, original version of a folk-song:[7]

> There is no 'original' in traditional art, and there is no particular virtue in the earliest known version.
>
> ***
>
> We folk-song collectors are often asked 'what is the origin' of a particular tune or 'how old' it is. There is no answer to either of these questions; there is no original version of any particular tune; any given tune has hundreds of origins.

The folk-song may in fact be spun from stock phrases of communal origin, with good practical reason:[8]

> The great difficulty is how to start, and the stock phrase solved this difficulty with the ballad maker. ... In the same way we find a common opening to many folk-tunes, and this opening would naturally be a variant of some musical formula which comes naturally to the human voice.

From his understanding of the aural folk tradition, Vaughan Williams fashioned an aesthetic. Its principal thesis is that 'perfection of form is equally possible in the most primitive music and in the most elaborate'.[9] He admired the spontaneous nature of folk-music-intuitive, not calculated; an applied art, not absolute in the sense of *l'art pour l'art*;[10] a music with a natural brevity and economy flowing directly from the limitations of memory. In answer to the criticism that second-hand versions of folk-songs are of secondary quality – he asserts that the final product can as easily be an improvement as a corruption of the original.[11] In this respect, folk music differs fundamentally from art music. An alteration of a Schubert song corrupts the original – the definitive version captured in print. We allow for interpretation according to the temperament of the singer, 'but these differences can never become very wide because we are continually referring back to the printed copy'.[12] But a folk-song improved upon survives, in the best sense of natural selection:[13]

> A folk-singer is a free agent, there is no necessity for him to pass on what he does not care about. Let us suppose an example. John Smith sings a song to two other men, William Brown and Henry Jones. William Brown is a real artist and sees possibilities in the tune and adds little touches to it that give it an added beauty. Henry Jones is a stupid fellow and forgets the best part of the tune and has to make it up the best he can, or he leaves out just that bit that gave the tune its individuality. Now what will happen? William Brown's version will live from generation to generation while Henry Jones's will die with him. So you see that the evolution of the folk-song is a real process of natural selection and survival of the fittest.

The thesis that alteration produces errors and corruption is implicit in written works. Not so with folk-songs. 'Corruptions', Vaughan Williams writes, 'are much more likely to creep in the written word than in the spoken. Any alteration in a written copy is likely to be due to carelessness or ignorance whereas when we do find variations in versions of traditional words and music these are as often as not deliberate improvements on the part of later reciters or singers.'[14]

Vaughan Williams's fascination with folk-song was also a matter of cultural politics.[15] His hopes and aspirations for a modern English music were frankly national and closely connected with folk-song: for a music to be vital, it must not mechanically imitate foreign models, but rather develop from its own milieu – 'the raw material of its own national song'.[16] He drew an analogy between an exotic hothouse flower and a garden rose – foreign music and native English music, respectively. At first appearance, the former outshines the latter, 'but in a short time the exotic will be a mere stalk, while the rose will live on, and even when it dies will be succeeded by others'.[17] In this spirit, I believe he cast about for a native idiom to, if not supplant, at least complement the cosmopolitan but foreign idioms in English music of his day (often the task of an English composer). Contrary to this notion of a national music based on folk-song runs the prejudice that by incorporating folk-song in concert music the composer is 'writing down' to the popular tastes of a public.[18] Vaughan Williams responded to such criticism by ruling out any simple adaptation of folk tunes: 'I do not imagine that one can make one's music national merely by introducing a few folk tunes into it.'[19] To do so would be a 'precious affectation'.[20] The composer must be uncompromisingly true to his vision and calling: 'The ordinary man expects from a serious composer serious music and will not be frightened even at a little "uplift".'[21]

In his writings, Vaughan Williams left unaddressed the particulars of translating folk idioms to the concert hall. The procedure that I have called centonization, as it stems from the idea of the aural folk tradition and is applied in the first movement to the Fifth Symphony, was perhaps a way of solving this problem, a way of fusing applied and absolute music, a task I shall return to shortly. The procedure is not confined to the first movement; the second movement also embodies flux and change in its thematic material.[22]

The principal thematic material of the second movement stems from a chain of fourths. A chain of fourths, however, is so neutral, so uninterpreted as to be hardly suitable for forming the thematic identity of a movement. In creating particular theme statements, Vaughan Williams makes slight alterations to the chain. For example, he duplicates pitches at the octave, and thus breaks the sequence of successive fourths. (For each theme statement of Table 2.3, octave duplicates are placed in brackets.) By breaking up the chain of fourths, Vaughan Williams creates a family of themes like the thematic families of the first movement.

There are certainly no immediate folk-song associations to be drawn with these themes built of fourths. Nonetheless, I note again the general association with the aural folk tradition: the thematic treatment is like that of the first movement – a family of themes derived from an *Urthematische* chain of fourths never stated in its original form, as if such an original were lost in antiquity.

One of Vaughan Williams's tasks in the Fifth Symphony, accordingly, was to bridge the worlds of folk-song and symphony – applied and absolute worlds respectively. For him, the folk-song was unquestionably an applied art, but the first and second movements of the Fifth Symphony seem to be among the most absolute of his works. They have neither text nor programme, apart from associations of calm and tranquillity that distinguish the symphony from its predecessor and successor, and these associations are hardly a bridge to the applied musical world.[23]

In search of a bridge true to both absolute and applied musical worlds, a bridge between farmer's field and recital hall, Vaughan Williams might have settled for the folk-song fantasy or suite, genres he adopted on occasion; he might have refrained

Table 2.3   Second movement theme built of fourths

from writing symphonies at all. But the folk-song fantasy is a shaky aesthetic proposition in both absolute and applied terms. Although the folk-song tune shorn of words may work well in the technical terms of absolute music, one runs the risk of recognizing the tune, perhaps recalling the text, and thus shattering that delicate suspension of association so essential to absolute music. In applied terms, the folk tune fixed as a theme is but a parody of the original: a fixed version of something unfixed and fluid at heart. When committed to paper it violates the state of flux so characteristic of the folk-song. One cannot capture the spirit of folk music – and thus express national identity – by simply borrowing folk tunes, tearing them from their context. As Vaughan Williams put it: 'I do not imagine that one can make one's music national merely by introducing a few folk-tunes into it.'[24]

The folk-song idea in the Fifth Symphony is not expressed by a folk-song theme but rather by the treatment accorded thematic material. Some of this material may eventually be allied with folk-songs, but it is the fluidity, the natural simplicity and ease of transformation, so common to folk-songs, that makes the symphony folk-like. The second movement is a case in point. We may discover versions of an English folk tune hidden in the first movement, but what I call the *Urthema* of the second – a chain of fourths – is hardly an English folk product.[25]

Now it might be argued that thematic fluidity and development are the hallmarks of late nineteenth- and early twentieth-century music. What is there then to distinguish Vaughan Williams's approach from what Schoenberg termed 'developing variation' in Brahms, for example?[26] It is in the very nature of the theme and its conception that the difference arises. For Schoenberg, themes are defined (as problems) at the outset and from their implications a piece proceeds; development follows definition, in other words.[27] The themes that I have traced in this chapter are never stated definitively, and thus can hardly be developed in the traditional nineteenth-century Teutonic manner.

Ralph Vaughan Williams's thoughts on the aural folk tradition and his Fifth Symphony have certainly not been influential in the way that the concept of developing variation or the notion of a 12-tone theme subject to inversion and retrogression has. Vaughan Williams spoke often in terms of cultural politics, seldom of technique. In his writings, technical matters – a compositional method or technique – appear as the property of the craftsman's shop, and, with typical self-deprecation, not worthy of being aired by a composer before the public. Since technical matters are so readily accessible to scholars, however, scholarly interest in Vaughan Williams has perhaps been eclipsed by interest in other twentieth-century composers. I argue, however, that in the Fifth Symphony Vaughan Williams sets us some important puzzles to ponder.

On the surface, we admire the symphony in traditional symphonic terms – the handling of large-scale proportion.[28] And we admire the evolving themes – their ill-defined quality underneath which we sense a common, even familial, relationship. But perhaps what lies at the heart of our admiration is the subtle incorporation of a folkloric, ultimately nationalistic, ideology in the absolute, nonprogrammatic context of the symphony. The themes themselves appear absolute, without programmatic association. And yet their folk-like treatment would seem to bear the ideology of Vaughan Williams's hopes and aspirations for a national music to serve the English concert hall.

Notes

1   I am indebted to the Carthusian Trust for granting me a fellowship in the summer of 1987 that allowed me to examine documents related to the composition of the Fifth Symphony; to Ursula Vaughan Williams, for permission to consult these documents; and

to Charterhouse – its former music director, William Llewellyn, in particular – under whose generous auspices this paper was conceived. A version of this paper was read at a meeting of the Northeast Chapter of the College Music Society, at Toronto, in April 1990.

2   Elsie Payne has drawn similar conclusions. She notes that Vaughan Williams's complex treatment of themes, his 'methods of expression', accords 'with the tunes themselves', and is 'fairly founded on these folk-song structures'. She is more concerned with folk tunes *per se*, however, than with their overall treatment and its implications for a symphonic medium. See Elsie Payne, 'Vaughan Williams and Folk-song: The Relation Between Folk-Song and Other Elements in His Comprehensive Style', *The Music Review* 15, no. 2 (1954), 103–26. See as well, Vaughan Williams's remarks on the first movement of the Eighth Symphony, as 'seven variations in search of a theme', (pace Pirandello?), in Michael Kennedy, *A Catalogue of the Works of Ralph Vaughan Williams*, rev. edn. (London: Oxford University Press, 1982), 235–6. Scott Goddard, in 'Ralph Vaughan Williams (1872–)', *The Symphony*, Ralph Hill (Harmondsworth: Penguin Books, 1949), 412, describes the first movement of the Fifth Symphony as if it were 'going on in some hidden region before its sound reaches our ears', referring to the opening sonority. I will argue much the same, but from thematic treatment (rather than sonority), which evokes some thematic source removed from the symphony proper.

3   The question of ideology and national music is discussed in a remarkable essay by Alan Frogley, 'Constructing Englishness in music: national character and the reception of Ralph Vaughan Williams', in Alan Frogley, ed., *Vaughan Williams Studies* (Cambridge: Cambridge University Press, 1996), 1–22.

4   A current debate in musicology concerns itself with the place of centonization in Gregorian chant tradition. See the 'List of Works Cited: Modern Editions and Secondary Literature', in Kenneth Levy, 'On Gregorian Orality', *Journal of the American Musicological Society* 43, no. 2 (Summer 1990), 222–7. The issue, to my knowledge, has not arisen in discussion of twentieth-century symphonic music.

5   Ralph Vaughan Williams, *National Music* (London: Oxford University Press, 1963), 31.

6   Quoted in ibid., 32.

7   Ibid., 28, 33.

8   Ibid., 18.

9   Ibid., 6.

10   I am thinking of Whistler: '[Art] is, withal, selfishly occupied with her own perfection only – having no desire to teach...'. James Abbott McNeill Whistler, *'Ten o'clock' by J.A.M. Whistler* (Boston and New York: Houghton Mifflin and Company, 1888), 8. And see: Arnold Schoenberg, 'New Music, Outmoded Music, Style and Idea', *Style and Idea*, ed. L. Stein, trans. L. Black (Berkeley: University of California Press, 1984), 124. For Vaughan Williams on Whistler see *National Music*, 1.

11   *National Music*, 28.

12   Ibid., 30.

13   Ibid., 32. Vaughan Williams would have recognized natural selection at work in music with a certain familiarity, through the influence of his great-uncle Charles Darwin. Another potent influence, in this regard, would have been Herbert Spenser, exerted through Vaughan Williams's teacher, Hubert Parry, author of *The Evolution of the Art of Music* (1893; reprint, New York: Greenwood Press, 1968). But see Julian Onderdonk 'Vaughan Williams's folksong transcriptions: a case of idealization?' in Frogley, *Vaughan Williams Studies*, 118–38, especially p. 138.

14   *National Music*, 28.

15   See Paul Harrington, 'Holst and Vaughan Williams: Radical Pastoral', in *Music and the Politics of Culture*, ed. Christopher Norris (London: Lawrence and Wishart, 1989), 114–15.

16　*National Music*, 41.

17　Ibid., 156.

18　Ibid., 64.

19　Ibid., 41.

20　Ibid., 66.

21　Ibid., 66.

22　The last movement is a passacaglia, with a recognizable theme fixed immediately at first appearance. Themes from the first movement return at the end of the last movement, however, to lend it a tension between fixed and fluid elements – one of the most attractive moments of the symphony. The third movement in large part uses material from the 'morality' *The Pilgrim's Progress*, and the nature of the movement's themes is colored by extra-musical associations to that drama.

23　For a discussion of programmatic aspects of some of Vaughan Williams's symphonies, the Ninth in particular, see Alain Frogley, 'Vaughan Williams and Thomas Hardy: "Tess" and the Slow Movement of the Ninth Symphony', *Music and Letters* 68, no. 1 (1987), 42–59. With regard to the Fifth Symphony, many programmatic allusions have been drawn by means of the musical connections between the work and the opera *The Pilgrim's Progress*. Compare Wilfrid Mellers, *Vaughan Williams and the Vision of Albion* (London: Barrie and Jenkins, 1989), 176–86. A particularly measured approach to this question is offered by Arnold Whittall in the introductory remarks to his essay on the symphony: ' "Symphony in D major": models and mutations', in Frogley, *Vaughan Williams Studies*, 187–93. See as well, Oliver Neighbour, 'The place of the Eighth among Vaughan Williams's symphonies', in Frogley, *Vaughan Williams Studies*, 223.

24　*National Music*, 40-41.

25　For a remarkable discussion of rhythm in this movement see Lionel Pike, 'Rhythm in the symphonies: a preliminary investigation', in Frogley, *Vaughan Williams Studies*, 168–72.

26　Walter Frisch, *Brahms and the Principle of Developing Variation* (Berkeley: University of California Press, 1984).

27　Arnold Schoenberg, *Fundamentals of Musical Composition*, eds G. Strang and L. Stein (London: Faber and Faber, 1967), 102.

28　This large-scale proportion has been addressed in Schenkerian terms by Arnold Whittall, 'Symphony in D major...', in Frogley, *Vaughan Williams Studies*, 193–212.

Chapter 3

A Deconstruction of
William Blake's Vision:
Vaughan Williams and *Job*

Alison Sanders McFarland

An enduring aspect of the biblical story of Job is the constant temptation on the part of the reader to redefine and reinterpret it in the light of personal experience and belief. Its timeless themes of the nature of good and evil and the problem of human suffering were natural material for William Blake, whose own life was marked by an alternation of suffering and spiritual rebirth.[1] The subject of Job was to occupy Blake for many years, beginning with a single drawing in 1785 and culminating late in his life with the cycle *Illustrations of the Book of Job*. Between 1820 and 1825 Blake produced two large watercolor sets of his cycle, as well as a half-sized series of engravings.[2]

The Blake illustrations in turn inspired Geoffrey Keynes, the noted surgeon and Blake scholar, who found them so suggestive of motion that they cried out for staging.[3] In the centenary year of Blake's death, 1927, he began to realize his conception of a ballet to be based on the Job illustrations. Keynes selected eight of the 21 drawings for his production, and enlisted his sister-in-law, Gwendolen Raverat, to supply the stage and costume designs and to help write the dramatic scenario. The selection of a composer began only later, and after much consideration Keynes offered the project to Raverat's cousin, Ralph Vaughan Williams. The composer's initial reaction was to decline, but eventually he accepted after specifying several conditions. For the choreography, Keynes turned to yet another family connection: his brother, John Maynard Keynes, had married Lydia Lopokova, formerly a dancer with Diaghilev's Russian Ballet. By the time Diaghilev was approached, however, Vaughan Williams had already begun composing, and had stipulated that there would be no dancing on point and that *Job* would not be a ballet but a masque, noting that the ballet 'has acquired unfortunate connotations of late years to me'.[4] Diaghilev was, predictably, not interested in these conditions and declined the invitation, rejecting the project as 'too English'.[5] Vaughan Williams was not really disappointed: in a letter to Raverat, he commented

I amused myself with making a sketch of Job – I never expected Djag w[oul]d look at it ... but it really w[oul]dn't have suited the sham serious ... decadent and frivolous attitude of the R.B. toward everything – can you imagine Job sandwiched between 'Les Biches' and 'Cimarosiana' – and that dreadful pseudo-cultured audience saying to each other 'My dear, have you seen God at the Russian Ballet?' No – I think we are well out of it – I don't think

this is sour grapes – for I admit that it would have been great fun to have been a production
by the R.B. – though I feel myself that they w[oul]d have made an unholy mess of it with
their over-developed calves.[6]

When it seemed that a production was not going to materialize, the composer
finished the music expecting that it should be performed as a concert suite, and
scored it for a very large orchestra.[7] But at the insistence of Vaughan Williams's
friend and colleague, Gustav Holst, *Job* was finally produced by the Camargo
Society, with choreography by Ninette de Valois.[8] It was first produced at London's
Cambridge Theatre in July 1931. The vagaries of its performance history have
resulted in the masque never being performed exactly as its creators imagined it.[9]

Job occupies a pivotal position in Vaughan Williams's works and belongs to a
period of transition. This is illustrated by a concern shared by Vaughan Williams and
Holst that they were drifting apart musically as their acceptance of each other's work
became less immediate (a thought that seemed to disturb Vaughan Williams more
than it did Holst).[10] *Job* is frequently acknowledged as a musically important work
because of its juxtaposition of several of the composer's styles: many of his idioms
are present to some degree, from his interest in English folksong heritage and the
pastoral passages reminiscent of *The Lark Ascending*, to the anticipation of the
harsh, dissonant elements of several of his later symphonies. It is also, as Kennedy
has observed, a successful fusion of literature, art, music and dance that helped
English ballet to emerge from the shadow of foreign models.[11] But the extra-musical
importance of *Job* has received less attention, and has significant implications for
others of the composer's works. At the heart of *Job* is a testament of personal
conviction that led Vaughan Williams to a deconstruction of Blake's basic premise.
While *Job* seems at first glance to be simply a theatrical representation of the
illustrations, the composer has completely altered their original meaning, and has
done so using Blake's own materials.

A study of the complicated creation of *Job* reveals that the dramatic concept went
through substantial changes, reflecting the inclination of each participant to impose
his or her own reading on the story. Once Vaughan Williams became involved in the
project there were at least two disparate interpretations of Job, perhaps three. From
the beginning, the composer made it clear that he was not merely providing music
for someone else's scenario, but wished to be an equal creative partner in the
development of the concept. By the end of the project he had become the dominant
voice, and the finished drama bore little resemblance to what Keynes and Raverat
initially had written.[12]

There are two basic interpretations of Job, which are mutually incompatible at the
core. The first treats the story as an insoluble problem of human suffering. Job, and
by extension the reader, cannot hope to understand why tragedy strikes the
seemingly just and upright man. The second approach explains Job's trials as the
result of his own, albeit unintended, sin: once Job has acknowledged his error, his
former life is restored to him. This second interpretation is a far more comfortable
one because it enables the reader to maintain a sense of control and even-handed
justice, and many, but by no means all, readings of Job have concentrated on
offering different explanations of Job's supposed sin. Many biblical scholars believe
that the book of Job itself contains a later interpolation of this nature – the character

of Elihu. Without Elihu, the only accusation of sin comes from Job's friends, who cling to the belief that such dire sufferings must be deserved: God himself does not suggest that Job has sinned, but instead shows him that the universe is beyond his understanding. Elihu, however, rebukes Job for an inflated sense of his own importance. If Job had not sinned through an earlier deed, he has done so now, in attempting to fathom God's justice. This act provides the basis for those who would see Job as sinner.

Blake's own interpretation of the book of Job is thoughtfully examined in Joseph Wicksteed's book on the drawings. This seminal study of Blake's cycle and its inherent symbolism was admired by Keynes, who had a close association with Wicksteed.[13] Wicksteed explains that Blake felt compelled to solve the insoluble problem of Job. He describes Blake as an 'avowed system-maker', highlighting the line from Blake's *Jerusalem*, 'I must create a system or be enslaved by another man's.'[14] The system that Blake created required that Job be in error. To Blake, reality was spiritual rather than material,[15] and because the Old Testament couched Job's sufferings and restored life in largely material and corporeal terms, Blake asserts that Job's very prosperity is the symbol of his error. Blake accuses Job not of sinning by deed, but rather by thought, by virtue of his dependence on material possessions and his overt, self-righteous acts of piety, at the expense of his seeking of spiritual wealth. Blake creates Elihu as the crucial turning point of Job's spiritual journey, and the struggle becomes one of good and evil within the self.

Wicksteed's brilliant discovery was that Blake represented this system of good and evil by the use of pervasive symbolism regarding spiritual and corporeal, that corresponds to right and left in the illustrations. Job's actions that betray his materiality are conveyed, in the age-old tradition of 'sinister', by his use of the left hand, or by the revealing of the left foot under his robe, and his spiritual side is indicated by the right; the other characters in the drawings observe this convention as well. The symbolism is extended to actual facial similarity: Job resembles God or Satan in turn, depending upon the events of the story.[16]

Keynes, as an enthusiastic admirer of Wicksteed's study, based the scenario for his ballet largely on this concept of the duality of good and evil. He later wrote that he and Raverat had chosen Vaughan Williams as the composer because they felt that he would have sympathy with Blake's symbolism, as disclosed by Wicksteed.[17] But the masque did not turn out to be simply a musical representation of Wicksteed's Blake: the subject of Job proved, once again, too much of a temptation for the participants, who were unable to put aside their own interpretations.

Vaughan Williams's initial refusal of the project centers around the issue of the scenario. He wrote to Keynes:

> I return your friends scenario I have looked over it carefully and shew it to one or two friends whose judgement I trust. And I have come to the conclusion that it is not for me Doubtless all my fault
> I have delayed returning it because I wanted to think it over ...[18]

But Keynes, in his memoirs, does not recall any reluctance on Vaughan Williams's part. He reports that after Raverat had shown Vaughan Williams the scenes in the toy theater she had made, the composer was so 'fired with enthusiasm that he became rather difficult to control'.[19] This eagerness later shows in a letter to Raverat, in which Vaughan Williams says he is 'anxiously awaiting your scenario – otherwise the music will push on by itself which may cause trouble later'.[20] This is a revealing statement: Keynes had insisted that the participants have a common understanding and purpose,[21] yet Vaughan Williams was already composing in advance of the completed dramatic concept. Having first refused the project on the basis of the scenario, something – perhaps the demonstration of the scenes in the toy theater – persuaded the composer to change his mind and accept. He then tried to wait for a revised scenario but it is apparent that, for him, the project assumed a life of its own.

The revision of the scenario for which he was waiting may have been one of the conditions for his undertaking the work. No fewer than seven scenarios survive in the Fitzwilliam Museum, Cambridge, and an examination of them shows that the dramatic concept changed throughout several stages.[22] Leaving aside minor differences, there are three different versions represented. Keynes's own scenario is missing from this collection but is available elsewhere, bringing the total of distinct versions to four. One of the points of contention of these scenarios, unsurprisingly, is the same one that had occupied so many others: the nature of Job's sin. Wicksteed and Keynes both agreed that Blake's Job had sinned through dependence on the material, rather than the spiritual. But what precisely constitutes 'materialism' must be defined with caution. Blake does indeed decry materialism, by which he means anything not inherently spiritual. The Druids and the Egyptians, for example, are 'materialistic' to Blake because their society incorporates highly mathematical architecture.[23] His dismissal of Newton and Locke, among others, is scathing, and reveals that Blake believed analytical thought to be a form of materialism.

The definition of materialism in the twentieth century was not as subtle. The first synopsis of the Job ballet, with Raverat as apparently the sole author, paints Job's sin in very bold strokes, and the sin is in action, not only in thought.[24] In this version there is no doubt that Job has sinned because of his accumulation of wealth and possessions: the typescript at times lapses into language reminiscent of a socialist tract. The drama begins with Job and his family, 'rich and prosperous shepherds, and a complacent materialism reigns all about them'. When Job and his family sit down to feast, Satan calls upon Jehovah, who is seen on his throne with his children dancing before him. 'Satan addresses Jehovah and accuses Job of the sin of materialism, pointing at Job as he sits in voluptuous contentment.' Jehovah agrees to the testing of Job, and allows Satan to take his place on the throne. The feast of Job's sons and their wives becomes riotous, and they begin a 'wild and drunken dance'. Satan appears before them and they fall dead. Messengers tell Job of the loss of his wealth and his sons, and Satan torments him with boils, but Job does not curse Jehovah. Job's friends enter, who perform a 'dance of pious complacency and self-esteem' and accuse Job of sin. Heaven is revealed to them, but it is Satan on God's throne, and all are terrified. At last 'Elihu enters and rebukes Job for his materialism ... Job understands how he has sinned and has a true vision of the Deity'. Job, his wife, and his daughters worship God and build an altar. The last scene mirrors the first, but now it is sunrise, and Job and his remaining family are surrounded not by livestock but by ripe corn. Satan enters again, unnoticed.

The socialist overtones are not altogether surprising. Wicksteed notes that Blake is often compelling to us precisely because he anticipated 'philosophical and ethical ideas that we almost regard as characteristically twentieth-century'.[25] Wicksteed and others recognized, in Blake's opposition to the Industrial Revolution and its economic consequences, quasi-socialist tendencies. Raverat was the granddaughter of Charles Darwin (the branch of the family by which she was also related to Vaughan Williams), and was raised and lived in Cambridge academic circles, then a center of socialist sympathy. The memoirs of her childhood certainly do nothing to dispel suspicions of this philosophy: her comments throughout are highly critical of the British upper class, its treatment of servants and working people, its self-righteousness, and its narrow and unrealistic moral values.[26] From an early age, Raverat considered theological issues that had a direct bearing on the later Job project. Raverat recalls that her aunt used to lie awake at night 'struggling with the problem of why God allowed suffering', and she recorded her belief even in childhood that God gives out good and bad things with different hands.[27]

The next three scenarios in the collection present the same basic plot as the first, with only minor changes in certain details. One typescript eliminates some text, mostly stage directions, which was visible but lined out in the earliest version. The next is labelled 'acting version' and is identical with the previous version except that the seven wives of Job's sons, although still present in the synopsis, are crossed out in the list of characters. The third restores the wives to the cast of characters and makes a few changes that seem to be motivated by concern for dramatic effect.[28] The second distinct version that appears in the Fitzwilliam manuscripts is the one submitted to Diaghilev, translated into French by Raverat. It is obvious from this version that the dramatic conception was far from sacrosanct: there are far more dances included, all highlighted in the script, and the drama is a less cohesive *mélange* organized around the dances. Because the project was rejected by Diaghilev, this version was discarded.

Keynes's scenario, which does not appear in the Fitzwilliam manuscripts,[29] offers several important points of contrast. His version is in nine scenes, rather than Raverat's five acts alternating between Heaven and Earth, and the pointed emphasis on materialism has disappeared. Instead of being identified simply as Jehovah, the Deity is referred to as the Godhead, or Job's Spiritual Self.[30] There are two explanations for this interpretation, both of which may have intersected. First, Wicksteed had seen the Blake cycle as a struggle between good and evil within Job, personified as his spiritual self and his materialistic self; and even though Wicksteed does not use precisely this language, Keynes's use is consistent with his premise. Second, the project would be at some small risk for blasphemy prosecution if the Supreme Being were characterized on stage.[31] Surprisingly, Keynes differs from his model Wicksteed in two respects. The issue of Job's sin is left unanswered: instead, Job's Spiritual Self consents 'that his moral nature be tested in the furnace of temptation'. Furthermore, Keynes differs from Wicksteed over an issue that seems to trouble nearly everyone. In the biblical account, Job's seven sons and three daughters are destroyed by Satan, and Job is given a new family when his trials are over. In Blake, however, Wicksteed determined that there were seven women killed along with the seven men, and that Blake must have intended them as the wives of the sons. This leaves Blake free to bring back the original three daughters of Job in his penultimate plate, before the restoration of Job's wealth and the rest of his family. Raverat took this interpretation for her scenario, in which only the daughters return at the end. In Keynes's version, however, the women killed are daughters, not wives, and the entire family is restored to the humbled Job in the last scene.

Keynes's scenario differs from Raverat's in two other ways. He depicts Satan's plagues as terrifying visions during Job's sleep, rather than the Biblical plague of boils, which would have been both difficult and distasteful to depict on stage. Keynes also makes an unprecedented departure in his labeling of Job's comforters. Here they are 'three wily hypocrites', a judgment far harsher than anything found in either the Bible or Blake.[32]

The scenario written by Vaughan Williams is included in the Fitzwilliam manuscripts.[33] It appears in the published score as well, in which it actually takes two forms: the synopsis printed at the beginning, and more detailed comments, including stage directions, written above the music as the drama unfolds. The score bears the disclaimer 'The following synopsis and the more detailed scenario printed with the music differs in some particulars from the original scheme of the authors. For these alterations the composer alone is responsible.'[34] Vaughan Williams's language is the most direct of the three authors: his Deity is not 'Job's Spiritual Self', the 'Godhead', or 'Jehovah': he is simply God. In many respects his scenario resembles Keynes's, but it is apparent that the composer has not simply accepted the earlier versions of the drama. Vaughan Williams returned to the original sources himself, both the Bible and Blake, and added biblical verses and references to illustrations not selected by Keynes, as well as extra staging and choreographic directions. Several of the details are included for dramatic effect: Vaughan Williams's addition of a funeral cortège to Scene V, the scene in which Job learns of his misfortunes, helps to create action at a point that was originally dangerously static. But some of the details written into the score subtly alter the meaning or even directly contradict the synopsis published with the score, and the composer's use of several of the Job illustrations out of their proper order does violence to Blake's philosophy.

One of the main differences between Vaughan Williams and Keynes is the vexing issue of the daughters/wives. In the synopsis, Scene III is labeled 'Minuet of the Sons and Daughters of Job', yet a few pages later in the score it becomes the 'Minuet of the Sons of Job and their Wives'. It seems the composer is following Raverat here, because at the end only the daughters are restored.[35] Vaughan Williams also obscures what is in the other scenarios the climax of the drama, for his Elihu does not rebuke Job, either for materialism or for any other sin, and there is no revelation of Job perceiving his error. Also, the composer's conclusion to the drama is more subdued than in Keynes. In addition to omitting the restored sons, Vaughan Williams is emphatic that Job should not play an instrument, even though the Blake illustration clearly shows him doing so. The composer also adds the illustration, from earlier in the cycle, of Job receiving charity. In Blake's sequence this was one of Job's darkest moments and an important step in his redemption, emphasizing that Job was reduced to accepting the charity he had once given. By invoking this image of Job's restored prosperity, by the prohibition against his playing an instrument, and by describing Job as an old and humbled man, Vaughan Williams clouds the unfettered rejoicing imagined by both Blake and Keynes.

Keynes and Raverat each had occasion to disagree with Vaughan Williams about his conception of the drama. Keynes said of the composer that

He wished to introduce features having no connexion whatever with the designs, whereas it was my intention that the entire conception should be unadulterated Blake. No compromise was possible. Ralph was a formidable, but generous, opponent and gave way with good grace. At one point he wrote a letter to Gwen telling her that I had made my objections to his proposals 'in sorrow rather than in anger', so that he had to agree with me.[36]

The extraneous elements to which Keynes refers must be the additional pictorial associations found only in the piano solo edition, that suggest resemblance between certain scenes, pictures in the National Gallery, and folk dances.[37] This piano version, originally meant for use in rehearsing the dancers, was arranged from the composer's two-piano score by Vally Lasker, an associate of Holst.[38] Because these additions occur nowhere but in Lasker's edition, they can only be securely linked to Vaughan Williams on the basis of Keynes's complaints.

Keynes had stated his intent was to stage Blake's *Job* 'as Wicksteed called it',[39] and the composer was obviously pressed to familiarize himself with Wicksteed's study. Again, Vaughan Williams asserted his independence. In the same letter to Raverat in which he asks for the revised scenario, he says, 'I've got the Wicksteed book – but I'm not going to worry about the left foot and the right foot.'[40] In another letter to her, he discusses scene ordering. Vaughan Williams had changed the order of events in Blake in order to make better dramatic sense. In the original, Job is sitting in front of his house when the messengers appear to tell him of his losses. Two plates later, a sleeping Job is being tormented by Satan. The composer has reversed the order so that Job is awakened by the messengers from his dreams of Satan's torments. This condensing of events calls for only one recumbent Job, rather than two, but Raverat and Keynes insist that the drama should follow Blake's sequence. As a footnote to this detailed and lengthy discussion, Vaughan Williams remarks

> I agree that this illustration is probably the finest but it doesn't follow that it makes a good *stage* climax. Also I don't feel inclined necessarily to read into it all that Wicksteed and other say that it means. I am only interested in the *picture itself* and the texts with which *Blake* surrounds it.[41]

The issue of the scene ordering was still being debated after the première, and the composer was continuing to advocate his own ideas as well as offer reproach that his concept was not fully realized. In a letter to Raverat, Vaughan Williams critiques the production, remarking that there would have been greater clarity if his stage directions had been carried out. Lamenting the lack of a procession where he had asked for one, he insists that if there is to be no procession, he will cut some of the music.[42] Vaughan Williams ultimately compromised on the issue of scene ordering to the extent that the printed score contains directions for a cut should future producers wish to follow Blake's original order.

Examination of the scenarios and correspondence sheds much light on the issue of *Job*'s creation, but because of the tantalizingly incomplete documentation, there are a few questions that cannot be answered. Conflicting evidence, and the one-sidedness of the extant letters, make it difficult to assign particular scenarios to specific events, and, unless the letters written to Vaughan Williams by Keynes and

Raverat come to light, the problem may never be solved. It seems curious that so many versions of Raverat's basic scenario exist, as though it was being fine-tuned, considering that it was so fundamentally different from Keynes's: it is hard to imagine Keynes approving any of her versions, since they differ in substantive ways from his.[43] But what Keynes sent to Vaughan Williams, and what the composer initially rejected, was apparently not his own scenario and was, presumably, Raverat's. The existing scenarios and letters are also contradicted by Keynes's memoirs, in which he asserts that he and Raverat sat down together to do the scenario.[44]

The differences between Keynes and Raverat were centered largely around her extravagant language, the question of the daughters/wives, and the restoration of the entire family. The fundamental shape of their scenarios always followed Blake's basic outline of events. It is clear that after Vaughan Williams joined the project, the two of them struggled to keep the composer from straying too far from Blake and Wicksteed. Just by means of his synopsis and stage details, the composer had already altered Blake's vision in several substantial ways; but the most important vehicle for his own interpretation was his music.

One indication that Vaughan Williams had constructed the music around his own interpretation appears in his letter to Edwin Evans of the Camargo Society, regarding the Society's proposed production of *Job* (note that the roles he attributes to Keynes and Raverat do not include authoring the scenario):

> The only condition as far as I am concerned, and I am sure the mention of it is a mere formality – *that I shall be allowed to veto anything in the production which to my mind does not agree with my music....* But I cannot move without Geoffrey Keynes & Mrs Gwen Raverat who are the prime instigators and have designed the scenery and costumes.[45]

In the letter written after the first performance, Vaughan Williams congratulated Raverat for her 'beautiful realization of Blake' and was 'pleased that my music seemed to fit in with your scenery and dresses'.[46] These letters reveal that the composer saw the potential for conflict between the staging and his music, and was not inclined to alter any aspect of his concept, instead being relieved when the costumes worked well with his music. Vaughan Williams, following an impulse similar to Blake's, was making a system to support his vision and wanted to ensure that none of the stage action would violate it. Analysis of the score reveals the structure of this system.

It has long been recognized that there are several different thematic associations in *Job*. In another letter to Evans of the Camargo Society, the composer offers an amusing critique of the programme notes for *Job* and regrets that musical excerpts are not included:

> Many thanks for the notes – which seem as good as they can be without musical quotations. Perhaps some of the accounts of modulations suggest rather a Mus Bac [Bachelor of Music] harmony creation 'start thus and modulate through p minor, Q major, R sharp minor back to the original key. Preserve some unity of style' – But I daresay this is necessary – and certainly if people like it, certainly let them have it.[47]

The composer may have been more satisfied with the programme for the Norwich Festival, because included with the programme notes was a page of music with the primary themes outlined.[48] Vaughan Williams had constructed a system of complex musical representations that corresponded to the characters on stage, and he wanted the audience to know this. Several studies have dealt with this basic motivic construction,[49] but the relationship of the motives to an underlying system of symbolism has not been recognized, nor have critical harmonic relationships been explored.

The system of symbolism that was the basis of Wicksteed's study is reflected in the musical treatment, despite the composer's ingenuous claims not to have been influenced by it. But crucial points of musical construction cannot be explained satisfactorily if Wicksteed's influence is not recognized. There is overwhelming evidence that Wicksteed's analysis of Blake was the guiding principle behind much of the project. Vaughan Williams read the book, apparently at the insistence of Keynes, and it was the subject of much discussion among the three participants. Even if Vaughan Williams was skeptical about some of Wicksteed's more complicated points, the basic and, to everyone else, unarguable discovery of the symbolism would have had to affect him on some level. Reduced to its simplest elements, Blake's cycle is about good versus evil, right versus left, with man and his opposing tendencies caught in the middle. Vaughan Williams reproduced this system, contrasting three compositional techniques to reflect the Heavenly, Earthly, and Satanic elements.

The music associated with Satan and his followers is highly constructivist, making extensive use of motives, ostinatios, and small recurring figures. This is an elegant musical manifestation of Blake's hatred of the analytical. Satan himself is portrayed by four distinct motives (see Example 3.1): (a) a staccato-leap, expanding chromatic figure, a minor seventh that opens in both directions to a major or minor tenth, (b) a brass fanfare characterized chiefly by a melodic minor third, although its harmonisation differs among its appearances, (c) a quartal figure, and (d) extensive use of the interval of the tritone.

Alternating major and minor thirds, which are related to the major or minor tenths of the chromatic staccato-leap motive, are also associated with Satan. The tritone or the minor third often form the limits of a number of repetitive figures. Scene II, Satan's dance, is constructed over a tritone-bounded ostinato, which shifts at letter Q to include alternating major and minor thirds within the boundaries of the tritone. Three different rhythmic patterns for Satan's ostinati create a constantly shifting metrical emphasis and add to the intricacy. Little or no tonal context can be determined for most of Satan's highly dissonant music.

One or more of these motives are prominent each time Satan appears, and in particular all four motives permeate Satan's dance. In addition, these motives represent Satan's involvement in various events, even when he is not present. Job's three comforters (Keynes's 'wily hypocrites'), for example, are introduced by the staccato-leap motive, and their false sympathy is further depicted by alternating major and minor thirds. Another musical association with the absent Satan is the arrival of the messengers, who tell Job of his misfortunes by means of *senza misura* runs in the oboe that outline interlocking quartal figures. These musical representations are analogous to the symbolism of the Blake illustrations, in which the left hand or foot betrays Satan's influence.

(a) Expanding chromatic figure, seven measures before E

(b) Fanfare with minor third, O

(c) Quartal figure, five measures after H

(d) Tritone forming the boundaries in an ostinato pattern eight measures before R

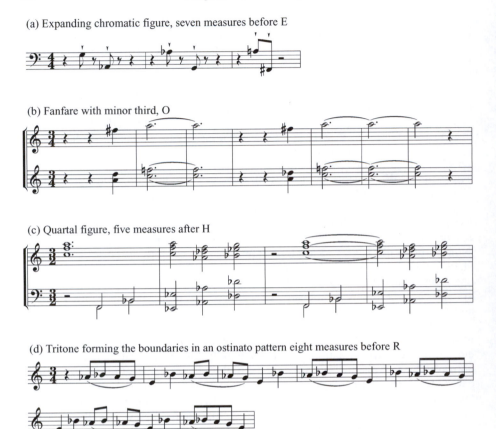

Example 3.1   Satan's four motives (a–d)

In contrast, the music of God and the angels is usually in a sharp key or mode, and is predominantly homorhythmic. Their material is broadly melodic rather than motivic, and with the one exception of the Pavane which returns in the altar dance, it is never heard more than once. Many of the expansive melodies, and certainly some of the most strikingly beautiful moments of the work, are found in these sections, and include the Tudor masque dances of the Pavane and the Galliard. The metaphor of dance as worship has a venerable history, and in *Job* the old masque dances serve to define the acts of homage. The music for Elihu, who is human but speaks for God, is similar to the heavenly music in its simplicity, melodic emphasis and sharp key. It consists of an expressive, minimally accompanied melody with strong connotations of English folk-song, alternating between modal and pentatonic.

Between the extremes of Heaven and Hell lies the middle ground of Job's music. Job is depicted by two themes, first heard in the introduction and in the music for his dream. These melodies are either modal or pentatonic, like those for the heavenly characters, and are equally expansive and lyrical. Yet they are not purely homorhythmic, but often treated contrapuntally. The theme of the introduction is heard against a counter melody in the lower strings, and the music for Job's dream is presented in canon (see Example 3.2).

Example 3.2   Theme of Job's dream

© 1934 Oxford University Press. Reproduced by permission.

In addition, each theme reappears in subsequent scenes: as a fragment such as the passage 'Hast thou considered my servant Job' from Scene I, or in more complete form at the end of the messengers' Scene V, in which the theme of Job's dream symbolizes that he is still at peace. The music associated with Job's dream returns in Scene VII, this time in combination with the other material of the altar dance. Thus Job's music is related to heaven in its melodic content, and to Satan in its recurrent and contrapuntal treatment.

The interchange between God and Satan in Scene I clearly illustrates this contrast of techniques. God is depicted by diatonic triads, whereas Satan is represented by an ascending linear quartal passage. This quartal figure is a parody of the fourth–fifth-octave ascent that had signified Heaven opening, just before the Saraband. It reveals that in addition to specific melodies or motives being associated with each group of characters, Satan's techniques can color the material of other characters. In Scene III, for example, the 'Minuet of the Sons and their Wives', a modal flute melody represents the dance; after Satan enters and the dancers fall dead, the melody continues, but now with chromatic and dissonant alterations that represent Satan's act. Vaughan Williams again chooses chromatic alteration for the dance of the sinister veiled figures in Scene VI. Their music is a parody of the 'Saraband of the Sons of God', interrupted by an ascending quartal figure when the dancers are revealed as Satan and his minions.

The association of thematic material and technique with character groups makes possible a complex layered texture in which the symbolism is clear. Aspects of the Heavenly and the Earthly are combined but plainly demarcated in the altar dance of Scene VIII. Its main melody is related to the beginning of the Kyrie of the Gregorian Mass VIII, the Kyrie de Angelis, and represents Job's worship.[50] Two themes from previous scenes reappear: the music of Job's dream, and the 'Pavane of the Sons of the Morning'. Each is in duple meter, and each frequently appears in conjunction with the altar theme, which is in compound meter, first 6/8, then 12/8. This clear metric contrast separates the material and highlights the continuous altar dance. The orchestration further distinguishes the three thematic layers, generally confining each melody to a specific family, the altar motive to the high winds, the heavenly

(a) Job: 'It may be that my children have sinned', ten measures after C

(b) God: 'All that he hath is in thy power', K

Example 3.3   Descent figures (a–d)

© 1934 Oxford University Press. Reproduced by permission.

Pavane to the harp and brass, and Job's theme to the strings. Eventually, the music of Job's dream gives way to the ongoing altar theme, suggesting Job's reconciliation with God and the end of his trials.

Elements of symbolism are thus inherent in the contrasting compositional techniques by which Vaughan Williams represents the various groups of characters, particularly in Job's position midway between the extremes. A critical aspect of this technique is the resemblance between descending figures that first link Job to God and then Job to Satan (Example 3.3).[51] In Scene I, at God's proclamation to Satan 'all that he hath is in thy power', the descending motive in the violins resembles that

(c) Job: 'Let the day perish wherein I was born', Pp

(d) Satan stands, nine measures after Qq

Example 3.3   (*continued*)

© 1934 Oxford University Press. Reproduced by permission.

heard in the first part of the scene when Job stands and blesses his children, one of the Bible verses Vaughan Williams added to this scene. Wicksteed had pointed out that one aspect of the symbolism in Blake is that Job resembles God or Satan in turn, depending upon his actions, as the story unfolds. This likeness is suggested not only by the use of right and left, as described earlier, but also by actual facial similarity. Thus when Job blesses his children, he is emulating God, and the music is related to that of God's proclamation. When Job, in Scene VI, is finally overcome by his trials and curses the day he was born, his anger is depicted by another chromatic descent figure, rhythmically and harmonically different from the first pair. Later in the same scene, when Satan stands and reveals himself to Job, the descent figure is essentially identical to that of Job's curse.

This situation is thus the exact mirror of the first, in which there was a resemblance between God and Job when Job was performing a pious act; here, Job's curse causes him instead to imitate Satan. Descent figures, usually involving triplets, are found throughout the masque at moments of particular drama, but the relationship between these pairs of descents is the most telling evidence of the influence of Wicksteed.

Harmonic aspects, particularly key relationships, also play a symbolic role in *Job*, and many of the harmonic relationships governing the masque grow out of the motivic relationships. The minor third and the tritone, two of the intervals associated with Satan that often form the outer boundaries of his ostinato patterns, are particularly important as key relationships. Scenes that contrast the Heavenly and the Satanic are frequently expressed by the tritone relationship: both the tonic Dflat/Csharp at the end of the messenger scene, and the D flat at the end of scene in which Satan reveals himself to Job, are contrasted against the tonic G of the 'Pavane of the Sons of the Morning', the representation of Heaven restored. The symbolism of the minor third appears in Scene IV, 'Job's Dream'. It begins over a pedal on E, but just before Satan's entrance, when Job begins to move uneasily in his sleep, the pedal becomes C sharp. This change of pedal is not included when the theme returns in the altar dance, because Satan plays no part in this scene of worship. Tonal centers related by minor thirds and tritones are seen even after Satan's defeat; in the Pavane, the movement is G–E–D♭–B♭–E–G, and that of the altar dance is B♭–G–D♭–E–G. Vaughan Williams's symbolism of evil in the tonal relationship of minor third becomes clearest in the final scene. The composer specifies that this scene is the same as the opening, but with the significant omission of Job's sons. The music is the same as that for the introduction; it is orchestrated a little less richly and there are very slight melodic variations, but the passages representing Job, his fields, and the entrance of his children are present in the same order and for the same number of measures. The critical difference is that the epilogue moves quietly and unexpectedly to end on B flat, rather than the tonic G of the introduction. Indeed, the entire masque up to this point generally revolves around G or, less frequently, the related centers of C and D. The only emphasis on a remote pitch occurs in the sections suggesting Satan's victory, when the movement is to the tritone relationship of D flat. So the arrival at B flat at the end of the masque does not fulfill a purely musical purpose; rather it exists solely to delineate Satan's interval of the minor third. Vaughan Williams is clearly symbolizing the persistence of evil even when all is seemingly resolved. This idea was undoubtedly taken from Raverat: her last line is 'Enter Satan to spy again?' and her scenario is the only one in which this direction appears. Vaughan Williams did not include it in the text of his own synopsis, perhaps because this interpretation entirely negates Keynes's reading of Job's complete restoration.

The expression of Vaughan Williams's own interpretation is found not only in the compositional structure of the masque but in its larger shape as well. Vaughan Williams reinforces musically his own dramatic scenario by displacing the climax of the work. The critical issue here is Job's redemption, and in Vaughan Williams's version it begins immediately after Job has cursed his fate. Satan's appearance forces Job to realize what is behind his questioning of God's justice, and that he has been misled by his comforters, who insist that he is being punished for his sins. Vaughan Williams emphasizes the drama of Job's realization by adding sinister veiled figures and directing that Satan stand before the terrified men. Job's enlightenment is the climax of the masque; but here it occurs earlier than in Blake and for different reasons, and the scene itself is not drawn from any Blake illustration.

In Blake's vision, Elihu is the pivotal figure in the turning of Job's fortunes; his arguments begin the process of Job's reconciliation with God. The illustration of Elihu is the model for the next scene, but the climax is now past, and Elihu no longer serves the same purpose. Vaughan Williams's Elihu is conciliatory, not the stern and wrathful figure seen in Blake; the music of his dance, revealingly labeled a dance of youth and beauty, is elegant and calm. The music of Satan's fall also has none of the drama of the Blake illustration. It is so curiously devoid of the intensity and emotion seen in the print that, for the only time in the masque, the directions in the score are crucial to an understanding of the composer's intent. Without seeing a staged production, the listener could never guess that this stately music represents Satan being driven out of Heaven. In Vaughan Williams's version, there can be no unequivocal victory over Satan, as evinced by his return at the end of the drama and the implication that the cycle might begin again.

There is no doubt that, to Vaughan Williams, the story of Job made splendid theater. He had a well-developed sense of the stage, and several of the changes he made to the scenario were motivated by his theatrical instincts, for example the reordering of Scenes IV and V, or the addition of the funeral cortege. He depended heavily on the pictorial aspects of the Blake cycle, studying it in its entirely rather than relying on Keynes's reduction, and added the numerous details in the score that incorporated events not found in the illustrations, as well as unrelated paintings, folk dances, and elements from the composer's own imagination.

But many of the changes to Blake's concept cannot be explained as concessions to staging or choreography. The common ground between Vaughan Williams's manipulation of the dramatic scenario and the organization of his music is the relentless deconstruction of Blake's vision. His changes to Raverat's and Keynes's texts were the beginning of the process that he completed in his music. His musical expression of Blake's symbolism as uncovered by Wicksteed is an effective dramatic device, one that created a work so cohesive that *Job* can satisfactorily be separated from its staging as concert music. But it also provided Vaughan Williams, by means of harmonic relationships derived from the motives, an opportunity to apply the symbolism to his own system. Finally, the composer deliberately distorted

Blake's conclusion by the larger-scale processes: he recombined elements that once represented distinct steps in Job's spiritual journey, and musically repositioned the climax to reflect an entirely different interpretation.

Thus, using the same symbolism that Blake invented, the composer has rewritten the meaning. This deconstruction actually brings him closer to the Job of the Bible than any of the other interpretations, but his goal was not a recension of the authoritative biblical text. Rather, it was to express his own beliefs through the nominal vehicle of Blake.

Wilfrid Mellers, in his thoughtful book on Vaughan Williams, discusses the impact on the composer of such literary influences of Whitman, Bunyan and Blake, and contends that the composer discovered in the Job illustrations a vision similar to his own.[52] There is little doubt that Vaughan Williams was attracted to Blake – his song settings attest to that. But at least in terms of *Job*, the critical issue is that his conception is not at all the same as Blake's. Vaughan Williams envisions a darker and more somber view of the story, and this is nowhere better illustrated than in the last scene. Blake's final drawing bears the caption 'So the Lord blessed the latter end of Job more than the beginning', and the illustration depicts Job with his restored wealth and complete family, as Keynes's scenario also reflects. The image is complementary to Blake's first print, but rather than sitting peacefully at prayer, the family is rejoicing, playing instruments, and even Job's sheep seem intangibly more content. Blake completes the symbolism by the addition of the rising sun, whereas in the first illustration it was setting. Compare to this Vaughan Williams's version, in which Job's wealth is not restored, nor are his sons; in the composer's description, Job is now an 'old and humbled man'; and he has been specifically prohibited from playing an instrument. Completing this impression is the reduced, sparse orchestral texture and the harmonic presence of Satan in the unexpected shift of tonal center.

The main element missing from the composer's interpretation of Blake is Job's role as a strong central figure attempting to make sense of his misfortunes. Instead, Vaughan Williams's Job is a passive, enduring figure, a pawn in the ongoing conflict of good and evil, who plays little or no part in his own redemption. His physical afflictions are represented but not his spiritual struggle and process of soul-searching; and even in the last scene he is still a victim, old and humbled, bereft of family and possessions. The philosophy that emerges is a de-emphasis of man's role in his own redemption, and a sense of resignation to the ongoing presence of evil, beliefs that would have been anathema to Blake.

There are striking resemblances between this interpretation and elements of the composer's life. Vaughan Williams insisted on enlisting in the army and served in the ambulance corps during the First World War, a harrowing experience of which he spoke little. Letters, and most particularly his biography by his second wife, Ursula, reveal that he came home a changed man, concerned that he would not regain his creative gifts and worried that they were lost permanently as a result of the horror he had seen.[53] Many of his closest friends, including several of his students and members of his compositional circle, had been killed. It is hardly surprising that he would have strong feelings regarding the issues of human suffering and the nature of evil, and that his interpretation would not emphasize man's redemption but instead his victimization.[54] Vaughan Williams's version of *Job* differs in important respects from all his models – the Bible, Blake, Wicksteed, Raverat and Keynes –

but in destroying Blake's system Vaughan Williams most closely approaches the original insoluble problem. Vaughan Williams's *Job* is no more a musical depiction of Blake than Blake is a mere illustration of scenes from the Bible. The greatness of Blake's cycle is that it is a powerful statement of individual belief. In his own interpretation Vaughan Williams has created a personal vision to rival that of Blake.

Appendix: Texts of the Scenarios for *Job*

A. Scenario by Gwen Raverat. First version[55]

The stage is divided into 2 parts; the back half is raised 1 or 2 steps and represents Heaven. The scene shows a night sky with stars. The drop scenes which represent Earth fall and hiding the raised part of the stage.
    In 5 acts with 1 interval.
Act 1 Earth: Sunset, pastoral scene [with sheep]
Act 2 Heaven: [night sky]
Interval
Act 3 Earth: Night, before Job's house
Act 4 Heaven: [night sky]
Act 5 Earth: Sunrise; pastoral scene [with ripe corn]

Act 1 *Earth*: (The front part of the stage only is seen)
Sunset. The scene represents hilly country, where many flocks of sheep are feeding. Job and his whole family are seated under a tree in the middle of the stage. They are rich and prosperous shepherds, and a complacent materialism reigns all about them. Job's children perform a *pastoral dance*. Satan comes in softly to spy, and dances among them.
    After the dance, Job and his children sit down to feast in 2 groups on each side of the front of the stage. Satan leaps into the middle of the stage behind them and appeals to Jehovah to show himself. The drop scene rises and reveals
Act 2 *Heaven*: (the back part of the stage is raised 2 steps above the front part). Night sky with stars. Jehovah is seated on his throne and his children are dancing before him. (*Dance of Jehovah's children.*) Satan addresses Jehovah and accuses Job of the sin of materialism, pointing at Job as he sits in voluptuous contentment in the front part of the stage. Jehovah authorizes Satan to tempt Job; he descends from his throne and with a gesture allows Satan to take his place. He goes out, followed by all his children. Heaven darkens. After a wild dance of triumph Satan leaps on to the throne. Thunder and lightning – Job and his wife and daughters bid farewell to their sons and the sons' wives. They go out, and the feast of the shepherds grows more riotous. They begin a *wild and drunken dance*. After gloating over them for a while with evil pleasure, Satan springs down among them and destroys them all. They fall dead in heaps. Triumph of Satan.
Curtain
Interval
Act 3 *Earth*: Before Job's house at night. Job and his wife are sitting at their door in peaceful happiness. Three messengers enter, one after the other. They bring the news

of the deaths of Job's sons and the destruction of all his wealth. Job mourns and rends his clothes and sits naked on the dunghill. Satan enters and torments Job in many ways and at last smites him with boils. Job is quite overcome and grows desperate, but he does not curse Jehovah.

His three friends enter. They perform a *dance of sympathy* which gradually becomes a *dance of pious complacency and self-esteem*. They accuse Job of sin. Job justifies himself and summons his vision of the Deity. They all assume attitudes of devotion and expectancy. The drop scene rises and reveals

Act 4 *Heaven*: but Satan on Jehovah's throne instead of Jehovah. Horror, terror, and despair of all. They cower and hide their faces.

Elihu enters and rebukes Job for his materialism. 'Ye are old and I am very young.' A dance of youth and beauty. Job understands how he has sinned and has a true vision of the Deity. Jehovah enters in majesty, followed by his children; he drives Satan from his throne and takes his place upon it in glory. Job and the other mortals worship. Job's daughters return; he embraces them. Shepherds enter; then all together fetch stones and build an altar before Jehovah (altar-building dance). They sacrifice and dance and play musical instruments while the sons of the morning dance in Heaven. (Two dances of glory, a heavenly and an earthly one.)

Act 5: During this dance the last drop scene falls hiding Heaven. The back cloth represents the same hills as in Scene 1, only it is now sunrise; instead of sheep there are fields of ripe corn. The shepherds repeat their pastoral dance, while Job and his wife sit under the tree – enter Satan to spy again? [My note – this last note about Satan is in brackets in the original]

Curtain

B. Scenario by Keynes

Scene I: Job is sitting in the sunset of prosperity with his wife, surrounded by his seven sons and three daughters. They all join in a pastoral dance. When they have dispersed, leaving Job and his wife alone, Satan enters unperceived. He appeals to Heaven, which opens, revealing the Godhead (Job's Spiritual Self) enthroned within. On the steps are the Heavenly Hosts. Job's Spiritual Self consents that his moral nature be tested in the furnace of temptation.

Scene II: Satan, after a triumphal dance, usurps the throne.

Scene III: Job's sons and daughters are feasting and dancing when Satan appears and destroys them.

Scene IV: Job's peaceful sleep is disturbed by Satan with terrifying visions of War, Pestilence and Famine.

Scene V: Messengers come to Job with tidings of the destruction of all his possessions and the death of his sons and daughters. Satan introduces Job's comforters, three wily hypocrites. Their dance at first simulates compassion, but this gradually changes to rebuke and anger. Job rebels: 'Let the day perish wherein I was born.' He invokes his vision of the Godhead, but the opening Heaven reveals Satan upon the throne. Job and his friends shrink in terror.

Scene VI: There enters Elihu who is young and beautiful. 'Ye are old and I am very young.' Job perceives his sin. The Heavens then open, revealing Job's Spiritual Self again enthroned.

Scene VII: Satan again appeals to Job's Godhead, claiming the victory, but is repelled and driven down by the Sons of the Morning. Job's household build an altar and worship with musical instruments, while the Heavenly dance continues.

Scene VIII: Job sits a humbled man in the sunrise of restored prosperity, surrounded by his family, upon whom he bestows his blessing.

C. Scenario by Vaughan Williams

Scene I 'Hast thou considered my servant Job?'
Introduction. Pastoral Dance. Satan's appeal to God. Saraband of the Sons of God.
Job and his family sit in quiet contentment surrounded by flocks and herds. Satan enters unperceived and appeals to heaven. God answers: 'All that he hath is in thy power.'

Scene II 'So Satan went forth from the presence of the Lord.' (Plate 1)
Satan's Dance
God's throne is empty. Satan in wild triumph seats himself upon it.

Scene III 'Then came a great wind and smote the four corners of the house and it fell upon the young men and they are dead.'
Minuet of the sons and daughters of Job
Job's children are feasting and dancing: Satan appears and destroys them.

Scene IV 'In thoughts from the visions of the night ... fear came upon me and trembling.'
Job's Dream. Dance of plague, pestilence, famine, and battle. (Plate 2)
Job is quietly asleep. Satan leans over him and evokes terrible visions which dance round him, foreboding his tribulation to come.

Scene V (no break between Scenes IV and V) 'There came a Messenger.'
Dance of the Messengers
The messengers announce to Job the destruction of all his wealth and the death of his sons and daughters. Job still blesses God.

Scene VI 'Behold, happy is the man whom God correcteth.'
Dance of Job's comforters. Job's curse. A vision of Satan.
Satan introduces Job's comforters, three wily hypocrites. Their dance is at first one of apparent sympathy, but gradually changes to rebuke and anger. Job curses God. 'Let the day perish wherein I was born.' Job invokes his vision of God. Heaven opens and reveals Satan seated on God's throne. Job and his friends cower in terror.

Scene VII (no break between Scenes VI and VII) 'Ye are old and I am very young'
Elihu's dance of youth and beauty.
'Then the Lord answered Job.'
Pavane of the Sons of the Morning.
Enter Elihu, who is young and beautiful. Heaven opens again and shows God sitting on His throne surrounded by the heavenly host.

Scene VIII 'All the Sons of God shouted for joy.' (Plate 3)
Galliard of the Sons of the Morning
'My servant Job shall pray for you.'
Altar dance and heavenly pavane.

Satan appeals to God but is driven down by the Sons of the morning. Job and his household build an altar and worship God with musical instruments. The heavenly dance continues.

Scene IX (no break between Scenes VIII and IX) 'So the Lord blessed the latter end of Job more than his beginning.'

Epilogue

Job, an old and humbled man, sits again surrounded by his family. He blesses his children. (Plate 4)

D. Vaughan Williams's additional stage directions. Roman type indicates the text found in the printed score and in the manuscript full score.[56] *Items in italics are the texts found only in the piano solo edition, arranged by Vally Lasker from the two-piano version*[57]

Scene I

Curtain rises. Scene (back cloth) as in Blake illustration I. Job with his wife and a few servants sitting. Shepherds and husbandmen cross the stage and salute him. / Here the distant landscape lights up suggesting the far off sounds of flocks and herds. / Here Job's children enter and group themselves round him. / Dance of Job's sons and daughters *(6 sons and 3 daughters). (The figures of this dance should take suggestions from the dances 'Jenny pluck pears' and 'Hunsdon House' also the dancing group in the 'Munich glyptothek'.)* First the women dance alone. / Here the men dance. / Here the women group themselves in the middle and the men move slowly round them. Then vice versa. / Here the dance becomes general. / Job stand ups and blesses his children, saying 'It may be my children have sinned.' The dance continues. / Everyone kneels. Tableau as in Blake I. Angels appear at the side of the stage as in Blake II and V. *Also see Botticelli's Nativity (Nat. Gall) and Blake's frontispiece.*[58]/ The group breaks up into two on each side of the stage. All go off except Job and his wife who are left in meditation down stage (the Angels however remain). / Enter Satan. / Satan appeals to Heaven. / Heaven gradually opens and displays God sitting in majesty, surrounded by the sons of God (as in Blake II). The line of Angels stretches of earth to Heaven. / All bow down in adoration. / God arises in His majesty and beckons to Satan. / Satan steps forward at God's command. / A light falls on Job. God regards him with affection and says to Satan 'Hast thou considered my servant Job.' / Satan says 'Put forth Thy hand now and touch all that he hath and he will curse Thee to Thy face.' / God says 'All that he hath is in thy power.' Satan departs (see Blake V). / The dance of homage begins again. God leaves his throne. / The stage darkens. Black-out.

Scene II

Stage gradually lightens. Heaven is empty and God's throne vacant. Satan alone on the stage. / A light falls on Satan, standing at the bottom of the steps of Heaven. / Here the dance begins. / Satan climbs up to God's throne. / Satan kneels in mock adoration before God's throne. / The hosts of Hell enter running, and kneel before Satan, who has risen and stands before God's throne facing the audience. / Satan with a big gesture sits in God's throne. / Black-out; a black curtain falls leaving the front quarter of the stage visible.

Scene III

This is now titled Minuet of the Sons of Job and Their Wives, in contrast to the sons and daughters in the synopsis.

Stage gradually lights up. Enter Job's sons and their wives and dance in front of the curtain. They hold golden wine cups in their left hands which they clash at + (each time). The Dance should be formal, statuesque, and slightly voluptuous, it should not be a minuet as far as choreography is concerned. *For the clashing of the wine cups suggestions should be taken from the Morris Dance 'Winster Processional'. See also Botticelli 'Marriage feast'.*/ Here the black curtain draws back and shows an interior as in Blake III. / Enter Satan above. The dance stops suddenly. The dancers fall dead. Tableau as in Blake III. / Gradual black-out. The black curtain descends.

Scene IV

The black curtain rises. Stage gradually lights up. Job is discovered lying asleep as in Blake VI. / Job moves uneasily in his sleep. / Enter Satan. Tableau as in Blake VI. Satan stands over Job and calls up terrible Visions of Plague, Pestilence, Famine, Battle, Murder, and Sudden Death who posture before Job (see Blake XI). Each of these should be represented by a group of dancers. The dance should be wild and full of movement, and the stage should finally be full. *(Suggestions may be taken from Rubens 'Horrors of War' (Nat. Gall))* / Enter Plague and Pestilence. / Enter Famine. / Enter Battle etc. / The dancers headed by Satan make a ring around Job and raise their hands three times. / The vision gradually disappears.

Scene V

Job awakens from his sleep and perceives three messengers, who arrive one after the other, telling him that all his wealth is destroyed. (See Blake IV.) / A sad procession passes across the back of the stage, culminating in the funeral cortege of Job's sons and their wives. / Job still blesses God. 'The Lord gave and the Lord hath taken away, blessed be the name of the Lord.'

Scene VI

Satan introduces in turn, Job's 3 Comforters (three wily hypocrites). Their dance is at first one of pretended sympathy. But develops into anger and reproach (see Blake VII and X). / Enter 1st Comforter. / Enter 2nd Comforter. / Enter 3rd Comforter. / Here the comforters return to their gestures of pretended sympathy. / Job stands and curses God, 'Let the day perish wherein I was born.' (see Blake VIII) / Heaven gradually becomes visible, showing mysterious veiled sinister figures, moving in a sort of parody of the Sons of God in Scene I. / Heaven in now lit up. The figures throw off their veils and display themselves as Satan enthroned, surrounded by the hosts of Hell. / Satan stands. Job and his friends cower in terror. / The vision gradually disappears.

Scene VII

Enter Elihu, a beautiful young man. 'I am young and ye are very old' (see Blake XII). / Heaven gradually shines behind the stars. Dim figures are seen dancing a solemn dance. As Heaven grows lighter, they are seen to be the Sons of the morning dancing before God's Throne (see Blake XIV).

Scene VIII

Enter Satan. He claims the victory over Job. / God pronounces sentence of banishment on Satan. / The Sons of the Morning gradually drive Satan down. (See

Blake V and XVI.) / Here Satan falls out of Heaven. (Blake XVI.) Black-out and Curtain. / Curtain rises. / Enter (on earth) Young men and Women playing on instruments; others bring stones and build an altar. Other decorate the altar with flowers (see Blake XXI). But Job must not play an instrument himself. / Job blesses the altar (see Blake XVIII). / The Heavenly dance begins again, while the dance on earth continues. / Tableau. / Gradual black out.

Scene IX (Epilogue)

Stage lights up again shewing the same scene as the opening. Job an old and humbled man sits with his wife. His friends come up one by one and give him presents (see Blake XIX). / Job stands and gazes on the distant cornfields. / Enter gradually Job's three daughters. / They sit at his feet. He stands and blesses them. (see Blake XX). / Very slow curtain, and black out.

Acknowledgements

This chapter is reprinted from the *International Journal of Musicology* 3 (1994): 339–71 by permission of Peter Lang GmbH Frankfurt. Portions of this chapter were presented at the meeting of the Pacific Southwest Chapter of the American Musicological Society, February 1990. I am grateful to The Carthusian Trust for a grant allowing subsequent research in England. I would like to thank the following people for conversations and advice regarding this article: Professors William F. Prizer and Alejandro Enrique Planchart of the University of California, Santa Barbara; Professors Byron Adams and Robert N. Essick, of the University of California, Riverside; Dr Alain Frogley of the University of Conneticut; Professor Carolyn Bremer of the University of Oklahoma, Norman; and Mr Robin Wells and Mr Geoffrey Ford, of Charterhouse School, England. I am also grateful to Mrs Ursula Vaughan Williams for her many kindnesses and suggestions.

Notes

1 Geoffrey Keynes, *Blake Studies: Notes on his Life and Works in Seventeen Chapters* (London: Rupert Hart-Davis, 1949), 123–4.
2 The first series was purchased by Thomas Butts and the second by John Linnell, who proposed and financed the series of copper-plate engravings. For a complete history of the Blake drawings and their current locations, see Keynes, *Blake Studies*, 124–45.
3 Keynes, *Blake Studies*, 149.
4 London, British Library, Add. MS 59814, ff. 28–30. *Job* was the composer's third work for dance. The first, the ballet *Old King Cole* (1923), incorporates old English folk dances. In *On Christmas Night* (1926) the composer had begun to explore the genre of the masque. It too contains traditional dances, including Hunsdon House, which Vaughan Williams cites as inspiration for the dance in Scene I of *Job*. See Michael Kennedy, *The Works of Ralph Vaughan Williams*, rev. edn (London: Oxford University Press, 1980), 178.
5 Ursula Vaughan Williams, *R.V.W.: A Biography of Ralph Vaughan Williams* (London: Oxford University Press, 1964), 183.
6 Cambridge, Fitzwilliam Museum, MS 1250–1985.
7 It received its première at the 1930 Norwich festival, conducted by the composer.

8   Vaughan Williams acknowledged that 'I owe the life of *Job* to Holst.' The two had spent
     countless of their 'field-days' over the masque. One of Holst's suggestions regarding *Job*
     was to beg the composer, almost on his knees, to reduce the complement of percussion,
     which Vaughan Williams considered but decided against. See Ralph Vaughan Williams,
     'A Musical Autobiography', in *National Music and other Essays*, 2nd edn (Oxford:
     Oxford University Press, 1987), 194; Ursula Vaughan Williams and Imogen Holst, eds,
     Heirs and Rebels: Letters Written to Each Other and Occasional Writings on Music (New
     York: Cooper Square, 1976), 76; and Kennedy, *Works*, 203.

9   Because of the limitations of the orchestra pit at the theater, the scoring had to be reduced;
     this was done not by the composer, but by Constant Lambert, who was to conduct. At the
     Covent Garden revival in 1948, Vaughan Williams was delighted that the size of the pit
     allowed the original orchestration to be heard for the first time in conjunction with the
     staging; and the conductor was Adrian Boult, to whom *Job* was dedicated. But the original
     scenery, designed by Gwen Raverat, had been abandoned in Holland when the Sadler's
     Wells Ballet had left at the outbreak of the war, and Vaughan Williams was unhappy with
     the new interpretation by John Piper. In addition, many of the stage directions which
     Vaughan Williams had written into the score were ignored. *Job* has been produced with
     new choreography and scene designs several times, including a 1977 production for
     Thames Television by Robert Cohan, and a 1992 version by David Bintley for the San
     Francisco Ballet.

10   Vaughan Williams and Holst, eds, *Heirs and Rebels*, 60–65.

11   Kennedy, *Works*, 225.

12   Vaughan Williams's feelings on the matter were so strong that when the project finally
     passed into the hands of its fourth collaborator, the choreographer Ninette de Valois, the
     composer was asked not to attend the early rehearsals, presumably to preclude his
     interference. His concern extended to the smallest details, including the size of the angels'
     wings. See Ursula Vaughan Williams, *R.V.W.*, 187.

13   Joseph N. Wicksteed, *Blake's Vision of the Book of Job* (London, 1910; reprint, New
     York: Haskell House, 1971). Keynes reviewed this book in the December 1, 1910, issue
     of *The Cambridge Review*, and discusses its importance in his *Blake Studies*, 146–7.

14   Wicksteed, *Blake's Vision*, 34–5.

15   Max Plowman, *An Introduction to the Study of Blake*, 2nd ed. (New York, Barnes and
     Noble, 1967), 58.

16   The explanation of Blake's system is found in the introductory material to Wicksteed,
     Blake's Vision, 13–43. The exposition of the symbolism of right and left is the main
     premise of the study and is discussed throughout the book in connection with each
     illustration.

17   Keynes, *The Gates of Memory* (Oxford: Clarendon Press, 1981), 204. A close reading of
     Wicksteed is essential to an understanding of *Job*. It is the only study securely associated
     with the creation of the masque (see also Vaughan Williams's acknowledgment of the
     book, quoted below). Some writers have turned to the work of Northrop Frye or Carl Jung,
     both published well after *Job* was composed, to help underscore Vaughan Williams's
     interpretation. These later studies, however well elements of them might agree with the
     composer's intent, have no relevance for Vaughan Williams's understanding of Blake or
     the biblical story. See Wilfrid Mellers, *Vaughan Williams and the Vision of Albion*
     (London: Barrie and Jenkins, 1989), and O. Alan Weltzien, 'Notes and Lineaments:
     Vaughan Williams's *Job: A Masque for Dancing* and Blake's *Illustrations*', *The Musical
     Quarterly* 76 (1992): 301–36.

18   Undated letter, Vaughan Williams to Keynes, Cambridge, Fitzwilliam Museum, MS
     1254–1985. The composer's erratic punctuation is preserved throughout. Vaughan
     Williams's reference to 'your friend' is problematic, given that the other participant was

his cousin, Gwen Raverat, and I considered the possibility of involvement by an unknown fourth party. But nothing in the surviving documents or in Keynes's own memoirs admits the participation of anyone else. Raverat's role in the production is the least credited and the most elusive to define: her presence is seen to a much greater extent in the documentary evidence than in any of the descriptions of her participation by Keynes, Vaughan Williams, or subsequent writers.

19   Keynes, *Gates of Memory*, 204.
20   Cambridge, Fitzwilliam Museum, MS 1251–1985.
21   Keynes, *Gates of Memory*, 203.
22   Cambridge, Fitzwilliam Museum, MS 3-1987. None of the scenarios are dated but their order in the manuscript reflects corrections that seem to appear chronologically. Some items are foliated, but many are not. The complete scenarios are reproduced in the Appendix.
23   Blake of course subscribed to the view of his century that the Druids built Stonehenge. Blake's amusing drawing of 'The Man Who Built the Pyramids', in which the man's nose and forehead slope at an alarming angle to form a pyramid with his rather pointed head, is reproduced by Keynes in his *Drawings of William Blake: 92 Pencil Studies* (New York: Dover, 1970), pl. 62. Keynes describes the drawing as illustrating Blake's 'hatred of the mathematical materialism of the Egyptians and their architecture'.
24   Cambridge, Fitzwilliam Museum, MS 3-1987, ff. 4ff., labeled 'draft by G.R'.
25   Wicksteed, *Blake's Vision*, 14
26   Gwen Raverat, *Period Piece: A Cambridge Childhood* (London: Faber and Faber, 1952).
27   Ibid., 136 and 213.
28   Cambridge, Fitzwilliam Museum, MS 3-1987, ff. 7ff; the third scenario directly follows the second but is unfoliated.
29   The scenario appears in 'Job and The Rake's Progress', *Sadler's Wells Ballet Books*, no. 2 (London: The Bodley Head, n.d.), 24–34. Reprinted and more easily accessible in Michael Kennedy, *A Catalogue of the Works of Ralph Vaughan Williams*, rev. edn (London: Oxford University Press, 1982), 138–44.
30   The last scenario of the Fitzwilliam MS 3-1987, ff. 15ff, is also couched in this language and must be related to Keynes's published version, although it is not attributed.
31   Keynes, *Gates of Memory*, 206–8. As an additional precaution, the dancer wore a mask to further depersonalize the character.
32   Michael Kennedy erroneously attributes the wily hypocrites to the original Blake. See *The Works of RVW*, 223–4.
33   Cambridge, Fitzwilliam Museum, MS 3-1987, ff. 9ff.
34   The full score to *Job: A Masque for Dancing* is published by Oxford University Press.
35   The synopsis seems to indicate the entire family is present, but only the daughters appear in the score details.
36   Keynes, *Gates of Memory*, 204. The publication of the composer's scenario with the score, rather than that of Keynes, suggests that perhaps Vaughan Williams had not capitulated quite in the manner described by Keynes.
37   The piano solo was first published by Oxford University Press in 1934. See the Appendix for a complete listing of the additions.
38   The two-piano score preceded the full orchestral score and contains a number of different readings. A discussion of the sketches and the different manuscript sources will form the basis for another study.
39   Keynes, *Gates of Memory*, 206.
40   Cambridge, Fitzwilliam Museum, MS 1251-1985.
41   Cambridge, Fitzwilliam Museum, MS 3-1987, unfoliated (italics original). The illustration to which the composer refers is Blake VI. The letter is reprinted in its entirety

in Kennedy, *Works of RVW*, 228. It is this comment that has caused other researchers to discount the importance of Wicksteed's study to the production, as does Weltzien in 'Notes and Lineaments', or to dismiss it entirely, as does Mellers in *Vaughan Williams and the Vision of Albion*.

42   Letter dated 12 July, no year. New York, Pierpont Morgan Library.

43   Kennedy lists Raverat as co-author of the scenario in *Catalogue* 138, and in the briefer catalog at the end of his *Works* 417. In the body of the latter volume, however, he explains that Keynes completed a scenario before turning to Raverat for scenery and costumes. If this were true, the Keynes scenario would have come first and there would have been little need for Raverat's; certainly there was no reason for Keynes to send it to the composer.

44   Keynes, *Gates of Memory*, 203–4.

45   London, British Library, MS 59813, ff. 28–30. Italics are the composer's.

46   New York, Pierpont Morgan Library.

47   London, British Library, MS 59813, f. 32.

48   Cambridge, Fitzwilliam Museum, MS 3-1987, f. 12.

49   Frank Howes, *The Music of Ralph Vaughan Williams* (London: Oxford University Press, 1954), 299–314. Mellers, *Vaughan Williams and the Vision of Albion*. Weltzien, 'Notes and Lineaments'.

50   This is the second appearance of Mass chants in the masque, the first being Satan's parody of the Gloria in Scene II.

51   Mellers identifies this as the 'blessing/curse' theme, recognizing its dual nature but not exploring its symbolism. *Vaughan Williams and the Vision of Albion*, 142–57, passim.

52   Ibid.

53   Vaughan Williams and Holst, eds., *Heirs and Rebels*, 44–8; Ursula Vaughan Williams, *R.V.W.*, esp. 132.

54   I am indebted to Professor Byron Adams for several conversations and suggestions on these points.

55   All text in brackets is crossed out but still visible in this version.

56   London, British Library Add. MS 54326

57   Published by Oxford University Press, 1934.

58   In the review of *Job* in the *Radio Times*, 17 February 1933, it is suggested that the separation of the stage in Heaven, Earth, and a flaming gulf in between resembles Botticelli's *Nativity*. This brings up the question of whether the reviewer knew of the composer's pictorial association, or whether Vaughan Williams adopted his idea later.

Chapter 4

Vaughan Williams and the 'night side of nature': Octatonicism in *Riders to the Sea*

Walter Aaron Clark

Ralph Vaughan Williams is often characterized by commentators as a master of the musical *pastoral*. Among the scores that are often deemed 'pastoral' are the *Norfolk Rhapsody No. 1* (1905–6), *In the Fen Country* (1904; rev. 1935), the Third Symphony (*Pastoral*) (1921), and *The Lark Ascending* (1914; rev. 1920). These works exhibit a diatonic, tonal (often modal) harmonic language and an evocative use of instrumental color. On their relatively placid surfaces, they exude a feeling of tranquil – at times mystic – reflection, tinged with melancholy, and are among the composer's most popular and enduring compositions. They have, however, inadvertently served to typecast him as a sort of bucolic bard, stubbornly resisting the encroachment of modernism and the eclipse of Albion.

Vaughan Williams was, however, far too great an artist to be reduced to simple formulae, and his relationship with nature was much more complex. As for most Romantics – and his aesthetic remained forever grounded in the nineteenth century – Vaughan Williams's view of nature encompassed tragedy as well as beauty. Nature's terrifying indifference to human destiny, what German Romantics called *die Nachtseite der Natur* ('the night side of nature'), is the central theme of Vaughan Williams's *Sinfonia Antartica* (1949–52), originally a film score (1948) which he transformed into his Seventh Symphony. The story of Scott's doomed expedition provided the inspiration for music that vividly portrays one man's heroic (but futile) attempts to wrest glory from nature. But no symbol of nature's eternally dichotomous relationship with man is more telling than that of the sea itself. Vaughan Williams's first major symphonic work was *A Sea Symphony* (1903–9; rev. 1923), a choral symphony using texts drawn from Walt Whitman's *Leaves of Grass*. Here, the sea becomes a metaphor for the ocean of existence, on whose 'limitless heaving breast' the reckless soul sails forth for deep waters, where no terrestrial mariner has dared yet to go. Though brave captains and intrepid sailors have gone down doing their duty, from their sacrifice is woven a pennant universal, 'subtly waving all time, o'er all brave sailors, all seas, all ships'.

Such transcendentalism posits nature as an emblem of a benign Eternal, ennobling and sublimating even violent death. This is an idealistic, if naïve, conception that did not survive the horrors of the First World War, a conflict the composer experienced directly.[1] In the 1920s a darker side of nature came to the fore in Vaughan Williams's music, giving rise to some of his most pessimistic works.[2] Perhaps the darkest of these is his one-act opera, *Riders to the Sea*. In *Riders to the Sea* Vaughan Williams achieved a greater cohesion of text, music and drama than any of his other operas. No other composition by Vaughan Williams provides a starker contrast with his 'pastoral' style, or more effectively challenges all consequent stereotypes. This chapter, then, is a detailed examination of *Riders to the Sea*, with particular emphasis on the advanced harmonic idiom that lies at the heart of the work's disturbing affective power. Of all the opera's facets, it is the harmony that has made the work less accessible, less obviously 'characteristic', than most of his other compositions.

Vaughan Williams's choice of J.M. Synge's one-act play *Riders to the Sea* was consistent with his fascination with the theme of man-against-nature.[3] In a tiny fishing village on an island off the west coast of Ireland, a family faces the loss of all its men to the sea. The old woman Maurya's husband and all but her youngest son have drowned in the roiling waters from which they eked out a meager living. In the brief span of the play's action, Maurya experiences the death of this last son, Bartley. Another son, Michael, has recently drowned, and shreds of his clothing are all that remain. Maurya's two daughters conceal these tattered remnants from their mother until they can positively identify them. Finally, Bartley sets out for the sea to take a boat to Connemara where he will sell a pony. He, too, meets a dire fate when his horse throws him into the surf. The crucial moment in the drama comes when Maurya accepts this final blow with stoic resignation; her acceptance of tragedy provides a bitter victory, in that the sea can no longer do her any harm.

Another aspect of the drama that undoubtedly resonated with Vaughan Williams's personal philosophy is the fact that the characters in the story find no consolation in religion. In the struggle between relentless nature and stoic human resolve, the deity appears to occupy a marginal position in the drama. Vaughan Williams's skepticism and outright agnosticism are often remarked upon, so speculation that this aspect of the play reflected his ambivalence towards organized religion is on firm ground.[4]

Although Vaughan Williams derived his libretto directly from this play and inserted nothing,[5] he excised much more material than previous commentators have noted, roughly 15 percent of the original. Some of the cuts tighten up Synge's dialogue, which is hardly prolix. When Nora and Cathleen, Maurya's daughters, secretly examine the bundle of clothes they fear to be Michael's, the composer omits several lines of dialogue dealing with a comparison of a shred of flannel with one of Michael's shirts. He includes only the portion of the dialogue where Nora discovers that a sock in the bundle is one she herself knitted for Michael. But several of the editorial changes cut closer to the bone. For instance, Vaughan Williams omits Maurya's scolding of Bartley for suggesting that his sister Cathleen could deal with farm business in his absence ('How would the like of her get a good price for a pig?'). Maurya's bitter premonition of helplessness adds vital tension to the drama's development. Nora's gruesome disclosure that the oar of a boat actually caught Michael's lifeless body floating in the water is mercifully omitted. Other excisions by the composer actually obscure the meaning of the dialogue. When Maurya prepares to go after Bartley to give him bread for his journey, Cathleen tells Nora to give their mother the walking stick so she won't slip 'on the big stones'. When Maurya declares that 'in this place it is the young men do be leaving things behind for them that do be old', Vaughan Williams's libretto withholds a crucial piece of information that Synge provided: the stick was Michael's.[6] At the end of the play,

Nora whispers to Cathleen that Maurya is 'quiet now and easy; but the day Michael was drowned you could hear her crying out from this to the spring well'. The opera requires us to deduce a reason for this, as the play states explicitly, 'It's fonder she was of Michael...'. In place of this, Vaughan Williams inserts a portion of Cathleen's text actually uttered previously, thus presenting a different explanation for Maurya's impassive response: 'It's getting old she is, and broken.'

Other seemingly minor changes in the Anglo-Irish dialect are not easily explained, given the importance of language to the story's locality. When Maurya first appears, she inquires about Bartley's whereabouts, 'Where is he itself?' Vaughan Williams alters the reflexive pronoun to the more grammatical but less idiomatic 'himself'. In another instance, a piece of rope that 'will be wanting in this place' becomes 'will be wanted'. One other characteristic aspect of the language that Vaughan Williams avoids is parallel clauses. Maurya declares in the beginning of the drama: '*He [Bartley] won't go this day* with the wind rising from the south and west. *He won't go this day*, for the young priest will stop him surely.' Vaughan Williams omits the first sentence and thus the repetition of a poignant phrase laden with futile hope. At the end of the play, another of Maurya's repetitions is removed: 'but *it's a great rest I'll have now*, and it's time, surely. *It's a great rest I'll have now*, and great sleeping in the long nights after Samhain...'. Here Vaughan Williams deletes the second statement, thereby excluding any chance for parallel phrasing in the music.

Vaughan Williams's second wife, Ursula, has stated that on occasion the composer simply forgot or overlooked passages in texts he was setting.[7] Oversight may explain some of the omissions, but certainly not all of them. The precise reasons for the cuts will never be known. In fact, the entire genesis of this work must remain somewhat obscure due to the paucity of sketches and manuscripts. Neither is his copy of the play extant, a source that might provide useful insights into his editorial decisions.

The composer's concert programme for the première at the Royal College of Music, which took place 1 December 1937,[8] states that the music was composed ten years earlier. Michael Kennedy posits 1925 as the year in which composition was begun.[9] The score was published by Oxford University Press over a decade later, in 1936. The sketches shed little light on the issue, as these are neither signed nor dated. They are now located in the British Library and are described below.

The initial sketches strongly suggest that Vaughan Williams was indeed working on *Riders* during the period 1926–27:

1   Add. MS 50481, f. 68bv. Graphite pencil on paper of 12 staves measuring 30.4 × 22.8 cm. On the reverse side of the last page of *Along the Field*, eight songs to words by A.E. Housman for voice and violin. Autograph of nos. 1–4 and 7–8, first performed 24 October 1927. This sketch page contains three passages, only the first of which is from *Riders*, a preliminary setting of the words 'they are all gone now'. Although Vaughan Williams indicated a grand staff by drawing bar lines through two staves, the lower staff contains but a single note, and no clef. All his ideas were poured on to the upper staff. These conceptions are the most revealing and significant of all the sketches and will be treated later in detail.

2   Add. MS 50412 A, f. 4b. Entitled 'Notes for Riders'. Graphite pencil on paper of six staves measuring 12.5 × 19.1 cm. This brief sketch corresponds with

rehearsal 28 in the printed score. The clef is not stipulated, but from the accidentals it would seem to be bass clef. This is further supported by the fact that Vaughan Williams wrote bar lines through two staves, but filled in only the lower line. However, the final version was transposed an augmented fifth below this excerpt. The remaining material on this sketch page was either discarded or used in other contexts; it appears to be an embryo of later material. The pencil has faded and the paper darkened, making this sketch page difficult to read.

3   Add. MS 50482 A, f. 1.[10] Graphite pencil on six folios of paper of ten staves. Although the British Library lists this as a *Riders* sketch, Vaughan Williams's handwriting makes identification uncertain. If any of this material was originally intended for *Riders*, it was winnowed out at an early stage.

The autograph scores also present an incomplete picture of the work's genesis:

1   Add. MS 50417. Partial autograph fair copy of the orchestral score. Sixty-one folios + i (blank). 118 pages. Black ink on paper of 20 staves, measuring 34.4 × 25.3 cm. Corrections, additions and conducting directions (cues, rehearsal numbers) in blue, red and orange pencil (not in the composer's hand). Some markings in regular pencil are in his hand; in some cases these have been written over and made clearer in colored pencil. The inscription states 'Ralph Vaughan Williams [illegible] Dorking The White Gates'. The paper has been cut, and part of the autograph is missing. Comparison with the printed full score reveals very few differences. Vaughan Williams originally marked the tempo Moderato 4/4. This was later altered, in blue pencil (by the composer?), to Lento 2/2, half note equals 60. This marking has been retained in the printed version. Some of Vaughan Williams's notational quirks include the omission of whole-measure rests; he simply leaves the measure empty. Like his friend Gustav Holst, he also made generous use of measure-repeat signs rather than writing the material over again. Clearly, writing out the music was a time-consuming task, and Vaughan Williams sought all available shortcuts.[11] This manuscript lacks many of the stage directions and metronome markings found in the printed version. When (and by whom) these were added is unknown. There are some curious anomalies in the manuscript. The vocal line is not in Vaughan Williams's hand, neither notes nor text. The ink is also different (lighter and grayer). The copyist may have obtained the music from a manuscript source that was subsequently discarded. The names of the characters were written in by Vaughan Williams only until three measures after rehearsal 5. Between Cathleen's entrances at rehearsal numbers 5 and 6, these names were inscribed in another hand (not that of the copyist writing the vocal line), in green ink. After that, they were written by the copyist. At certain points (for example after 12 where Maurya says, 'You'd do right to leave that rope, Bartley, hanging by the boards'), the copyist apparently forgot to add the text. The conductor added it in blue pencil; this was later erased and written over in ink by yet another hand. At least two copyists worked on this manuscript.

2   Add. MS 50416. Labeled by Vaughan Williams 'Rough Copy'. An orchestration of a now missing piano-vocal score. On paper of 28 staves in black ink with some corrections in pencil and a lighter shade of black ink. A few additions in

red ink. Thirty-four folios (folio 1 title page recto only; folio 34 recto only) measuring 31.5×44.5 cm. Interestingly, a staff is reserved for the voice parts and chorus where appropriate, and this is indicated in the left margin. But no notes are written in. Only occasionally does text appear, for example, in the ninth measure after rehearsal 5 (including that measure), where 'Clean burial by the...'. (Nora's line) is added. Such insertions served as points of reference. Another curiosity is the composer's carelessness about key and time signatures and clefs, which he includes only sporadically. Mistakes are either crossed or scratched out. Although his notoriously difficult handwriting is hard to read, the music corresponds closely to the final version. The frequent use of measure-repeat signs indicates not only a desire to save writing time and effort but also his thinking in terms of periodicity and blocks of material. Bowings, dynamics, slur and phrase markings are applied inconsistently.

Though the manuscripts shed little light on the opera's creation, the finished product furnishes plenty of material for consideration. Of particular interest is Vaughan Williams's careful attention to correct prosody when setting Synge's text. He employs a dramatic kind of recitative that approaches actual lyricism only occasionally, especially at the cathartic conclusion of the drama. Scott Goddard described Vaughan Williams's recitative as 'some modern projection of plain-song', finding that 'though the voices are given no set melody yet they are fully eloquent'.[12] Hugh Ottaway states that 'the voices, for the most part, are restrained and subdued, and never soar away from their earth-bound existence at Maurya's cottage'.[13] Edmund Rubbra went so far as to declare:

> The melody is no longer shackled to a chord, but is free to companion the subtleties of speech-rhythm. I have no hesitation in saying that, in 'Riders to the Sea', Vaughan Williams has succeeded in discovering a recitative or free declamation that is as important in twentieth century music as the recitativo stromentato of the seventeenth century. Such a musical approach to Synge's beautiful play is, of course, the only possible one. In no sense is this an opera: rather is it spoken drama raised in emotional power and expressiveness to the nth degree ... This work is England's 'Pelléas et Mélisande'.[14]

Frank Howes also made a connection with Debussy's opera (and with Musorgsky as well) in Vaughan Williams's 'true representation of real people'.[15] Most other writers have discounted any similarity to *Pelléas*. Ottaway notes that *Riders* possesses a 'stark earthiness quite foreign to Debussy's conception'.[16] But the most revealing commentary about the relationship of text and music comes from the composer himself in a quote from an essay that dates from the early twentieth century:

> *The duty of words is to say just as much as the music has left unsaid, no more.* Now, music, expressing as we have seen emotion only, will demand least of the words at the most emotional moments, and the words will stand out most clearly at those explanatory passages where the music is almost non-existent. (Emphasis added.)[17]

This declaration forms an interesting counterpoint to Rubbra's suggestion that Vaughan Williams viewed the purpose of the music chiefly as enhancing the meaning of the text. In fact, the music clearly does more than merely augment the play: it assumes a life and direction of its own.

Earlier examination of the music of *Riders* has tended largely, though not entirely, toward the descriptive. Goddard noted it as 'a complete microcosm of the fateful circumstances of man's existence'.[18] Kennedy rightly saw it as a precursor to the Sixth and Seventh Symphonies, as well as a descendant of *On Wenlock Edge* and the *Pastoral* Symphony. Warrack characterized Vaughan Williams's musical depiction of the sea as a 'force so inexorable [that it] must be the ultimate victor ... and the musical realisation of this, planted surely in our minds, carries us more directly to the centre of the hopeless conflict'.[19] Other authors have waded into more substantial analyses of the opera. Hugh Ottaway noted the 'polytonal dissonance' as one way that Vaughan Williams enlarged 'his creative materials' during the 1920s. Ottaway perceived that 'the sense of key is generally fluid and indeterminate, but there is always some tonal entity, some chord or pedal note, however short-lived, exercising a sort of gravitational pull'.[20] Frank Howes makes the only attempt to describe the musical evolution of the work in its entirety.[21] More recently, an article by Anne-Marie H. Forbes has brought the work's motivic coherence into sharper focus.[22] She labels motives and makes connections between them, which, after the fashion of Wagnerian leitmotif, exhibit consistent associations with certain characters and events (which is unsurprising given Vaughan Williams's lifelong love of Wagner).

Those who have analyzed *Riders to the Sea* have noted Vaughan Williams's use of harmonic devices quite advanced for the 1920s, especially bitonality. But the most unconventional procedure that Vaughan Williams employs, one with few precedents in his works before 1920, is the use of the octatonic scale. The octatonic collection constitutes a scale made up of alternating half and whole steps. Its use in Stravinsky's *Petrushka* is the subject of a detailed examination by Van den Toorn in his book on Stravinsky,[23] in which he sets forth the two fundamental varieties of octatonic scale, each beginning with either a whole or half step. But its appearance in Vaughan Williams comes as something of a surprise. However, since he had used other symmetrical scales in other works (whole-tone and chromatic), it seems plausible that he would also have experimented with octatonicism. The octatonic scale contains a tritone between the first and fifth degrees of the scale, the 'tonic' and 'dominant', which is an important factor in creating the dark mood of this work. In fact, the octatonic is the among the 'darkest' of scales precisely because it combines the minor scale with the absence of a true dominant.

From where did Vaughan Williams derive his use of octatonicism? Does this reflect the influence of Stravinsky and Bartók, composers with whose works he was quite familiar? It is entirely possible that Vaughan Williams employed octatonicism in this opera without placing himself under debt to any other composer. In one way, asking such a question insults Vaughan Williams by insinuating that he must necessarily have borrowed such a procedure from more forward-looking, continental composers. Indeed, he could just as easily have been introduced to this scale by his countryman Gustav Holst, who used octatonicism in 'Saturn' from *The Planets* (1913) and in the *Hymn of Jesus* (1920). In any event, Vaughan Williams was undoubtedly familiar with the octatonic scale and its peculiar quality before 1911 and *Petrushka*. Ravel's 'Noctuelles' and 'Oiseaux tristes' from *Miroirs* for piano (1904–5) both contain octatonicism, as do his *Shéhérazade* (1903), *Rhapsodie espagnole* (1907–8), and *Daphnis et Chloé* (1912). During Vaughan Williams's period of study with Ravel in 1907–8, he was often assigned bits of the French composer's piano music to orchestrate. Moreover, there is perceptible influence of 'Vallée des cloches' from *Miroirs* on 'Bredon Hill' from Vaughan Williams's *On Wenlock Edge* (1908–9). On the basis of this we can be certain Vaughan Williams was intimately familiar with *Miroirs*. There is also a possible Russian connection. Ravel also had Vaughan Williams orchestrate bits of Russian piano music (perhaps Musorgsky, whose 'Gnomus' from *Pictures at an Exhibition* is octatonic). Vaughan Williams was also a friend of M.D. Calvocoressi, an expert on Russian music, and we know that Vaughan Williams admired Stravinsky's *Firebird*.[24] As Richard Taruskin has pointed out, *Firebird* is a work in which octatonicism symbolizes 'dark forces' while diatonicism represents the 'daylight' world.[25] It will become clear in the course of the following analysis that similar associations are established between the music and the drama in *Riders to the Sea*.

Why no one has previously applied set theory to Vaughan Williams's works can probably be explained by two factors. First, few would have associated such a procedure with Vaughan Williams, who was regarded, especially after the Second World War, by certain critics as a musical reactionary. But the second and more specific reason has to do with the fact that the octatonic collection frequently appears in the vocal part of *Riders*, and the vocal part has, as noted above, received little attention for its inherent musical, rather than primarily textual, value. Clearly, the vocal part is an important vehicle for the exposition of musical as well as textual material, as Vaughan Williams's own statements concerning the supremacy of musical over textual expression attest.

The opera begins with an orchestral introduction that represents the sea in all its violence and unpredictability (Example 4.1). This introduction is also an exposition that generates all the significant thematic material of the opera.[26] It opens with a highly discordant sonority. A quartal–quintal stack on A flat in the bass constitutes a diad whose root is D flat. It is juxtaposed against a C minor triad in first inversion in the right hand, with an accented appoggiatura on D. This top note clearly presages the tonal destination of the first seven measures of the work and, commencing at measure 5, persists as a pedal until measure 8. The bass line progresses by a descending whole-tone tetrachord to D, a tritone away. The soprano line follows in parallel motion, landing, however, on A rather than A flat, the dominant of a cell of relative stability in D Dorian achieved in measure 8. These initial seven measures include all the notes of the chromatic scale, except for A and B. They are provided at measure 8, forming an elision between this scale and the new collection of pitches that coalesces into D Dorian (Example 4.2).

Vaughan Williams then introduces a pentatonic theme on E over the D diad in the bass. This theme returns at the end of the opera, where it is sung offstage by a wordless chorus. The C minor chord of the first four measures is recalled on the final upbeat of measures 9–11 by the intrusion of E flat, contrasted against E natural of the pentatonic scale. Such cross-relations are found throughout the score and generate considerable surface tension. This relative calm is overwhelmed by the return of instability at measure 13. Here D Dorian continues in the treble while diads on A flat and B appear in the bass. Measures 8 through 15 are connected by another pedal

Example 4.1 *Riders to the Sea*, Introduction, measures 1–44

point, this time on B, whose enharmonic equivalent C flat fits into the A flat diad (to make A flat minor), thus providing greater harmonic continuity both horizontally and vertically. Vaughan Williams's penchant for enharmonic spellings is apparent in measures 16–21, where the opening opposition of chords a semitone apart reappears. Now, however, a C diad is present in the bass while D flat major is enharmonically spelled (C#–F–Ab) in the treble. The F of the enharmonically spelled D flat major triad serves as a common tone to another, more extensive passage of modality at rehearsal 2 (measure 23), this time in B flat Aeolian, the relative minor of D flat major. This haunting melody recurs at no other point in the opera.

B flat Aeolian dominates the remainder of the orchestral introduction to rehearsal 4, but at measure 31 the struggle between the D flat minor and C minor triads recurs, harking back to the opening sonority, though less forcefully now in a

Example 4.1 (*continued*)

Example 4.2 *Riders to the Sea*, **chromatic pitch-class set, measures 1–7, completed in measure 8 with notes in the D Dorian scale**

horizontal rather than vertical arrangement. The use of D flat major to harmonize much of the melody between rehearsal numbers 3 and 4 creates a certain ambiguity about the real tonal center, though the melody emphasizes in its undulating contour the tonic and dominant of B flat Aeolian. The juxtaposition of D flat major and B flat minor is, at all events, somewhat less discordant than earlier bichordal passages, and the reduced harmonic tension prepares for Nora's entrance. D flat is the unequivocal tonal center at rehearsal 4, though the tremolo between E and F leaves open the question of modality. The C minor triad in first inversion on the second upbeat again recalls and confirms the underlying harmonic relationships of the first measures of the work.

At measure 44 (counting each *senza misura* passage as a single measure), Cathleen sings on a collection of pitches that forms an octatonic scale on E. This constitutes the third of the three possible octatonic collections, that is, [0,1,3,4,6,7,9,10] (Example 4.3).[27]

Example 4.3 *Riders to the Sea*, **principal octatonic pitch-class set, measure 44**

The bichordal juxtaposition of D flat in the bass and a C major triad in the treble at the beginning of this measure (refer to Example 4.1) comprises pitches that are part of this octatonic scale. The transition from D flat major/minor to E octatonic is seamless to the point of being scarcely perceptible. Insofar as B flat is the fifth degree of an E octatonic scale, the preceding extended passage in B flat Aeolian clearly constitutes a kind of 'dominant' preparation for the arrival of this new collection, further clarifying the close relationship between these two seemingly disparate scales. In this light, the opening tritone descent from A flat to D is clearly a premonition of this essential feature of the octatonic scale, though the scale *per se* does not appear until Nora's entrance. Before pursuing the octatonic connection further, let us recapitulate the main features of this opening, perhaps the most remarkable 44 measures of music composed by Vaughan Williams.

Although Vaughan Williams employs a degree of dissonance approaching atonality, pedal points perform a vital unifying function. Areas of chromaticism and polytonality alternate with more stable, diatonic, modal passages, and these areas are connected by traditional means of common tones or elision of various scales. Double-inflected chords and cross relations color the harmonic surface with added dissonance but do not alter the underlying harmonic relations, which can be summarized as follows:

c/D♭–E pentatonic/D Dorian–E Phrygian/a♭[g#]–C#[D♭]/C–b♭/D♭–D♭–E octatonic

D flat is clearly the center of tonal gravity in the introduction, with digressions to D Dorian and B flat Aeolian, but it appears unalloyed only before the entrance of Nora and E octatonic. The ultimate destination of E forms a polar opposite to B flat, with the semitones C to D flat and D flat to D clustered in between. Both E and B flat are equidistant from this cluster, that is, a whole step (all the notes of this cluster are contained in the opening chord). Traditional fifth-related movement is utterly absent. All of the important tonal centers except D are part of the octatonic collection on E. The symmetrical arrangement of important tonal centers in the initial forty-four measures of the opera (Example 4.4) clearly points to the importance of E–B♭ as a tonal axis, an axis that will reappear at other points in the opera, especially at the conclusion.

Example 4.4 *Riders to the Sea*, symmetrical arrangement of important tonal centers, measures 1–44

An interesting feature of this opening octatonic gesture is the three-note motive at the end of Nora's statement. This motive recurs throughout many of Vaughan Williams's works and is a veritable *idée fixe* in *Riders*. The drooping figure encompasses a major and then a minor third, and can be linked in a descended sequence to modulate to any tonal center (Example 4.5).

Example 4.5 *Riders to the Sea*, three-note motive, measure 44

Octatonic collection 3 on E pervades the first half of the opera. At measures 53–54 Vaughan Williams presents this same collection rearranged on C sharp (Example 4.6).

Example 4.6 *Riders to the Sea*, rearrangement on C# of the octatonic scale, measures 53–4

This lasts until measure 91, where this collection on E once again asserts itself. A motive associated with Maurya at measures 94–5 is a singularly conspicuous assemblage of notes from this scale (Example 4.7).

At measure 121 Vaughan Williams employs collection 1, [1,2,4,5,7,8,10,11], on D, and again at measure 132. At measure 148 collection 2, [2,3,5,6,8,9,11,0], appears on E flat, and at rehearsal 14 (measure 161) collection 1 re-emerges on B.

Example 4.7 *Riders to the Sea*, **Mauyra's octatonic motive, measures 94–5**

Other instances of collection 1 can be found at measures 240–44 (rehearsal 20), on E; at measures 268–85 (rehearsal 23), on B; measure 314, on D; and measure 315 (rehearsal 27), again on E.

At measure 317 (two before rehearsal 28) collection 2 is arranged on C. At measure 319 occurs a series of notes in the bass part that appeared in the sketch Add. MS 50412A, f. 4b, but here transposed an augmented fifth below, to C flat. This particular scale hardly plays a central role in the piece, but its appearance in the sketches is an intriguing occurrence (Example 4.8).

Example 4.8 *Riders to the Sea*, **transposition to pitch class C of Maurya's**
**   octatonic motive, measures 319–21, with a bass line that appears**
**   in the sketch on London BL Add. MS 50412 A, f. 4b**

If the notes D flat, G natural, and B flat can be considered 'passing tones', then the pitches fall into this same collection 2 on C (Example 4.9).

Example 4.9 *Riders to the Sea*, **octatonic collection derived from the bass line of**
**   measures 319–22**

This provides a sharply dissonant juxtaposition to the upper line. However, when the scale is viewed out of context, it exhibits a peculiar symmetry. It begins with a series of three whole steps (the augmented fourth from C flat to F), followed by five half steps (comprising a perfect fourth from F to B flat). Perhaps Vaughan Williams's fascination with symmetrical scales led him to the creation of this unique arrangement.

Other examples of collection 2 can be located at the following points: measure 345, on E flat; measure 357, on C; measure 388, on E flat. Finally, collection 3 recurs at measure 425, on E. At measure 447 (rehearsal 39), however, the harmonic syntax becomes diatonic, a development that coincides with the return of Maurya to the cottage and her report of having had a vision. This is a crucial moment because she has, through this vision, confronted the reality of the deaths of Michael and Bartley. Thus, the listener is prepared for the climax of the drama: Maurya's stoic resignation to her loss.

At measure 468 (rehearsal 41) Maurya's realization that Michael is dead is accompanied by a passacaglia-like figure in the bass. Maurya's realization is quickly succeeded by the announcement that Bartley has just been killed. During this climactic part of the drama, any hint of octatonicism is banished, and the music becomes completely diatonic. At measure 489 Maurya reflects on the disaster that has befallen her with utter resignation. D major/minor dominates the scene. The sketches reveal an intriguing aspect of Vaughan Williams's approach to this poignant moment. His preliminary setting of the words 'They are all gone now' is found in Add. MS 50481 on f. 68bv, and probably dates from 1926 or 1927. This initial setting is reproduced below and is followed by Vaughan Williams's final draft (Example 4.10–11). The horizontal melodic contour makes no gesture on the word

Example 4.10   *Riders to the Sea,* sketch on London BL Add. MS 50481, f. 68b rev.

Example 4.11   *Riders to the Sea,* final setting of the words 'They are all gone now', measures 495–6

'all', as had the earlier version. Maurya's submission to her tragic destiny is, in the final version, completely devoid of hysteria.

At the end of the opera, E major emerges as the final tonal area, though there is still an absence of fifth-related movement or dominant motion. The final bitonal

Example 4.12   *Riders to the Sea*, **final juxtaposition of E and B flat, rehearsal 55**

sonority of the work, at rehearsal 55, pits B flat against E, one last backward glance at the essential tonic–dominant relationship in the E octatonic scale (Example 4.12).

The work ends with the chord in the treble, that is to say a simple E-major triad in second inversion. The 'triumph' of this tonal center, however, is somewhat mitigated by the unsettling effect of a closing chord in other than root position, which creates the sense that though the tonal conflict may have been resolved in favor of a conventional sonority, the larger conflict between man and nature is ongoing. This represents a final demonstration that, along with his tightly organized manipulation of leading motives, the extraordinary cohesion and emotional impact of this work are indebted to the composer's skillful handling of his harmonic materials to express, in every measure, the underlying currents of the drama. Octatonicism plays a central role in conveying the 'night side' of nature and its terrifying aspect, while diatonicism is clearly associated with the 'daylight' of stoic resolve and its triumph over adversity.

Vaughan Williams's use of octatonicism in *Riders to the Sea* is evident, but the question arises: did he employ octatonic collections in any of his other scores? Although there are no other examples of octatonicism so obvious or pervasive in his output, there are significant octatonic passages in *Flos Campi* (for viola solo, wordless chorus, and orchestra) from the same year of 1926, and in the oratorio *Sancta Civitas* (1923–25). There are undoubtedly other passages as well, especially from this experimental period of the 1920s and 1930s, but these must await further exploration. Certainly he employed the technique in the Fourth and Sixth Symphonies (1931–34 and 1944–47; rev. 1950, respectively), as well as in the *Magnificat* (1932). Above and beyond the use of certain scales, we note the very effective use of wordless chorus in a number of his works. Here, the 'keening' of the women represented by the wordless chorus at the end of the opera is a premonition of the offstage women's chorus at the end of the *Sinfonia Antartica*. Perhaps all of these passages ultimately derive from the haunting soprano solo in the *Pastoral* Symphony.[28]

Riders to the Sea may never figure as one of Vaughan Williams's more popular works, but it remains one of his finest achievements. This work refutes any suggestion of an 'amateurish technique' (which Vaughan Williams once imputed to his early work) and reveals that he was fully in command of a wide range of harmonic resources when it suited his aesthetic purposes. What we admire in Vaughan Williams is his dedication to the cause of expression in music above all else, rather than a slavish devotion to technique and innovation for their own sake. Innovation and expression find a harmonious union in this otherwise disquieting and dissonant composition, compelling us to challenge the received notion of Vaughan Williams as a conservative 'pastoral' composer out of step with his time.

Acknowledgements

The author wishes to express his gratitude to the Carthusian Trust, whose generous support made this research possible, and to the faculty and staff of Charterhouse School. He especially appreciates Mrs Ursula Vaughan Williams's gracious hospitality. Finally, he gratefully acknowledges the assistance of Professor Byron Adams as well as of Professors Charles Hoag, Deron McGee and Ruth Robertson.

Notes

1   See Byron Adams, 'Scripture, Church, and culture: biblical texts in the works of Ralph Vaughan Williams', in *Vaughan Williams Studies*, ed. Alain Frogley (Cambridge: Cambridge University Press, 1996), 112–13.

2   Although I have cited the Third Symphony as an example of his 'pastoral' style, it should be remembered that it was inspired by his experiences during the First World War and possesses a greater sense of tension and conflict than most of his other works in this vein.

3   Was Vaughan Williams also attracted to the Celtic ambiance of the story? Anne-Marie Forbes in her article 'Celticism in British Opera: 1878–1938', *The Music Review* 47, no. 3 (August 1986/7), 176–83, treats briefly the question of Celtic nationalism in *Riders to the Sea*. Forbes points out that by the 1930s, when *Riders* premièred, Celticism was on the wane. It should be remembered, however, that the opera was composed a decade earlier, in the 1920s, when the Celtic twilight still glimmered. But Forbes correctly points out that the setting and language of the play were subordinate to its 'musical representation' and its universal theme. That this is not, ultimately, a product of Celticism is also borne out by the absence of any use of folk music to mark the score as 'Irish'.

4   For more on this, see Adams, 'Scripture', 102–3.

5   Vaughan Williams occasionally mixed textual sources, as in his *Oxford Elegy*, for which he combined portions from Matthew Arnold's *Thyrsis* and *The Scholar Gypsy*. This last poem he at one time considered as the basis for an opera. The textual observations here are based on the following edition: J.M. Synge, *The Complete Plays*, intro. and notes by T.R. Henn (London: Methuen, 1988).

6   Michael Kennedy makes this observation in *The Works of Ralph Vaughan Williams*, 2nd edn (London: Oxford University Press, 1980), 274.

7   Ursula Vaughan Williams, in a conversation with the author on 7 June 1992.

8   A private dress rehearsal took place on 30 November.

9   Kennedy, *Works*, 420. According to Kennedy, the work was completed by 1932.

10   This manuscript was not available at the time the author was doing his research in the British Library, and though he now possesses a microfilm of it, its exact measurements cannot be determined.

11   Vaughan Williams was left-handed but learned to write with his right hand, which contributed to his poor penmanship. See Byron Adams's essay in this volume (Chapter 1).

12   Scott Goddard, 'The Operas of Vaughan Williams', *The Listener* 20, no. 511 (27 October 1938), 917.
13   Hugh Ottaway, 'The Operas of Vaughan Williams', *Musical Opinion* 74, no. 880 (January 1951), 141.
14   Edward Rubbra, 'The Later Vaughan Williams', *Music and Letters* 18, no. 1 (January 1937), 6.
15   Frank Howes, *The Dramatic Works of R. Vaughan Williams*, Musical Pilgrim Series (London: Oxford University Press, 1937), 70.
16   Hugh Ottaway, ' "Riders to the Sea" ', *Musical Times* 93, no. 13 (August 1952), 359.
17   Ursula Vaughan Williams, 'VW and Opera', *Opera* 23, no. 11 (November 1972), 960.
18   Goddard, 'The Operas', 917.
19   John Warrack, 'Vaughan Williams and Opera', *Opera* 9, no. 11 (November 1958), 699.
20   Ottaway, 'Riders', 359.
21   Howes, *The Dramatic Works*, 65–80.
22   Anne-Marie H. Forbes, 'Motivic Unity in Ralph Vaughan Williams's Riders to the Sea', *The Music Review* 44, nos 3/4 (August/November, 1983), 234–45.
23   Peter C. Van den Toorn, *The Music of Igor Stravinsky* (New Haven, CT: Yale University Press, 1983), 131–72. It is well known that Bartók used the octatonic scale as well.
24   See Michael Kennedy, *Works*, 376.
25   Richard Taruskin, *Stravinsky and the Russian Traditions*, vol. 1 (Berkeley and Los Angeles: University of California Press, 1996), 602.
26   See Forbes, 'Motivic Unity', 245.
27   According to Joseph N. Straus, *Introduction to Post-Tonal Theory* (Englewood Cliffs, NJ: Prentice Hall, 1990), 97. The three possibilities are collection 1, [1,2,4,5,7,8,10,11]; collection 2, [2,3,5,6,8,9,11,0]; and collection 3, [0,1,3,4,6,7,9,10]. *Riders* employs all of them.
28   In the opinion of Byron Adams, to whom the author is grateful for this and many other insights.

Select Bibliography

Adams, Byron, 'Scripture, Church, and Culture: biblical texts in the works of Ralph Vaughan Williams', *Vaughan Williams Studies*. Alain Frogley, ed. Cambridge: Cambridge University Press, 1996.
Bayliss, Stanley A., 'The Operas of R. Vaughan Williams', *Musical Opinion* 60, no. 719 (August 1937), 950–51.
Butterworth, N., *Ralph Vaughan Williams: a guide to research*. New York: Garland, 1990.
Douglas, Roy, *Working with Vaughan Williams: the correspondence of RVW and Roy Douglas*. London: The British Library, 1988.
Forbes, Anne-Marie H., 'Celticism in British Opera: 1878–1938', *The Music Review* 47, no. 3 (August, 1986/7), 276–83.
Forbes, Anne-Marie H., 'Motivic Unity in Ralph Vaughan Williams's Riders to the Sea', *The Music Review* 44, nos. 3/4 (August/November, 1983), 234–45.
Foss, Hubert, 'Vaughan Williams and the Stage', *The Listener* 42, no. 1083 (27 October 1949), 740.
Goddard, Scott, 'The Operas of Vaughan Williams', *The Listener* 20, no. 511 (27 October 1938), 917.
Howes, Frank, *The Dramatic Works of R. Vaughan Williams*. Musical Pilgrim Series. London: Oxford University Press, 1937.

Kennedy, Michael, *The Works of Ralph Vaughan Williams*. 2nd edn. London: Oxford University Press, 1980.

Littler, W., 'Riders to the Sea Toronto: Opera in Concert'. Reprinted from the *Toronto Star. Opera Canada* 22, no. 2 (1981), 25–6.

Lunghi, F.L., ' "Calvacate a mare" di Ralph Vaughan Williams', *Sancta Cecilia* 8 (1959), 49–50.

Mellers, Wilfrid Howard, *Vaughan Williams and the Vision of Albion*, London: Barrie and Jenkins, 1989.

Ottaway, Hugh, ' "Riders to the Sea" ', *The Musical Times* 93, no. 13 (August 1952), 358–60.

Ottaway, Hugh, 'Ralph Vaughan Williams', *The New Grove Dictionary of Music and Musicians*, 1980 ed.

Ottaway, Hugh, 'The Operas of Vaughan Williams', *Musical Opinion* 74, no. 880 (January 1951), 141.

Reber, William Frances, 'The Operas of Ralph Vaughan Williams', D.M.A. thesis, University of Texas, Austin, 1977.

Review of première, *The Royal College of Music Magazine* 34, no. 1 (March, 1938), 42–3 Opera and Drama section.

Rubbra, Edward, 'The Later Vaughan Williams', *Music and Letters* 18, no. 1 (January 1937), 1–8.

Straus, Joseph N., *Introduction to Post-Tonal Theory*, Englewood Cliffs, NJ: Prentice Hall, 1990.

Taruskin, Richard, *Stravinsky and the Russian Traditions*, vol. 1. Berkeley and Los Angeles: University of California Press, 1996.

Van den Toorn, Peter C., *The Music of Igor Stravinsky*, New Haven, CT: Yale University Press, 1983.

Vaughan Williams, Ursula, *R.V.W.: a biography*, London: Oxford University Press, 1964.

Vaughan Williams, Ursula, 'VW and Opera', *Opera* 23, no. 11 (November 72), 960–62.

Warrack, John, 'Vaughan Williams and Opera', *Opera* 9, no. 11 (November 1958), 698–703.

Chapter 5

'Full of fresh thoughts':
Vaughan Williams,
Whitman and the
Genesis of *A Sea Symphony*

Stephen Town

... another, and very different, kind of writer was beginning to fill his mind. Walt Whitman's *Leaves of Grass*, in several editions, from a large volume to a selection small enough for a pocket, was his constant companion. It was full of fresh thoughts, and the idea of a big choral work about the sea – the sea itself and the sea of time, infinity, and mankind, was beginning to take shape in many small notebooks. It was an ambitious and terrifying project, for the scope was to be unlike that of any choral work he had yet attempted. ... but he kept it very much to himself, sketching and re-sketching the text, using, discarding, and re-arranging poems.

Ursula Vaughan Williams, *R.V.W.: A Biography of Ralph Vaughan Williams*

In *R.V.W.: A Biography of Ralph Vaughan Williams*, Ursula Vaughan Williams reveals that her husband was absorbed with the poetry of Walt Whitman as early as 1903. The *Leaves of Grass*, 'in several editions, from a large volume to a selection small enough for a pocket, was his constant companion'.[1] It is not surprising, then, that the American poet appealed to Vaughan Williams, for during his youth Whitman's work became something of a *cause célèbre* among British literati.

After the appearance in America of the first edition of *Leaves of Grass* (1855), it was disseminated rapidly in England: by the 1860s Whitman had many prominent British admirers, including such major figures as Swinburne and Tennyson.[2] Chief among them was William Michael Rossetti (1829–1919), brother of Dante Gabriel and Christina, and a noted critic, editor and translator. In 1868, Rossetti produced the first English edition of Whitman's work, a bowdlerized anthology entitled *Poems of Walt Whitman*.

Rossetti's edition of *Leaves of Grass* was created almost by chance. A few months after the failure of the first edition in America, Thomas Dixon, a cork cutter of Sunderland, purchased a copy from an itinerant merchant, James Grinrod. Dixon sent this copy to his friend William Bell Scott, a minor poet and sculptor and an associate of the Pre-Raphaelite Brotherhood, who in turn presented this volume to Rossetti as a Christmas gift in 1856. The impact of the American poet on Rossetti and his associates was immediate, lasting and profound. More than a decade later, Rossetti published an appraisal of *Leaves of Grass* in a *Chronicle* article of 6 July 1867. The long interval had given him the time to contemplate Whitman's poetic aesthetic. When Rossetti at last produced his magazine article, its significance could hardly be over-estimated, as Harold Blodgett notes, for 'it resulted in the first English selection, Rossetti's own *Poems of Walt Whitman* (1868)'.[3] Rossetti's edition contained about half the poems of the fourth American edition of *Leaves of Grass* (1867) as well as Whitman's original preface. This edition was distinguished by its careful prudence, for Rossetti expurgated some of Whitman's more 'objectionable' lines.

Rossetti's younger contemporary, John Addington Symonds (1840–93), was one of the most discriminating students of Whitman's work in the nineteenth century. (Symonds 'became acquainted with Whitman's writings in 1865 at Trinity College, Cambridge, through his friend Frederic Myers'.[4]) In 1893, Symonds produced *Walt Whitman, A Study*, a book whose insights remain valid. Blodgett opines that Symonds's reading of Whitman's work 'was fundamentally a religious experience', even though Symonds was surely attracted by Whitman's unbuttoned expression of homoeroticism.[5] In his *Study*, Symonds identifies four distinct and predominant themes in Whitman's verse: (i) religion or the idea of the universe; (ii) personality or the awareness of self and sex; (iii) love, deviating into the amativeness of sexual love and the adhesiveness of comradeship; and, (iv) democracy, or the theory of brotherhood and human equality.[6] Like Symonds, Vaughan Williams was introduced to Whitman's poetry at Cambridge; his fellow-student Bertrand Russell directed his attention to the American poet in 1892.

Vaughan Williams responded at once to the contradictions and inner oppositions mirrored in the lyrical beauty and magical lines of Whitman's utterances. It is more likely, however, that he was attracted by a limited number of Whitman's themes, such as in those poems that Symonds identifies as expressing Whitman's transcendent strain. Vaughan Williams was often inspired by texts that deal with the destiny of the soul, a subject that is endowed with an emotional power in Whitman's work. Like Whitman, Vaughan Williams often muses on pilgrimages and voyages but declines to provide an unambiguous sense of arrival in harbor. Therefore, the English composer was particularly enchanted by the meditative and elegiac qualities of the mystical or religious sections found throughout *Leaves of Grass*, or by its poetic diction, frequent use of parallelism and lovely cadences. Perhaps Vaughan Williams discerned a connection between Whitman's work and the Pre-Raphaelite poetry with which he was fascinated in 1896.[7]

For Michael Kennedy, the explanation for Whitman's appeal to Vaughan Williams is clear:

> In Vaughan Williams's nature there was a strong vein of mysticism veiled by a thoroughly down-to-earth commonsense approach to his art. He was a romantic; he was also an agnostic, a questioner; he believed in the strength of national roots and he looked to the past in order to venture into the future.

Whitman articulated a pantheism that expressed transcendent aspirations in plain masculine diction; as Kennedy cannily notes, Whitman 'drew, like the folk singers, on vivid verbal material shorn of academicism'.[8]

Given the English composer's taste for Whitman's poetry, it is scarcely surprising that he should be inspired by *Leaves of Grass* and, as Ursula Vaughan Williams reports, begin to ruminate on 'the idea of a big choral work about the sea – the sea itself and the sea of time, infinity, and mankind, [which] was beginning to take shape'.[9] Of course, Whitman's 'fresh thoughts' appealed to many composers during Vaughan Williams's formative years.

Vaughan Williams's principal teacher, Sir Hubert Hastings Parry (1848–1918), is rarely thought of in connection with Walt Whitman, 'whom Parry greatly admired but never set himself'.[10] Vaughan Williams regarded highly the democratic idealism, and transcendent agnosticism exemplified by both Parry and Whitman, and may well have associated the two men in his mind.

Parry's setting of Robert Bridges's poem *Invocation to Music* for soprano, tenor and bass soli, chorus and orchestra, which was performed at the 1895 Leeds Festival, clearly influenced Vaughan Williams when he came to compose certain sections of *A Sea Symphony*. Vaughan Williams must have been particularly impressed by two passages from Parry's score. The episode 'Down from the gardens of Asia descending' from the finale of *A Sea Symphony* (p. 85)[11] is reminiscent of the solemn march 'Man, born of desire' in Parry's ode (p. 45)[12] (Example 5.1). The similarity is due, in part, to timbre: the pizzicato accompaniment used by both composers in these respective passages creates a mood both dignified and solemn. Moreover, in both examples the transition from the preceding numbers – a bass solo in Parry and a choral episode in Vaughan Williams – is achieved by a concentric harmonic progression: in the former, from the tonic major, C, to the major submediant, A flat; in the latter, from E flat to the minor mediant, G minor (though the episode is in D minor). The poetic thrust is not dissimilar: the episode from Parry's ode begins with 'Man, born of desire,/Cometh out of the night,/A Wandering spark of fire,/A lonely word of eternal thought,/Echoing in chance, and forgot[,]' and, later, includes 'He striveth to know,/To unravel the Mind/That veileth in horror', while the passage from Vaughan Williams's choral symphony begins 'Down from the gardens of Asia descending,/Adam and Eve appear, then their myriad progeny after them,/ Wandering, yearning, with restless explorations...'.

After this majestic march, the emotional climax of Parry's ode occurs in the eighth movement, 'Rejoice, ye dead, where'er your spirits dwell'. A forthright unison choral declaration of the words 'Now have ye starry names' grandly proclaims the imperishable fame of the artist. This stirring episode is followed by a concluding passage of great beauty for solo soprano and chorus (p. 60). Parry's haunting music may have been in the back of Vaughan Williams's mind when he composed the conclusion of *A Sea Symphony* (see especially p. 122, 13 measures after rehearsal letter Aa), for there Parry's soprano floats radiantly above the chorus and orchestra in a manner that forecasts his setting[13] (Example 5.2).

Towards the end of his career, Parry completed a number of ethical choral works (variously labeled symphonic ode, motet, sinfonia sacra, symphonic poem, and so on), to texts that were partially or completely his own, 'in a style somewhat akin to the manner of Walt Whitman, a poet very much in vogue and one Parry had for many years admired for his "lack of elaborate speechmaking and elegance of literature" as well as his own powers of ethical affirmation and belief in the justice of democracy'.[14] It is thus entirely in character that Parry would advise Vaughan Williams to 'write choral music as befits an Englishman and a democrat'.

In many ways, the career of Sir Charles Villiers Stanford (1852–1924) parallels that of Parry. Stanford was a composer and scholar, as well as one of Vaughan

Example 5.1   Movement 7, 'Man, born of desire', from *Invocation to Music*
(pp. 45–6, six measures after letter L, of the vocal score)

Example 5.2 Movement 8, 'Now are ye sphered' (codetta for soprano and chorus), from *Invocation to Music* (p. 60, from letter X, of the vocal score)

Williams's teachers. Stanford's highly successful choral scores, especially *Songs of the Sea* and *Songs of the Fleet*, were often performed at the Leeds Triennial Festivals. Vaughan Williams knew both works intimately. Stanford's nautical choral works are saturated with the atmosphere of the sea and vary in mood from poignant expression to breezy boisterousness in a manner that surely provided a potent model for *A Sea Symphony*. Significantly, it was Stanford who, as conductor to the Leeds Festival from 1901 to 1910, persuaded the Leeds Committee to include *A Sea Symphony* by Vaughan Williams in the 1910 festival performances.[15]

In view of the obvious influence of *Songs of the Sea* and *Songs of the Fleet* on *A Sea Symphony*, Stanford's single setting of a Whitman text for large performing forces, *Elegiac Ode*, Op. 21 (1884) must be briefly examined. Like *A Sea Symphony*, Stanford's *Elegiac Ode* is a four-movement work, though of much smaller dimensions, for baritone and soprano soli, large chorus and orchestra. Stanford assembles moving excerpts from Whitman's 'When Lilacs Last in the Dooryard Bloom'd' for his text in a manner strikingly similar to the process by which Vaughan Williams would adapt parts of *Leaves of Grass* for *A Sea Symphony*. Furthermore, the passages scored for women's chorus in *Elegiac Ode* are particularly suggestive of episodes in the finale of *A Sea Symphony*; Stanford's pensive setting of Whitman's great poetic eulogy for Lincoln may well have served as an exemplar for Vaughan Williams's work.

The names of Stanford and Parry are often linked with that of Edward Elgar (1857–1934) in relation to a perceived late nineteenth-century renaissance in English music. Elgar's oratorio *The Dream of Gerontius*, a setting of a skillful redaction of the poem by Cardinal Newman, has been identified by Wilfrid Mellers, among others, as one of the most influential works of early twentieth-century British music. 'Conceiving oratorio as inner strife', writes Mellers, Elgar 'refashions the prototype in highly personal music approaching Verdi in lyrical ardour, Wagner in harmonic expressiveness.'[16] Vaughan Williams related that he spent hours studying the full score of *The Dream of Gerontius* in the British Library and candidly acknowledged the influence of Elgar's oratorio upon *A Sea Symphony*.[17] Mellers considers the seraphic F major opening of the second part of *The Dream of Gerontius* to be a direct and unique prophecy of Vaughan Williams's mature style:

> Flowing from god-like fourths, it is at first not only diatonic, but modal, limpidly scored for woodwind. Within this modality, chromatic oscillations and enharmonic mysteries acquire a new significance; for what had been, in relation to the hero's inner life, anxiety, is now release. Materiality becomes spirit; and spirit is materialized, since Gerontius's soul, having 'passed over', converses with an angel whose music is posed between Gerontius's dreamy enharmony and the modal purity of stepwise-floating alleluyas.[18]

Mellers does not make a further obvious connection between the two scores, for the mighty imperative injunction for unison chorus, 'Sail forth', in the last movement of *A Sea Symphony* (p. 111) produces the same exhilarating effect as the magnificent exhortation for unison chorus, 'Go forth', from the end of Part One of *The Dream of Gerontius* (p. 41).[19] Vaughan Williams may have created this splendid moment in *A Sea Symphony* by combining Elgar's choral unison, 'Go forth', with the first two chords that introduce the line sung by Gerontius in Part Two (p. 112, rehearsal number 71), 'But hark! A grand mysterious harmony!'

Perhaps the words sung next by Gerontius, 'It floods me, like a deep and solemn sound/Of many waters', were similar enough in tone to 'Sail forth – steer for the deep waters only', to prompt Vaughan Williams to combine the harmonic progression with the choral unison ('Go forth'/'Sail forth') that Vaughan Williams uses to usher in the enthralling penultimate conclusion to the fourth movement, 'Reckless O Soul, exploring, I with thee, and thou with me,/For we are bound where mariner has not yet dared to go.' Notice, too, how these choral exhortations of 'Sail forth' (at pp. 113–14 of *A Sea Symphony*) are not unlike those of 'Praise' (at p. 105, rehearsal number 68 *passim*, Part Two of *The Dream of Gerontius*), before the interruption of 'But hark! A grand mysterious harmony!'

Finally, the manner in which the soul sets sail for uncharted waters at the end of *A Sea Symphony* is remarkably similar to the end of Part One of *The Dream of Gerontius*. In the latter, the death of Gerontius occurs in the presence of friends around his bed, who sing the 'Subvenite', serene and hushed, with the priest (p. 45 *passim*). Significantly, the return of similar material in Part Two (p. 151, after rehearsal number 103), though modified and abbreviated, is reached by the last statement of the two chords of the 'grand mysterious harmony' (at p. 150, mm. 5–8) which, as part of the complete harmonic progression or as a fragment of it, have been reiterated at important junctures as the soul approaches 'the veiled presence of our God' (p. 151, before rehearsal number 103). Of course, while the musical content of the visionary choral epilogue of *A Sea Symphony* is different from the end of Part One of *The Dream of Gerontius*, as is the key (E flat rather than D), both Elgar and Vaughan Williams strive to express that which lies beyond sense and knowledge and transport their listeners into a state of transcendent, mystical rapture.

Returning to Vaughan Williams's comment about the opening pages of the last movement, it is curious that he did not mention Elgar's *The Light of Life* as well, for the phrase at the line 'Below, the manifold grass and waters' in the fourth movement, 'The Explorers', of *A Sea Symphony* (p. 211, orchestral study score)[20] is reminiscent of the fourth theme, the motive symbolizing 'Light', introduced in the orchestral introduction to the short oratorio (at p. 12, rehearsal letter G, and again four measures before rehearsal letter H, of the orchestral full score).[21] The contour of Vaughan Williams's phrase – the graceful melodic gesture, leaping then gently falling; the initial segment of the harmonic progression, $I^bV^{7c}I^bV^{7d}I^bVI^7$ in E flat major; the scoring, especially the use of the harp and timpani – all suggest an indebtedness to the Elgar motive. (Note the similar features of the first passage at letter G: the melodic gesture; the initial segment of the harmonic progression, $I\ V^{7c}I^bIII^7IV\ II^7I^cV$ in G major; the scoring – see Example 5.3.) Though the first performance of *The Light of Life* took place in Worcester Cathedral in 1896, and was revived four years later during the Worcester Three Choirs Festival, the full score was not published until 1908. However, the first part to appear in print, and to gain wide currency, was the 'Meditation', the orchestral introduction that features the melodic phrase under discussion, which was published separately in 1903.[22]

A fourth creator whose work may have influenced *A Sea Symphony* was Frederick Delius (1862–1934), a cosmopolitan composer who was born in Yorkshire. Of all Vaughan Williams's older contemporaries under consideration

Example 5.3   Motif of 'Light' from *The Light of Life* (p. 12, letter G of the orchestral score)

here, Delius is the one most closely identified with the writings of Walt Whitman: Delius composed several large-scale works using texts drawn from *Leaves of Grass*. Vaughan Williams, who later did not dissimulate an almost visceral dislike of Delius and his music, played portions of *A Sea Symphony* for the older composer in 1907. Despite Vaughan Williams's oft-expressed distain for Delius's music, one of Delius's settings of Whitman clearly had an influence on *A Sea Symphony*. Delius's *Sea Drift* (1903–4) for baritone soloist, chorus and orchestra, which pre-dates Vaughan Williams's score by some six years, was first performed in Essen in 1906, and is considered by most discerning critics to be its composer's finest achievement.[23]

For his setting, Delius chose the first of Whitman's 'Sea-Drift' poems, 'Out of the Cradle Endlessly Rocking'. He omitted the initial verse and began the choral recitative with the main body of the poem, 'Once Paumanok,/When the lilac-scent was in the air and Fifth-month grass was growing', the narrator's account of his observing a pair of amorous mockingbirds on the Long Island shore when he was a child. Delius deleted the long philosophical conclusion of the poem, the final six verses about death beginning with 'The aria sinking'. The formal structure of Whitman's poem may well have suggested a formal design to Delius: a rhapsodic colloquy between soloist and chorus. Whitman, however, 'italicized portions of the main narrative to suggest the bird's lament, leaving in roman type the narrative of the boy'.[24] Delius ignored this distinction and distributed the lines of the poem between the baritone and chorus as suited his expressive purpose.

That Delius may have detected that his *Sea-Drift* had exercised a certain influence on *A Sea Symphony*, is evinced by his odd comment to Vaughan Williams: 'Vraiment, il n'est pas mesquin' ('Truly, it is not shabby'). The hypnotic and almost static equanimity of the hushed introduction of *Sea-Drift*, produced by the seamless flow of chromatic chords in the strings, punctuated by ascending melodic gestures in the bass instruments and harp and descending filigree in the winds, may have suggested to Vaughan Williams the brooding, quiescent and mysterious introduction of the second movement, 'On the Beach at Night Alone', produced by the juxtaposition of tenebrous C minor and E major chords in the strings, punctuated by a descending melodic motive in the bass instruments but without the embellishing descending figures in the winds (see Example 5.4). The rapt conclusion of *Sea-Drift*, which recalls the surging of waves, rising (to reach their apex with a chromatic chord at p. 48, m. 5), falling, then dying away, may have combined with Elgar's example to persuade Vaughan Williams to end his transcendent choral epilogue of *A Sea Symphony* in a similar fashion (Example 5.5).

The expressive content of *Sea-Drift* is quite similar to the second movement of *A Sea Symphony*. In *Sea-Drift*, Delius initiates and continues the choral writing (p. 3, rehearsal number 3) in a manner that is echoed in 'On the Beach at Night Alone' (p. 49, rehearsal letter F). Perhaps the felicitous details of Delius's expert scoring for winds, two harps and solo violin in *Sea-Drift* at 'He call'd on his mate,/He poured forth the meanings which I of all men know' (p. 44, m. 248, 11 measures before rehearsal number 13, of the orchestral study score) prompted Vaughan Williams to orchestrate the section which immediately precedes 'O soul thou pleasest me, I thee' in the finale for solo instruments and two harps (p. 262, ten measures before rehearsal letter P and following, of the orchestral study score). Despite Vaughan

Example 5.4   Introduction of '*Sea-Drift*' (p. 1 of the orchestral study score)

Example 5.5   Conclusion of 'Sea-Drift' (p. 48 of vocal score)

Williams's later demurrals, Delius's evocative work profoundly influenced *A Sea Symphony*.

Like Delius, Vaughan Williams assembled his text from Whitman's *Leaves of Grass* in order to conform to his own aesthetic vision. Vaughan Williams selected excerpts from 'Song of the Exposition', 'Sea-Drift' and 'Passage to India'. Ursula Vaughan Williams writes that he worked hard over the task of 'sketching and re-sketching the text, using, discarding, and re-arranging the poems'.[25] He avoided those Whitman texts that center on the autonomous self in favor of those that reflect universal philosophic, moral, or transcendent themes. Vaughan Williams then entered these, together with his compositional ideas, 'in many small notebooks'.[26] This is a slightly misleading phrase as it does not fully describe the complex state of the manuscripts of *A Sea Symphony*. During the seven-year period from 1903 to 1910, Vaughan Williams's choral score slowly expanded from its original conception as *Songs of the Sea* (in five movements, though the projected fourth, called 'The Steersman', was discarded) through an intermediate phase as *Ocean Symphony* (1906) to become, finally, *A Sea Symphony*.

There are twenty four volumes, containing sketches and drafts of the composition in its various stages of completion, housed in the British Library along with most of Vaughan Williams's other papers. Ursula Vaughan Williams's initial bequest forms British Library Add. MSS 50361–50482, but many more items have since been added to the collection.[27] These range from the 'small notebooks' of Add. MS 50361, which are probably the ones mentioned by Ursula Vaughan Williams, of the kind that are easily pocketed when walking, travelling or conducting field work, to the larger 'music books' of Add. MS 50362. Thus there exist a wide variety of manuscript sources: the sketches and drafts (Add. MS 50363); the first proofs of the Breitkopf and Härtel vocal score; the handwritten full scores (Add. MS 50365); and the printed full scores (Add. MS 50366). (For a complete description of the manuscripts, see the Appendix.)

In assorted sizes and shapes, the manuscripts have a collage-like appearance caused by Vaughan Williams's peculiar compositional methods. As the composer revised his material, he attached new manuscript paper (from small fragments to entire pages) over the original, using paste or brown, silver or transparent tape; he frequently crossed out measures and pages, deleting what he found unacceptable or tentative; and he used black, blue and red graphite, and black, dark blue, red and green ink.

An examination of the manuscripts is necessarily conditioned by these features and by several other significant factors, as well. Vaughan Williams's calligraphy is far from tidy; he was naturally left-handed but was trained to write with his right hand in childhood. This difficulty, 'combined with the nervous rapidity with which he notated his music', contributed to the creation of an individualistic style of writing which is virtually illegible. Indeed, Byron Adams has labeled it 'striking, unwieldy, and occasionally obscure'.[28]

The order of the manuscripts represents their relative chronology only approximately. Each of the groups of notebooks, drafts and sketches that make up the manuscript collection of *A Sea Symphony* traces the genesis of the first to the fourth movement; however, the relationship of this material within each volume, and to each succeeding volume, is difficult to determine. As Alain Frogley writes, 'Vaughan Williams rarely dated sketchbooks or other manuscripts and moved frequently (and sometimes haphazardly) between different sketchbooks and full-score material.'[29] To examine the manuscripts consecutively would be both confusing and misleading; the clearest way to discuss these materials is to sift back and forth as needed, in an order that follows the presentation of Whitman's literary themes and Vaughan Williams's musical ideas as they appear in isolated manuscripts. Wherever possible, the manuscript sources will be compared and contrasted, taking into account revisions and refinements made by the composer.

'Behold the sea itself'

In crafting the first movement of *A Sea Symphony*, Vaughan Williams chose five lines from section eight of 'Song of the Exposition', beginning with 'Behold, the sea itself', which he combined with 'Song for All Seas, All Ships' from 'Sea-Drift'. Although 'Song of the Exposition' commemorates a celebration of America's industrial achievement, as do many of the poems in *Leaves of Grass*, Vaughan Williams carefully omitted all references, here and elsewhere, to any specific place or time and, instead, focused on the universal fraternity of sailors, or, as A.E.F. Dickinson wrote, focused on thoughts 'which most consistently and evocatively lead from common experience at sea to the boundless vistas of every pioneer'.[30]

Many commentators have remarked upon the unforgettable opening of the symphony with its enthralling sequence of musical gestures: the bold fanfare of the brass, a B flat minor to D major harmonic progression, the exultant choral response, 'Behold, the sea itself', and the sublime orchestral passage illustrating the swelling ocean's 'limitless heaving breast'. We first encounter this splendid paragraph in the initial notebook, Add. MS 50361 A, of the series that constitutes Add. MS 50361, all condensed scores, where (at f. 2r) the chorus follows the entrance of brass to a fragment of the words ('Behold, the ...') and the first theme with only a bass line. The sketch of this initial section is remarkable because there is very little deviation from the original powerful gesture, although an abbreviated form of the opening theme may be seen (at f. 1v) in Add. MS 50361 C.

This paragraph, concluding with the first theme and a transition, leads to the second subject of the baritone's 'rude brief recitative of ships sailing the seas' (at ff. 5r–6r), section one of 'Song for All Seas, All Ships'. The composer penned a note (at f. 7r), rather difficult to read, that seems to say, 'work out this figure'. The figure in question, to 'Of dashing spray', is rhythmic and, indeed, is solved in the first few pages (at ff. 2v–6r) of the succeeding notebook, Add. MS 50361 B. Familiar lines of the poem with music follow, until (at f. 8r) we find only a text with a clear diagram of how it is to be set and who is to sing it – 'Picked sparingly without noise by thee old ocean/Thou sea that pickest and cullest the race in time/and unitest the nations/ Suckled by thee (solo), Embodying thee (chorus), Indomitable (no indication)' – although, ultimately, it did not assume this form.

Other sketches of the second subject section may be found in Add. MS 50363, a voluminous compilation of several drafts and sketches 'in vocal score'. Folios 1–23 [1], a draft of the first movement described as a 'rough sketch' by the composer, feature (at f. 8r) the baritone solo, 'Thou sea, that pickest ...' with a slightly different melodic profile, while (at f. 8v) 'untamed as thee', its conclusion, is in the key of B flat minor rather than the final choice, C minor. Folios 22–70v [2], a second draft of the first movement, consists of (at f. 39v) the choral statement of 'Today a brief rude [*sic*] recitative' in the key of C minor rather than D, while (at f. 44v) the melodic content of 'Thou sea, that pickest and cullest ...' is also varied.

Of Vaughan Williams's mastery of prosody, Michael Kennedy writes, 'it is still a matter for wonder that Whitman's words should have found music which fits them so naturally, the speech-rhythms having an inevitable musical cadence'. In this and in other aspects of the opening paragraph of *A Sea Symphony*, Kennedy detects the influence of Purcell, for 'the baritone's phrases are first answered by the chorus and then accompanied by it, to end in a forceful declaration of "untamed as thee", builds up a tension released by the return of the opening fanfare and the dramatic entry of the solo soprano with her "Flaunt out O sea your separate flags of nations" '.[31]

Section two of 'Song for All Seas, All Ships', 'Flaunt out O sea your separate flags of nations', represents the development section of the first movement. This material may be found initially in Add. MS 50361 B, where (at f. 8r) it is in a different key and, although the barring is in an incomplete state, the partitioning of the statements is in its final form. The music for 'But do you reserve especially for yourself ...' appears (at f. 10r) without text, but in Add. MS 50361 C this passage is clearly designated (at f. 13v) for baritone rather than soprano, although many other folios are illegible.

Referring, again, to the second draft of Add. MS 50363 [2], there are found markedly inferior versions (at ff. 52v and 53r) of the episode from V in the orchestral score to the thrilling soprano statement (at f. 54r) of 'Token of all brave sailors', which is notated in rhythmic augmentation. Then (at ff. 57v–61v), there are different versions of the material from four bars before Z to one bar before the *Animato*. The composer replaced this passage with another (at ff. 62r–63v) at the *Animato*, and recast the music in 4/4 rather than 2/2. In the first draft found in Add. MS 50363 [1], the strenuous lines associated with 'Emblem of man' of the *Ancora piu mosso* are set (at f. 19v) to 'Token of all brave sailors'.

Add. MS 50362 A presents the least altered version (at ff. 2r–6v) of the mighty climax, 'One flag above the rest'. A different setting of choral homophony was contemplated (at ff. 3v and 5r) for the section 'Behold, the sea itself'. Vaughan Williams decided against this version, pasting a folio (f. 4) over the first (f. 3r) and crossing out the second (f. 5v).

Then, the conclusion, 'All seas', proceeds (at f. 6). The evanescent choral epilogue has an orchestral ritornello of fifteen measures as an appendage, repeating the main theme imitatively in the pattern of S/A/T/B (for instruments).

'On the Beach at Night Alone'

For the second movement, Vaughan Williams selected the poem 'On the Beach at Night Alone' found in the section of *Leaves of Grass* entitled 'Sea-Drift'.

The composition of this second movement must have had a special significance for Vaughan Williams, for among the early sketches and drafts may be found a penultimate version in choral score that exhibits evidence of extraordinary care by the composer:[32] it is in a coherent form, unlike the sketches for the first, third and last movement which are episodic in nature, and the calligraphy is unusually neat.

A comparison of the penultimate version with the published vocal score reveals that the former has the shape and outline, as well as many of the characteristic features, of the latter. However, the manuscript features neither a baritone soloist nor a semi-chorus of women.

It is in the second section of the movement where the penultimate version diverges most significantly from the published score. The key change from C minor to E flat major (at measure 54) ushers in a livelier theme and a processional passage in triple meter that is underscored by a passacaglia-like bass. The choral fugato unfolds in a similar fashion, but the lines are distributed differently than in the final draft. This earlier version of the fugato begins just as in the final version with the bass; however, a tenor soloist (notated on the tenor staff) is used rather than a baritone. Then, the altos sing the line designated for soprano; sopranos, the line for tenors; and, tenors, the line for altos. In measure 65, the tenors resume momentarily their (slightly altered) line, while the basses follow with a melodic fragment that was ultimately excised. At letter G, the sopranos assume the solo part briefly, then in measure 69 move to their line to execute higher pitches (e–g–f#–e–d). The tenors take the second soprano line only to revert to their part in measure 71. A few subsequent alterations of this type precipitate the *Largamente* climax (at measure 81).

In the published score, the thematic fragment seen at measure 85, first sung by the baritone soloist, is developed sequentially and with chromatic alterations, concluding on C minor at letter K. However, in the penultimate version, the solo is taken first by the soprano and then by the alto (at measure 93) and accompanied in both instances by imitative choral passages. Vaughan Williams alters the harmony at the cadence at measure 93 (from D minor to D major) and the bass line is different at measures 96–97. At letter K, the sequential passages continue with a weak choral episode that Vaughan Williams replaced with the more effective and emphatic compositional material from measure 99 through 123. The manuscript features the *fff tutta forza* and *allargando* choral declaration, 'and shall compactly hold and enclose them', found at measures 125–6.

The final section begins at measure 131 with an inversion of the opening chord progression (C minor triads juxtaposed with A major triads). As in the opening of the movement, the phrase sung by bass and tenor is answered by soprano and alto. The bass follow with 'at night alone' as printed. The remainder of the movement (from letter Q) is a quiet postlude, largely as it appears in the published score, except for a few minor alterations.

'After the Sea-Ship'

A corybantic tribute to both ships and the 'emulous' waves of the sea, the third movement of *A Sea Symphony*, cast as a Scherzo, provides an exuberant foil to the brooding second movement. The Scherzo opens with an arresting variant of the first movement fanfare. Michael Kennedy's description of the bulk of the movement is apt:

> the sensation of a stormy sea is exhilaratingly communicated – whistling winds and flying spray and 'waves, undulating waves' (a thrilling part for the chorus). Whirling chromatic scales for the orchestra, with the folk song 'The Golden Vanity' quoted in the woodwind, prepare the way for the fine, broad, Parry-ish tune of the Trio to depict the great vessel ploughing her way through the tumultuous ocean, with a snatch of 'The Bold Princess Royal' in the harmony.[33]

Other musicologists have discerned that the refulgent nobility of these passages is strongly influenced by Parry's music. Perhaps this connection prompted Parry to note in his diary that *A Sea Symphony* was 'full of impertinences and noble moments'.

Only fragments of the Scherzo are found in Vaughan Williams's sketchbooks. The sketches and single extant draft of this movement (Add. MS 50362 C, D, E and F) are complicated and obscure. Moreover, none of the sketches are complete and Add. MS 50362 F, which has been catalogued by the British Library as a draft, is filled with deletions, erasures and paste-overs, and is sadly truncated.

Add. MS 50362 C is (on ff. 12v–17v) a skeletal or preliminary portion of the Scherzo. The 124 bars are written in black ink in vocal score format; however, much of the sketch, on manuscript paper ruled by Vaughan Williams himself, presents only a choral passage here, a melody line or occasional choral line there, an intermittent harmonic progression, and an abundance of empty staves.

Perhaps the sketches contained in Add. MS 50362 D preceded those of C, inasmuch as an indication on the outer cover reads 'Copy of Notes for/After the Sea Ship'. Indeed, the initial folios (ff. 2–4r) seem organized like an inventory, with the important themes, motives, harmonies and rhythms displayed by sentence or section in an abbreviated fashion. There are in addition some annotations for instrumentation, choral unison or harmony.

Add. MS 50362 E may be Vaughan Williams's attempt to copy out a neat, legible copy of previous work, but it is discontinued abruptly (at f. 11v). The 169 measures of music in black ink (to f. 11v) parallel the completed version, in outline, but the transitional passages are greatly lengthened. Thereafter, the manuscript looks like Add. MS 50362 C, with partially sketched passages (mostly in pencil) as the composer plotted out his ideas quickly.

Add. MS 50362 F, undoubtedly based on the contents of the book E, may have been written over a relatively lengthy period of time. The handwriting exhibits various degrees of legibility; the attached fragments and numerous deletions, emendations (in pencil, blue pencil and red ink) and erasures give the autograph a disorganized appearance. Lastly, Add. MS 50363 contains an incomplete draft (at ff. 81–8) in vocal score and a quite untidy organ part [6] in black and blue ink (at ff. 89–94).

'O vast Rondure, swimming in space'

For the finale of the symphony, Vaughan Williams chose lines from sections five, eight and nine of one of Whitman's most ecstatic and metaphysical long poems, 'Passage to India', which eschews terrestrial striving in favor of cosmic transcendence.

The soft, unison opening (*grave e molto adagio*), with an initial theme based on a rising fifth, perfectly depicts section five, 'O vast Rondure', one of the most mystical images found frequently in *Leaves of Grass*: that of a great round globe sailing through the heavens. James E. Miller notes that this image, derived from Emerson, 'serves to project both poet and reader into the universe as cosmic observers witnessing the dramatic progression of the earth'.[34] Poet and reader thus become performers and listeners 'swimming in space' to music endowed with Elgarian solemnity; or, as Wilfrid Mellers notes, 'the noble span of the lines and the diatonically dissonant texture resemble the Elgar of *Gerontius* rather than the blander sobrieties of Parry'.[35]

The initial draft for this opening paragraph is contained in Add. MS 50361 C, where (at ff. 2v–4r) there are embryonic sketches of 'O Vast Rondure' with indications of orchestration and harmony such as 'This in F# m[inor]' after six measures, and 'Chiefly strings'. Additional sketches are found in Add. MS 50361 D (at ff. 2r–6v), E (at f. 3), and in Add. MS 50362 G (at ff. 6v–15v), where Vaughan Williams makes a pencil notation in the top left-hand corner of a page (f. 8r) that reads 'Handelian Syncopation'. A later stage of the opening may be viewed in a disorganized, early draft (at ff. 95r–96r) contained in Add. MS 50363 [7].

When Michael Kennedy wrote that the sketchbooks of *A Sea Symphony* 'contain the equivalents of pieces of a jig-saw puzzle before they are fitted into the main picture',[36] he may have been referring specifically to the last movement, because the extant autograph material is exceedingly abundant and at times confusing to contemplate. Nevertheless, after reassembling the 'pieces' from the diverse manuscripts, Vaughan Williams's creative process can be profitably observed. His method allows the music to unfold gradually, with the manuscript revealing his first thoughts, repetitions and afterthoughts.

The section 'Down from the Gardens' gave Vaughan Williams a great deal of trouble. This passage exists in a number of sketches, from the tentative and somewhat illegible sketches of Add. MS 50361 C (f. 4v), E (at f. 5v), in the key of E flat major rather than F major, F (at f. 2), and H (at f. 13), mentioned by Michael Kennedy[37] and I (at f. 1v), to the discarded version of D (at ff. 7r–13v) – which Kennedy castigates as 'Sullivan-ish'[38] – in 3/4 and F Major. A later variant, mentioned by A.E.F. Dickinson,[39] exists in Add. MS 50362 G (at f. 9v), where the beginning 'Down from the Gardens' is found as a lyrical phrase in F mixolydian, while a very rough scribbling may be seen in J (at ff. 11v–12v). A late version, followed by the music that ultimately supplanted it, may be found (at f. 101v and 102v) in the fairly complete draft of the fourth movement contained in Add. MS 50363 [8].

The ensuing measures lead to one of the magical moments in the fourth movement, 'Wherefore unsatisfied soul?/Whither, O mocking life?' Hubert Foss describes this music eloquently: 'The voices sing in *oratio obliqua*, as in the Rossetti works. ... For a moment the universe stands still. The echo is equally immobile and remote: we are transported to Stevenson's "infinite shining heavens".'[40] The fourth movement exists in a fairly complete draft in Add. MS 50363 [8]. This draft features (at f. 103r) a version of the passage described by Foss that is cast in 3/4 as well as a version of the passage that follows, 'Ah who shall soothe' (in 2/4), both of which were rejected by the composer.

The next section of the finale, 'Yet soul be sure', exists in Add. MS 50361 D (at ff. 14v–15r), E (at f. 2), F (at f. 5), where it is found in a very early version, and finally in a much more complete form at H (at f. 17v and 20v). This section also appears in Add. MS 50362 G (at f. 15r), notated in D-flat major and cast in 3/4 time, and in book I (at f. 4r), after a fragment of 'Down from the Gardens' (at f. 1v) that culminates in the last 'Wherefore' (f. 3v); this is abruptly discontinued. The line 'Perhaps even now the time has arrived' is not set, and there is a compression of material before 'Finally' (f. 5v), with an inferior statement of 'Singing his Songs' leading directly into a version of 'O we can wait no longer'. The extensive draft of the fourth movement (Add. MS 50363 [8]) features (at f. 105r) a version of 'Yet soul be sure' which, after ten measures, is altered considerably. This variant is abandoned by the composer (at the bottom of f. 106r). The section 'After the seas are crossed' follows closely (at ff. 107r–107v), leading to 'Finally shall come the poet', which breaks off after one measure of 'O we can wait no longer' (at f. 108r). The verso of this folio (f. 108v) features 'Singing his songs', starting in the middle and, then, the orchestral interlude before 'O we can wait no longer'.

In the passages of these fragments, Vaughan Williams is working toward 'the supreme climax of the symphony,' reached, as Michael Kennedy writes, 'with a thrice repeated "Finally" and then "shall come the poet worthy that name, the true son of God shall come singing his songs", a moment of high ecstasy with an elaborate melisma on the word "singing".'[41] As described by Wilfrid Mellers, this music is a 'fugued climax ... hinting at the grandeur of Elgar and the majesty of Handel, and ending with Purcellian shifts to chords of the flat seventh, triple *forte*'.[42]

To paraphrase Miller's description, Whitman's poem has shifted from the initial spatial view of the earth 'swimming in space', through the temporal view, 'of time as it has been embodied sequentially in myth and as it has been set forth in history', to this moment: the desire 'of the mystic to transcend time and space and to merge with the Transcendent'. Section eight of 'Passage to India,' beginning with the line 'O we can wait no longer', is 'a dramatization of that merging as only Whitman can portray it in the ecstasy of his vision',[43] while the ending lines of section nine are its culmination, as Whitman exclaims: 'Sail forth – steer for the deep waters only,/ Reckless O soul, exploring, I with thee, and thou with me,/For we are bound where mariner has not yet dared to go.' Hugh Ottaway suggests that these lines virtually compelled Vaughan Williams to set them: the great ship of the third movement becomes man himself, and the ocean the infinite expanse of his unappeasable soul. As Ottaway notes, 'quite apart from its intrinsic appeal, this theme has the merit of linking up with thoughts expressed in the slow movement and of raising the finale to a higher plane'.[44]

To symbolize this shift in emphasis, Vaughan Williams provides a new melody, 'O we can wait no longer' that initiates an impassioned duet by the soprano and baritone. Embryonic ideas for 'O we can wait no longer' appear in Add. MS 50361 D, where the recto of one folio (f. 14r) is headed 'Notes for phrases in 2nd part "O we can wait no longer" ' followed by compositional notations (on f. 15v), and in Add. MS 50361 G (at f. 2r). Evolving from the latter are sketches, some rough and some more polished, found in Add. MS 50362 H (at ff. 8r–8v) and J (at f. 2r). The first version of the orchestral interlude before 'O we can wait no longer' is found in Add. MS 50363 [8] (at f. 108v). A more advanced version of 'O we can wait no longer', which presents some of the features of the soprano and baritone duet, appears in the fragment (at ff. 108v–112v) that ends with 'Away, O soul'. Other fragments of the duet, beginning after 'O we can wait no longer', exist in two sources: in Add. MS 50362 K (at 3r), where it begins at 'Amid the wafting winds', and starting with the words 'caroling thee' in Add. MS 50363 [8] (at f. 113r). (Vaughan Williams later discarded this variant for a stronger setting of these words.)

In Whitman's lovely, intimate poetic lines, the soul ventures further and further in its explorations:

O soul thou pleasest me, I thee,
Sailing these seas or on the hills, or waking in the night,
Thoughts, silent thoughts, of Time and Space and Death, like waters flowing,
Bear me indeed as through the regions infinite,
Whose air I breathe, whose ripples hear, lave me all over,
Bathe me O God in thee, mounting to thee,
I and my soul to range in range of thee.

In order to bathe these lines in appropriately warm and liquid sonorities, Vaughan Williams first composed and then discarded two episodes of 'O soul thou pleasest me' on the harmonic level of E7 in Add. MS 50362 J (at f. 4r) and in K (at f. 4v) for one on the level of B7 in Add. MS 50363 [8] (at f. 113v). Here, the baritone entrance is on the harmonic level of B7 for the first time, preceded by the orchestral interlude now in its ultimate form, although a variant occurs at 'lave me all over' (at f. 114r).

The most beautiful part of the finale reaches its pinnacle at 'Bathe me O God in thee'; but, before finding the final version of his eloquent music, Vaughan Williams experimented with its contour and articulation. Measures of 'Bathe me O God in thee' may be found, first, in Add. MS 50362 J (at f. 5v), although a pencilled phrase, 'Notes for "Bathe me O God."', succeeds these (at ff. 14v–14r). There is an ascending variant in K (at f. 6v). Still another version may be examined in the early draft contained in Add. MS 50363 [7] (at f. 97).

At this point in the poem, 'O thou transcendent', the poet attempts to name the 'Nameless', 'the fibre and the breath', the 'Light of the light', 'but always one metaphor is abandoned in its inadequacy for another'.[45] In version after version, Vaughan Williams struggled to match the intensity of Whitman's vision. In Add. MS 50361 G, 'O thou transcendent' is sketched in various forms (at ff. 2r, 3v and 7r), the most interesting of which is imitatively set for chorus (at f. 11r). A variant is found at Add. MS 50361 J (at ff. 6r–8v). A more developed version of this passage can be examined in the early draft (at ff. 97v–98v) contained in Add. MS 50363 [7]. Vaughan Williams finally discovered a solution: the chorus delivers Whitman's lines in block harmony, 'O thou transcendent', and so on, after the orchestra executes the 'Limitless heaving breast' melody. This setting, with the orchestral interlude preceding it for the first time, may be found in Add. MS 50363 [8] (at f. 114v).

After articulating his mystical rapture, Whitman lowers his poetic gaze towards his own being, and 'is more successful in conveying the sense of Union, the mingling of the self with the All':[46]

> Swiftly I shrivel at the thought of God,
> At Nature and its wonders, Time and Space and Death,
> But that I, turning, call to thee O soul, thou actual Me,
> And lo, thou gently masterest the orbs,
> Thou matest Time, smilest content at Death,
> And fillest, swellest full the vastnesses of Space.

By continuing the orchestral triplet figuration from the previous section and adding the alternating minor to major chords, giving the music a dilating effect, Vaughan Williams aptly matches Whitman's metaphor. An interesting variant of 'Swiftly I shrivel' is contained in Add. MS 50363 [8] (at f. 115v), after which the remainder of the movement follows the final version with only a few variations, the most notable of which is the contrapuntal passage of 11 measures before the epilogue (beginning at f. 120v).

Thereafter, the choral block harmonization of the lines 'Greater than stars or suns/ Bounding O soul thou journeyest forth' erupts with the exciting shouts of 'Away, O Soul' and the fervent exclamation 'Sail forth'. These passages went through a series of variants until they reached their final form. A sketch of 'Greater than stars or suns', set to a version of the music for 'O Thou transcendent', and an unsuccessful choral draft in Add. MS 50362 K (at f. 7r) are followed by a very rough outline of the last portion of the movement, abbreviated in places, but recognizable. A later version of 'Greater than stars or suns' exists in the fairly complete draft of the fourth movement in Add. MS 50363 [8] (at ff. 108v–112v). The rudimentary sketch of 'Away, O Soul', seen in Add. MS 50361 H (at f. 8), does not resemble 'fanfares on rising fourths and fifths, garlanded with trills', the aural image depicted by Wilfrid Mellers, who opines that 'the shimmering orchestra sounds like the angelic music in *Gerontius*, though the sounds also have much in common with Delius's nature-noises'.[47]

Vaughan Williams altered the final climax of the movement as late as the first proof of the vocal score prepared by Breitkopf and Härtel in 1909 (Add. MS 50364, at pp. 119–20/ff. 121–2). Using red ink, Vaughan Williams replaced nineteen bars of contrapuntal choral music elaborating the text 'Sail forth, steer for the deep waters only' (three bars before Z) with twelve measures that Kennedy characterizes as 'the mighty, imperative injunction, in unison, merely to "sail forth"'.[48]

After a pause, the movement concludes with the wave-like undulations of the choral epilogue, 'O my brave soul! O farther sail'. With but a few exceptions, the virtually complete draft of the fourth movement in Add. MS 50363 [8] presents the epilogue in its final version (at ff. 121r–123). There is one inspired alteration, however, for in this penultimate draft the symphony ends unambiguously with root position chords, rather than the haunting ultimate version of the final cadence that uses inverted triads.

As noted above, Vaughan Williams spent seven years creating *A Sea Symphony*; it was his first published large-scale symphonic composition, created in the optimistic first decade of the twentieth century. During this period, British composers were expected to produce large choral works, as did Parry, Stanford, Elgar and Delius. Although composed within this venerable tradition, *A Sea Symphony* is neither a perfunctory nor conventional composition: the score goes far beyond the musical expectations of its era by extending the symphonic principle over a vast and complex four-movement span.

The autograph manuscripts of *A Sea Symphony* provide precious insights into Vaughan Williams's compositional method. A meticulous craftsman, he first created and then revised ceaselessly; discarded inferior material with ruthless self-criticism; and he recast passages until he realized fully his artistic vision. Thus, through an extended and at times painful process of emendation and refinement, his music gradually attained clarity and concision. That Vaughan Williams worked so arduously and diligently, that there exist so many sketches and drafts, is hardly surprising, for as the composer himself wrote:

> Only the merest amateur imagines that a composer when he sets out to write a piece of music sits down and deliberately writes out bar one complete, followed by bar two complete and so on; Beethoven's notebooks disprove this, nor does anyone who knows think that ideas invariably spring from a composer's head 'ready to wear', or that there are never any lucky accidents.[49]

Though a comparatively early work and indebted to its British predecessors, *A Sea Symphony* was an augury of even finer works to come, for Vaughan Williams, initially inspired by his love of Whitman's exhilarating poetry, 'was full of fresh thoughts'. While he never revisited the genre of the choral symphony, Vaughan

Williams built a capacious symphonic legacy on the foundation of *A Sea Symphony*. From the grandeur of the *London* Symphony to the refulgent suffering of the *Pastoral*, from the bruising violence of the Fourth to the contemplative mysticism of the Fifth, from the anguished nihilism of the Sixth to the polar landscape of the *Sinfonia Antartica*, and from the exuberant Eighth to elegiac Ninth, Vaughan Williams created a symphonic legacy that remains unsurpassed in the history of British music.

Acknowledgements

The author wishes to thank Hugh Cobbe and the staff of the Manuscript Reading Room of the British Library for their assistance; he is also indebted to Peter Ward Jones and Peter Horton of the Bodleian Library (Oxford University) and of the Library of the Royal College of Music (London), respectively; and, he extends his gratitude to Glenn Morrow of the Owens Library of Northwest Missouri State University, who met his frequent, assiduous requests for interlibrary loan books, scores and journal articles with alacrity. It is a joy to circulate one's work to respected and trusted colleagues for their constructive comments and a great debt is owed to Dr Steven Brown, Chair of the Department of Music, University of Mississippi, Oxford, who read earlier versions of the manuscript and improved them considerably through his perspicacious remarks. The author takes great pleasure in acknowledging the Carthusian Trust and Northwest Missouri State University for financially supporting the felicitous ardour of his archival endeavours. Lastly he gladly thanks his wife, Denise, to whom this essay is dedicated.

Appendix: A Description of the Manuscripts of *A Sea Symphony*

Add. MS 50361 A–H consists of eight commercially produced manuscript notebooks [boxed] mainly 'in condensed score'. In fact, the notebooks measure 9¼" × 5¾" and have six (6) staves on each of the 24 pages (recto/verso). The outer cover has printed within a decorative border 'Manuscript/Music Book'.

Add. MS 50361 A. The folios have been numbered 1–23, but following f. 4 there are two unused (and hence, unnumbered) folios. Pencil is used throughout with but one minute exception. Folios 2–7 contain sketches of the first movement; ff. 7v–10 and 12v–14 are of the projected but discarded fourth movement, 'The Steersman'. The reverse (and upside down) of 23v–14v contain sketches of folk-songs. On f. 1r: 'Manuscript/Music Book' [Outer cover, written in black ink in the top, left-hand corner:] '1st Sketches for Sea Symph'. On f. 7v: transition, using first theme material, to the discarded fourth movement: 'Aboard, at the Ship's Helm'. On f. 8r: discarded 'Aboard, at the Ship's Helm' which uses both the introductory rhythmic cell and the 1st theme.

Add. MS 50361 B. The folios have been numbered 1–21, but following f. 19 there are four unnumbered folios (hence, blank). Pencil and black ink are used. Folios 2–13v continue the first movement from the point where it was broken off in MS 50361

A (for the discarded fourth movement), that is, 7r. Folk-songs may then be found at ff. 14–19b, followed by a fragment of 'The Wasps' (f. 21). On f. 1: [Again, outer cover:] '1st sketches for Sea Symph'.

Add. MS 50361 C. This notebook has a different outer cover than the preceding two (A and B), that is, a textured dark red with 'MUSIC' printed in the center. It is identical in size and the number of staves. The folios have been numbered 1–15. Black ink is used for ff. 1–3; pencil for the remaining folios. Michael Kennedy, in *A Catalogue of the Works of Ralph Vaughan Williams*, rev. edn (London: Oxford University Press, 1982), 54, indicates that *A Sea Symphony* began as 'Notes for Choral Work "Songs of the Sea"'. He must have been referring to this notebook, because it begins in this fashion. However, there is no explanation for this notebook being labelled 'C' instead of 'A' by the British Library staff. On f. 1r: Notes for Choral Work 'Songs of the Sea' [and a $1\frac{1}{2}$ measure statement of 'Token of all brave captains' with the text and designated for alto]. On f. 1v: abbreviated form of opening theme with the indication 'Note for return of the tune'. On f. 2r: [Headed] 'Beginning of the Whole thing'. [Music looks like the beginning of the Scherzo and it is juxtaposed with 1st theme of 1st movement.]

Add. MS 50361 D. The folios have been numbered 1–17 (but f. 17 is followed by two unused folios). Black ink and pencil are used throughout. This notebook contains sketches of the opening of the fourth movement, 'The Explorers', and notes for later passages.

Add. MS 50361 E. This notebook has no outside cover. It contains 14 numbered folios; however, there are five blank folios after f. 10 and three after f. 13. It is mostly in pencil. The British Library catalogue indicates that it contains sketches of the fourth movement and folk-song fragments; however, it is extremely difficult to decipher.

Add. MS 50361 F. This notebook contains nine numbered folios; however, one blank folio follows f. 3, 11 succeed f. 8. As in the above, not all folios use recto/verso. Again, the British Library catalogue indicates that this notebook contains sketches of the fourth movement, a fragment of 'The Steersman' (f. 4), and a folk-song, 'The Golden Vanity' (f. 7v); but, the writing is extremely messy.

Add. MS 50361 G. This notebook contains 16 numbered folios; however, one blank folio follows f. 10, while three follow f. 15.

Add. MS 50361 H. This notebook contains 24 numbered folios; however, as in the above notebooks, not all versos are used. The handwriting, too, is extremely hard to decipher, as it is so untidy. On f. 14v: a crude fragment of the motive at p. 222 of the full score.

Add. MS 50362 A–K consists of 11 commercially produced manuscript books [boxed] containing sketches and drafts, mainly 'in vocal score'. The music books measure $9\frac{1}{2}'' \times 11\frac{1}{2}''$ and have 12 staves on each of the 16 pages (recto/verso). This series of 'music books' differs from the preceding 'notebooks' chiefly in size. The notebooks are of the kind easily pocketed when walking or travelling and, perhaps, Vaughan Williams used this kind of notebook when conducting field-work (that is, gathering folk-songs).

Add. MS 50362 A. There are 22 numbered folios. However, f. 4 has been pasted over f. 3r. Half of f. 15 (six staves) is found on the verso of f. 14 pasted on at the top. Folio 17 is pasted over f. 16r. F. 18 is found on the verso of f. 17; f. 20 is pasted over f. 19r and f. 22 is affixed to the inside back cover of the music book. A folio, between f. 10 and f. 11, has been removed (by cutting). Black ink is used with abundant cancellations appearing in blue and red pencil. On f. 1r: [Outer cover, written in black ink in the top, right-hand corner:] 'Symphony of the Sea/3'. [The outer corner has printed within a decorative border the following: *'No. 1.*/THE/ SIXPENNY/MANUSCRIPT/MUSIC BOOK/No. 1. Ordinary 12 Stave, Open./'2. For Piano Music/'3. For Vocal Music. (The last two lines are together bracketed with clefs/and Brackets.)/London:/WEEKES & Co.,/14, Hanover Street, Regent Street, W.] Folios 7v–22 deal exclusively with a version of the second movement. Folios 7v–8r present an 'Adagio' section with the familiar music to D in the full score. At this point, there is a passage reminiscent of O. However, Vaughan Williams cuts 36 measures of this music with large, red Xs. Effectively, he tightens the introduction by compression. Two indications of instrumentation, oboe and clarinet, may be seen on f. 8r.

Add. MS 50362 B. There are 17 numbered folios. After f. 10r, the folios are blank. Pencil is used on f. 1r; thereafter, the notation is in black ink with a few corrections in pencil and blue pencil. On f. 1r: [Outer cover is identical to book A. In the upper right hand corner is written in pencil:] 'Sea Symph II'. Folios 2v–10r contain a 'recopy' of the second movement found in book A. It is, obviously, a neat, fair copy of work done at another sitting. The 'Adagio' marking, begun (as 'Ad') but not completed, has been changed to 'Largo sostenuto'. In general, the score has additional markings indicating levels of dynamics, mood/character ('misterioso', 'ma marcato', 'Tranquillo ma maestoso', 'dolce e cantabile', 'Poco animando', 'ancora animando', 'cantando', 'tempo del comincio'), and suggestions for instrumentation ('stopped Horn', 'cello', '3 flutes'), to name a few. The passage after the cadence on 'Bodies' is the excrescence which Vaughan Williams deleted. Also, the cadence after the chromatically ascending bass line ('though they be ever so different'), see p. 116 in the full score, is on D major rather than D minor.

Add. MS 50362 C. There are 17 numbered folios, but ff. 8v and 10 are blank. This music books contains an 'Imitation' of Mozart's string quartet in D, K. 499 (ff. 2–5) [in skeletal form] and of Beethoven's Pastoral sonata, Op. 28 (ff. 5v–6) [also in skeletal form], and sketches for the second movement of the *Sea Symphony* (ff. 7v–12) and the scherzo (ff. 12v–17v). Although this music book has been catalogued by the British Library staff as 50362 C, it pre-dates books A and B. The sketch of the second movement introduction is 'in condensed score' and represents the composer's first thoughts on paper. He writes 'On the Beach Notes' in the upper left-hand corner. The writing is in pencil and has the appearance of being very quickly done. The passage that accompanies 'as I watch the bright stars' appears as a progression from E to E flat. Although the remainder of the second movement sketches are in vocal score, they too are very skeletal and in a preliminary stage. One note about the skeletal sketch of the scherzo following the second movement material: on f. 12v, following the opening choral statement, Vaughan Williams has written in pencil, 'String passage like Don Juan here'.

Add. MS 50362 D. There are 7 numbered folios. Two folios have been removed (by cutting): one each between ff. 4 and 5, and 5 and 6. Folios 2–4r are written in black ink, as are ff. 6–7r, while ff. 4v–5 and f. 7v use pencil. On f. 1: [Outer cover indicates in the upper, right-hand corner that this Music Book contains the:] 'Fair Copy of Notes for/After the Sea Ship'.

Add. MS 50362 E. There are 17 numbered folios. Folios 2r–11v are written in black ink. This appears to be an attempt to pen a neat, legible copy of previous work. On f. 1: [In the upper, right-hand corner the composer has penned the following:] 'Symphony of the Sea Book 4/No 3 "After the Sea Ship"'.

Add. MS 50362 F. There are 33 numbered folios; however, these are not consecutive. The pagination is as follows: 1–8, 10, 14–17, 20, 22, 24–26, 30, 33. Removed by cutting, then, are ff. 9, 11, 12, 13, 18, 19, 21, 23, 27, 28, 30, 31, 32. Fragments of these, mostly in two-stave format, have been affixed to other folios. A strip of f. 9 is glued to the bottom of f. 8v. Strips of ff. 11, 12 and 13 are glued to f. 10r. Strips of ff. 18 and 19 are glued to f. 17v. A strip of f. 21 is glued to the bottom of f. 20v. A three-measure strip of f. 23 is glued to f. 22r. One-half page of f. 27 is glued to the top of f. 26v, and a four-staved strip of f. 28 is glued beneath this example. Folio 29r is completely obscured by fragments of ff. 30 and 31, while a strip of f. 32 is placed at the top of what was f. 29v. The draft begins on f. 5v. An incomplete copy of Bach's fugue in A minor, from Book 2 of *Das Wohltemperierte Klavier*, appears on ff. 2–3r. Folios 4r and 5r are unused; f. 4v features an unidentified composition. The last four folios are extremely messy; after having covered 388 measures, the draft is discontinued.

Add. MS 50362 G. This volume contains the discarded fourth movement, 'The Steersman' (ff. 2–6), dated (f. 6) 'Aug 17th 1906' and the last movement, 'The Explorers', beginning 'O vast rondure' (ff. 6v–15v). There are 15 folios written in black ink, with emendations – deletions (Xs through measures) and additions – in black, blue and red pencil. In *A Catalogue of the Works of Ralph Vaughan Williams* (p. 55), Michael Kennedy writes: 'The main theme of the first movement is quoted in this discarded movement, diminished and agitato. A derivation of this passage found its way into the finale at the "allegro animato" section ... (nine bars after K).' On f. 1: [At the top of the outer cover may be seen the following:] Book V. Sea Symphony No 4 'The Steersman'.

Add. MS 50362 H. The British Library catalogues this music book as the 'continuation' of G. That it is, briefly, but it quickly becomes a jumble of mostly illegible squiggles. There are 18 numbered folios, but not all of them are used: 9v, 10r, 17v–18r are blank. The writing is in black ink and pencil. On f. 1: [At the top, right-hand corner is written:] Symphony of the Sea Book 6/No V (continued/The Explorers).

Add. MS 50362 I. There is no outer cover to this music book. It consists of 16 folios of manuscript pages, ten of which have been numbered (thus, the remaining six are blank). The British Library catalogues this book as a continuation of H 'The Explorers,' beginning (f. 1v) at 'Down from the Gardens'. Folios 1v–7r are in black ink with some additions and cancellations in blue ink and pencil. Folios 7v–10v are in pencil and, as these sketches have the appearance of scribblings, are unreadable.

Add. MS 50362 J. There are 17 numbered folios; however, two complete folios after f. 13v are blank and, thus, unnumbered. Black ink and pencil are utilized.

Add. MS 50362 K. There are 20 numbered folios; however, these are not in consecutive order. There is no f. 6; yet a fragment of f. 6 (written on manuscript paper of a different type) has been glued on to f. 5. Folio 14 (of the same type paper as f. 6) has been inserted between ff. 12 and 13. The writing is in black ink with emendations entered in pencil, as well as blue and red pencil (boldly marked).

Add. MS 50363. This volume is a multiple compilation (at 123 folios) of several drafts and sketches 'in vocal score' of *A Sea Symphony*. Quite obviously, it contains work that was executed over the course of months and, perhaps, years. The manuscript paper is of various types; there are numerous examples of cuttings and paste-ins; and so forth. The physical dimensions of the volume are $12'' \times 14''$ and, as usual for the British Library volumes, the binding is finished in red leather (spine and corners) and cloth (boards). The notable contents follow.

Add. MS 50363 [1] ff. 1–23 constitute a draft of the first movement described as a 'rough sketch' by Vaughan Williams. Folios 2 and 3 are inserts. Folio 2 consists of four staves only; f. 3 of eight staves.

Add. MS 50363 [2] ff. 24–70v constitute a second draft of the first movement described by the British Library as 'somewhat later'. Most of the folios are of one kind (with printed brace) but different from the manuscript paper in (1). Having said that, the second draft has a mosaic-like appearance, for there are *many* insertions and paste-ins. Folio 25 is a two-measure fragment attached to f. 24r. Folios 26 and 27 are two-measure corrections attached to f. 24v. Folio 29, a two-measure fragment, and f. 30, a one-measure fragment, are attached to f. 28r. Folio 32r has two, one-measure fragments labeled f. 33 and f. 34. A five-stave, eight-measure correction (f. 36) is attached to f. 35r. A three-stave, four-measure fragment (f. 37) is attached to f. 35v. A two-measure, four-staved fragment (f. 39) is glued to f. 38v. Folio 45, 20-staved orchestral paper, is inserted before f. 46. Folios 53, 62, 63, 65 and 67r are plain manuscript paper (that is, they do not have printed braces on them). Folio 65 is a half-page insertion; f. 67r is blank. Folios 57v–61v have a different version of the material from four measures before Z in the full score to one measure before the *Animato*. Vaughan Williams replaced this with ff. 62r–63v. This second version is also different, especially at the *Animato*, in 4/4 rather than 2/2.

Add. MS 50363 [3] ff. 71–3 are three formerly loose sheets referring to the passages indicated in ff. 57v and 61v, and ff. 62r–63v; nevertheless, this fragment is still a penultimate version.

Add. MS 50363 [4] ff. 74–79v, written on 12-stave manuscript paper with no braces, constitute a penultimate version of the second movement in a very rough outline. It has features similar to those seen in the music books of Add. MS 50362: the chorus sings the opening material in a BT/SA format; 'A vast similitude' is in D major and sung by chorus.

Add. MS 50363 [5] ff. 81–8, written on 12-stave manuscript paper, represent a very untidy, incomplete draft in vocal score of the third movement. Folio 84 is an insert of four staves; f. 87, of eight measures.

Add. MS 50363 [6] ff. 89–94, written on 12-stave manuscript paper different from that in (5), represent an organ part for the third movement. Very messy, it is penned in black and blue ink.

Add. MS 50363 [7] ff. 95–8v constitute a very messy, early draft of the fourth movement.

Add. MS 50363 [8] ff. 99–123 consist of a fairly complete draft of the fourth movement, including the discarded sections. It uses 20-stave orchestral manuscript paper, but it is in vocal score. On f. 99r: [in bold red pencil is written:] Symphony of the Sea/Finale/The Explorers.

Add. MS 50364. This volume is the *first proof*, with corrections by Vaughan Williams, of the Breitkopf and Härtel vocal score, prepared at Leipzig in 1909. This fourth volume in the Vaughan Williams Collection is bound (by Breitkopf and Härtel) in green leather (spine, corners and titled centerpiece) and cloth (boards); it is embossed in gold, and stored in a red British Library box. It is 126 folios in length, the score is 11″ × 14″, while each folio is about 6½″ × 9¾″, printed recto only, with a generous border for editorial emendations. With the single exception on f. 11r of a pencilled emendation, the editorial markings in Vaughan Williams's hand are in red ink and are of the usual type one finds displayed in a proof copy. They deal with the additions and deletions of accidentals and dynamics, corrections to the text, changes to rhythms and rehearsal letters (upper case to lower case, and vice versa), and the like.

Add. MS 50365 A. This is an *autograph* full score of the first, third, and fourth movements. Additionally, letters and papers from Frank Kidson, Ralph and Ursula Vaughan Williams are bound in at ff. i–vi. The letter of U.V.W., dated 24 November 1960, is of the greatest importance. It reads:

> *IMPORTANT*/As this score has been used by/many conductors no marks/should be taken to be the composer's/own without reference to his copy/of the printed score./[signed] Ursula Vaughan Williams/[date]

We can identify two conductors, at least, from a letter published in the *Musical Times* in April 1923 by Edward C. Bairstow, who complained of the physical abuse the full score had received from a previous user (particularly by Sir Henry J. Wood). He wrote that the score was literally covered with enormous blue-pencil marks (but pencil, red and green ink have been used, too). They included the final consonants of every sustained word sung by the choir inserted in all four parts; huge breath marks before, in the course of, and at the end of each phrase, not only for choir but for soloists; the names of instruments written in full before any passage they had to play; the words 'Cue for Chorus' inserted some bars before the chorus entries; and when any bars come along with a different number of beats from those preceding and following it, the score is *heavily* marked with the new time signature and beats. Significantly, Bairstow acknowledges that he spent hours erasing the marks. However, the score remains covered with similar markings *in profusion*. Upon the evidence of U.V.W. and Bairstow, we are forced to conclude that this score is useless as a manuscript source.

The manuscript paper is *c.* 11½″ × 16½″ in size and consists of 34 staves. It is bound in red leather (spine and corners) and cloth (boards). The pagination (recto/verso) is as follows: ff. 2–51v make up the first movement; ff. 52–136v make up the third movement; ff. 137–228 make up the fourth movement. The score exhibits abundant revisions pasted over the original paper. These invariably alter some facet of scoring or in a few instances change notes without harming the overall design of a passage. The correction to the contrapuntal passage for chorus before the epilogue has been done in green ink (compare f. 219 on recto of f. 218, a one-measure, four-stave fragment, where the contrapuntal passage begins, and f. 220 on verso of f. 218, a five-measure, four-stave fragment, where the passage continues).

Add. MS 50365 B. This is an elegant *copy* of the second movement. Since it is not in the hand of Vaughan Williams, it is useless as a manuscript source. Bound in a similar fashion as Add. MS 50365 A, it has the same physical dimensions. Consisting of fourteen folios, it is heavily marked with blue pencil and red ink.

Add. MS 50366 A-D. These four volumes, bound separately in red leather (spine and corners) and cloth (boards), make up the four movements of the *printed* full score by Stainer and Bell in 1924. Physically, each is *c.* 12¼″ × 18″. The British Library catalogue indicates that each score contains the composer's corrections. There are red ink, and black and blue pencil annotations. Red ink is used to indicate which part is playing (for example, Tuba; I Trb, II Trb; and so on). Add. MS C (third movement) has an organ part written in on f. 32v to the end. Many other markings of the kind found in the autograph full score (for example, when time signatures change, boldly written numbers count out the beats; circles and arrows to cue entering instruments and voices are abundant; and so on) make it quite likely that these printed full scores were used as performance material. The annotations are very much what a conductor, reading from the score during a performance, would need, and how he would complete them. The bottom corners have been completely destroyed from turning, although the British Library has repaired them by using matching paper and paste. Red ink annotations indicate reduced orchestration, as Vaughan Williams writes on the fourth volume, and it is usually entered into the brass and reed instrumental sections (for example, Trpt II; I Horn, II Horn; II Fag; and so on). The organ part has been entered into the harp line.

Notes

1. Ursula Vaughan Williams, *R.V.W.: A Biography of Ralph Vaughan Williams* (London: Oxford University Press, 1964), 65. Reprinted (with corrections) in 1984 and first published as a Clarendon paperback in 1992.
2. The reception and influence of Walt Whitman's poetry in the British Isles during his lifetime has been superbly treated in Harold Blodgett, *Walt Whitman in England* (Ithaca, New York: Cornell University Press, 1934). Throughout this essay I quote from the inclusive edition *Leaves of Grass by Walt Whitman*, edited by Emory Holloway (Garden City, New York: Doubleday and Company, Inc., 1926).
3. Blodgett, *Whitman*, 20–22.
4. Gay Wilson Allen, *The New Walt Whitman Handbook* (New York: New York University Press, 1986), 273–4. Allen notes that the Rossetti edition was reprinted in England in 1886, 1892, 1895, 1910 and 1920 by Chatto and Windus, 270–71.

5   Blodgett, *Whitman*, 59.
6   Ibid., 69–70.
7   Vaughan Williams set the poems of both Rossetti's about the same time he was considering the Whitman texts as a source for his first symphony, cf. *Willowwood* (D.G. Rossetti), cantata, 1902–3 cantata [for lv, pf], rev. for Bar/Mez, female chorus, orch, 1908–9; *The House of Life* (D.G. Rossetti), 1903.
8   Michael Kennedy, *The Works of Ralph Vaughan Williams* (London: Oxford University Press, 1964), 82.
9   Ursula Vaughan Williams, *R.V.W.*, 65. By the time Vaughan Williams was beginning to sketch *A Sea Symphony*, he was in the midst of composing a less ambitious setting of Whitman for chorus and orchestra, *Toward the Unkown Region* (1907).
10   Jeremy Dibble, *C. Hubert H. Parry: His Life and Music* (Oxford: Clarendon Press, 1992), 227.
11   Ralph Vaughan Williams, *A Sea Symphony*, pianoforte arrangement by S.O. Goldsmith and the composer (London: Stainer & Bell, Ltd, 1918) [plate number: S. and B. 1961].
12   C. Hubert H. Parry, *Invocation to Music*, for Soli, Chorus, and Orchestra; vocal score (London: Novello, Ewer and Co., 1895) [plate number: 8232]. Bodleian Library Mus.20d.1(2). Unless otherwise noted, all references are to vocal scores of both works and those cited in following discussions.
13   Bernard Benoliel has made the same observation in 'A Modern Choral–Orchestral Tradition', 82, in *Parry before Jerusalem: Studies of his Life and Music with Excerpts from his Published Writings* (Aldershot: Ashgate Publishing Limited, 1997).
14   Dibble, *Parry*, 392.
15   Kennedy, *Works*, 99. An earlier setting of Whitman by Vaughan Williams, *Toward the Unknown Region* for chorus and orchestra, had been successfully premièred during the 1907 Leeds Festival, thus paving the way for *A Sea Symphony* three years later; see Charles Edward McGuire's essay in this volume (Chapter 11).
16   Wilfrid Mellers, *Vaughan Williams and the Vision of Albion* (London: Barrie and Jenkins, 1989), 8.
17   Ralph Vaughan Williams, 'A Musical Autobiography',188, in *National Music and Other Essays*: 'I spent several hours at the British Museum studying the full scores of the *Enigma Variations* and *Gerontius*. The results are obvious in the opening pages of the finale of my *Sea Symphony*.' In 'What Have We Learnt From Elgar?', *Music and Letters*, xvi/1 (1935), 17, the composer wrote: 'I find that the Elgar phrase which influenced me most was "Thou art calling me" in *Gerontius* (vocal score, p. 7, fifth bar of figure 22), not so much perhaps in its original form as when it comes later on in combination with another theme (e.g., p. 19, figure 37). For proof of this see *Sea Symphony* (vocal score, p. 84, nine bars before letter B).'
18   Mellers, *Vaughan Williams*, 9–10.
19   Edward Elgar, *The Dream of Gerontius*, rev. edn, vocal score (Great Britain: Novello, 1978).
20   Ralph Vaughan Williams, *A Sea Symphony*, orchestral score (London: Stainer and Bell, Ltd, 1918).
21   Edward Elgar, *Elgar Complete Edition*. Series I: Choral Works. Vol. 3: *The Light of Life* [full score]. Edited by Robert Anderson and Jerrold Northrop Moore (London: Novello & Company Limited, 1989). The vocal score was published in 1896 by Novello, Ewer and Co. [plate number: 8246].
22   *Elgar Complete Edition*, viii–ix.
23   Frederick Delius, *Sea Drift*, Hawkes Pocket Scores [orchestral score] (London: Boosey & Hawkes, Ltd, 1939) and *Sea Drift*, rev. and ed. Sir Thomas Beecham, Bart., C.H.,

Vocal Score by Siegfried Fall, ed. Robert Threlfall; *New edition, entirely re-engraved in 1991* (London: Boosey and Hawkes, Ltd., 1991).

24 Joseph Gerard Brennan, 'Delius and Whitman', *Walt Whitman Review*, xviii/3 (1972), 92.

25 Ursula Vaughan Williams, *R.V.W.*, 65.

26 Ibid., 65.

27 Cf. Pamela J. Willetts, 'The Ralph Vaughan Williams Collection', *British Museum Quarterly* xxiv (1961), 3–11. (For a summary list of acquisitions up to the mid 1960s, see: Willetts, *Handlist of Music Manuscripts Acquired 1908–67*, London, 1970.)

28 See Byron Adams, 'The Stages of Revision of Vaughan Williams's Sixth Symphony', Chapter 1 of this volume, 4.

29 Alain Frogley, 'Vaughan Williams and Thomas Hardy: "Tess" and the Slow movement of the Ninth Symphony', *Music and Letters* 68 (1987), 48.

30 A.E.F. Dickinson, *Vaughan Williams*, first published in 1963 by Faber and Faber, Ltd; reprinted by Scholarly Press, Inc., 19722 E. Nine Mile Rd, St Clair Shores, Michigan 48080, n.d., 183.

31 Kennedy, *Works*, 127. As for Purcell's influence upon *A Sea Symphony*, it should be remembered that Vaughan Williams edited a volume of *Welcome Songs* in 1905 for the Purcell Society.

32 As mentioned in the Appendix, Add. MS 50362 B is a recopy of the material found in Add. MS 50362 A (ff. 7v–22), i.e. it appears to be a neat, fair copy of work done at another sitting. Add. MS 50362 C also contains sketches for the second movement (ff. 7v–12). Although it has been catalogued as 'C', it pre-dates A and B. (The sketch of the second movement introduction is 'in condensed score' and represents the composer's first thoughts on paper; the remainder of the movement is very skeletal and in a preliminary stage.) Consult Add. MS 50363 (4), too, in the Appendix.

33 Kennedy, *Works*, 128.

34 James E. Miller, Jr, *Walt Whitman,* updated edn (Boston: Twayne Publisher, A Division of G.K. Hall and Co., 1990), 109.

35 Mellers, *Vaughan Williams*, 23.

36 Kennedy, *Catalogue*, 57.

37 Ibid., *Catalogue*, 55.

38 Ibid., 55.

39 A.E.F. Dickinson, 'The Vaughan Williams Manuscripts', *The Music Review*, xxiii (1962), 181.

40 Hubert Foss, *Ralph Vaughan Williams* (New York: Oxford University Press, 1950), 97.

41 Kennedy, *Works*, 130.

42 Mellers, *Vaughan Williams*, 23.

43 Miller, *Whitman*, 85.

44 Hugh Ottaway, *Vaughan Williams Symphonies* (London: first published by BBC Books, 1972, reprinted by Ariel Books, 1987), 18.

45 Miller, *Whitman*, 135.

46 Ibid., 135–6.

47 Mellers, *Vaughan Williams*, 23.

48 Kennedy, *Catalogue*, 57.

49 Ralph Vaughan Williams, 'What Have We Learnt From Elgar?', 18–19.

Chapter 6

Hymn Tunes from Folk-songs: Vaughan Williams and English Hymnody

Julian Onderdonk

In December 1903, Vaughan Williams heard an elderly agricultural worker, Mr Potiphar, sing 'Bushes and Briars'. The experience proved to be overwhelming, and brought Vaughan Williams 'face to face' with English folk-song for the first time. From this beginning, he undertook to travel throughout England collecting folk-songs, a labor of love which occupied him for the next ten years and ultimately resulted in the notation of over 800 tunes and songs.[1] A year or so later,[2] an equally important event occurred in the composer's career. Percy Dearmer, vicar of St Mary's, Primrose Hill, appeared at his door to offer him the musical editorship of a new hymn-book. Despite reservations about the assignment, Vaughan Williams accepted the task and so began an association with Dearmer that spanned 32 years and the production of *The English Hymnal* (1906; rev. 1933), *Songs of Praise* (1925; rev. 1931) and *The Oxford Book of Carols* (1928), as well as several smaller singing books derived from these publications.

Given this chronology, it is no surprise that Vaughan Williams's encounter with folk-song and his engagement with hymnody have been closely linked in the literature. Ursula Vaughan Williams's account of her husband's work on *The English Hymnal*, for example, follows directly upon the story of Vaughan Williams's discovery of folk-song and his initial attempts to collect it.[3] James Day remarks that Vaughan Williams's work with folk-song 'dovetailed in an interesting manner' with his work on hymn tunes, and considers the two as interrelated.[4] The reasons for the pairing go well beyond the coincidence of their occurrence, however, and derive from long-standing perceptions about the role of English folk-song and hymnody in the development of the composer's 'national' style. Writers as diverse as Frank Howes, Percy Young and Elliott Schwartz have stressed the impact of both folk-song and hymnody on Vaughan Williams, and A.E.F. Dickinson goes so far as to devote a single chapter to each in his volume on the composer's music.[5] Writing in 1964, Michael Kennedy aptly summarized such views:

> Through a conscious nationalism [Vaughan Williams] discovered a means of self-expression. Upon a foundation of folk-song and other equally important influences – Purcell, the Tudor composers, and the hymn-tunes – he erected his own personal style which was his natural voice'.[6]

By explicitly connecting the two fields of interest, Kennedy suggests that Vaughan Williams's work with hymn tunes 'was, in fact, by coming as a tributary from, and corollary to, his folk-song collecting, another "liberating" influence'.[7]

Yet there is another, more practical, reason why commentators have grouped folk-song and hymnody together in discussions of Vaughan Williams – the fact that the composer *adapted* folk-songs when setting hymn texts and other religious verse to music. Such adaptations included versions of folk-songs belonging to various continental nations (France, Germany, Italy) as well as to Scotland, Ireland and Wales. But by far the majority of the traditional tunes he adapted were English, taken from the collections of friends and contemporaries active in the Folk-song Revival – collectors like Lucy Broadwood, W.P. Merrick and Cecil Sharp. In some cases, Vaughan Williams adapted folk-songs from his own collection. Of the 43 English traditional tunes he adapted for the 1906 *English Hymnal*, 12 come from his own manuscript folk-song collection.

Viewed within this context, Vaughan Williams's engagement with folk-song was intimately connected to his editing of hymn tunes. But the roots of this connection derive as much from the humanitarian dimensions of his nationalism as from its musical and stylistic goals. For Vaughan Williams, nationalism was fundamentally a *cultural* matter, a question of shared language and tradition, and his transformation of folk-songs into hymn tunes was much more than an attempt self-consciously to create a 'national style'. Rather, Vaughan Williams's ambition was to establish the conditions by which his compatriots might come into a more profound relation with a common English heritage. Folk-song, he believed, was 'the spiritual life-blood of a people',[8] a positive force for social and cultural regeneration, and he conceived of its use in Church services as a means to forge connections between social classes. Hymn tunes contained a similar communal potential since, in his view, the music of the Church – notably plainsong, but also psalmody and hymnody – had directly evolved from folk-song.[9] Moreover, hymn tunes were fundamentally congregational in character, sung by people sharing the same language, customs and experiences. For these reasons, Vaughan Williams did not hesitate to speak of hymn tunes as a form of 'national music'[10] in their own right, and he considered his efforts to fashion hymn tunes from recently-collected folk-songs as part of a long and distinguished tradition. As he put it in a 1956 radio broadcast discussing this aspect of the *English Hymnal*: '[By 1906] Cecil Sharp had just made his epoch-making discovery of the beautiful melody hidden in the countryside: why should we not enter into our inheritance in the church as well as the concert room?'[11]

Religious motivations, understood in the conventional sense, had little to do with this conjoining of sacred and secular. A great-nephew of Charles Darwin who was conversant from his teenage years with nineteenth-century rationalist debates, Vaughan Williams was an atheist at Cambridge and only later drifted into what Ursula Vaughan Williams termed a 'cheerful agnosticism'.[12] Rather, his immediate concern was to reform the music of the Established Anglican Church, which he believed had fallen into sentimentality at the hands of Victorian composers like Joseph Barnby and J.B. Dykes.[13] Folk-song, with its clean diatonic outlines and restrained emotional character, was the perfect antidote to sentimentality; indeed, its inherent reticence may even have influenced Vaughan Williams's 'austere' selection of material for *The English Hymnal*.[14] More importantly, by reforming the music of the Anglican Church, Vaughan Williams was in effect reforming the music of the *national* Church, itself a cultural institution and an instrument of the English state. The significance of this to his own nationalist agenda, as outlined above, will be clear. This agenda, it should also be noted, was not much different from that of the High Church clerics who initiated *The English Hymnal*. Percy Dearmer, Canon Scott Holland and the various members of the editorial committee of *The English Hymnal* were nationalists and Church reformers who believed in the power of art to bring together different social strata in a common democratic cause.[15] For these clerics, as for Vaughan Williams, nationalism was a tool for reform, and there can be little doubt that they too valued English folk-song for its humanitarian potential and welcomed its inclusion in the new hymn-book.

The full story of the cultural negotiations surrounding Vaughan Williams's engagement with folk-song and hymnody has yet to be written. Early commentators have tended to discuss the connection between folk-song and hymn-tune in superficial terms, as twin facets of the composer's 'English' background.[16] More recent scholarship has addressed the subject more thoughtfully, but generally only in passing.[17] Given the enormous complexity of the issues involved – complicated yet further by the fraught question of Vaughan Williams's own religious beliefs – this is unsurprising. This chapter does not attempt to tell this story either, but rather seeks to work towards it by filling in gaps in the known record. First, there currently exists no complete list of the folk-songs *from his own collection* that Vaughan Williams adapted as hymn tunes. Given the importance that his own collecting activities had upon his decision to adapt folk-songs at all, such a list would provide many insights, as would a cross-index of the publications where he published and reprinted those adaptations. Second, while all observers comment on the significance of the composer's adaptation of folk-songs as hymn tunes, no one has carefully examined the editorial process whereby he converted one into the other. Such an investigation reveals much about his editorial and creative methods and gives us insight into his musical ideas and assumptions. In particular, it clarifies the extent to which Vaughan Williams's translation of folk-songs into hymn tunes reflected, on the detailed editorial level, his nationalist convictions and activities. This essay will take up each of these points in turn.

Establishing an Inventory

There does exist a certain amount of published information concerning the folk-songs that Vaughan Williams adapted from his own collection for use in hymn-books. Michael Kennedy has provided thorough lists of the traditional melodies that the composer selected and arranged for hymnals.[18] With the exception of his impeccable entry for the 1906 *English Hymnal*, however, Kennedy has not always indicated which folk-songs came from Vaughan Williams's own collection and which from those of other collectors. This represents a modest lacuna, as all but four of his folk-song adaptations for hymn-books were first published in *The English Hymnal*. Nevertheless, when the importance of these adaptations to Vaughan Williams's nationalist vision is put in proper perspective, it seems important not only to trace these four but also to uncover as much information as possible about the corpus as a whole. A complete roster of the publications in which the folk-song adaptations appeared would be especially useful, for while Vaughan Williams published the majority of his adaptations in the 1906 *English Hymnal*, he continued to reprint them in various publications thereafter.[19] These included the 1933 edition of *The English Hymnal*,[20] of course, but also *Motherland Song Book, Vol. 1* (1919), *Songs of Praise* (two editions 1925, 1931), *The Oxford Book of Carols* (1928), and *The Oxford Book of Carols for Schools* (1956).

It must be noted, however, that this chapter is exclusively concerned with adaptations of folk-songs into hymn tunes, not with the folk carols that Vaughan Williams arranged for these publications. The folk-songs that he turned into hymn tunes were originally sung to secular words, and this meant that Vaughan Williams had to 'fit' the tunes with substitute Christian texts. By contrast, the carols that he arranged already had their own, Christian, words (Christmas and Easter being the usual subjects), and they consequently required little or no textual alteration. This distinction is an important one, for while the addition of Christian text compromised the original 'folk' identity of the traditional melodies in their transformation into SATB hymn tunes, the retention of original text in the carols meant that this repertory maintained its 'folk' status even as it underwent similar musical treatment. This may be why Vaughan Williams typically published his carol arrangements not in hymn-books but rather in carol-books and other anthologies of 'traditional' music – for example, *The Oxford Book of Carols* (1928), *English Traditional Carols* (1954), and *The Oxford Book of Carols for Schools* (1956). For this reason – and also the fact that the composer's hymn tune adaptations are far more revealing from an editorial perspective than are his carol arrangements – Vaughan Williams's carol arrangements, and the sources in which they appear, lie outside the parameters of this investigation. (For the sake of completeness, however, Table 6A.1 in the Appendix lists the 13 carols from his collection that he arranged for congregational singing, along with appropriate manuscript and publication information.[21])

This distinction between 'adapted' hymn tunes on the one hand and 'arranged' carols on the other does, however, make for a certain untidiness *vis-à-vis* the source materials. For one thing, both *The Oxford Book of Carols* and *The Oxford Book of Carols for Schools* contain hymn-tune adaptations of folk-songs along the lines of those published in *The English Hymnal*. That is, they contain reworked versions of 'secular' folk-songs whose original folk text has been replaced with a Christian one. Although these adaptations are only two in number, their appearance in these sources requires that both carol-books be added to our roster of relevant publications. A second anomaly concerns the fact that Vaughan Williams reprinted his hymn tune *King's Lynn* (an adaptation of 'Van Dieman's Land') in the specifically non-Christian *Motherland Song Book, Vol. 1* (1919). At first glance, it is surprising that he should have done so, given that the hymn tune has a decidedly Christian text and was originally conceived for the Church liturgy. But the choice seems less odd when the fundamentally civic and national tone of *Motherland Song Book* – it contains examples of traditional and early English songs, and advertises itself as appropriate to local events and national occasions – is taken into consideration. Indeed, given Vaughan Williams's abiding belief in the social and cultural links between folk-song and hymnody, the appearance of the hymn tune in the collection seems consistent with his cultural nationalism.

By acknowledging these caveats, it is possible to proceed to an accounting of the individual folk-songs collected by Vaughan Williams and adapted by him for use as hymn tunes. Table 6.1 summarizes this information and reveals that he adapted 16

Table 6.1 Folk-songs collected and adapted as hymn tunes by Vaughan Williams

No.	Manuscript title	Manuscript location	Hymn tune name	Publications						
				1906 English Hymnal	Motherland Song Book	1925 Songs of Praise	Oxford Book of Carols	1931 Songs of Praise	1933 English Hymnal	Oxford Carols for Schools
1.	The Bailiff's Daughter	54191, f. 166r	Rodmell	186 611	–	441	–	221	611	–
2.	The Bailiff's Daughter	54190, f. 148v	Farnham	525(i)	–	156	–	285	525(i)	–
3.	A Brisk Young Farmer	54191, f. 12v	Danby	295	–	12 (new arr.)	–	16 (1925 arr.)	295 (1906 arr.)	–
4.	The Brisk Young Lively Lad	54190, f. 183v	Gosterwood	299 572 594	–	107(i) 137 169	–	21	299 572 594	–
5.	In Jessie's City	54187. f. 3r	Herongate	597	–	321 428	–	602	597	–
6.	The Fisherman	54190, f. 54v	East Horndon	595	–	427	–	–	595	–
7.	Newport Street	54190, f. 51v	Essex	–	–	352(ii)	–	637(ii)	–	–
8.	Our Captain Calls	54190, f. 199r	Monks Gate	402	–	255	–	515	402	–
9.	The Ploughboy's Dream	54188, f. 15v	Forest Green	15	–	53	138	79(i)	15	32
10.	Psalm Tune	54191, f. 190r	Dunstan	–	–	–	–	393(ii)	638 (alt.)	–
11.	The Red Barn	54190, F. 161v	Job	–	–	–	App.6(n)	–	–	–
12.	The Royal George	54191, f. 153r	Sussex	239 385	–	190 229	–	321	239 385	–
13.	The Sheffield Apprentice	54188, f. 15r	Ingrave	607	–	–	–	–	607	–
14.	Tarry Woo	54191, f. 20r	Dent Dale	23	–	248	–	88	23	–
15.	Van Dieman's Land or Young Henry the Poacher	54191, f. 81v	King's Lynn	562	13	177	–	308	562	–
16.	Virgin Unspotted	54189, f. 157v	Hardwick	–	–	438	–	34	–	–

folk-songs from his collection and that these appeared in seven different publications.[22] The left-hand column of Table 6.1 lists the songs alphabetically by title and provides vertical columns for manuscript location[23] as well as for the 'tune name' Vaughan Williams used to identify the hymn tune derived from each.[24] The remaining columns indicate the seven publications – listed, from left to right, by date of publication – in which the various hymn tunes were printed and reprinted.[25] Throughout Table 6.1, the numbers in these columns refer to the number of each hymn, not to the pages where the hymn tune is found.

As for the number of times Vaughan Williams published and republished his folk-song-derived hymn tunes in these sources, Table 6.1 shows that he did so 66 times. This may seem a surprisingly large figure given the small body of sources and tunes, but Vaughan Williams reprinted the same hymn tunes again and again, especially when it came to the later editions of *The English Hymnal* and *Songs of Praise*. It might be argued that these later editions do little more than reprint their first editions, and as such do not constitute 'separate' publications. Yet later editions of both *The English Hymnal* and *Songs of Praise* show clear evidence of editorial revision and reconsideration in their preparation for print. Another factor contributing to the high number of reprintings is Vaughan Williams's practice of using certain hymn tunes more than once in a given publication. For example, the tune *Sussex*, adapted from the folk-song 'The Royal George', appears twice in the 1906 and 1933 editions of *The English Hymnal*, as well as twice more in the 1925 *Songs of Praise*. In these duplicate cases, the tune is coupled with different texts, each reflecting various seasons of the Church calendar. The use of 'alternative' texts was (and still is) standard practice in hymnody, and by treating his folk-song adaptations in this way Vaughan Williams further evinced his belief in their centrality to Church tradition.

It remains only to comment on Vaughan Williams's SATB arrangements in regard to this duplication pattern. Generally speaking, Vaughan Williams provided a single arrangement for each hymn tune, so that the same version of each tune was used for all publications. Thus all ten appearances of *Gosterwood* listed in Table 6.1 use the same arrangement that first appeared in the 1906 *English Hymnal*. The one exception is *Danby*, No. 3 in the Table, which is found in different arrangements in *The English Hymnal* and *Songs of Praise*. This difference is clearly indicated in the table.

From Folk-song to Hymn Tune: The Editorial Process

Generally speaking, Vaughan Williams's attitude towards the arranging of folk-songs was consistently open-minded. So long as the arranger's settings grew 'out of the love of a tune [and not] from a mistaken idea that it is necessary to "make something of it"',[26] he welcomed a wide range of compositional solutions. But when it came to adapting folk-songs for use in hymn-books, he took a narrower view. There were sound reasons for this, for the restrictions imposed by hymn-tune adaptation were necessarily more stringent than those imposed by a solo, choral or instrumental arrangement. In the latter, a certain skill in performance could be taken for granted – trained choirs, expert pianists, sensitive instrumentalists – and this made more sophisticated arrangements not only feasible but desirable. Hymn tunes, by contrast, were meant to be performed by congregations, motley assemblages of individuals whose musical abilities are widely varied. In addition, hymn-tune arrangements had to be sensitive to the constrictions of vocal range and clear part-writing, and this presented the composer with a formidable technical challenge.

Given such restrictions, Vaughan Williams tended to adapt folk-songs into hymn tunes in a simple and direct manner. Whereas his arrangements of folk-song for secular contexts often employ elaborate and even experimental techniques,[27] those prepared for Church performance bring the tune forward as clearly and forcefully as possible. His adaptation of Mr Walter's 'The Bailiff's Daughter' for the hymn tune *Rodmell* offers a case in point. Example 6.1 gives Vaughan Williams's manuscript transcription of the original folk-song as well as the hymn tune version he produced for *The English Hymnal*:[28]

The purpose of the setting, clearly, is to place the tune in strong relief. The block chords in the lower three parts provide a solid and uncomplicated harmonic basis for

(a) 'The Bailiff's Daughter', Add. MS 54191, f. 166r (originally collected without text)

(b) 'When Christ Was Born in Bethlehem' *(Rodmell), The English Hymnal,* No. 611

When Christ was born in Bethlehem,
Fair peace on earth to bring,
In lowly state of love he came
To be the children's King.

Example 6.1   Manuscript transcription of 'The Bailiff's Daughter', 1st version with hymn-tune adaptation

the tune. The lower parts proceed in even crotchets throughout, even where the melody departs from that rhythm. (The tenor and alto do occasionally deviate from the crotchet pattern to follow the melody.) As befits the tune, the chords are unremittingly diatonic. The arrangement, in short, closely concurs with the methods of Cecil Sharp, about whose 'best' folk-song arrangements Vaughan Williams said 'it is the tune that counts and the arrangement falls into its proper background'.[29]

But even as it subordinates itself wholly to the tune, the arrangement of 'The Bailiff's Daughter' is neither dull nor pedestrian. Vaughan Williams revered Bach's settings of chorales, and his study of the German composer results in subtle part-writing that lends interest to the accompaniment and serves to enhance the tune. He adds variety to the prevailing diatonic harmony with an occasional suspension (bar 4) and the deft use of a passing tone (bar 7). He uses a wide variety of chord voicings and inversions, most notably in bar 2 where the 'melodic' bass descending by step results in a succession of inverted tonic and dominant chords. Vaughan Williams also cleverly withholds the vi chord until the start of the fourth phrase, where it adds weight to the conclusion of the tune. Finally, the nuanced handling of the related second and third phrases of the tune (bars 3–5) is particularly effective. The part-writing for both phrases, which seems similar, proves to be subtly different through chord substitution and inversion, and this makes for variety even as it draws attention to the unified structure of the melody.

A similar balance between the necessity for emphasizing the tune and providing elegance of accompaniment can be found in his adaptation of Mr Garman's 'The Ploughboy's Dream' for the famous Christmas hymn tune *Forest Green* (Example 6.2 – note that the hymn-tune version doubles the value of the original beat).

Vaughan Williams matches the measured serenity of Mr Garman's tune with simple diatonic chords that closely follow the rhythm of the melodic line. Indeed, Vaughan Williams is so sensitive to the tune's overall shape that when the rhythm becomes more animated at the beginning of the third phrase, his accompaniment keeps pace and becomes more active. But observe how the setting unobtrusively exceeds the implications of the original tune. The shifting chords over the repeated Fs of the primary strain (bars 1, 5 and 13) provide a sense of forward motion at a static point in the tune. The same is true of the crotchets passed from bass to tenor to alto during the gradual slowing of the melodic line in the second half of the third phrase. Note, finally, the skill with which Vaughan Williams imbues the final phrase (bars 15–16) with a sense of finality lacking in earlier statements (bars 3–4, 7–8): increased bass and tenor activity in bar 15 facilitates the earlier arrival at the dominant and results in a firmer cadence.

Rodmell and *Forest Green* may be taken as representative of the hymn tunes Vaughan Williams adapted from folk-songs in his collection. Both demonstrate his skill in creating accompaniments that adhere to the tune but derive imaginative inspiration from the contours of the original melody. They also demonstrate something more: Vaughan Williams did not invariably reproduce the melody exactly as his informants sang it. A comparison of the manuscript fair copies with the hymn-tune versions in the two examples above reveals that he ignored variants, changed rhythms and altered individual pitches during the process of transferring the tunes from manuscript to print. The crotchet B variant that Mr Walter sang in bar 6 of 'The Bailiff's Daughter' is missing from *Rodmell*, for example, while Mr

(a) 'The Ploughboy's Dream', Add. MS 54188, f. 15v

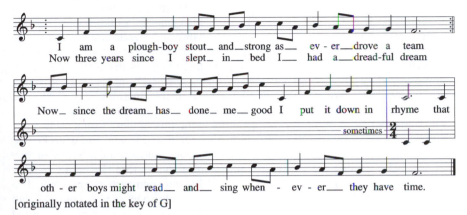

I am a plough-boy stout__ and__strong as__ ev - er__drove a team
Now three years since I slept__ in__ bed I__ had a__dread-ful dream

Now__ since the dream__ has__ done__ me__ good I put it down in rhyme that

sometimes

oth - er boys might read__ and__ sing when - ev - er__ they have time.

[originally notated in the key of G]

(b) 'O Little Town of Bethlehem' *(Forest Green), The English Hymnal,* No. 15

O little town of Bethlehem
How still we see thee lie!
Above thy deep and dreamless sleep
The silent stars go by.
Yet in thy dark streets shineth
The everlasting light;
The hopes and fears of all the years
Are met in thee to-night.

**Example 6.2   Manuscript transcription of 'The Ploughboy's Dream' with
hymn-tune adaptation**

Garman's 2/4 variant measure in 'The Ploughboys Dream' has disappeared entirely from *Forest Green*. The rhythm sung by Mr Walter in the second half of bar 2 – dotted crotchet D followed by quaver D – has been changed in the final version to repeated crotchet Ds. And *Forest Green* contains three wholesale alterations of pitch in bars 2, 6 and 14 – that is, at the same point in each statement of the primary strain – as well as at the anacrusis to bar 9. Nor are these isolated instances of editorial alteration. Of the 16 folk-songs Vaughan Williams selected from his own collection, 14 (or 88 percent) have melodies that have been altered in some way during the process of their transformation into hymn tunes.

Of course, Vaughan Williams was under no obligation in these instances to leave what his informants sang in its original, pristine condition. In the case of folk-song arrangements published in 'secular' singing books and anthologies, Vaughan Williams believed that the collector/arranger must 'put before the public exactly what he has heard – neither more nor less'.[30] But no such restrictions applied to folk-songs arranged as hymn tunes since these were published 'out of context' – that is, with the original folk lyric excised and with a substitute Christian poem inserted in its place. As noted above, the Church's long tradition of incorporating folk-song and other popular material for the liturgy had always resulted, Vaughan Williams believed, in the 'transformation' of that material.[31] Thus he had no compunction about altering the tunes from his collection when adapting them for hymn-books. He never disguised the alterations that he made to the original folk-songs when turning them into hymn tunes, and he forthrightly printed the words 'from an English traditional melody' or 'adapted from an English traditional melody' at the head of several tunes.[32]

But even if Vaughan Williams's editorial alterations of traditional melodies are justified by a long precedent and are entirely acknowledged, there is still considerable interest in examining the details – the how and why – of their occurrence. The study of such changes throws light upon Vaughan Williams's process of creating hymn tunes, especially where the adaptation of folk-songs is concerned. More than this, a close investigation of the editorial process gives us insight into Vaughan Williams's unique concerns and preferences. In particular, it enables us to grasp, on the detailed musical level, the extent to which his editorial decisions were in fact determined by the larger goals of his nationalist agenda.

A first explanation for Vaughan Williams's alterations of folk melodies when transferring them into hymn tunes is found in the very reasoning that prompted him to adapt folk-songs simply and directly: his sensitivity to the limited musical abilities of the congregation. Organist and choirmaster of St Barnabas, Lambeth, for four years, from 1895 to 1899, Vaughan Williams had first-hand experience with congregations, and knew what they could reasonably be expected to sing. His expertise in this regard is evident from the selection of variants he made in Examples 6.1 and 6.2, above. Variant selection was to some extent unavoidable in these instances, of course, since hymn tunes demand a strict adherence to strophic formats that Mr Walter and Mr Garman, in common with most folksingers, did not feel constrained to employ. The essential point, however, is that Vaughan Williams invariably chose the variant best suited to *simplify* the melody and therefore to make the tune more accessible to the earnest but inexperienced singers in the congregation. In the case of Mr Garman's tune, for example, he selected the 4/4 variant in bar 12 because the 2/4 variant interfered with the rhythmic flow of quadruple time (4/2 in published version) and disrupted the expected cadential pause between phrases 3 and 4. (In the effort to regularize this cadence further, Vaughan Williams substituted even notes – in this case minims – for the dotted rhythm of the original 4/4 variant.) By contrast, Vaughan Williams rejected Mr Walter's crotchet B variant in bar 6 of 'The Bailiff's Daughter' because the alternative quaver G–B variant followed more logically (and easily) from the flowing rhythm of the third phrase. He may also have chosen the G–B variant because he believed congregations would find it easier to move to the closer pitch G (rather than to the higher B) from the previous phrase ending on E. That the C major triad with which he harmonized the E contains a G, but *not* a B, may well have influenced his selection.

Considerations of congregational ability also explain those instances where Vaughan Williams altered what his informants sang. One instance of this, the rhythmic change in Mr Garman's 4/4 variant measure, has been discussed above; a parallel example comes in bar 2 of *Rodmell*, where Vaughan Williams changed the rhythm of Mr Walter's repeated Ds. In both cases, the change regularized the rhythm on both sides of a cadence and, with the help of a breathing indication and traditional double bar, eased the transition from one phrase to the next. Vaughan Williams's substitution of a minim A for Mr Garman's quaver C–A figure in bars 2, 6 and 14 of *Forest Green*, meanwhile, served to encourage congregational involvement by simplifying both the rhythm and the melody. His alteration of Mr Garman's quaver A–B flat to a crotchet F–A at the pick-up to bar 9 was made with the same intention. With F as the final note of the previous phrase, Vaughan Williams clearly felt that a jump to A would confuse some singers and so created a new figure that started on F. Harmonic considerations – here, the abrupt movement to a D minor chord – may once again have influenced his choice.

Congregational concerns prompted editorial alterations and omissions in other hymn tunes as well. 'The Royal George', 'Tarry Woo', 'Van Dieman's Land', and 'Virgin Unspotted' all contain variant passages that had to be omitted if the original melody was to conform to the strophic requirements of the text. Vaughan Williams made the necessary selections, of course, but always with an acute understanding of congregational expectations: in every case, the chosen variant simplified the melody and promotes ease of singing in a way that the rejected variant would not.[33] As for outright alterations, his adaptation of 'Virgin Unspotted' eliminated fermatas sung by Mr Lewis, establishing instead a rhythmic regularity that encourages the untutored singer. His reworking of Mr Baker's 'The Brisk Young Lively Lad' brought an anomalous 6/4 bar into conformity with the 4/4 norm by shortening the durations of the original rhythm. His adaptation of 'Psalm Tune' raised the initial anacrusis to Mr Thompson's tune a full octave so that the vocal range was reduced from an eleventh to a more manageable octave.

It might be argued that such changes are precisely what one might expect in that they result less from a nationalist agenda than from an uncomplicated desire to revive these tunes for public consumption. The omission of fermatas is surely a sensible change that allows a congregation to sing a hymn tune successfully. The same may be said of alterations that bring the vocal range of a tune within reasonable limits, regularize anomalous metrical passages, standardize rhythms around cadences, or simply serve to make a tune more comfortable to sing. But when such procedures are placed within the wider cultural context – Vaughan Williams's stated desire to bring English citizens together in a common heritage – the nationalistic implications of his alterations become harder to dismiss. The very changes he wrought on these melodies allowed him to turn folk-songs into hymn tunes in the first place, and so bring them before the English nation. Indeed, Vaughan Williams succeeded in this aim beyond his initial imaginings: the folk-songs that he published as hymn tunes have reached far more people than those he published in other forms of arrangement. By establishing the conditions by which his message of social and cultural renewal reached its widest audience, Vaughan Williams's 'congregational' alterations reflected, albeit indirectly, his nationalist agenda.

Other forms of editorial manipulation reflected that agenda more directly. Certain alterations that Vaughan Williams introduced when adapting folk-songs as hymn tunes often went well beyond the mere simplification of the melody for congregational purposes and resulted instead from his desire to clarify the rhythmic and melodic parallels that he believed had been obscured by his singers' performances. Here the nationalist implications of his work of adaptation are made manifest, for what he sought to do in these instances was not to 'clean up' these melodies for public consumption but rather to uncover something far more fundamental about them. Drawing out such 'hidden' melodic connections and relationships by means of editorial alteration and correction, Vaughan Williams sought to demonstrate nothing less than the melodic coherence and structural integrity of English folk-song itself.

This programme can best be illustrated by first taking a slight detour in order to examine Vaughan Williams's handling of verbal texts in the adaptation process. The question of text substitution was one of major importance in deciding which folk-songs were to form the basis of new hymn tunes. For a folk-song to be converted into a hymn tune, after all, it had to be matched with Christian words that were more or less compatible with it. Compatibility in this case was determined less by a convergence of verbal meaning in the two texts, which, given the secular message of most folk texts, would have been improbable, than by the relative concurrence of their verbal meters, or syllabic counts. It is not always clear whether Vaughan Williams searched for folk-songs that fit pre-chosen Christian texts or whether those texts were selected (or newly written) to match folk-songs he had already chosen. What is clear, however, is that Vaughan Williams and his literary co-editor (usually Percy Dearmer) did their best to find compatible texts. Of the 16 hymn tunes listed in Table 6.1, only four carry texts whose verbal meters do not match those of the original folk texts.[34] (Neither of the musical examples discussed above posed a textual problem of this sort – not even Example 6.1, despite the fact that Vaughan Williams neglected to transcribe the original folk text.[35] Examination of the melodic rhythm of Mr Walter's tune shows that his text conformed to the 8 6. 8 6. 'common meter' of the substitute Christian text.)

It is instructive to look closely at some of these 'incompatible' text substitutions because the grafting of 'alien' Christian texts on to folk tunes reveals yet another reason for Vaughan Williams's editorial alterations. Quite simply, if the syllabic count of both folk and Christian text were not exact, or nearly so, some form of alteration to the original folk-song had to be made to accommodate the imposed text. This was the case when Vaughan Williams reworked Mr Punt's 'The Fisherman' for

Jemima Luke's religious verses for children, 'I think when I read that sweet story of old', one of the four incompatible texts mentioned above (Example 6.3).

The metrical incongruity of Punt's and Luke's text is readily apparent. The former consists of 28 syllables per stanza grouped according to the 8 6. 8 6. metrical pattern of common meter, while the latter runs anywhere from 79 to 81 syllables per stanza and is arranged in a consistently asymmetrical sequence. (The apparent irregularity of Luke's first stanza, where lines of between 11 and 12 syllables alternate with those containing eight or nine, is confirmed by later stanzas which introduce variations on this pattern.) Vaughan Williams's solution to this metrical quandary, after he expanded the overall beat from a quaver to a crotchet, was to provide a repetition of the entire tune to accompany the second half of Luke's stanza. Such a

(a) 'the Fisherman', MS 54190, f. 54v

(b) 'I think when I read that sweet story of old' *(East Horndon), The English Hymnal,* No. 595

I think when I read that sweet story of old,
    When Jesus was here among men,
How he called little children as lambs to his fold,
    I should like to have been with him then.
I wish that his hands had been placed on my head,
    That his arm had been thrown around me,
And that I might have seen his kind look when he said,
    'Let the little ones come unto me.'

Example 6.3 Manuscript transcription of 'The Fisherman' with hymn-tune adaptation

radical step was not enough to accommodate all the poet's syllables, however, so he not only suppressed the few melismas found in Punt's tune but extended the melody by adding quaver beats to all 5/8 measures. In an effort to accommodate the metrical and prosodic irregularities of the new text, finally, Vaughan Williams provided alternate rhythms – indicated by smaller notes – in bar 2 and at the upbeat to bar 1.

These additions do not merely accommodate Luke's text; they also make it easy to sing. With its shifting meter, Mr Punt's tune would have been too difficult for congregations to grasp and remember, so that the changes described above – which also include the doubling of note values in bars 4 and 8 – serve to place the entire melody in a 'regularizing' 6/8 meter (6/4 in the published version). And yet, Vaughan Williams's alterations transform the melody in unexpected ways. His conversion of the 5/8 bars into 6/8 bars involves the introduction of a dotted rhythm (♩. ♪♩ in the published version) that has little real basis in the original tune, which is cast almost wholly in even quavers. It is true that a comparable dotted figure appears in Mr Punt's bar 3, but only at the *end* of the measure, not in the beginning as here. Note, moreover, that this figure is omitted from the published version, where it is replaced by even quavers.

These last-mentioned changes demonstrate the strength of Vaughan Williams's interest in the structural cohesion of English folk-song, for they are motivated less by congregational concerns than by an interest in tightening the melodic structure and clarifying the rhythmic and melodic parallels that had been obscured by Mr Punt's performance. The placement of the new dotted figure at the beginning of bars 1 and 3 establishes a stronger, more overt connection between the first two phrases of the tune than had previously existed. The appearance of this dotted figure in bars 5, 6 and 7, meanwhile, strengthens the outlines of the less 'classically' balanced third and fourth phrases. Above all, the appearance of the figure throughout the hymn tune provides a unifying rhythmic motive throughout the entire melody. Nor is it a coincidence that this 'unifying' dotted figure derives from the same dotted rhythm found in Mr Punt's bar 3, the one that Vaughan Williams removed from its original place in the hymn tune version. Vaughan Williams's use of this rhythm, albeit in different parts of the melody, signals his desire to construct something like an 'ideal' version of the tune, drawn from the various elements of Mr Punt's performance.

Another example of this 'tightening' process comes in Vaughan Williams's adaptation of Mr and Mrs Verrall's 'The Royal George' for Love M. Willis's hymn 'Father, hear the prayer we offer'[36] (Example 6.4).

Once again, the metrical incompatibility of text with tune prompts melodic change. The beaming and general rhythm of the Verralls's melody – Vaughan Williams again collected the tune without notating the text – show that their text approximated a poetic meter of 9 7. 9 7., not the 8 7. 8 7. of Willis's text. The discrepancy meant that Vaughan Williams had to eliminate space for two syllables from the tune, and he did so by dropping the anacruses to the first and third phrases. By contrast, his rejection of the 'original' bar 5 in favor of the lower variant relates to his congregational concerns since the choice considerably simplifies the melody. Even his decision to remove the two anacruses reflects this sensitivity to communal performance, for that removal creates room in bar 4 for a proper half-cadence (complete with semi-breve pause) without any of the awkward interruptions of the

(a) 'The Royal George', MS 54191, f. 153r (originally collected without text)

* [variant]

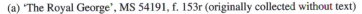

(b) 'Father, hear the prayer we offer' *(Sussex), The English Hymnal,* No. 385

Father, hear the prayer we offer;
Not for ease that prayer shall be,
But for strength that we may ever
Live our lives courageously.

Example 6.4   Manuscript transcription of 'The Royal George' with hymn-tune adaptation

beat that the Verralls's fermata creates for singers. And yet, the removal of the anacruses and the switch of variants do not represent all of Vaughan Williams's editorial changes. He also takes liberties with the rhythm, substituting a dotted figure (♩. ♪ in the published version) for the original rhythm in bars 1, 3 and 6. In all cases, the new figure – which in bar 1 actually provokes changes in pitch as well – serves to strengthen the structure of the tune: it brings out the parallelism between the first and second phrase, underscores the ties between the third and fourth, and ultimately points up connections between all four phrases. As with *East Horndon* above, the figure is not imposed on the tune from outside but is derived from the original tune itself – specifically, from the Verralls's dotted figure in bar 7. Once again, Vaughan Williams rearranges what his informants sang in order to create an 'ideal' version that brings out structural parallels obscured in performance.

Admittedly, there is a fine line between the act of drawing out the hidden structural relationships of folk-songs and efforts to 'regularize' them for purposes of singing ease. On one level, emphasizing melodic parallels and clarifying rhythmic relationships can only facilitate a congregation's initial grasp and ultimate memorization of a tune. Yet it is clear that such 'structural' alterations often go well beyond what is required for this purpose and that they do not invariably add to the 'singability' of these tunes. If simplicity was Vaughan Williams's sole intention, for example, it would have been enough to create for *East Horndon* a new figure comprised wholly of *even* crotchets rather than the dotted figure he decided upon. This solution would in fact have been more in keeping with Mr Punt's tune, in which even quavers predominate. The same can be said of *Sussex* where, after accommodating the stresses of the new text, the original melody would surely have posed no problems for congregational singing. Indeed, a close examination of the Verralls's tune discloses that a certain amount of rhythmic parallelism exists between the beginnings of the first, second and fourth phrases. Eager to tighten the tune yet further, however, Vaughan Williams brought the dotted figure from the fourth phrase to bear on all *four* phrases, thus emphasizing that parallel all the more.

The simple truth is that Vaughan Williams was fascinated with the structural possibilities of folk-song. He theorized traditional music as the unsophisticated and half-conscious utterance of unlettered and untraveled peoples, but resisted the ingrained prejudice common among 'sophisticated' musicians that dismissed folk-song as primitive and inept. Indeed, viewing folk-song as a primal embodiment of the human need for artistic expression, he argued, 'there is no difference in kind but only in degree between Beethoven and the humblest singer of a folk-song'.[37] In these terms, folk-song possessed within its narrow compass an inherent structural integrity equal to that of the great classics, and it was with intent to demonstrate this contention that he presented detailed melodic analyses of folk tunes in his prose essays.[38] It was also this insistence on the structural integrity of folk-song that prompted him to alter what his informants sang. Vaughan Williams believed that English folk-song existed in an essentially unchanging (or at least slowly changing) repertory of songs, and that each collected song embodied the singer's personal response to that repertory. He further believed, rightly or wrongly, that the advanced age of many of his singers, their uncertainty in both memory and voice, often rendered them incapable of correctly performing their songs. And it was usually with the intention of bringing the performances of these elderly singers into conformity with the presumed 'original' or exemplar – to recapture the tune 'behind' their performances – that he editorially altered what they sang.[39]

This editorial practice was the direct result of a nationalist agenda. By working backwards to the structurally perfect 'original', Vaughan Williams sacrificed his singers' individual melodic contributions to his ambition to reconstruct the *repertory* of songs from which they drew them, a repertory that collectively represented the corpus of 'English folk-song'. Nothing better demonstrates that the 'structural' alterations we have been tracing in his hymn tune adaptations have a nationalist impulse at their core. Vaughan Williams typically published his editorial reconstructions in secular sources, such as in singing books and anthologies as well as in the *Journal of the Folk-song Society*, the literary organ of the Folk Revival.

But it is also clear that the alterations he introduced into folk-songs adapted for *The English Hymnal* and other publications designed for the national Church derive from the same motive. There is no other possible explanation for the way in which the innocuous dotted figure from 'The Fisherman' is transformed into the pervasive rhythmic motive of *East Horndon*; or for the manner in which the first three phrases of 'The Royal George' are manipulated in order to clarify the melodic interconnections lying just beneath the surface of *Sussex*. Further evidence is found in Vaughan Williams's adaptation of Mr Adams's 'The Bailiff's Daughter' for Charles Kingsley's hymn 'From Thee All Skill and Science Flow' (Example 6.5).

Once again, some of the alterations can be attributed to metrical differences between the two texts as well as to Vaughan Williams's efforts to facilitate congregational involvement. The textual problems are minimal, however, for even though Mr Adams's one stanza embodies an irregular 10 7. 9 6. syllabic count, it is easily reduced to the 8 6. 8 6. common meter of Kingsley's text by replacing the repeated quavers in bars 1 and 2 with crotchets, and by setting the B flat–C quaver

(a) 'The Bailiff's Daughter', MS 54190, f. 148v

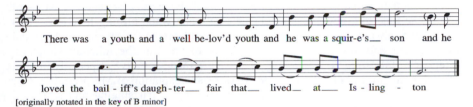

There was a youth and a well be-lov'd youth and he was a squir-e's son and he

loved the bail - iff's daugh - ter fair that lived at Is - ling - ton

[originally notated in the key of B minor]

(b) 'From Thee All Skill and Science Flow' *(Farnham), The English Hymnal*, No. 525

A - men.

From thee all skill and science flow,
All pity, care, and love,
All calm and courage, faith and hope –
O, pour them from above!

Example 6.5 Manuscript transcription of 'The Bailiff's Daughter', 2nd version, with hymn-tune adaptation

figures in bars 3 and 4 to a single syllable. The 'congregational' alterations are also minor and are limited to regularizing the pause between the first two phrases by substituting even crotchets Ds for the dotted figure in the second half of bar 2. But all other changes in *Farnham* stem from a desire to draw out the melodic and structural connections that had been obscured in performance. The alterations in the first two phrases – the switch from G to D at the opening anacrusis and the replacement of the D–C quaver figure in bar 3 with a crotchet C – strengthen the melodic and rhythmic parallels between them. The changes in pitch and rhythm in bars 5 and 7 establish closer ties between the last two phrases and, what is more, unify the entire melody under a basic rhythmic framework. The rhythmic figure generated as a consequence of these changes – ♩. ♪♩♩ – in phrase 3, ♩. ♪♩♫ in phrase 4 – relate far more closely to the central rhythms of bars 1 and 3 than had been the case before, and this underscores the connection between all four phrases. As with *East Horndon* and *Sussex*, these changes go far beyond the few modifications that would have been required to 'clean up' the tune for public consumption; Vaughan Williams clearly sought to reconstitute the tune as it might have existed anterior to performance, its original symmetries intact.

Does this mean, then, that Vaughan Williams's editorial alterations exclusively stem from nationalist motivations? That over and above the practical necessities of fitting the tune to a new text, the changes he made when turning folk-songs into hymn tunes always relate, on the one hand, to his efforts to facilitate congregational involvement and, on the other, to his desire to uncover the inherent structural integrity of folk-song? It is tempting to answer in the affirmative, especially in light of such hymn tunes as the famous *Monks Gate*, an adaptation of Mrs Verrall's 'Our Captain Calls' where, for reasons of both congregational singing and structural coherence, Vaughan Williams goes so far as to rearrange the original order of the tune's four phrases from ABBC to AABC.[40] Yet such a conclusion fails to acknowledge other factors that also contributed to the composer's editorial decisions. Vaughan Williams may well have believed that his efforts to reconstruct the melodic 'original' were the inevitable consequence of 'flawed' performances, but it is obvious that his reasons for doing so ultimately originated in his own musical needs and tastes. If he reworked folk-songs from his collection in order to bring out their 'lost' melodic parallels and connections, it was because of his immersion in the Western tradition of art-music, a tradition that notoriously valorizes melodic coherence and structural unity. Given that he was writing for the Anglican Church, a distinctly Western institution with a long and distinguished musical tradition, his manipulation of folk-tunes in the interests of melodic cohesion is entirely understandable and even appropriate in context. This point underscores the fact that Vaughan Williams's 'structural' alterations, far from being mere 'correctives' to his singers' perceived shortcomings, constitute an active aesthetic response to the challenge of fashioning hymn tunes from folk-songs. And understood in these terms, it becomes clear that Vaughan Williams's pursuit of the folk-song 'ideal' was not the sole reason why he altered what his informants sang.

Quite simply, questions of harmony and harmonization, and concerns about the overall shape and general effectiveness of the SATB arrangement, also played a role in Vaughan Williams's editorial decision-making. This is hardly surprising. As the detailed discussion of Examples 6.1 and 6.2 above shows, Vaughan Williams was a consummately skilled arranger and harmonist, and it would have been strange indeed if his attention to harmony and form had not resulted in significant melodic alteration. In fact, some of the editorial changes we previously attributed to 'congregational' factors might more properly be consigned to Vaughan Williams's harmonic and formal concerns. For example, his selection of variants in 'Virgin Unspotted', discussed above in passing, derives at least as much from a wish to create a consistent underlying harmony as from the effort to simplify the melody for singing purposes. The same can be posited of a passage in *Monks Gate* where the substitution of a crotchet D for Mrs Verrall's original quaver C–D figure in bar 3 clearly relates to the underlying B♭ $\frac{4}{3}$ harmony.[41] Even Vaughan Williams's rejection of the crotchet B variant in bar 6 of *Rodmell* (Example 6.1 above) may derive from formal considerations, for the quaver G–B variant maintains the flowing rhythm of the second half of the tune, and thus is more consonant with the 'arrangement' as a whole.

No doubt a further fine line exists here between Vaughan Williams's practice of altering a tune for harmonic or formal reasons and his doing so for purposes of singing ease. As with the clarification of hidden melodic parallels, manipulating a folk-song melody to fit a chosen harmony or to improve the formal design can only enhance a congregation's affection for a tune. Nonetheless, the distinction is important for it underscores the role that traditional 'compositional' considerations played in the adaptation process. Take, for example, Vaughan Williams's alteration of Mr Garman's quaver A–B♭ to a crotchet F–A at the pick-up to bar 9 of *Forest Green* (Example 6.2 above) – an alteration previously ascribed to congregational factors. Is it not equally plausible that this change originates just as much in the composer's need to establish continuity, however briefly, with the three-voice texture with which the previous phrase ends as in his compulsion to simplify the melody? As for his substitution of a minim A for Mr Garman's quaver C–A figure in bars 2, 6 and 14, is it not possible that the change derives not just from an impulse to streamline the melody but from a preference for the underlying D minor harmony? That chord marks a fresh and surprising arrival at the sixth scale degree and thus achieves a splendid effect by permitting the bass to descend by a fifth and then rise by step to the dominant. Admittedly, the change created a difficulty, for the D minor harmony did not 'fit' the C of the original C–A quaver figure. Vaughan Williams might have overcome this in the hymn-tune version by introducing two *crotchet* chords, one each for the C and A of the melody, but this solution would have interfered with the measured minim chords with which he carefully constructs his accompaniment. Exchanging a minim I or iii chord for the vi chord was also an alternative, but one that would mean forfeiting the compositional possibilities opened up by the D minor harmony. Given a choice between a strict but dull adherence to the given notes of the tune and an opportunity to create a more satisfying musical effect, his substitution of the minim A was well-nigh unavoidable.

'Compositional' considerations were thus not only central to the editorial process, but at times competed with congregational factors in determining Vaughan Williams's editorial choices. Such considerations of taste and style also vied with the composer's 'structural' concerns such as his desire to reconstruct 'ideal' versions of his singers' melodies. In certain instances, compositional considerations *outweighed* structural concerns, which were simply cast aside in order to secure formal continuity and accompanimental elegance. Upon closer examination of the example just cited, it appears that Vaughan Williams's substitution of the minim A eliminates a motivic parallel (between the C–A quaver figure and its A–F quaver 'echo') that originally existed in Mr Garman's tune. The selection of the G–B quaver variant over the crotchet B variant in *Rodmell* offers another example of the same process, as it turns out, for that choice means forfeiting the crotchet pick-up figure shared by all previous phrases. But the strongest evidence that Vaughan Williams was willing to sacrifice his impulse towards 'idealization' of a folk-tune to the shape and overall effect of the arrangement comes in his adaptation of Mr Bowes's 'A Brisk Young Farmer' for Samuel Longfellow's hymn ''Tis Winter Now; the Fallen Snow' (Example 6.6).

The most important change comes in bar 5 of the hymn-tune version where, after allowing for the expanded beat, Vaughan Williams has shortened the high D from a dotted minim to a simple minim and lengthened the following C and B to crotchets. (Exact doubling of the beat would result in quavers.) At first glance this alteration is surprising since it actively disrupts the parallel with the other three phrases, all of which employ a dotted minim followed by one crotchet (or alternatively, two quavers heard in the space of the crotchet) at the same point in the phrase. The metrical differences in the third line of text – Mr Bowes's phrase occupies nine syllables, Longfellow's eight – do not explain the change since Vaughan Williams's 'solution' to the problem, setting the C and B to a single syllable, could just as easily have been accomplished had those pitches conformed to the original quaver rhythm. Indeed, given that the syllable in question belongs to the inconsequential word 'the', the original rhythm would have been textually more convincing. Harmonic considerations do not fully explain the change either, as Vaughan Williams might just as easily have harmonized the original C–B quaver figure with a single triad (perhaps D major) without any disruption to the succeeding chords. Instead, his motivation appears to have been a subtle attempt to control the architecture and sweep of the arrangement as a whole. The obvious emotional climax (and highest note) of the tune occurs in phrase three, and it seems likely that Vaughan Williams wished to provide a smoother denouement from that climax than the one provided by Mr Bowes's original melody. The altered rhythm – ♩ ♩ ♩ and not ♩. ♫ – effects this perfectly, and precisely because it runs contrary to the prevailing rhythm of the other phrases. Adding to the impression of melodic 'slowdown' is the plangent harmonization of the phrase, notably the E minor seventh chord on the downbeat to bar 5, and the unusually voiced dominant seventh chord (in third inversion and with dissonant passing tone in the tenor) occurring at the end of the same bar.[42]

Nothing could better demonstrate that Vaughan Williams's editorial alterations did not invariably originate in nationalist motivations. Indeed, the striking aspect of *Danby* is that the changes introduced there for 'compositional' reasons actively clash with both the composer's structural and congregational concerns. The changes in bar 5 not only disrupt the otherwise symmetrical architecture of the tune, but also eliminate thereby a strict rhythmic parallel that presumably would have helped the congregation to learn the tune more quickly. Nor is this an isolated instance. Adapting Mr Anderson's 'Van Dieman's Land', an ABBA tune, for G.K. Chesterton's poem 'O God of Earth and Altar', Vaughan Williams deliberately

(a) 'A Brisk Young Farmer', Add. MS 54191, f. 12v

A brisk young farm - er cour-ted me he stole a - way my__ li - ber-ty he

stole my heart with my free good-will I must con - fess I love him still

[originally notated in the key of C major]

(b) ''Tis Winter Now; the Fallen Snow' *(Danby), The English Hymnal*, No. 295

In moderate time ♩ = 104 (♩ = 52)

WINTER

'Tis winter now; the fallen snow
Has left the heavens all coldly clear;
Through leafless boughs the sharp winds blow,
And all the earth lies dead and drear.

Example 6.6   Manuscript transcription of 'A Brisk Young Farmer' with hymn-tune adaptation

leaves unchanged the singer's third phrase even though it differs from the second only in three variant pitches. As with *Danby*, the decision means forfeiting a potential structural parallel that might have made the tune easier to sing, but also lends greater excitement to the tune and establishes a sense of forward motion that a restructured version would lack. Ignoring the structural and congregational implications of both tunes in the interests of creating a vital and effective arrangement, Vaughan Williams here sacrifices nationalist goals to compositional taste.

This is just what one expects from such a composer of course. Vaughan Williams may have been animated by nationalist concerns in many of his musical projects and activities, but he was first and foremost a *composer*, and by virtue of his dedication to craft he maintained a final independence from all ideologies and agendas. This is a crucial point to bear in mind, especially in view of the evolving image of Vaughan Williams as a more cosmopolitan and international figure than had previously been supposed.[43] Nevertheless, few musical projects were as inherently 'nationalistic' as that of preparing indigenous folk-songs for use by the Anglican Church, and it would be surprising if some nationalist objectives did not find their way into the editorial process. Perhaps the most fascinating and revealing aspect of Vaughan Williams's hymn-tune adaptations is that they demonstrate in miniature how intimately his compositional and nationalist concerns were conjoined. Editorial changes aiming at melodic simplification, textual substitution, structural tightening and compositional 'effect' can all be found in the same hymn tune, sometimes in the very same bar. Demonstrating the range of forces – ideological, musical, and practical – influencing the composer's choices, Vaughan Williams's adaptations from folk-songs are a fascinating study and merit close attention.[44]

Appendix: Vaughan Williams's Carol Arrangements

In addition to crafting hymn tunes from folk-songs he collected, Vaughan Williams arranged 13 folk carols from his collection for congregational performance. Because carols originally had Christian texts, he viewed them differently from his hymn-tune adaptations, and generally published the two separately. The composer's carol arrangements have not been discussed in this essay, but because they closely resemble the hymn-tune adaptations in their general musical treatment – both were

Table 6A.1   Folk carols collected and arranged for congregational performance by Vaughan Williams

No.	Manuscript title	Manuscript location	Published title	Oxford Book of Carols	English Traditional Carols	Oxford Carols for Schools
1.	All You that are to Mirth Inclined	54189, f. 100r	The Sinner's Redemption	51	–	
2.	Angel Gabriel	54189, f. 148r	Hereford Carol	7	–	37
3.	Carnal and Crane	54189, f. 149r	The Carnal and the Crane	53	–	–
4.	Dives and Lazarus	missing	Dives and Lazarus	57	2	–
5.	Down in Yon Forest	54189, f. 103r	Down in Yon Forest	61	4	11
6.	Gloucestershire Wassail Song	54189, f. 158r	Gloucestershire Wassail	31	20	45
7.	May Song	54189, f. 51r	May Carol	47	–	7
8.	On Christmas Day	54189, f. 100r	All in the Morning	17	–	–
9.	On Christmas Day	54187, f. 51r	Coverdale's Carol	131	–	–
10.	On Christmas Night	54190, f. 103v	Sussex Carol	24	16	33
11.	The Seven Virgins or Under the Leaves	missing	The Seven Virgins	43	–	–
12.	There is a Fountain	54189, f. 162v	Joseph and Mary	115	12	–
13.	This is the Truth	54189, f. 161v	The Truth from Above	68	19	42

written with groups of vocal amateurs in mind – it seems appropriate to list them here and the publications in which they appeared. As with the hymn-book sources included in Table 6.1 above, the three publications listed here represent the only carol-book sources that Vaughan Williams actively saw into print. (See Kennedy, *Catalogue*, for publication details.) It should also be noted that the 13 carols listed here do not constitute the sum total of his carol arrangements, but rather only those arrangements he intended primarily for congregational performance.

Notes

1   For a recent examination of the events leading to his first collected folk-song, see Tony Kendall, 'Through Bushes and Through Briars: Vaughan Williams's Earliest Folk-Song Collecting', in *Vaughan Williams in Perspective: Studies of an English Composer*, ed. Lewis Foreman (Albion Press, 1998), 48–68. According to Kendall, the singer's name was Potiphar, not the 'Pottipher' usually cited.

2   The precise date is uncertain. In 'Some Reminiscences of the English Hymnal' (*The First Fifty Years: A Brief Account of the English Hymnal from 1906 to 1956*, Oxford, 1956, 2), Vaughan Williams simply stated the year 1904, and most commentators have followed him in this. In her biography of her husband, *The Life of Percy Dearmer* (London: Jonathan Cape, 1940), 178, Nan Dearmer incorrectly cites February 1905 as the month when Dearmer approached Vaughan Williams.

3   Ursula Vaughan Williams, *R.V.W.: A Biography of Ralph Vaughan Williams* (Oxford and New York: Oxford University Press, 1964), 66–72.

4   James Day, *Vaughan Williams* (London: J.M. Dent and Sons, 1961), 18–22 (quotation at 20).

5   Frank Howes, *The English Musical Renaissance* (London: Martin Secker and Warburg, 1966), 232; Percy Young, *Vaughan Williams* (London: Dennis Dobson, 1953), 27, 35; Elliott Schwartz, *The Symphonies of Ralph Vaughan Williams* (Amherst: University of Massachusetts Press, 1964), 13–14; A.E.F. Dickinson, *Vaughan Williams* (London: Faber and Faber, 1963), 101–42.

6   Michael Kennedy, *The Works of Ralph Vaughan Williams*, rev. edn. (London: Oxford University Press, 1980), 38.

7   Ibid., 74.

8   R. Vaughan Williams, *National Music and Other Essays*, 2nd edn. (London: Oxford University Press, 1987), 23.

9   'The Influence of Folk-song on the Music of the Church', in *National Music*, 74–82.

10   Quoted in Kennedy, *Works*, 33–4.

11   Holst, Gustav, and R. Vaughan Williams, *Heirs and Rebels: Letters Written to Each Other and Occasional Writings on Music by Ralph Vaughan Williams and Gustav Holst*, ed. Ursula Vaughan Williams and Imogen Holst (London: Oxford University Press, 1959), 38.

12   Ursula Vaughan Williams, *R.V.W.*, 29. See Byron Adams, 'Scripture, Church and Culture: biblical texts in the work of Ralph Vaughan Williams', in *Vaughan Williams Studies*, ed. Alain Frogley (Cambridge: Cambridge University Press, 1996), 99–117, for a detailed investigation of Vaughan Williams's religious views.

13   One of the reasons Vaughan Williams undertook the musical editorship of *The English Hymnal* was that Walford Davies, a deeply religious man with whose musical and liturgical ideas Vaughan Williams strongly disagreed, would be given the job if he refused it. Ursula Vaughan Williams, *R.V.W.*, 71.

14   In his editorial preface to the 1906 *English Hymnal*, rev. edn. (London: Oxford University Press, 1933), x, Vaughan Williams argued that his efforts to raise the standards of hymn

tunes included in *The English Hymnal* 'does not mean that austerity has been unduly sought'. But his words imply that he understood well enough how austere his editorial selections might be perceived. Note that the *Standard* of 30 November 1904 remarked that Vaughan Williams's appointment as musical editor 'ensures purity of musical taste, perhaps even leaning to the side of severity'. Quoted in Kennedy, *Works*, 68.

15 See Nan Dearmer, *Life of Percy Dearmer*, 178–85, and *passim*; also Horton Davies, *Worship and Theology in England, Vol. 5: The Ecumenical Century 1900–1965* (Princeton: Princeton University Press, 1965), 110–17, 284–7.

16 See especially Hubert Foss, *Ralph Vaughan Williams: A Study* (London: George G. Harrap & Co., 1950), 49–76.

17 See many of the essays in Frogley, *Vaughan Williams Studies*, notably Jeffrey Richards, 'Vaughan Williams and British Wartime Cinema', 139–65 (esp. 145), and Adams, 'Scripture, Church and Culture', 106. See also Robert Stradling and Meirion Hughes, *The English Musical Renaissance 1860–1940: Construction and Deconstruction* (London and New York: Routledge, 1993), 65–6; and Wilfred Mellers, *Vaughan Williams and the Vision of Albion* (London: Barrie and Jenkins, 1989), pp. 257–8.

18 *A Catalogue of the Works of Ralph Vaughan Williams*, 2nd edn (London: Oxford University Press, 1996), 30–33, 84, 110–12, 127–9, 136–7, 140–41, and 156. See also Kennedy, *Works*, 71–3.

19 Literally hundreds of hymn-books contain hymn tunes adapted from folk-songs collected by Vaughan Williams, but this essay only touches on the publications in which the composer took an active role. This limitation immediately rules out hymn-books published for Protestant bodies other than the Church of England, though the importance of these in disseminating Vaughan Williams's adaptations throughout the English-speaking world cannot be minimized. (See 'A Concordance of Hymn-tune Books' in Dickinson, *Vaughan Williams*, 488–93, for some idea of the range of hymn-books reprinting his adaptations.) When we consider publications made under the auspices of the Anglican Church, however, the question of Vaughan Williams's personal involvement becomes somewhat more difficult to determine. Oxford University Press, the publisher of *The English Hymnal, Songs of Praise* and *The Oxford Book of Carols*, constantly drew from these sources to produce smaller volumes for a specialized market – *Hymns Selected from the English Hymnal* (1921) and *Songs of Praise for Boys and Girls* (1929) are typical examples – and these often reprint the adaptations in question. Vaughan Williams's name sometimes even appears among the editors. (Kennedy's *Catalogue* lists some of these publications, but is far from complete.) Yet there is little real evidence that Vaughan Williams played any significant role in the selection of hymn tunes for these smaller publications, and I therefore exclude them from consideration here. The two exceptions to this – *Motherland Song Book, Vol. 1* (1919, published by Stainer & Bell) and *The Oxford Book of Carols for Schools* (1956) – are based on internal evidence of Vaughan Williams's personal involvement in their production.

20 An 'Abridged Edition' of *The English Hymnal* appeared in 1907, but this was merely a reprinting of the 1906 edition without five 'Catholic' hymns to which various Church leaders had objected (Dearmer, *Life of Percy Dearmer*, 182–5). From an editorial standpoint, the 1907 edition was virtually the same as the 1906 edition, and it is therefore not considered separately in this essay.

21 Once again, I include in Table 6A.1 only those publications in which Vaughan Williams took an active role.

22 A seventeenth folk-song from Vaughan Williams's collection, 'Lullaby' (manuscript location: British Library Add. MS 54191, f. 189r), was adapted by Martin Shaw, and published in *The Oxford Book of Carols* (No. 130) and in the 1931 edition of *Songs of Praise* (No. 382).

23 The manuscript folk-song collection is housed in the British Library and has been grouped into Add. MSS 54187–91. For convenience, the 'Manuscript Location' column here indicates the members of this series by the five-digit shelfmark alone (e.g. '54187').

24 Vaughan Williams was in the habit of naming his hymn tunes after the place where he collected the original folk-song. The only exception to this in Table 6.1 is No. 11, 'The Red Barn', which because it was published in *The Oxford Book of Carols* is called 'Job' after the substitute carol text with which it was published.

25 For publication details on these seven publications, see Kennedy, *Catalogue*, 30–33, 76–7, 110–12, 117–19, 136–7, 141, 119.

26 R. Vaughan Williams, 'Review of *Six Suffolk Folk-Songs*, collected and arranged by E.J. Moeran', *Journal of the English Folk Dance and Song Society* 1/3 (1934), 173. See also his complimentary review of settings by Benjamin Britten and Herbert Murrill in 4/4 (1943), 164, of the same journal.

27 See, for example, the elaborate arrangements in *Five English Folk-songs* (1913, for SATB chorus) and *Six Studies in English Folk-song* (1926, for cello and piano). See also the extraordinary setting for three unaccompanied women's voices of 'The Unquiet Grave', using a folk-song from W.P. Merrick's collection, in *Folk-songs of the Four Seasons* (1949).

28 In this and subsequent examples taken from manuscript, I attempt to reproduce all musical notation just as it appears in the original. The three exceptions to this are that (1) original manuscript staff changes are not retained, (2) clefs and key signatures have routinely been added to the beginning of lines, and (3) tunes have been transposed in order to facilitate comparison with the hymn-tune version. In the last case, all notational details appearing in the original are left intact, only now shifted in accordance with the new key. Any other additions are bracketed. In the case of verbal text, limitations of space permit the transcription only of the first verse. (Those instances where Vaughan Williams has collected tune but no text are duly noted.) Transcriptions of hymn tunes, by contrast, simply reprint the tunes as they appear in *The English Hymnal* (for convenience, the 1933 edition is used), although space limitations again dictate that only the first verse of text appear. My thanks to Ursula Vaughan Williams for permission to quote both music and text from the folk-song manuscripts; and to Oxford University Press for permission to print hymns and hymn tunes from *The English Hymnal*.

29 R. Vaughan Williams, 'Cecil Sharp's Accompaniments', in A.H. Fox Strangways, *Cecil Sharp* (London: Oxford University Press, 1933), 217.

30 R. Vaughan Williams, 'English Folk-Songs', reprinted in Young, *Vaughan Williams*, 202. The entire passage reads, 'But nowadays a new spirit animates the collector: he wishes to preserve and put before the public exactly what he has heard – neither more nor less – and we can be sure that whatever we find in the collections of modern investigators is an accurate transcript of the songs of the traditional singers.'

31 *National Music*, 77.

32 See *Farnham, Monks Gate, Dunstan* and *Sussex* in *The English Hymnal* and *Songs of Praise*.

33 Vaughan Williams's handling of 'The Royal George' is discussed in more detailed below.

34 Besides *East Horndon* and *Sussex*, discussed below, these include *Dent Dale* and *Hardwick*.

35 Vaughan Williams has been strongly criticized by folklorists and cultural historians for neglecting to note text as well as tune in such instances. See, for example, Roy Palmer, *Folk Songs Collected by Ralph Vaughan Williams* (London: J.M. Dent and Sons, 1983), xi–xvii.

36 This tune also appears in *The English Hymnal* set to Althelston Riley's 'Saints of God! Lo Jesu's people' (No. 239). Since it appears there without harmony, however, I print the Willis version here.

37 *National Music*, 6.

38 See, for example, *National Music*, 19–20; and 'Dance Tunes', *The Music Student*, 11/12 (August 1919), 453–7.

39 For an analysis, see my 'Vaughan Williams's Folk-song Transcriptions: A Case of Idealization?' in Frogley, *Vaughan Williams Studies*, 118–38; for a more extended discussion, see my 'Ralph Vaughan Williams's Folk-song Collecting: English Nationalism and the Rise of Professional Society' (Ph.D. diss., New York University, 1998), 312–83.

40 See Dickinson, *Vaughan Williams*, 127–8, for a reproduction of the manuscript version of 'Our Captain Calls'. Note that Dickinson explains this reordering – as well as other alterations in the hymn tune version – purely in terms of congregational facilitation, explaining that 'the a–b b–c pattern is wrong, and a a–b c sounds right'. Vaughan Williams no doubt did alter the tune because he recognized that an AABC phrase pattern was more in keeping with melodic, and thus congregational, expectations than an ABBC pattern. At that same time, he surely could not resist the structural implications of the tune – A material reappears at the end of the C phrase – which provided all the excuse he needed to repeat the A section earlier in the tune.

41 Again, see Dickinson, *Vaughan Williams*, 127, for a reproduction of the manuscript version of 'Our Captain Calls'.

42 As noted earlier, Vaughan Williams presents a different arrangement of *Danby* in *Songs of Praise*. There, the tune is precisely the same as in *The English Hymnal* version, but now set to a somewhat austere two-voiced accompanying texture. The chord progression is more or less the same, although he replaces the crucial vi chord on the high D in bar 5 with a ii chord in which the D serves as an upper neighbor. The general effect is comparable, however, for the writing in the third phrase provides for harmonic tension and a similar sense of melodic and harmonic slowdown.

43 Alain Frogley, 'Constructing Englishness in Music: National Character and the Reception of Ralph Vaughan Williams', in *Vaughan Williams Studies*, 1–22.

44 I would like to thank Drs Byron Adams, Jesse Rosenberg and Cary McBeam for help and advice during the preparation of this chapter.

Chapter 7

Robert Louis Stevenson, Ralph Vaughan Williams and their *Songs of Travel*[1]

Rufus Hallmark

I like biography far better than fiction myself; fiction is too free. In biography you have your little handful of facts, little bits of a puzzle, and you sit and think, and fit 'em together this way and that, and get up and throw 'em down and say damn, and go out for a walk, and it's real soothing; and when done, gives an idea of finish to the writer that is very peaceful. Of course it's not really so finished as quite a rotten novel; it always has and always must have the incurable illogicalities of life about it ... Still, that's where the fun comes in.

Robert Louis Stevenson[2]

Vaughan Williams composed his *Songs of Travel* in the first years of the last century, and today we know them as an integral cycle of nine numbers;[3] but it was not always so. In his 1950 book on Vaughan Williams, for example, Hubert Foss wrote the following:

Out of Stevenson's verses he made the two books of *Songs of Travel* (1905 and 1907 respectively) and one separate song, 'Whither must I wander'.[4]
Of the two books ... the first, containing 'The Vagabond', 'Bright is the Ring of Words', and 'The Roadside Fire'..., won for itself and still keeps a considerable popularity. The second book ['Let Beauty Awake', 'Youth and Love', 'In Dreams Unhappy', 'The Infinite Shining Heavens'] attracted far less attention, and is not remembered now .... Stevenson's verses had a wider vogue then than they have today, though there are signs of a revival of interest.[5]

How did this close student of Vaughan Williams's works come to have such an erroneous impression of these songs? Foss's remarks evoke two issues: the misleading initial publication of the Vaughan Williams songs, on the one hand, and the general reception of the works of Robert Louis Stevenson, on the other. The bare facts of the original, piecemeal publication of these songs is generally known,[6] but I shall flesh out their history with new information and interpretation. I shall also argue that there is a relation between the Vaughan Williams songs and the vicissitudes of Stevenson's posthumous reputation. Finally, I shall raise a question about authorial intentions with respect to the posthumously published cycle of nine songs.

I

On 17 December 1894, the London press announced the death two weeks earlier in Samoa of Robert Louis Stevenson. *The Times* ran a two-and-a-half-column obituary, 'Death of Mr. R.L. Stevenson', on page six, the first article following official reports, advertisements and 'intelligences' about government, politics, empire and economics. After brief reports of the circumstances of the writer's death ('suddenly of apoplexy') and the reaction of the Samoans (who 'bore his body to its last resting place, at the top of Pala Mountain'), there was an 'Appreciation from France' and a discussion of his life and career.

The more literarily and artistically inclined *Pall Mall Gazette* offered more extensive coverage, including both a front-page notice and a substantial 'Special Biography and Literary Appreciation' inside (p. 7). The notice on the first page was headed elegantly 'R.L.S'. and read effusively:

> It is not too much to say that the untimely death of Mr. Robert Louis Stevenson takes from us the most notable man in English letters. Wherever he be placed among his compeers and contemporaries, he had the distinction of being vastly better known among his readers .... He loomed on the horizon, mistily, as a personage, in a sense [in] which neither Mr. Meredith, nor Mr. Hardy, nor even Mr. Kipling, has been yet received.

The *Pall Mall Gazette* also printed a new poem along with Stevenson's obituary (p. 2). It was none other than 'Whither must I Wander?'. Over the next several weeks the paper continued its homage to the writer by printing more hitherto unpublished poems: 'In the highlands, in the country places' (December 21), 'Over the Sea to Skye' (December 31), 'I will Make you Brooches' (January 3), 'To the heart of youth' (January 17).[7]

These poems, along with 39 others, appeared two years later in the collection titled *Songs of Travel and Other Verses*, with a prefatory editorial note by Sidney Colvin, Stevenson's close friend and editor.[8] Published by Chatto & Windus, the book is a small, compact volume bound in black cloth with gold imprints on the spine, the format that the publishing house had been giving to all their editions of Stevenson's works.

Three of the poems that had been printed in the *Gazette* – 'Whither must I wander', 'I will Make you Brooches', and 'To the Heart of Youth' – are among those that Ralph Vaughan Williams set to music a few years later, and naturally one wonders if he first came upon these verses in the newspaper. Indeed, one is led to speculate further about the young composer's acquaintance with Stevenson's work altogether. Twenty-two-year-old Vaughan Williams was in the middle of his last year at Cambridge when Stevenson died in the South Seas. He may well have read several of Stevenson's books and stories, which had been published during his youth. *Treasure Island* appeared in 1883, Vaughan Williams's eleventh year; *The Strange Case of Dr Jekyll and Mr Hyde* and *Kidnapped* in 1886; *The Master of Ballantrae* in 1889; and *Catriona*, the sequel to *Kidnapped*, in 1893.

Though Vaughan Williams probably knew the fiction, it is unlikely that he had read Stevenson's poetry earlier. He was, after all, 13 when the writer's *A Child's Garden of Verses* was published in 1885; as a young adolescent, Vaughan Williams likely had little interest in these verses for children. Conversely, Stevenson's first collection of more serious poems, *Underwoods*, was published in 1887, when Vaughan Williams was fifteen and perhaps at that age not yet disposed to an interest in adult verse. But Stevenson's *Songs of Travel* may have caught his imagination in his university years.[9] Ursula Vaughan Williams notes that 'Stevenson was a poet that everyone knew well in the early years of the century', ... 'Ralph read a great deal of poetry – as well as practically everything else, particularly history and novels'.[10]

'Whither must I Wander?' was the first *Travel* song Vaughan Williams composed and published. As mentioned above, this poem was the first one of a series printed in the *Pall Mall Gazette* immediately after Stevenson's death. Vaughan Williams might also have made prior acquaintance with portions of it in *The Master of Ballantrae*, where Stevenson puts some of its verses in the mouth of the Master at the head of Chapter Nine (see further in Appendix II). Vaughan Williams's song was published in a new magazine called *The Vocalist* in June 1902, where two earlier songs, 'Linden Lea' and 'Blackmwore by the Stour', had preceded it in April and May, respectively. These three songs were Vaughan Williams's first three published works, and he refers to the publication arrangement in a letter to his cousin Ralph Wedgwood in early 1902.

> I've not much to chronicle except that I've sold my soul to a publisher – that is to say I've agreed not to sell songs to any publisher but him for 5 years. And he is going to publish several pot boiling songs of mine – that is to say not real pot boilers – that is to say they are quite good – I'm not ashamed of them – as they are more or less simple and popular in character. They are to come out in a magazine called 'The Vocalist' and then to be published at 1/0 – which is a new departure – and I'm to get penny halfpenny on each copy – so you see I'm on the high road to fortune.[11]

Aside from the amusing appraisal of his compositional achievement, this letter is also important for the business agreement he describes with the publisher.

Whether the other *Songs of Travel* were composed in conjunction with 'Whither' or some time later in the next two years, that is, whether Vaughan Williams had a cycle in mind from the start or made this plan later, may be impossible to determine. In any event, Vaughan Williams finished the set by 1904 at the latest, for the cycle was premièred in December of that year.

What may have been some of the factors guiding Vaughan Williams's choice of Stevenson's verse? In comparing the song cycle with its literary source, one is immediately struck by several things. First, most obviously, Vaughan Williams retained the title of Stevenson's collection and also used its initial poem, 'The Vagabond', to open his cycle.[12] Perhaps he kept Stevenson's title out of respect, but as a young, little known composer, he surely also wished to capitalize on the ready association with the famous writer.

Vaughan Williams's choices of poems for *Songs of Travel* grow more interesting as we look closely at Stevenson's collection. At first glance, it seems curious that all nine of his songs are chosen from among the first twenty two of Stevenson's fourty four poems. One notes, however, that most of the poems in the latter half of Stevenson's collection are occasional poems dedicated to family and friends, including both English and Hawaiian acquaintances (for example, No. XXXVI 'To S.C'. (Sidney Colvin); No. XXIX 'To Kalakaua', of Honolulu; No. XXX 'To Princess Kaiulani', of Waikiki). Many of these latter poems also have much more geographical specificity, particularly the South Pacific; and some depart from lyric into narrative mode (for example, XXXVII 'The House of Tembinoka'). One would hardly expect Vaughan Williams to shift his travel cycle, some of which is tinged with a Scottish atmosphere, to the tropics. There are nevertheless some lyric poems among the latter half of the collection that Vaughan Williams likely considered; poems XXIII, XXIV, XL, XLI, XLII and XLIV all have to do with farewells, endings, death, and so on, and may have been considered by Vaughan Williams for the concluding songs of his cycle.

Another observable feature of the composer's selection and ordering is both the retention and the disturbance of the order of the source collection.[13] Consider the correlations between the published order of Stevenson's poems and the final ordering they have in Vaughan Williams's songs as shown in Table 7.1. There are consistencies between the two lists as well as differences. As already remarked, the first poem of Stevenson's collection becomes the first song; and the highest numbered poem chosen from the collection, no. XXII, becomes the last song. Poems III, IV and VI are preserved in this order in Vaughan Williams's song cycle, though they are shifted in place; similarly, Stevenson's poems IX and XI remain in sequence, though exchanged with the latter group of three. Poems XIV and XVI are reversed.

Table 7.1   RLS (ed. Colvin, 1896) and RVW orderings compared

Poems (RLS) (poem's title or first line)		Songs (RVW) (song's title)	
I.	The Vagabond (To an air of Schubert)	1.	The Vagabond
III.	Youth and Love – II[1]	2.	Let Beauty Awake
IV.	In Dreams, Unhappy	3.	The Roadside Fire
VI.	The Infinite Shining Heavens	4.	Youth and Love
IX.	Let Beauty Awake	5.	In Dreams
XI.	I Will Make You Brooches and Toys	6.	The Infinite Shining Heavens
XIV.	Bright is the Ring of Words	7.	Whither must I Wander?
XVI.	Home, no more Home (To the tune of Wandering Willie)	8.	Bright is the Ring of Words
XXII.	I have Trode the Upward and the Downward Slope	9.	I have Trode the Upward and the Downward Slope

[1] Vaughan Williams's song 4 is poem III in the Stevenson anthology, not 'II' as listed by Kennedy, *Catalogue*, 25. This tiny oversight is understandable because poems II and III in the anthology are headed 'Youth and Love – I' and 'Youth and Love – II'.

This selection *and* reordering of the poems was probably made before Vaughan Williams began to compose his songs, and this inference comes from internal, musical evidence. 'Youth and Love', which preceded 'Roadside Fire' among Stevenson's poems, follows it in Vaughan Williams's reordering and contains musical allusions to 'Roadside Fire' (as well as to 'The Vagabond'). In this instance the composer had switched the order of these poems before he fashioned his musical settings of them.

Why did Vaughan Williams depart from the published ordering of the poems? What was he creating with his selection and sequence? While some commentators have addressed the general tone and topics of *Songs of Travel*, no one has examined closely the musical or literary coherence and meaning of Vaughan Williams's *Songs of Travel* as a cycle. In his thorough-going survey of early twentieth-century English song, Stephen Banfield, for example, wrote:

> The dominant impression is one of absolute integrity to the spirit of Stevenson. Vaughan Williams's capacity for empathy ... blots out the obvious dissimilarity between the frail, tubercular, restlessly wandering and sensitively observing poet and the solid, slowly achieving, upper-middle-class composer, and produces instead a work as fertile in its Romantic wayfaring images for early-20th-century England as was *Die Winterreise* for early-19th-century Vienna. The images themselves are different ... but the Wanderer impulse, associated with both joy and sorrow, pervades ... Vaughan Williams [and] Schubert ... alike. Perhaps it is part of an escapist dream; perhaps it stems from a desire to experience all things, to observe rather than judge.[14]

But even though the full cycle has been published as a unit since 1960, Banfield and others still appear to regard *Songs of Travel* merely as a collection of loosely related mood pictures. While I shall not attempt an extended discussion here, it is worth trying to construe a meaning in the particular sequence of these songs.

First it is important to note a connotation of the vagabond spirit of the protagonist that comes through the imagery and events of the poems. This spirit, imbued with images of creativity, arguably represents the artist, who stands on the edge of society, dips his bread in the river, makes palaces in the wild, has dreams, rises in the night to see the stars, and transmutes his experience into art. This is most explicitly felt in the penultimate song, 'Bright is the Ring of Words',[15] but it can be perceived in many of the others as well.

While the Stevenson collection has no presumption to narrative, Vaughan Williams's cycle suggests stages in the vagabond–artist's life and career. 'The Vagabond' establishes the character of the wanderer, who seeks nothing but 'the earth around', 'the heaven above', and 'the road before me'. The Stevenson poem strikes a familiar chord in late nineteenth-century English literature that is different from the German wayfarer; or at least it is less like Müller and Schubert's unhappy *Wanderer* and more like the Kerner-Schumann *frohe Wandersmann*. This English vagabond may have its roots in the popular novels of George Borrow – *Lavengro* and *The Romany Rye*[16] – and be a cousin to Matthew Arnold's 'Scholar Gypsy'.[17] The character of this vagabond also has much in common with the gypsy knife grinder Stevenson wrote about in his essay 'Beggars':

> If he had no fine sense of poetry in letters, he felt with a deep joy the poetry of life. You should have heard him speak of what he loved; of the tent pitched beside the talking water;

of the stars overhead at night; of the blest return of morning, the peep of day over the moors, the awaking birds among the birches; how he abhorred the long winter shut in cities; and with what delight, at the return of the spring, he once more pitched his camp in the living out-of-doors.[18]

Of course the vagabond spirit also reflects Stevenson's own peripatetic nature; and it corresponds to Vaughan Williams's own fondness for countryside treks as well as for the metaphysical journies that one finds in several other works such as *Toward the Unknown Region, A Sea Symphony, The Pilgrim's Progress.*[19]

The next song, 'Let Beauty Awake', can be read as the dawn of romance in the vagabond's life or interpreted as the artist's awakening to his calling. Responding to his beloved or to his muse, the young lover or artist creates beauty of out of a void in the third song, 'I will Make you Brooches' (entitled 'Roadside Fire' by Vaughan Williams). These two poems were shifted by Vaughan Williams so as to precede the next three, and this reversal places two poems that speak of youthful love in the present *before* poems that refer to love in the past. Thus in 'Roadside Fire' the young man relishes his beloved, but in 'Youth and Love' he is taking leave of her, as the artist abandons his first inspiration – indeed these may be one in the same thing. He will move beyond the pleasure of early romance; he leaves behind his 'boyish stave', turning his back on his earlier and easier conventional art to venture toward 'his nobler fate'. (Note that in 'Youth and Love' the piano quotes the opening melodic phrase of 'The Vagabond' at the text 'He to his nobler fate/ Fares' and elaborates on the main tune of 'Roadside Fire' at the words 'Cries but a wayside word to her ... /Sings but a boyish stave', thus insinuating the earlier song as the very 'boyish stave' the wanderer had sung. These are not just thematic unification devices, then, but narrative signifiers.) In fact, in retrospect, the second and third songs seem a kind of flashback or reminiscence that come between 'The Vagabond' and 'Youth and Love'. In the latter song the present journeying begun in song 1 is rejoined in song 4 after a momentary recollection of the past in songs 2 and 3.[20]

In the fifth song, 'In Dreams' – an extremely Heine-esque poem – we learn that the protagonist will always remember his first love, though he has left her behind. His outlook is now a colder realism, but his earlier experience, transmuted through time, still enriches his creativity. In 'The Infinite Shining Heavens' the happiness he seeks (or the art he yearns for) seems as out of reach as the stars in the sky, and he becomes cynical about his chances, 'Till lo! I looked in the dusk/ And a star had come down to me'. Now that he has found his own place in the world, he can accept the past with equanimity in 'Whither must I Wander?'. He will still 'go on forever and come again no more', but now he can contemplate his past with equanimity. The springtime of creativity (third stanza) always returns. He acknowledges, in 'Bright is the Ring of Words', his own mortality, but is consoled by the endurance of his creations. In the final song he looks back with satisfaction on his life and achievement: 'I have lived and loved.' Fittingly this closing song contains reminiscences of 'The Vagabond', 'Whither Must I Wander?', and 'Bright is the Ring of Words'.[21]

By reading such a narrative into Vaughan Williams's cycle, one recognizes the latent dramatic nature of the poems as selected and reordered by the composer and thereby demonstrate plausible grounds for his decisions. The cycle does not consist solely of the shared themes and imagery of the poems and of the musical cross-references in the songs; these features work together to create a satisfying whole, which is greater than the sum of its parts. By composing a group of songs that was not just a lyric anthology, but had a coherent, narrative design, Vaughan Williams joined Arthur Somervell (*Maud*, 1898 and *A Shropshire Lad*, 1904) in establishing the story-telling cycle in twentieth-century English music.

The cycle was premièred on Monday, 2 December 1904, at London's Bechstein Hall (Wigmore Hall today). The programme consisted of vocal works by both Vaughan Williams and by Gustav Holst, and featured Vaughan Williams's two recently completed cycles, *House of Life* and *Songs of Travel*. The latter was performed by baritone Walter Creighton, with Hamilton Harty at the piano.[22] With regard to the purported narrative content of *Songs of Travel*, it is worth noting that the programme informs the audience, 'The songs of this cycle will be sung in continuity'.[23] No such comment is appended to the listing of *House of Life*, which is subtitled only 'A Cycle of Sonnets'. The recital drew mostly positive reviews. The *Daily News* critic preferred the 'open-air feeling' of the Stevenson cycle, as compared with the songs based on Pre-Raphaelite Dante Gabrieli Rossetti's poems, and he found the Stevenson group 'far the more original and real of the two'.[24]

Perhaps more important for the eventual popularity of these songs was the adoption of them by the well-known bass-baritone Harry Plunket Greene. Greene included five of the *Songs of Travel* in his recital two months later, on February 3, 1905. Vaughan Williams was almost certainly present, or soon heard Plunket Greene perform these songs, for he subsequently dedicated them to this singer. Plunket Greene added *Songs of Travel* and other Vaughan Williams songs to his repertory and later cited 'The Vagabond' and 'The Roadside Fire', as well as 'Silent Noon' from the *House of Life* cycle, in his book *Interpretation in Song*.[25] The support of this celebrated and crusading singer helped situate *Songs of Travel* in the repertory. Though he gave only incomplete performances of the cycle, Plunket Greene made many of these songs staples in the repertoire of English song recitals.

Having enjoyed the initial success of this cycle, the composer must have been sorely disappointed to have to give in to the cold reality of the piecemeal fashion in which the songs were published. Because he had already sold 'Whither must I Wander?' to *The Vocalist*, and because Boosey wanted to venture into print with only three of the most popular of the remaining numbers, *Songs of Travel* was published in pieces and did not appear as a cycle for over half a century, and then only posthumously.[26] Boosey brought out 'The Vagabond', 'Bright is the Ring of Words', and 'The Roadside Fire' (nos 1, 8 and 3 of the cycle) as *Songs of Travel* in 1905. These were probably the most popular songs in the set (along with 'Whither must I Wander?', already in print), being tuneful and harmonically accessible, and perhaps the easiest of the songs.[27] Two years later the publisher reissued these three songs as *Songs of Travel* Part I, and also brought out four others as Part II: 'Let Beauty Awake', 'Youth and Love', 'In Dreams', and 'The Infinite Shining Heavens' (nos 2, 4, 5 and 6 of the cycle, but numbered I, II, III and IV in this print). Noteworthy is the inscription – and marketing ploy – on the title pages: 'Dedicated to and Sung by Mr. Plunkett Greene'. In 1912 Boosey acquired the rights from *The Vocalist* to 'Whither must I Wander?' and published it as a single song.[28]

In November 1905, 11 months after their première, Vaughan Williams orchestrated the three songs of Part I. Neither Ursula Vaughan Williams's biography nor Michael

Kennedy's catalogue cites a first performance of these orchestrated versions, so one is left to speculate about the composer's reasons for making them.[29] It was in 1904 and early 1905 that the Leith Hill Musical Festival in Dorking was planned and that Vaughan Williams was appointed as conductor. It is tempting to believe he may have orchestrated Part I of *Songs of Travel* for Dorking, but if it was his hope to include the orchestrated songs in the Festival, this plan never materialized. (Individual songs from the cycle, however, with piano accompaniment, did make appearances in the Festival through the years.[30]) Sir Adrian Boult conducted a performance of the three orchestrated songs as part of a festival at the Royal College of Music in July 1919.[31] Markings in the autograph score suggest that they were performed on several other occasions. (See Appendix I.) In 1954, Vaughan Williams's friend, baritone Keith Falkner, then a member of the Cornell University Faculty, performed the set with the Buffalo Philharmonic Orchestra in Ithaca, New York, during the composer's visit to Cornell.[32]

Despite the fragmentary publication and the consequent public ignorance of the cycle as a whole, the individual *Songs of Travel*, particularly the 1905 set of three and 'Whither must I Wander?', became very popular and helped establish Vaughan Williams's reputation. In a 1928 survey of Vaughan Williams's songs, Hermon Ould wrote of the *Songs of Travel* (meaning the three 1905 songs), 'which Mr. Plunket Greene made popular', that they were 'popular in the best sense: tuneful, singable, even catchy, yet they show a musicianship which would be quite beyond the capacity of a mere ballad-writer'. He commented separately on 'Whither must I Wander?', noting what he perceived as its 'northern, even Scottish, pathos'.[33] A measure of the esteem in which these songs came to be held can be found in other musicians' impressions. In his autobiography Arthur Bliss wrote, 'To us musicians in Cambridge Vaughan Williams was the magical name; his *Songs of Travel* were on all pianos'.[34] In her biography of her husband, the tenor Steuart Wilson, Lady Wilson recalled, 'As for Vaughan Williams, Steuart once wrote that he had revered him "this side of idolatry" from the moment when, as a schoolboy "muddling around with music" he first discovered *Songs of Travel*'.[35]

II

For twenty years following Robert Louis Stevenson's death, his high reputation was maintained, his works enjoying popularity and respectability. At the same time, it must be noted that his admirers were worshipful and uncritical, and that he was held in fond memory as much for his personality, romantic wanderlust, exotic abode and early death as for his literary achievements. The quintessential stylist that the astute and critical Henry James found in his friend Stevenson went largely unappreciated by the reading public and critics alike.

Stevenson's poetry, understandably, had generated less interest than the novels and stories. The writer himself made light of his poetry, describing himself as a 'poetaster' and 'a weak brother in verse'.[36] Writing to John Addington Symonds about *Underwoods*, Stevenson said, 'I do not set up to be a poet. Only an all round literary man: a man who talks, not one who sings ... Excuse this little apology for my muse; but I don't like to come before people who have a note of song, and let it be supposed I do not know the difference.'[37]

What Stevenson was calling attention to through such disingenuous disparagement was the simplicity and naturalness of his verse. His language is not self-consciously 'poetic' in the sense of using archaic or stilted vocabulary, uncommon syntax, or traditional high-culture forms such as the sonnet. In the same passage of the letter quoted above, Stevenson continued, 'I believe the very fact that it [his verse] was only speech served the book [*Underwoods*] with the public. Horace is much a speaker, and see how popular!'[38] Probably it was in part the more natural diction of Stevenson's poetry and its contrast with that of Rossetti's sonnets that led the reviewer of the song cycle's première to speak of the 'open air' style of *Songs of Travel*. As for Stevenson's influence as a poet, it has been argued that both A.E. Housman and Rupert Brooke, and the succeeding generation through them, profited from Stevenson's example.[39] And no less than Robert Graves called attention to the fine qualities of poems like 'The Vagabond'.[40]

One book of Stevenson's poetry achieved tremendous popularity. Though there were two collections of his serious poems – *Underwoods* and *Songs of Travel*, these were eclipsed in the public response by *A Child's Garden of Verses* (1885). The vogue of popularity of his children's verse was in keeping with the sentimental and adulatory affection for Stevenson. And consistent with its lopsided popularity were the many illustrated editions and musical settings made from *A Child's Garden of Verses*. Vaughan Williams likely knew at least some of these songs; a set of nine had been composed by his teacher Charles Villiers Stanford and published as *A Child's Garland of Songs* (1892). These were republished with 11 settings of the *Child's Garden* poems by other composers in 1897 as *The Stevenson Song-Book* (Scribner's, New York). In addition to Stanford's settings, there were songs by Reginald de Koven, Homer Bartlett, C.B. Hawlet, W.W. Gilchrist, Arthur Foote, and George W. Chadwick.[41] There were also *Child's Garden* settings among Liza Lehmann's two cycles *The Daisy Chain* (1900) and *More Daisies* (1902). Other composers who set *Child's Garden* verses before Vaughan Williams turned his hand to Stevenson include Nathalie Curtis, Elvira Gambogi, Thomas Shepard, Henry Hadley, and, last but not least, Ethelbert Nevin.[42]

By contrast, before Vaughan Williams's *Songs of Travel* settings, only a handful of songs had been composed to any of Stevenson's serious or adult poems. These include a single song each by Elliott Schenck (1902), Graham Peel (1903), and Robert Clarke (1903), two by Bertram Shepleigh (1901), and a set of six by American composer Sidney Homer (*Six Songs from Underwoods*, 1904).[43]

Now let us consider Vaughan Williams in this context. A theme of his post-university aesthetic attitude is what several scholars have characterized as his 'cultural nationalism'.[44] Vaughan Williams was vitally interested in the best England had to offer in the arts, of the present and of the past. He was committed to working to uncover and raise awareness about those elements of English culture he thought great and good, the most obvious being folk-song. As a corollary to this conviction, he worked to improve music in areas where he felt standards had been abased. Thus he took up the commission to prepare a new English hymnal, and of course his love and respect of folk-song fed into this project.

Vaughan Williams made it clear in his writing about the musical scene that he thought the general artistic level of vocal recitals was appallingly low. In his peppery 1902 essay, 'A Sermon to Vocalists', he castigated singers for lack of intelligence and taste. 'The music and the words provided at these entertainments vie with each other for the first prize in utter lack of meaning', he wrote. 'Is your voice such a wretched thing that it can only be shown off by pronouncing bad poetry to worse music?' Toward the end of the essay Vaughan Williams relents a bit, admitting, 'I know there is a great difficulty in getting good English songs; we seem to come to grief between the pedant and the confectioner ... But if you want a rich storehouse of national tune, why do you not go to our own dazzling treasury of British folk-tunes?'[45]

The singer Harry Plunket Greene, the dedicatee of *Songs of Travel*, shared these aesthetic convictions and worked by his example to foster improved song recitals. He programmed good material and allowed his name to be associated by music publishers with the better composers in their lists of publications.[46] Steuart Wilson wrote of his achievement and influence: 'The effect of Greene on his generation was remarkable: it was due ... above all to his fresh-air outlook which banished the hackneyed insincerities of the shop-ballad and raised the standards of public taste.'[47]

Given these two desires – to promote all that was good in the British arts and to improve vocal recitals – it is reasonable to posit that Vaughan Williams felt the serious poetry of Stevenson gave him an ideal opportunity to realize both goals.[48] Stevenson's *Songs of Travel* – fine, well-crafted poems, refreshingly varied in structure, direct in sentiment, plain in diction, and often quite singable – provided him with excellent material for his intertwined cultural imperatives. His songs to these poems would provide singers with well-crafted material for their programmes and at the same time call the public's attention to the neglected side of Stevenson's poetic achievements. It probably did not go unnoticed at the time that 2 December 1904, being the eve of the tenth anniversary of Stevenson's death, was a timely occasion for the première of *Songs of Travel*. One doubts this was merely coincidence and even wonders if Vaughan Williams may have composed the cycle as a commemoration.

Setting Stevenson's verse gave Vaughan Williams the additional satisfaction of working with another artist who occasionally drew inspiration from the 'rich storehouse of national tune'.[49] For Stevenson wrote some of his poems to be sung to folk tunes (as well as other pre-existent melodies). It surely was not lost on Vaughan Williams that Stevenson had penned 'Whither must I Wander?' to an actual folk-song, 'Wandering Willie'. (See further in Appendix II.)

Vaughan Williams's ambitions were not disappointed; his songs were taken up by singers, admired by colleagues, and enjoyed by the public. And as for championing Stevenson, while few composers preceded Vaughan Williams in setting Stevenson's serious poetry to music, many followed his example. They include Samuel Coleridge-Taylor, Ivor Gurney, Ernest Farrar, John Ireland, George Butterworth, Cyril Scott, Roger Quilter, Cecil Armstrong Gibbs, and Walford Davies – just to name the estimable composers of this generation. Many more settings follow these, even up to the present day. Alain Frogley has argued that not only did 'Englishness' in its manifold manifestations help shape Vaughan Williams, but also reciprocally that his music and aesthetic contributed to the definition of that very 'Englishness'.[50] By analogy I am proposing that Vaughan Williams's settings of *Songs of Travel* were not only a result of the general posthumous regard for Stevenson, but also a positive factor contributing specifically to the reception of his serious poetry.

Plate 1. Satan goes forth from the presence of the Lord: *Blake, Illustrations of the Book of Job, Plate 5*. Note the facial and postural resemblance between Job and God, and the presence of Job's right foot as he is performing an act of charity to a beggar.

Plate 2.   Job's evil dreams: *Blake, Illustrations of the Book of Job, Plate 11*. Note the facial and postural resemblance between Job and Satan.

Plate 3.   When the morning stars sang together: *Blake, Illustrations of the Book of Job, Plate 14.*

Plate 4.   Job with his restored family and posterity: *Blake, Illustrations of the Book of Job, Plate 21*. Note that Job plays an instrument.

Plate 5.   Piero di Cosimo: A Satyr mourning over a Nymph, copyright National Gallery, London. Reprinted with permission.

Plate 6.   Apollyon and the Doleful Creatures. Photograph by Angus Mcbean, copyright the Harvard Theatre Collection, The Houghton Library, Frederic Woodbridge Wilson, Curator. Reprinted with permission.

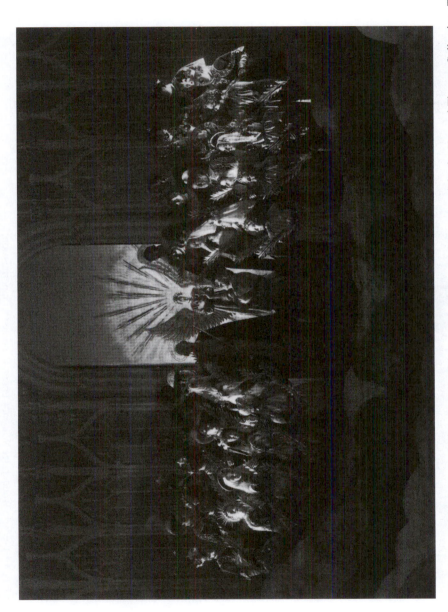

Plate 7. Act Four, Scene Three: Pilgrim in the Celestial City. Photograph by Angus Mcbean, copyright the Harvard Theatre Collection, The Houghton Library, Frederic Woodbridge Wilson, Curator. Reprinted with permission.

Plate 8.   Act One, Scene Two: Pilgrim is received at the House Beautiful.   Photograph by Angus Mcbean, copyright the Harvard Theatre Collection, The Houghton Library, Frederic Woodbridge Wilson, Curator. Reprinted with permission.

During and after the First World War, a reaction to Stevenson's unmoderated popularity set in. Writers and critics began to eschew the nostalgic, sentimental regard for Stevenson. A particular volume is usually cited as the origin of this critical downturn: Frank Swinnerton's *R.L. Stevenson. A Critical Study* (New York, 1914). 'It is no longer possible for a serious critic to place him among the great writers', wrote Swinnerton.[51] For the next thirty years, while Stevenson's books remained popular reading, they suffered a loss of prestige in the literary and academic communities. His novels were characterized as adventure fiction for boys and were thereby effectively eliminated from the critical eye. The films made during this period of favorite Stevenson novels did not help. The cinematic versions of *Treasure Island* portray Jim Hawkins as younger than he is in the book, and Long John Silver is sentimentalized almost into gentility. The fascinating and obscuring narrative manner in *The Strange Case of Dr Jekyll and Mr Hyde* is destroyed in straightforward dramatic adaptations, and the underlying philosophical and moral issues are subordinated to the sensational horror story.[52]

After the Second World War, and probably stimulated by the approaching centennial of the writer's birth, the scholarly community began a reappraisal of Stevenson, the 'revival of interest' to which Foss alluded. The turn-about began with a handful of new critical studies and the new biography by J.C. Furnas, *Voyage to Windward: The Life of Robert Louis Stevenson.*[53] After this volume, Stevenson's work has attracted increasing attentions and scholarly respect. At least three other biographies have followed Furnas's,[54] a complete critical edition of the correspondence has appeared,[55] many articles and books of critical studies have been published,[56] new scholarly editions of individual novels, essay collections, and poetry have appeared,[57] and a new edition of the complete works is being planned. As if to clinch the much bolstered regard for Stevenson, three complementary biographies of his wife Fanny have also been produced.[58]

Bearing this revival in mind, let us turn to the post-Second World War history of Vaughan Williams's *Songs of Travel*. In 1950 Hubert Foss published his important study of Vaughan Williams. In his prefatory note, Foss thanks the composer for 'looking over the list of works'.[59] In that list several statements occur that are incorrect or misleading without the larger context: 'Whither must I Wander?' is listed separately and as having been composed 'c. 1894'; *Songs of Travel* is listed, without further qualification, as the two separate collections, and the date of composition of volume I is given as 'before 1905' and of volume II as 'before 1907', which are, of course, their respective years of publication.[60] It is clear that Foss was both unaware that these songs formed a cycle and that they had been premièred as such in 1904.[61]

Of course the songs had not been published as a cycle by the time Foss was writing, but it comes as a surprise that Vaughan Williams did not point out the errors, which he should have inferred from the works list that Foss asked him to inspect. In defense of Vaughan Williams, he had not yet seen the discussion within the body of the book; Foss reports that 'the composer ... has resolutely and rightly taken the fatherly view that he would not read my manuscript'.[62] But Vaughan Williams did read the book after publication, and he wrote to Foss on 7 February 1951. Here is the relevant excerpt from his heretofore unpublished letter:

I have been through the book carefully, as you asked, and I have found a certain number of misprints and mistakes ...

As regards 'Songs of Travel'. It was originally written and sung as one cycle. The order was quite different from what it is as now published and included 'Whither must I wander', which had already been published, but not by Boosey's though Boosey's have it now. Boosey's originally refused to publish the whole cycle and chose three – then published the others later.

I don't know whether it is worth doing anything about that.[63]

Over the next seven years before his death Vaughan Williams apparently did not do anything outright about it. He did, however, make a fresh, unaccompanied male chorus arrangement of 'The Vagabond', which was published in 1952. There is also some tantalizing evidence that awareness of the existence of these songs as a cycle began to take hold in the post-war period. In a BBC broadcast of 25 April 1954, a recording was played of baritone Arthur Cranmer and pianist Philip Cranmer performing songs 1, 2, 3, 4, 7 and 8. The BBC note acknowledges the existence of a cycle, albeit of only eight songs: 'These eight settings of Robert Louis Stevenson's poems ... have never been published as a complete cycle: seven of them appeared in two sets and the remaining song was published separately. In the ... recording Arthur Cranmer sings only six of the settings, but in their original order'.[64] Where did the BBC obtain this information?

Finally, here is Roy Douglas's account of the dénouement of the publication history:

In a trunk in the boxroom I discovered a song ... It was labeled *Songs of Travel* No. 9: 'I have trod the upward and the downward slope'. When I showed this to Ursula she was delighted, for the existence of this song had been known, but it had been mislaid for many years. A copy was sent to Boosey and Hawkes ... and they were at last able to issue the complete cycle in the order in which the composer wished the songs to be sung.[65]

Boosey and Hawkes did bring out the complete cycle in 1960, putting the seven songs it had published as Parts I and II in correct order, inserting 'Whither must I Wander?' (which Boosey had acquired and published separately in 1912),[66] and adding 'I have Trod the Upward and the Downward Slope' as No. 9 at the end.[67] This version was first performed by baritone Hervey Alan with pianist Frederick Stone, on 21 May 1960, and broadcast by the BBC.[68] In 1961 Boosey and Hawkes commissioned Douglas to orchestrate the six songs that the composer had not transcribed for orchestra. Douglas did so, faithfully retaining the instrumentation the composer had employed for the full scores of the three songs of 'Part I' in 1905.[69]

One wonders whether and to what extent all this posthumous activity concerning Vaughan Williams's *Songs of Travel* may have been influence to the continuing Stevenson revival. Why did Vaughan Williams voice such pointed concern about Foss's erroneous understanding of these songs in his 1950 book when over the preceding forty or so years the songs had continued to be available only in the two misleading Boosey sets and the singly issued 'Whither must I Wander?', and missing the final song? Why is it only now that the composer wonders 'whether it is worth doing anything about that'? Did the composer seek to persuade Boosey and Hawkes to re-publish the songs as a cycle in 1933, when it was time for copyright renewal on Parts I and II? Why after so many years did he return in 1952 to arrange 'The Vagabond' for male chorus? Was it the composer who gave the BBC the correct information for the 1954 broadcast of six songs from the cycle in the correct order?[70] When the ninth song was discovered, were Roy Douglas, Ursula Vaughan Williams and Michael Kennedy concerned only to publish the cycle as originally conceived, or were they perhaps also, even unconsciously, motivated by the Stevenson revival? Boosey and Hawkes not only published the complete cycle for voice and piano, but also commissioned Douglas to complete the orchestration of *Songs of Travel*. Was the firm aware of and eager to take advantage of the renewed regard for Stevenson's work?

While there is no incontrovertible evidence that Vaughan Williams was aware of a Stevenson revival *per se*, there is a circumstance that makes it practically certain that the composer was acquainted with some of the renewed academic discussion of Stevenson's works, and specifically of his poetry. In 1948 Vaughan Williams published an essay, 'A Minim's Rest', in a *Festschrift* for Sir Humphrey Milford, head of Oxford University Press.[71] In that same volume appeared an essay on 'The Poetry of R.L. Stevenson' by H.W. Garrod.[72] Surely Vaughan Williams at least browsed through this essay, since he would have been curious about the other writings in the same volume and since the essay in question concerned the poetry of a writer whose verse he had set to music.

When the complete cycle was published as piano-accompanied songs and also complete in an orchestrated version, one wonders whether its appearance and performances may have been used to enhance further the Stevenson revival? In December 1994, during the centennial of Stevenson's death, the BBC broadcast a series of programmes about the author with the general title 'Songs of Travel'. Of all the possible titles the creators of this series could have used, they chose this particular one. On 16 December, Radio 3 presented a programme entitled 'Bright is the Ring', which was proudly listed as 'Poems of Robert Louis Stevenson as set by Vaughan Williams in his *great song-cycle "Songs of Travel"* ' (my emphasis).[73] Thus each work provides a mirror for the other.

III

One more troublesome matter requires discussion: the ninth song, 'I have Trod the Upward and the Downward Slope'. That Vaughan Williams and Boosey published it in neither set of the *Songs of Travel* in 1905 or 1907, nor separately, is of course understandable. Containing as it does musical reminiscences of 'The Vagabond', 'Whither must I Wander?', and 'Bright is the Ring of Words' (song nos 1, 7 and 8), it depends on the context of at least these three songs to make sense. But it is curious that there is no indication of its existence before it was discovered in 1960. This song was not included in the première of the cycle.[74] Vaughan Williams, in his letter to Foss quoted above, refers to the earlier-published 'Whither must I Wander?' and to the seven songs published as Parts I and II, but does not mention 'I have Trod'. In a heretofore unpublished letter of 24 August 1949, to Anthony Vercoe, a student at the Royal College of Music, who had evidently written to enquire about the order of the songs in preparation for a student recital, the composer wrote:

The order of my 'Songs of Travel' is as you state in your letter.
When they were first published Messrs. Boosey would only take three of them – 'The Vagabond', 'Roadside Fire' and 'Let Beauty Awake'. The others were published later and 'Whither must I wander' had already been published.
That is why, in the published version, the order is all wrong.[75]

There are several things to glean from this letter,[76] but the one that concerns us here is that the composer again *fails to mention the ninth song*.

There are, then, two possible conclusions: either Vaughan Williams had not yet composed 'I have trod the upward and the downward slope' and must have done so after 1951 (his letter to Foss), or even after 1954 (the BBC mention of eight songs); *or* if he had written it along with the others, he had deliberately rejected it or even forgotten it. The first hypothesis is appealing for the biographical picture it paints: a composer returns to one of his earliest works and completes it in his eighties with a lyric that he could view as a capstone motto for his own career. Consistent with this view is the fact that the sentiments of song no. 8, 'Bright is the Ring of Words', which was the original final number in the première, had offered a fitting conclusion to the cycle. Furthermore 'The Vagabond' and 'Bright is the Ring of Words', according to one interpretation of the sources, were at some preliminary stage in the same key, so that the cycle would have begun and ended in D (see Appendix I). Thus much of the evidence supports the conclusion that 'I have Trod' was, as James Day has recently speculated, 'a later afterthought'.[77]

Yet the manuscript of this song – the one that was discovered among Vaughan Williams's papers after his death – points strongly, if not indisputably, to a date of composition that is contemporary with the other songs. The separate bifolio on which 'I have Trod' is written is like the 12-stave paper of the other extant manuscripts (see Appendix I), and the handwriting is comparable.[78] It is therefore entirely possible that Vaughan Williams composed this final song along with the others, but subsequently decided to omit it before the question of publication arose, indeed even from before the first performance. Or we might imagine that he composed it after the première, feeling that the cycle as it stood needed a firmer conclusion, with summary musical references to some preceding songs. But this plan, if he ever conceived it, was thwarted both by Boosey's disruption of the cycle and by the agreement with *The Vocalist*, which prevented the inclusion of 'Whither must I Wander?', one of the songs alluded to in 'I have Trod'.

In the end there is no way to be certain when Vaughan Williams wrote this song or what he intended to do with it. Yet one unambiguous and novel fact emerges: the only form of the cycle that has the explicit approval of the composer is that of the eight songs in the correct order, without the ninth. This is testified to by the première performance, his letters to Anthony Vercoe (1949) and to Hubert Foss (1951), and by the information he (or someone close to him) reported to the BBC (1954). Although it was certainly understandable for Douglas, Kennedy and Ursula Vaughan Williams to take the manuscript of 'No. IX' at face value when they – laudably – had the cycle republished as a whole, one can, with the benefit of hindsight seriously question whether the composer would have approved of their decision.

Without more evidence there is no entirely satisfactory solution to this riddle. That Vaughan Williams could have either restored the cycle to its eight-number correct sequence or republished it with the ninth song, but in fact did neither, suggests an indecision on his part borne of dissatisfaction or indifference.[79] Perhaps, on the one hand, the final cadence of 'Bright is the Ring of Words', leaving the voice on the fifth degree of the scale and providing no piano postlude, seemed too abrupt an ending and in need of more closure. On the other hand, maybe 'I have Trod the Upward and the Downward Slope' seemed too slight and too self-conscious with its three musical allusions to earlier songs crowded into *and* accounting for at least 15 of the song's 25 bars.[80] In the end, though his creative fountains were still flowing, Vaughan Williams may not have been able after fifty years to return to this early work and revive it to his complete satisfaction. Of this cycle, for better or worse, he was in effect saying:

Lone stands the house, and the chimney-stone is cold.
...
Birds come and cry there and twitter in the chimney –
But I go forever and come again no more.

Having painted a picture of the intertwined histories of the *words* of Robert Louis Stevenson and the *music* of Ralph Vaughan Williams, it is appropriate to close with a passage from Stevenson's *Weir of Hermiston*, the novel left incomplete at the author's death. In this scene Archie Weir, the protagonist, is in conversation with Kirstie Elliott, probing to discover whether she may be a kindred soul. Archie begins:

On days like this – I do not know if you feel as I do – but everything appears so brief, and fragile, and exquisite, that I am afraid to touch life. We are here for so short a time; and all the old people before us ... that were here but a while since ... why, where are they now? It's deadly commonplace, but, after all, the commonplaces are the great poetic truths.
....
'Have you mind of Dand's song?' she answered. 'I think he'll have been trying to say what you have been thinking'.
'No, I never heard it', he said. 'Repeat it to me, can you?'
'It's nothing wanting the tune', said Kirstie.
'Then sing it me', said he.

Appendix I: The Source Materials

The extant autograph material for *Songs of Travel* is not extensive.[81] The British Library manuscripts of 'The Vagabond', 'Bright is the Ring of Words',[82] and 'The Roadside Fire'[83] are fair copies bearing the numbers '1', '2' and '3'; these are plainly Boosey's copies for preparing the initial publication of these three songs. At the bottom of 'The Roadside Fire' manuscript one reads the reminder in pencil: 'Write to Lloyd Osbourne for permis[sion]. Chatto and Windus, Pubs'. Lloyd Osbourne was Fanny Stevenson's grown son, Robert Louis Stevenson's stepson, friend, partner in amateur music making, and sometime literary collaborator (for example, co-author of *The Wrong Box*). Chatto and Windus published many of

Stevenson's works, including *Songs of Travel*. It is not clear whether this annotation about obtaining the publisher's permission is the composer's or Boosey's. Interestingly, the title page of 'Bright is the Ring of Words' bears three different numerations. The original inked '7' is overwritten with a larger '8' in blue pencil, and then these two are cancelled in plain pencil and the number '2' is substituted. The final number is clear; this is the second song in Boosey's grouping in the 1905 publication. But the first two numbers are intriguing. This song is, of course, the eighth in the cycle, which accounts for the '8'. There are at least two possible explanations for the '7'. One is that in his original conception Vaughan Williams had not included the earlier-composed 'Whither must I Wander?' in the cycle, and 'Ring of Words' thus stood in seventh place. Another possibility is that these two songs were originally reversed in the seventh and eighth places. The fact that these canceled numbers stand here at all strongly indicates that the composer had indeed submitted the complete cycle to Boosey for publication.

Another manuscript of 'The Vagabond' is at the Royal College of Music;[84] in this manuscript the song is in F minor, but it bears the note 'Original key D. Minor'. Another copy of 'Bright is the Ring of Words' is in the collection of the Cornell University Music Library;[85] its key is D flat major.

There is also a manuscript of the last song, 'I have Trod the Upward and the Downward Slope', the one that Douglas found after the composer's death.[86] On its first page the song title preceded by the arabic numeral '9' are written in ink. In pencil, written above and below the song title, respectively, are the cycle's title 'Songs of Travel' and the roman numeral 'No. IX'. The double, apparently redundant, numeration is puzzling.[87]

No manuscript materials have been located for the other five songs; that is, there is no autograph of 'Whither must I Wander?' or of the four songs that were published by Boosey in 1907 as Part 2.[88]

The composer's manuscript score of the orchestral versions of songs 1, 3 and 8 exists.[89] Interpretative markings in this score and a list of six different dates indicate that they were indeed performed on several other occasions.[90]

The various manuscripts and primary printed sources present a puzzling array of keys for these songs. (See Table 7A.1.) One is tempted to infer that Vaughan Williams was not too particular about keys, and indeed there seems to be anecdotal evidence to support that inference.[91] One does not even know for sure in what key the first song 'The Vagabond' was performed at the première. The autograph is written in D minor; it cannot be ascertained when the annotation 'C Minor' was added (see Figure 7A.1, note 2). The composer's final choice of keys is clear from the C Minor autograph of the orchestral score. The one serious anomaly is the publication by Boosey & Hawkes in 1960 of Song no. 8 'Bright is the Ring of Words' in C major, which clearly contradicts the earlier sources (see Table 7A.1, note 8).

Table 7A.1 Annotated chart of keys of the songs in various sources

Song	Autograph MSS	1st edition 1905	1907	Autograph MS Orch.	Full cycle 1960	Other[1]
1. Vagabond	d;c[2]	c	–	c	c	d, f[3]
2. Beauty	–	–	f#	–	f#	–
3. Roadside	D/Db[4]	Db	–	Db/C[5]	Db	C
4. Youth	–	–	G	–	G	–
5. In Dreams	–	–	c	–	c	–
6. Infinite	–	–	d	–	d	–
7. Whither	[c][6]	–	–	–	c	–
8. Bright	E;D[7]	D	–	D	C[8]	D,C,Db[9]
9. I have Trod	d/D	–	–	–	d/D	V

[1] Keys in secondary autographs, manuscripts and in separate, single-song editions or other formats, if different from preceding sources. I consider these to be practical transpositions, not bearing on the question of the 'right' key, the key in which the composer intended the song to be performed as part of the cycle.

[2] This song is notated in D minor; note on title page says 'C Minor'; note at beginning of music appears to read 'C# minor'.

[3] Royal College of Music, MS 4128, annotated 'Original key D minor'.

[4] Song was originally notated in D major, but sharps are canceled on first staff and note says 'Five flats Db'. Title page is annotated 'Db', in another place is written 'C & Db', but this is canceled.

[5] The score is notated in D flat, but a note says 'Parts in key C'.

[6] Key of the original publication in *The Vocalist* (1902).

[7] The song is notated in E major. Penciled at top of title page: 'D'; and penciled above top staff on next page: 'flats – Eb & D'.

[8] In his orchestral score of the songs, Roy Douglas notes: 'In the complete edition for low voice and piano [i.e. Boosey and Hawkes 1960], No. 8 is in C major' but D major is the original key, in which the composer scored it. Boosey and Hawkes, rental full score (which reproduces Douglas's next autograph score) is in C major. This indeed is an anomaly of the 1960 print: is it possible that the 1905 plates for the original print in D were lost or damaged, so that the publisher substituted the plates for the alternate key, single-issue edition in C? This seems unconscionable. But it is the easiest explanation.

[9] Cornell University, MS M1621 V37.S6. 1904.

Appendix II: Stevenson's Use of Pre-existent Tunes

Music held a significant place in Stevenson's life.[92] His letters include frequent references to music he has heard, to music he is playing (on the penny whistle, later on the flageolet, and 'pickling' – his word for two-finger playing on the piano), to music he has asked to have sent to him, and even sometimes to music he has composed. His writing, prose and poetry, is infused with musical imagery, and incidents and even plot lines in the novels and stories involve music. The piping contest between Alan Breck and Rob Roy Macgregor's son Robin Oig, for example, is one of the finest scenes in *Kidnapped* (Ch. 25 'In Balquidder'); Gideon, the central character in *The Wrong Box*, which Stevenson wrote with his stepson Lloyd Osbourne, sets out to create a false identity for himself, and he chooses to impersonate an opera composer.

Stevenson also composed some of his verse to pre-existent tunes. Sometimes he identified his sources specifically, sometimes only vaguely, and – one suspects – sometimes not at all even when he made use of them (for instance, see the discussion of 'Sing me a song of a lad that is gone', *Songs of Travel* XLII, below). Two instances occur among the *Songs of Travel* poems that Vaughan Williams set and are worth discussing here. As mentioned earlier, 'Home no more home to me' ('Whither must I Wander?') bears the specific inscription 'To the tune of Wandering Willie'. This traditional Scottish song can be found in several anthologies, with only minor variants. Robert Burns had also penned verse to this tune. Stevenson refers to his contrafact and that of Burns in a letter to his friend Charles Baxter (November 1888):

> I am so besotted that I shall put on the back of this my attempt at words to *Wandering Willie*; if you can conceive at all the difficulty, you will also conceive the vanity with which I regard any kind of result; and whatever mine is like, it has some sense, and Burns's has none.[93]

The tune is printed here with the initial stanzas of the traditional folk text, and of the Burns and Stevenson texts, underlaid (Example 7A.1).

Also as alluded to earlier, Stevenson places some of his verse in the mouth of the title character in *The Master of Ballantrae* (Chapter Nine), and has the narrator (McKellar) comment on it:

> he began to whistle and then to sing the saddest of our country tunes, which set folks weeping in a tavern, 'Wandering Willie'. The set of words he used with it I have not heard elsewhere, and could never come by any copy; but some of them ... linger in my memory. One verse began –

> Home was home then, my dear, full of kindly faces,
> Home was home then, my dear, happy for the child.

> And ended somewhat thus –

> Now when the day dawns on the brow of the moorland,
> Lone stands the house, and the chimney-stone is cold,
> Lone let it stand, now the folks are all departed,
> The kind hearts, the true hearts, that loved the
>   place of old.

> I could never be a judge of the merit of these verses; they were so hallowed by the melancholy of the air, and were sung ... to me by a master singer at a time so fitting. He looked in my face when he had done, and saw that my eyes watered.[94]

'The Vagabond', the first poem in the collection, carries a vague attribution, 'To an air of Schubert'. We know from his correspondence that Stevenson was familiar with German *Lieder*; he adored Beethoven's 'Adelaide', and refers in more than one

Folk-song:	Here	a - wa',___	there	a - wa',	here	a - wa',	Wil - lie,
Burns:	Here	a - wa',___	there	a - wa',	wan - der - ing		Wil - lie,
RLS:	Home	no more___	home	to me,	whi - ther must I		wan - der?,

Here	a - wa',___	there	a - wa',	here	a - wa'	hame;
Here	a - wa',___	there	a - wa',	huad	a - wa'	hame;
Hun - ger my___		dri - ver,	I	go	where I	must.

Lang	have	I	sought___	thee,	dear___ have I bought___	thee,
Come	to	my	bo - som,	my	ain___ on - ly dear - ie,	O
Cold	blows	the	win - ter	wind	o - ver hill and hea	ther;

Now	have	I	got - ten	my	Wil - lie a -	gain.
Tell	me	thous	bringst	me my	Wil - lie the	same.
Thick	drives	the	rain,	and my	roof is in the	dust.

Example 7A.1   Folk-song 'Wandering Willie'* as model for the contrafact by Robert Burns and the model for 'Whither must I wander?' by Stevenson

*Source: *The Songs of Robert Burns*, ed. James Dick (London, 1903), 128, quoted from James Johnson, *The Scots Musical Museum*, Vol. I (Edinburgh, 1787), no. 57.

place to Schubert's cycles *Die schöne Müllerin* and *Winterreise*. Identifying the particular 'air' to which Stevenson wrote 'The Vagabond' seems to be like looking for a needle in a haystack, until one notices the trochaic meter of the poem. This meter is a relative rarity in German verse, and thus a rare occurrence in Schubert's songs. Perusing Volume I of the familiar Peters edition of Schubert's songs, one finds very few trochaic lines, and only one song in this meter whose alternating tetrameter and trimeter lines fit Stevenson's poem. That song is 'Mut', No. 22 in *Winterreise*. Its rhythm, its melody, and the bluster of its sentiments fit Stevenson's poem like a glove. The tune with the original Müller verse and Stevenson's contrafact are shown in Example 7A.2.

This apparent solution, however, is complicated by the fact that one manuscript copy of this poem is inscribed 'Schubert's Ninth'.[95] A search through Schubert's great symphony in C Major reveals no themes with a trochaic metrical profile. Of course in order of their discovery in the nineteenth century, someone may have incorrectly numbered Schubert's symphonies '7' (great C Major), '8' ('Unfinished', B Minor), and '9' (E Minor). The last work was realized from Schubert's sketches by John Francis Barnett and first performed at the Crystal Palace in May 1883.[96] The *Adagio* introduction of the first movement comes very close to the rhythm of 'The Vagabond' (see Example 7A.3).

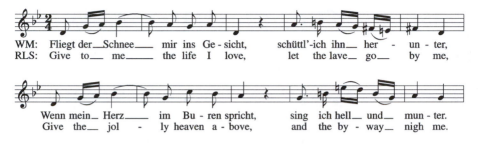

Example 7A.2 Schubert's 'Mut' (*Winterreise*, no. 22) as possible model for Stevenson's 'The Vagabond'

Another *Travel* song, though not one of Vaughan Williams's selections, merits inclusion in this discussion since it is a further instance of Stevenson's penning a lyric to an extant melody and because the song wedding Stevenson's text with the tune model is well known in Britain.[97] The tune is found in numerous Scottish folk-song anthologies, variously referred to as an 'old sea shanty', 'old Highland rowing measure', and the 'Skye Boat Song'.[98] To this melody Stevenson wrote his poem 'Sing me a song of a lad that is gone'. Fanny Stevenson left this account of the origin of this poem-song:

> The writing of *Over the Sea to Skye* grew out of a visit from one of the last of the old school Scots gentlewomen, Miss Ferrier ... Her singing was a great delight to my husband, who would beg for song after song, especially the Jacobite airs, which had always to be repeated several times. The words to one of these seemed unworthy, so he made a new set of verses more in harmony with the plaintive tune.[99]

Though in the published form of the poem – *Songs of Travel* XLII – no musical model is identified, Stevenson did acknowledge the debt in his manuscript. There, below his notation of the tune with his text, headed 'Gaelic boat-song', Stevenson wrote a note making clear that he has written down a tune he knew by ear, indeed, as we know from his wife's account above, a tune he had learned from Mrs Ferrier:

Example 7A.3 *Adagio* introduction from Schubert's E minor Symphony as possible model for Stevenson's 'The Vagabond'

[H]ere is the best I can make of it; the time I can only pray God is somewhere about right ... Note that this is a real Scotch air; no fourths or sevenths; it has not been doctored.[100]

Example 7A.4 shows the melody with Stevenson's first stanza.

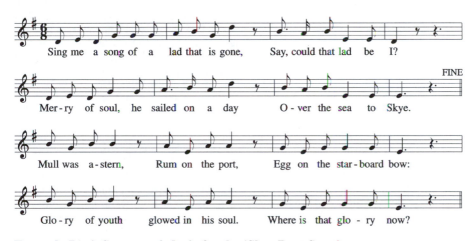

Example 7A.4 Stevenson's lyric for the 'Skye Boat Song'

Notes

1 I wish to acknowledge with gratitude the support for my research that has been provided by the Vaughan Williams Trust and the Research Foundation of the City University of New York. Also I want to thank the faculty and staff of Charterhouse School, especially Robin Wells, for their administrative support, encouragement and hospitality; and also Byron Adams, for his early and continued enthusiasm and counsel about my subject, and for the welcome he gave me to Vaughan Williams scholarship. My work could not have been accomplished without the cooperation, information, assistance and advice I have received from Paula Best, Lenore Coral, Roy Douglas, David Fallows, Susan Harris, Michael Kennedy, Valerie Langfield, Ernest Mehew, Ursula Vaughan Williams, the British Library Music Section, and the Beinecke Rare Book Library at Yale University (Stevensoniana Collection); they are individually noted below. Finally I am especially grateful to Stephen Banfield, Hugh Cobbe, Alain Frogley and Roger Savage for their advice and assistance along the way and above all for reading an earlier version of this paper and offering many fine suggestions, many of which I have with acknowledgement incorporated into this article.

2 From a letter to Edmund Gosse, as quoted in J.C. Furnas, *Voyage to Windward: The Life of Robert Louis Stevenson* (New York: William Sloane, 1951), iii.

3 Especially with the recent recorded performance by Bryn Terfel (*The Vagabond and Other Songs by Vaughan Williams, Butterworth, Finzi, Ireland*. Malcolm Martineau, piano. DGG 445 946–2). Other recent recordings include those by Benjamin Luxon (*Vaughan Williams: Songs of Travel*, David Willison, piano. Chandos 8475) and

Thomas Allen (orchestral version: *Vaughan Williams. Songs of Travel*, City of Birmingham Symphony Orchestra, Simon Rattle, cond. EMI Classics 7 64731 2).

4 Hubert Foss, *Ralph Vaughan Williams: A Study* (London: Harrap 1950), 80.

5 Ibid., 85. Other writers misrepresented *Songs of Travel*. Simona Pakenham (*Ralph Vaughan Williams. A Discovery of his Music*, London: Macmillan 1957) writes of 'two song-cycles, of which the first is the better known and the second the more varied' (32). By the time James Day wrote his biography for the Master Musicians Series (*Vaughan Williams*, London: Farrar, Straus and Cudahy 1961), the musical community was in the know about the single cycle of nine songs; but apparently Day's text was submitted before the complete cycle was published as such by Boosey, for he takes pains to explain how the songs as theretofore known are to be fitted together to make the whole set (88).

6 One can find the essential facts in Michael Kennedy's *A Catalogue of the Works of Ralph Vaughan Williams*, 2nd edn. (Oxford: Oxford University Press, 1996), 25–7.

7 J.W. Robertson Scott, in the second of his books on the history of the *Pall Mall Gazette, The Life and Death of a Newspaper* (London: Methuen, 1952), mentions that during his research on the newspaper he had 'come on the MS. of the lovely verses of R. L. Stevenson's which were published in the *Pall Mall*: "In the highlands in the country places/Where the old plain men have rosy faces/And the young fayre maidens quiet eyes", (366).

8 Colvin (1845–1927) had been Slade Professor of Art at Cambridge, Director of the Fitzwilliam Museum, Keeper of Prints and Drawings at the British Museum, and was the author of two highly esteemed books on Keats. Though he wrote no biography of Stevenson, he did edit his correspondence. Colvin also contributed regularly to the *Pall Mall Gazette* as art critic. Given these circumstances, and the warm and hyperbolic tone of the front-page notice cited earlier, it seems reasonable to infer that it was Colvin who penned the obituary notices for the *Gazette*. And it was surely Colvin who furnished the poems for insertion in the paper since it was to him that Stevenson had sent his latest poetry from Samoa.

9 Vaughan Williams may also have known some of Stevenson's essays; he would have found much to sympathize with in the essay on Walt Whitman (in *Familiar Studies of Men and Books* [London: Chatto and Windus, 1882]), whose poetry inspired several early works, including *Toward the Unknown Region* and *A Sea Symphony*.

10 Private communication to me, 16 September 1994. In an interview in the summer of 1995, Mrs Vaughan Williams reported that there was no copy of Stevenson's *Songs of Travel* in her possession.

11 I am indebted to Hugh Cobbe for sharing with me this letter from his forthcoming edition of Vaughan Williams's correspondence.

12 Similarly he retained Rossetti's title *House of Life* even though he picked only six sonnets from the 59 in Part I of the sonnet sequence; the first song of the cycle is Rossetti's fourth sonnet. By contrast, he named his cycle of six songs from Housman's *A Shropshire Lad* by a different title, *On Wenlock Edge*, taken from the thirty-first poem, which is the text of the opening song. Of the well-known nineteenth-century song cycles that Vaughan Williams would likely have known, the composers of some took over a poetic cycle more or less intact and retained the poet's title (for example, Schubert's *Die schöne Müllerin* and *Winterreise*, Schumann's *Frauenliebe und-Leben*), while others picked and chose poems and fashioned a reordered subset and provided their own titles (for example, Schumann's *Dichterliebe* based on 16 poems from Heine's 66-poem collection *Lyrisches Intermezzo*).

13 At this point, one should take note of the fact that the published sequence of the poems is not Stevenson's, at least not entirely. According to Sidney Colvin, Stevenson 'had tried them in several different orders and under several different titles, as "Songs and Notes of Travel", "Posthumous Poems", etc., and in the end left their naming and arrangement to

the present editor ...' (Robert Louis Stevenson, *Songs of Travel and Other Verses*, London: Chatto and Windus, 1896, [v]). So it is actually with Colvin's ordering that Vaughan Williams was dealing. Nevertheless, recurring images, phrases, and sentiments or complementary relations between adjacent poems strongly suggest that certain pairings and other groupings within the larger collection reflect Stevenson's own intentions. Note, for example, the two 'Youth and Love' poems (II and III); the related imagery in IV and V ('He came and went ...' IV, line 9 and 'She came, she went...' V, line 5); the travel *à deux* of X and XI; the similar farewells of XXII, XXIII and XXIV. Similarly, it is hard not to believe that Stevenson wanted the collection to begin with 'The Vagabond'.

14 Stephen Banfield, *Sensibility and English Song* (Cambridge: Cambridge University Press, 1985), 83.

15 Augustus Saint-Gaudens's relief medallion of Stevenson (1887) bears as part of its inscription the first stanza of 'Bright is the ring of words'.

16 Borrow's *Lavengro* was the composer's favorite novel, one which he long hoped to turn into an opera. See Roger Savage, 'Vaughan Williams, the Romany Ryes and the Cambridge Ritualists' (read at the British Library Vaughan Williams conference, November 1999; forthcoming in *Music and Letters*), in which Vaughan Williams's strong interest in gypsy lore and travel is documented. Savage goes on to discuss the origins of *Hugh the Drover* and *An Oxford Elegy* and to argue the influence of contemporary ideas and attitudes about gypsies and related archetypes on these works. I am grateful to Stephen Banfield for alerting me to Professor Savage's paper and to the author himself for sending me a copy.

17 A poem which Vaughan Williams excerpted in *An Oxford Elegy*, along with verses from the same poet's 'Thyrsis'.

18 'Beggars', first published in *Scribner's Magazine*, 3 (March 1888), and subsequently in *Across the Plains* (1892), Here quoted from *R.L. Stevenson. Essays and Poems*, ed. Claire Harman (London: Dent, 1992), 26.

19 I am grateful to Stephen Banfield for sending me to M.A. Crowther's essay 'The Tramp' in *Myths of the English*, ed. Roy Porter (Cambridge: Porter Polity, 1992), which in turn led me to other materials. For further discussion of travel and voyaging as a theme in Vaughan Williams's works, see Savage, 'Vaughan Williams, the Romany Ryes and the Cambridge Ritualists'. See note 16.

20 To my ear, sensitized to this interpretation, the tonal disjunction of these songs now sounds quite appropriate. The closely related keys of songs 1 and 4 – C minor and G major – are interrupted by the foreign keys F sharp minor and D flat major of songs 2 and 3, keys which are enharmonically compatible with each other. So present and past are characterized by distinct tonal areas.

21 Stephen Banfield in a private communication suggested the narrative interpretation of the cycle be taken further. 'I think the lad takes his "boyish stave" with him because he's an artist, a singer. This is therefore the archetypal romantic, *Bildungsroman* plot: artist had to leave love behind and be lonely for the sake of his muse, who visits him in the image of the beloved who becomes his inspiration ... The star that comes down is this image of the beloved, this muse, this touch of inspiration that will make something immortal out of his loneliness and sufferings. "Whither must I Wander?" ... then becomes what he composes ... [I]t's in a different style ... a folk style. The other songs aren't. So he's a "folk" singer, and in this cycle VW dramatises his ideal of the folk process: an anonymous individual's suffering gets transmuted into art and passed down to other lovers ("Bright is the Ring of Words").'

22 According to Michael Kennedy (*Catalogue*, 25) the cycle at this performance included only the first eight songs, omitting 'I have Trod the Upward and the Downward Slope'. Paula Best, Publications Manager at Wigmore Hall, kindly confirmed that the original

programme in the Wigmore archives lists only the first eight songs. This leads one to speculate that either Vaughan Williams was not satisfied with this song or *had not yet composed it*, a point to which I shall return.

23 I am grateful to Valerie Langfield, who furnished me with this annotation and referred me to Paula Best at Wigmore Hall for confirmation.

24 Quoted from Michael Kennedy, *The Works of Ralph Vaughan Williams* (London: Oxford University Press, 1964), 61.

25 Harry Plunkett Greene, *Interpretation in Song* (London, 1948), *passim*.

26 English publishers were unaccustomed to cycles, so perhaps Boosey ought not be singled out for criticism. Stephen Banfield observes that '... no British composer seems to have published a volume of more than six or at the very most seven songs between Somervell's *Maud* and *A Shropshire Lad* at the turn of the century and Britten's *Les illuminations* (1940) – that is unless they had charitable backing or financed it themselves'. *Gerald Finzi. An English Composer* (London: Faber, 1997), 204.

27 At least for the singer, the accompaniment figuration being awkward for the piano (though very string-like, especially 'Roadside Fire'). Ursula Vaughan Williams said of the initial Boosey publications: 'The first publisher insisted on publishing them in two books – choosing those that he considered the easiest for the first volume' (letter to the author dated 16 September 1994). Her assertion implies that Boosey had in mind publishing all the songs from the outset, but there is no supporting evidence for this.

28 Boosey not only acquired the rights, but took over the plates from *The Vocalist*; an inspection of the original magazine print and of the Boosey print reveals them to be identical. How Vaughan Williams got out of his agreement with *The Vocalist* 'not to sell songs to any publisher but him for 5 years' is not clear. Perhaps the magazine was interested only in single songs and released him from his obligation for cycles. Obviously he had likewise not been bound to them for *House of Life*. He did publish further individual songs in *The Vocalist*: 'A Cradle Song' (Kennedy 1905/3), 'The Splendor Falls' (1905/5). After these, there are no other songs before 1908, by which time the agreement had expired.

29 In the private letter cited earlier, Roy Douglas states: 'As for the orchestral versions: RVW obviously chose – or was asked – to orchestrate the three which had been published in 1905.'

30 'Bright is the Ring of Words', 28 April 1909; 'The Vagabond', 11 April 1923; 'The Roadside Fire', 21 April 1925; 'Bright', 25 April 1933; 'The Vagabond', 17 April 1934; 'Whither must I Wander?', 6 April 1937; and a male chorus arrangement of 'The Vagabond', 30 April 1954. The Leith Hill programmes in the possession of Ursula Vaughan Williams were consulted by the author in June 1995. Throughout the course of the Festival's history while Vaughan Williams was at the helm (1905–55), orchestrally accompanied opera arias and piano-accompanied songs were the solo vocal works presented.

31 Ursula Vaughan Williams, *R.V.W.: A Biography of Ralph Vaughan Williams* (Oxford: Oxford University Press, 1964), 136.

32 Ursula Vaughan Williams, *R.V.W.*, 354.

33 'The Songs of Ralph Vaughan Williams', *The English Review* 46 (1928), 606–7. This journal cannot be found in New York, and I am grateful to Susan Harris for sending me a copy from the Pennsylvania State University library.

34 Arthur Bliss, *As I Remember* (London: Faber, 1970), 26.

35 Margaret Stewart (Lady Wilson), *English Singer. The Life of Stueart Wilson* (London: Duckwork, 1970), 265. Stueart Wilson was considered one of the great interpreters of *On Wenlock Edge*, having taken it up in 1911 or 1912, after the première by Gervase Elwes. Vaughan Williams wrote *Four Hymns* for Wilson (36).

36 Quoted from H.W. Garrod, 'The Poetry of Robert Louis Stevenson', in *Essays mainly on the Nineteenth Century presented to Sir Humphrey Milford*, intro. by G.F.J. Cumberlege (Oxford: Oxford University Press, 1948), 42.

37 Dated 6 December, 1887, in *The Letters of Robert Louis Stevenson*, eds, Bradford A. Booth and Ernest Mehew, 8 vols. (New Haven: Yale University Press, 1994–95), VI, 65.

38 Ibid.

39 Garrod, 'The Poetry of R.L. Stevenson', 57.

40 Frank McLynn, *Robert Louis Stevenson: A Biography* (London: Hutchinson, 1993), 6.

41 I consulted copies of the original Stanford songs and of this anthology in the Yale Music Library.

42 Some of these songs I stumbled on in libraries, but Stephen Banfield introduced me to the Bryan Gooch and David Thatcher index *Musical Settings of Late Victorian and Modern British Literature. A Catalogue* (New York: Gooch and Thatcher Garland, 1976), which simplified and amplified the identification of these settings.

43 See for example Gooch and Thatcher, op cit.

44 Byron Adams, 'Scripture, Church, and culture: biblical texts in the works of Ralph Vaughan Williams', in *Vaughan Williams Studies*, ed. Alain Frogley (Cambridge: Cambridge University Press, 1996), 110.

45 *The Vocalist*, I/8 (November 1902), 227–9.

46 In the Boosey lists on the rear covers of their song publications, the following are some of the works associated with Plunket Greene: Arthur Somervell's *A Shropshire Lad*, Stanford's *Songs of the Sea*, Edward Elgar's 'After'.

47 *Dictionary of National Biography 1931–1940* (Oxford: Oxford University Press, 1949), 360.

48 Roger Savage (private communication) has wisely reminded me that Stevenson was Scottish, not English; hence the cautious 'British' used here. Interestingly he notes, however, that the poems Vaughan Williams chose are free of Scottishness, except for the mention of 'heather' (not exclusively Scottish, of course) and the use of the Scots 'lave' (remainder, rest) in 'The Vagabond'. Though reluctant to charge Vaughan Williams with deliberate 'cultural appropriation' in his selection of poems, Savage does detect a 'faint whiff of it'.

49 *The Vocalist*, see note 45.

50 Alain Frogley, 'Constructing Englishness in music: national character and the reception of Ralph Vaughan Williams', in *Vaughan Williams Studies*, 1–22, esp. 2–4.

51 As quoted in *Robert Louis Stevenson. The Critical Heritage*, ed. Paul Maixner (London: Routledge and Kegan Paul, 1981).

52 See 'The Dialectics of a Reputation', in Furnas, *Voyage to Windward*, 436–55.

53 (New York: William Sloane, 1951; London: William Sloane, 1952.)

54 James Pope Hennessey, *Robert Louis Stevenson* (New York: Simon and Schuster, 1974); Jenni Calder. *Robert Louis Stevenson. A Life Study* (London: Hamilton, 1980); Frank McLynn, *A Biography of Robert Louis Stevenson* (New York: Random House, 1994).

55 *The Letters of Robert Louis Stevenson*, eds Bradford A. Booth and Ernest Mehew, 8 vols (New Haven: Yale University Press, 1994–95).

56 For example, Edwin Eigner, *Robert Louis Stevenson and the Romantic Tradition* (Princeton: Princeton University Press, 1966); Maixner, ed., *Robert Louis Stevenson. The Critical Heritage* (London: Routledge and Kegan Paul, 1981); Andrew Noble, ed., *Robert Louis Stevenson* (London: Vision, 1983); Alan Sandison, *Robert Louis Stevenson and the Appearance of Modernism. A Future Feeling* (London: Macmillan, 1996).

57 For example, *Collected Poems*, ed. Janet Adams Smith 2nd edn (New York: Viking Press, 1971); *The Strange Case of Dr. Jekyll and Mr. Hyde and Other Stories*, ed. Jenni Calder (London: Penguin, 1979); *Weir of Hermiston and Other Stories*, ed. Paul Binding

(London: Penguin, 1979); *Treasure Island*, ed. Emma Letley (Oxford: Oxford University Press, 1985); *Essays and Poems*, ed. Claire Harman (London: Dent, 1992); *Travels with a Donkey in the Cevennes and Selected Travel Writings*, ed. Emma Letley (Oxford: Oxford University Press, 1992).

58 Margaret Mackay, *The Violent Friend: The Story of Mrs. Robert Louis Stevenson* (Garden City, NY: Doubleday, 1968); Alanna Knight, *The Passionate Kindness: The True Love Story of Robert Louis Stevenson and Fanny Osbourne* (Aylesbury: Milton House, 1974); most recently Alexandra Lapierre, *Fanny Stevenson. A Romance of Destiny*, trans. from French by Mary Cosmas (London: Fourth Estate, 1995).

59 Foss, *Ralph Vaughan Williams*, 5.

60 Ibid., 204.

61 At least Foss lists eight Stevenson songs. The reader is reminded of Hermon Ould's 1928 article (see above), in which only the three 1905 songs were discussed as the *Songs of Travel* and 'Whither Must I Wander?' was mentioned separately.

62 Foss, *Ralph Vaughan Williams*, 5.

63 Again I am grateful to Hugh Cobbe for sharing with me this excerpt from his edition (in preparation) of the composer's correspondence.

64 I am grateful to the BBC for providing me with records of the broadcasts of *Songs of Travel*.

65 Roy Douglas, *Working with Vaughan Williams*, 2nd edn (London: British Library, 1988), 107.

66 Boosey plate no. H.7547. British Library, Music Division H.3951(5) is an exemplar of this edition.

67 In the original key (baritone) publication of the complete cycle, Boosey & Hawkes understandably, but a little shoddily, reused the plates from its earlier publications. Songs nos 1, 8 and 3 use the 1905 plates (H. 4743), songs nos. 2, 4, 5 and 6 use the 1907 plates (H. 5557), and song no. 7, Boosey's edition of 'Whither must I Wander?' uses its 1912 plates (H.7547, which are in fact those of *The Vocalist* with a B&H plate number added; see above). Only song no. 9 is newly engraved (B&H 18741). Shamelessly the publisher made no effort to make the title matter at the head of all the songs consistent. In the initial edition of 1960, the publisher even left the Roman numerals I, II, II and IV from the 1907 'Part II' at the head of songs 2, 4, 5, and 6. Cf. British Library, Music Division, H. 3951.g.(5). The edition was subsequently cleaned up, though not re-engraved. Song no. 9 was also issued separately, presumably out of consideration for those who already owned the eight other songs. The ninth song, in the complete edition as well as in the separate issue, bears the cautionary note: 'This little epilogue to the Song Cycle "Songs of Travel" should be sung in public only when the whole cycle is performed.'

68 From the BBC print-out of its computerized records furnished to me in 1995.

69 The orchestral score is not published; Douglas's autograph score of the whole cycle has been photocopied by Boosey & Hawkes for rental.

70 Roger Savage points out (private communication) that 1951 was also the time of the premières of *The Pilgrim's Progress* and of *A Cotswold Romance* (a cantata version of *Hugh the Drover*). 'Perhaps finishing work on these two "travelers' tales" drew Vaughan Williams's attention to tidying the traveler-cycle (especially now people were getting to like the poetry again)'.

71 Ralph Vaughan Williams, 'A Minim's Rest', *Essays Mainly on the Nineteenth Century Presented to Sir Humphrey Milford*, 113–16; reprinted in Vaughan Williams, *National Music and Other Essays* (London: Oxford University Press, 1963), 166–9. Milford edited works of Leigh Hunt (1923), William Cowper (1926), and Robert Browning (1941) for Oxford University Press, as well as compiling a book of essays (1931) and *The Oxford Book of English Verse of the Romantic Period* (1951). At Oxford University

Press, Milford apparently oversaw the publication of Vaughan Williams's works; Adrian Boult solicited his support for the production of a score of *Job* (Kennedy, *Works*, 229, note 2). His son Robin Humphrey Milford was a composer who studied with Vaughan Williams in the 1920s (Ursula Vaughan Williams, *R.V.W.*, 136) and whose work Vaughan Williams championed in later years (ibid., 380).

72 Garrod, 'The Poetry of R.L. Stevenson', 42–55.

73 The performers were baritone Stephen Roberts and pianist John Constable. From computer printouts from the BBC's archives.

74 The programme that is transcribed in Kennedy's *Works*, 60–61, cites the two cycles by title only without listing individual songs. The original programme, a copy of which can be found in the records of Wigmore Hall, does indeed list the individual songs, and the cycle ends with 'Bright is the Ring of Words'. As noted earlier, Paula Best at Wigmore was kind enough to check this for me. (Before I learned of the existence of this programme in the archives at Wigmore, I sent Professor David Fallows of Manchester University and Hugh Cobbe of the British Library on wild goose chases, respectively, among Kennedy's papers related to Vaughan Williams in the John Rylands Library in Manchester and among the recital programmes from this period still in the possession of Ursula Vaughan Williams; I thank them for their efforts and apologize for the unnecessary inconvenience.)

75 Again I am indebted to Hugh Cobbe for supplying me with this letter from his forthcoming edition of selected Vaughan Williams correspondence.

76 Vaughan Williams had a momentary lapse of memory and listed 'Let Beauty Awake' instead of 'Bright is the Ring of Words' as the third song in the first volume; and this letter again confirms that it was known in some quarters that these songs had originally formed a cycle whose order was skewed by the Boosey publications.

77 In the revised editon of his Master Musicians biography, *Vaughan Williams* (London: Oxford University Press, 1998), 113.

78 Hugh Cobbe also examined the manuscript at my request and is of the strong opinion that it is roughly contemporary with the other songs.

79 Hugh Cobbe points out that since Oxford University Press had become Vaughan Williams's principal publisher, it may have been unlikely that Boosey or the composer would have rekindled a relationship at this point. On the other hand, Boosey was unquestionably interested when the (sales?) prospect of a revised and unified edition with a new song came their way after the composer's death.

80 Stephen Banfield, following through on his own construction of the narrative of the cycle (see note 21 above), suggests that Vaughan Williams could have been 'ambivalent about the epilogue' because 'it brings [the cycle] back to the self-aware composer, adding a fourth narrative layer (to the tramp, his song, his folk legacy) rather than leaving the last word to the folk process' (private communication).

81 Michael Kennedy lists the known manuscripts in the second edition of his *Catalogue*, 26–7. Before this edition appeared, I wrote to both Kennedy and Roy Douglas about the existence and location of manuscripts for this cycle. Kennedy (letter of 29 September 1994) referred me to the forthcoming new edition of his book and wrote: 'Diligent search was made for autograph scores, but they seem to be lost except for one or two which have turned up.' Roy Douglas (7 November 1994) wrote: 'Regarding the original MSS of "Songs of Travel" for voice and piano: if these are not with Boosey and Hawkes or with the British Library, I can only surmise that RVW may have given them away (perhaps to a singer), or even torn them up.' One other manuscript has turned up at Cornell University; see further below.

82 Included in British Library, Add. MS 62906. 'The Vagabond' consists of two folios stitched together: title page, pp. 2–7 containing the song, last page blank. 'Bright is the

Ring of Words' is a single folio with title page, two written pages of music, and a blank page.

83 In British Library Add. MS 59796. 'The Roadside Fire' consists of two nestled folios, with title page and seven written pages of music. The 12-stave paper seems the same or very similar to that for Add. MS 62906.

84 RCM MS 4128.

85 M1621.V37.S6.1904. I am grateful to Lenore Coral, Music Librarian at Cornell University, for supplying me with information about this manuscript. Like the other manuscripts, this is a bifolio, with the song notated on the inner pages (1v and 2r). Folio 1r is blank, and 2v contains a sketch.

86 British Library Add. MS 50480. One bifolio, with title page and two written pages of music.

87 On the verso of the title page at the top is written 'Songs of Travel (no IX) (22 in the book)', referring to the fact that this is a setting of the twenty-second poem in Stevenson's collection.

88 Stephen Banfield, drawing on his extensive research on English song, says that very few of the manuscripts of songs published by Boosey around this time have survived (private communication).

89 British Library, Add. MS 50438 A.

90 At the bottom of page 1 are found the following dates: 13th Oct., 31 Aug., Sept 14, 14 Aug, 10 June, 17 May, all without years given. There are markings in the inked score in three different pencil colors: black, blue and red.

91 In response to something he had heard Vaughan Williams say, Gerald Finzi commented, 'It is delightful to hear Vaughan Williams's remark about not being able to tell whether a movement ended in the same key. That is really encouraging.' Banfield, *Gerald Finzi*, 302.

92 For a broader discussion of Stevenson and music, see Ernest Mehew's introduction to his edition of *The Wrong Box* (London: Nonesuch, 1989), xx–xxii.

93 *The Letters of Robert Louis Stevenson*, ed. Booth and Mehew, 222.

94 Stevenson, *The Scottish Novels*, intro. by Jenni Calder (Edinburgh: Canongate, 1995), *The Master of Ballantrae*, 151.

95 Beinecke Library, Yale University, MS Vault Stevenson 7078.

96 The *Musical Times* vol. 24, No 484, June 1, 1883, p. 319. Schubert's sketches had belonged to Mendelssohn and were given to Sir George Grove, who lent them to Barnett to prepare a score for performance. A piano reduction of Barnett's realizations was published by Breitkopf and Härtel, a copy of which was acquired by the British Museum in 1895 (n. 3183.C/8). See the Vorwort of the latter.

97 I am indebted to Stephen Banfield for calling this to my attention. The song was published in 1912 as *Over the Sea to Skye*. Words and Music [sic] by Robert Louis Stevenson, Piano Accompaniment by H.J. Stewart (Boston: Boston Music Company, 1912).

98 The latter title comes from the association of the tune with a text about the escape of Bonnie Prince Charlie to the Hebridean Isle of Skye after the defeat at Culloden Moor by the Duke of Cumberland in 1745.

99 Fanny Stevenson, prefatory note to *Underwoods*, in *The Works of Robert Louis Stevenson*, the Vailima Edition, ed. Lloyd Osbourne, vol. 8 (1922), 89, where the tune with Robert Louis Stevenson's first two stanzas is printed.

100 *Over the Sea to Skye*. The printed song is prefaced with a facsimile of Stevenson's autograph manuscript.

Chapter 8

A Critical Appraisal of the
Four Last Songs

Renée Chérie Clark

After the death of Ralph Vaughan Williams on 26 August 1958, his widow and the Oxford University Press decided to make public four previously unpublished songs that the composer had been working on intermittently during the four last years of his life. They were published together in 1960 under the title *Four Last Songs*. These songs, each a setting of a poem by his wife, are among the most intimate of his art songs, and the four of them, as a set, are representative of his contributions to the genre both in compositional process as well as in performance history.

Surprisingly, these songs have elicited very little comment in scholarly studies of Vaughan Williams's works or in examinations of English art song in general, even though their very existence raises a number of questions. In the 1964 edition of Michael Kennedy's catalog of Vaughan Williams's compositions, he remarks that 'Marriage to a poet re-stimulated the lyrical gift which had been so pronounced at the start of his career, and in the *Four Last Songs* there are fragments of song-cycles which might have been memorable'.[1] The most recent criticism of the set (and by far the most extensive) appears in the third (1998) edition of James Day's volume *Vaughan Williams*. Here Day describes the songs as having 'tenderness without nostalgia, austerity of expression but not of feeling, the passion of the early Rossetti settings seen through the eyes (or rather heard through the ears) of long experience, a return to port after a long spiritual voyage ... a new lucidity'.[2] Day's penultimate comment, 'a return to port after a long spiritual voyage', is perhaps the most poignant statement in this passage, for in many ways these songs are representative of the varied aspects of both Vaughan Williams's life and music.

Information on these songs appears in Kennedy's catalogue, as well as in Ursula Vaughan Williams's biography of her husband. However, the most extensive information available appears in a series of unpublished letters sent back and forth between Ernest Chapman, The Honourable Secretary of the Macnaghten Concerts, and Ursula Vaughan Williams in the autumn of 1959. In the year just after the composer's death, a performance of three of the four songs was planned for the 27 November concert of the Macnaghten series. It is through these existing letters that we discover that Oxford University Press and Mrs Vaughan Williams had decided to publish, as a group, four songs that were supposedly fragments of two projected song cycles. In the first letter of this series, dated 21 September 1959, Chapman explains that the Macnaghten Concert Committee has been unable to arrange the billing of Vaughan Williams's songs as was agreed between Ursula Vaughan Williams and the Oxford University Press. He promises that on the night and in future the Committee will add that the songs are part of 'Four Last Songs'. The second letter is dated 3 November 1959. Here Chapman asks Mrs Vaughan Williams to provide him with a short programme note. He requests that the programme not include the dates of composition and suggests that it mention the previous performance of one of the songs. He also makes the suggestion that, since he has agreed with the Oxford University Press to list them as three songs from 'Four Last Songs', Mrs Vaughan Williams refer briefly in the programme note to the song that is not included on the programme.[3] Mrs Vaughan Williams answers as follows:

November 15th 1959
Dear Mr Chapman,
    Thank you so much for your letter [and] the extra tickets for the 27th. I enclose the words of the songs and a programme note, which I hope will do.
                                With kind regards,
                                Ursula Vaughan Williams[4]

[typed enclosure]
    Four Last Songs are the fragments of two projected song cycles.
    Procris was suggested by the picture by Piero di Cosimo in the National Gallery.
    Menelaus was written by both author and composer after reading about the return from Troy in T.E. Lawrence's translation [of] the Odyssey: this song is dedicated to Keith Falkner who sang it as one of the Arts Council's recitals of English Songs at the Wigmore Hall in 1955.
    Tired belongs to a second cycle, as does the fourth song, which is a woman's song and so cannot be included in the group tonight.
    All the songs were written between 1954 and 1958.
                                U.V.W.[5]

Because of the information provided in the programme note, performers and scholars have taken for granted two pieces of information: the contents of the two projected song cycles – that is to say, which songs would, had the cycles been completed, have appeared together and which would not – and that 'Hands, Eyes and Heart' should be sung by a woman. Indeed, this information appears subsequently in Michael Kennedy's catalogue, as well as in the latest edition of James Day's monograph.[6] In addition, the songs, divided in such a way, would be grouped according to general subject matter. 'Procris' and 'Menelaus', two that would have comprised one cycle, involve figures from classical mythology, while 'Hands, Eyes and Heart' and 'Tired' are settings of texts that deal with love. Mrs Vaughan Williams's insistence that 'Hands, Eyes and Heart' is a woman's song is simply a matter of text ('Hands, give him all the measure of my love ...').

Despite the programme note, there is evidence that suggests that Vaughan Williams, at least at one point, had something quite different in mind. In 1954, the distinguished baritone, Keith Falkner, who was then Professor of Music at Cornell University, invited Vaughan Williams to be visiting professor at Cornell for the autumn term. In her biography of her husband, Mrs Vaughan Williams tells us that during their stay, Professor and Mrs Falkner (who was an accomplished pianist), shared a words and music recital with the poet and Cornell professor Morris Bishop.[7] At this recital, Falkner sang a new song Vaughan Williams brought for him as a present, 'Menelaus on the Beach at Pharos', a setting of one of Ursula Vaughan

Williams's poems. Upon returning to England in December of 1954 after his American lecture tour, the composer set another text by his wife, 'Hands, Eyes and Heart', and sent it, along with the following letter, to Falkner in March of 1955.

> March 7th 1955
> My dear Keith,
>   Here is a short pendant to Menelaus, but,
> 1. You may not like it,
> 2. You may think it unsuitable for a man,
> 3. You may think it too intimate for public singing,
> but if not, would you feel inclined to sing it at the B.B.C. Concert in May?
>   Thank you very much for you[r] card from Niagara. You can sing it in any key you like.
>   Love to you from both of us.
>   RVW[8]

While Vaughan Williams recognized that the text of 'Hands, Eyes and Heart' may have been considered by some to be inappropriate for a male singer, he still apparently thought it could be sung by a man. According to the BBC Written Archives, there is no record of Keith Falkner performing these songs for the BBC in May 1955. However, he is listed as singing this particular one at its first public performance on 21 December 1956, accompanied by his wife.[9] In addition, this letter reveals that, at least at the time of composition, Vaughan Williams intended 'Menelaus' and 'Hands, Eyes and Heart' to be grouped together – not separated into two different song cycles.[10]

There are two main sources of sketches and drafts for this group of songs: the British Library collection of Vaughan Williams's manuscripts, and Cornell University Music Library's holdings of the papers of Professor Keith Falkner, although these are not extensive. What one learns from these materials is that Vaughan Williams sketched these songs by noting down basic ideas for the introduction and the vocal melody. Once the basic idea is in place, he then returns to his material and rapidly expands it, solidifying the vocal melody with regard to rhythm and prosody, and by expanding the introduction of the piano accompaniment.

'Menelaus on the Beach at Pharos'[11]

You will come home, not to the home you knew
that your thought remembers, going from rose to rose
along the terraces and staying to gaze
at the vines and iris beside the lake
in the morning haze.

Forgetting the place you are in where the cold sea winds go
crying like gulls on the beach where horned sea poppies grow.

Homesick wanderer, you will come home
to a home more ancient, waiting your return:
sea frets the steps that lie green under waves
and swallows nest below lintel and eaves:
there lamps are kindled for you, they will burn
till you come, however late you will come,

till the west wind's sheltering wing
folds round your sail and brings you to land.

Stretch out your hand,
murmuring lapping sea and the lamps are the welcome wait
to draw you home to rest.
you shall come home and love shall fold you in joy
and lay your heart on her breast.

The text for 'Menelaus' was published in 1959 as part of Ursula Vaughan Williams's collection *Silence and Music*.[12] As Mrs Vaughan Williams explains in her programme note,[13] both the text and the music for 'Menelaus' were written after she and her husband had been reading aloud from T.E. Lawrence's translation of *The Odyssey*. In her biography of her husband, Ursula Vaughan Williams further explains that during the previous summer, after reading from Book Four, she wrote some verse and left it on his desk and went out into the garden. When she came back in, the song was virtually complete.[14]

Menelaus was the younger brother of Agamemnon and the husband of Helen, whose abduction resulted in the Trojan War. In Book Four of *The Odyssey*, Menelaus is the King of Sparta, living with great wealth and reunited with Helen. At this point in the story, Telemachus, the son of the absent Odysseus, is visiting Menelaus in the hope of learning some news of his father. Telemachus asks Menelaus to tell him about Odysseus; Menelaus complies with this request. The passage that inspired Ursula Vaughan Williams and, subsequently, her husband, is a quotation from Menelaus as he recounts the end of Proteus's speech telling him what he needs to do to return home: 'from the river of earth the west wind ever sings soft and thrillingly to reanimate the souls of men – there you will have Helen for yourself and will be deemed of the household of Zeus'.[15]

There are four manuscript sources available for this song, three in the British Library's collection of Vaughan Williams's manuscripts (BL Add. MS 65088, ff. 1–14, 15–18 and 19–30), and one in the Cornell University Music Library (Locked Press ++M1621.2V37, folder 2). Folios 1–14 of BL Add. MS 65088 are bound together in a 32-page 12-stave manuscript music notebook with the title 'Menelaus' written both in block capitals and in Vaughan Williams's hand on the front. The earliest sources for this song are included in the first 14 folios of this notebook. These sketches represent his initial conception and proceed through the earliest sketch, which is in graphite pencil and uses a two-stave format for a brief melodic and harmonic outline (f. 2r), to a more complete sketch of a setting for the entire text. By folio 2v he uses standard piano–vocal format (with four complete sets of three staves on the page). This represents a more advanced idea of the vocal melody and the piano accompaniment, which is now sketched both melodically as well as harmonically, all in black ink with corrections, additions and annotations in graphite pencil. At this point, Vaughan Williams conceived of the introduction and the subsequent accompaniment line as ascending first, then descending, rather than the other way around, as it appears in publication (Example 8.1a). In addition to the change in direction from these sketches to the published version, this sketch, along with the earliest incomplete draft of the song (ff. 7v–10r) shows a four-measure introduction. In the published version the introduction has been reduced to one full measure plus one beat, but the essence of the initial idea remains. That is to say, in the draft the piano introduction alternates between two measures each of a C minor triad that lasts for the duration of a dotted minim and a measure of semiquaver septuplets. Vaughan Williams clearly thought four measures were too long.

In his published collection of letters with commentary, Roy Douglas notes the difficulty of reading both Vaughan Williams's handwriting and music manuscript.[16] The composer's script did not alter much throughout the course of his life and his idiosyncratic handwriting is found throughout the holograph manuscripts of these songs. While the sketches are occasionally difficult to decipher, it is possible to see that throughout the process of notating the piano accompaniment, the composer occasionally uses chord symbols (for example, 'E♭m', indicating E flat minor, found in measure 9 of folio 2v of Add. MS 65088, which corresponds to the E flat minor triad found in measure 7 of the published version). Careful reading of the sketch is necessary here, because Vaughan Williams also uses letters when clarifying a dubious note.

By folio 3v the manuscript provides only the barest sketch of the vocal melody with intermittent accompaniment pitches and harmonies. Another feature of the composer's manner of sketching is his frequent practice of omitting bits and pieces of the text. Occasionally he just uses the first letter of a word to indicate where he is in the text, for example, using 'w' for wing ('Sheltering wing folds round your sail') on folio 4v. By the bottom of folio 5r, Vaughan Williams is no longer really using standard piano–vocal format and is simply sketching notes. Resurgence of the piano–vocal format appears in folio 5v, written in pencil with the upper two staves crossed out. (Folio 6r is in both graphite pencil and black ink, 6v is blank, and 7r is devoted to working out 'staying to gaze ...' in black ink.)

In this draft of 'Menelaus' (ff. 7v–11r), Vaughan Williams omits both the text and the music to almost three complete lines of text ('terraces and staying to gaze/at the vines and iris beside the lake/in the morning').

The two remaining sources for 'Menelaus' in the British Library, the incomplete draft on ff. 15–18 and the complete draft with a typewritten copy of the poem (f. 21) on ff. 19–30, follow in their chronological order. Folios 15–19 present a rather rough form of the piece, and there are instances where Vaughan Williams sketches through certain measure (f. 16r, in particular). (A sketch for the Eighth Symphony appears in the middle of the draft [f. 17v].) Here he still retains the idea of the four-measure introduction. (Ff. 15–18 are on RC1 12-stave manuscript paper, but are not bound together in the same booklet with any other sketches or drafts.) This stage still resembles a sketch in many ways: the melody is not necessarily the same as the published version and the accompaniment is often sparse.

The remaining source for 'Menelaus' in this collection of manuscripts (ff. 19–30) is the one closest to the published version. It is a complete draft of the song with a typed title page (f. 20) and a typed copy of the poem (f. 21). On folio 23 Vaughan Williams has written 'Menelaus' in the centre of the top of the page, and in the upper left-hand corner 'for UVW' in black ink. The words '(for Keith Falkner)' are written in blue ink underneath the title, suggesting perhaps that this dedication was a later thought. In this draft he has sorted out the introduction, and the draft is written almost completely in black ink in piano–vocal score format with three blank staves between each set of three used staves. Vaughan Williams used graphite pencil, blue pencil, and a bit of blue ink to make corrections and annotations and omissions. In addition, he seems to have used a small knife – a penknife or, perhaps, a razor blade – to scratch out errors (ff. 25r and 25v).

   The extant draft in the Cornell University Music Library (Locked Press ++M1621.2V37, folder 2) is presumably the one Vaughan Williams brought as a present for Keith Falkner. It is the latest draft of the song, written entirely in black ink. A pencil is used in certain places to clarify specific notes, to add an accidental,

(a) BL Add. 65088

(b) BL Add. 65088 f. 31v

became:

which ends up as:
the published version

(c) BL Add. 65088 f 31v
1st sketch:

Example 8.1   'Menelaus' introductory measures (a–d)

2nd sketch:

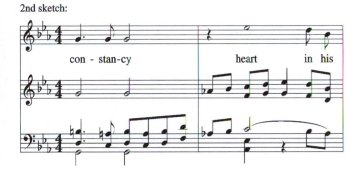

Published version, which is the same as the 2nd sketch:

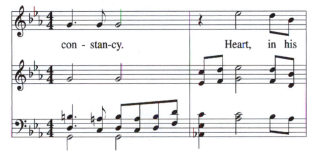

(d) BL ADD. 65088, f. 54v

Published version, measures 8-10

Example 8.1   (*continued*)

or to cross out the odd measure. Included in the same folder with the holograph draft of 'Menelaus' is a typewritten copy of the poem, one typescript recording schedule, and two handwritten leaves which are labeled as notes written by Keith Falkner. These miscellaneous papers are what make this source particularly interesting. This is the only song of the four for which there exists a draft of the text. Both typescript copies of the text, BL Add. MS 65088, f. 21 and the one in Locked Press ++M1621.2V37, folder 2 are slightly different than the published version of the poem. In both copies, the changes are minute, and in the version in the British Library's collection, the alterations are even less pronounced than in the one in the Cornell University Music Library. The draft in the British Library is virtually the same, with the exception of punctuation, line breaks, and the existence of one preposition and one article that do not exist in the published version. In the typescript copy held in the Cornell University Music Library, the changes involve, in addition to variations of punctuation and line breaks and the odd addition of an article here and there, actual alteration of the text. (For example, the fourth line in the published version reads 'at the vines and iris beside the lake', and in the draft at Cornell, this same line reads 'at the hills and vines and iris along the lake, in the morning haze', which is how the passage appears in the holograph draft. At this point in the published edition of the song, however, the line reads 'at the vines and reeds and iris beside the lake'. The published version of the music is as it appears in the Cornell draft.) This copy of the text is titled 'You Will Come Home', with the subtitle 'Proteus to Menelaus on the Beach at Pharos' typed underneath the text proper.

The three remaining articles in folder 2 (two handwritten and one typescript) have to do with broadcast performances of both 'Menelaus' and 'Hands, Eyes and Heart'. The handwritten pages include an explanation of two of the songs being sung and the text to 'Menelaus'. The former reads as follows:

Wasleys [?] Track
The next two songs were written by Dr and Mrs V.W. during their stay at Cornell University in 1954. The poems are by Ursula Wood Mrs Vaughan Williams a[nd] since this is the first broadcast performance in N.2 I would like to take the liberty of reading the words to you. The first is called Menelaus with a subtitle 'Proteus to Menelaus on the beach at Pharos'. The second [song] is called Hands Eyes [and] Heart. When Dr V.W. sent it to me he wrote' [the text ends here][17]

The subsequent recording schedule indicates that the pieces to be recorded were 'Let Beauty Awake', 'Menelaus', 'Hands, Eyes and Heart', 'The Vagabond', and 'Linden Lea', in that order. The schedule also indicates that the recording was supposed to take place on Friday, 21 December (1956) in the 'a' Studio.[18] There is a brief paragraph attached to the bottom of the schedule and reads as follows: 'No. 2 & 3. First broadcast performance in New Zealand. Both written for and given to Keith Falkner and Mrs Keith Falkner when Ralph Vaughan Williams was Visiting Lecturer at Cornell University 1954'.[19] The text goes on to state that it was the first performance anywhere for No. 3 (that is, 'Hands, Eyes and Heart'). It is not clear whether the handwritten memo by Falkner and the typescript recording schedule were meant to go together, but it is highly probable. The header to Falkner's text indicates a recording track, and the wording is much the same as in the recording schedule. This is the first instance of

'Menelaus' and 'Hands, Eyes and Heart' being sung together in a set; it is also the earliest example of 'Hands, Eyes and Heart' being sung publicly by a baritone.

'Hands, Eyes and Heart'

Hands, give him all the measure of my love
surer than any word.
Eyes, be deep pools of truth, where he may see
a thought more whole than constancy.
heart, in his keeping, be at rest and live
as music and silence meet and both are heard.

'Hands, Eyes and Heart' is part VI of 'Prologue', which was published in 1941 as part of *No Other Choice*, Ursula Vaughan Williams's first collection of poetry. There are five extant manuscript sources of this song: four in the British Library's manuscript collection (BL Add. MS 65088, ff. 31r–2r and ff. 33r–5v). At the top left middle of the second of these the query '?1956' is written in pencil, quite obviously not in Vaughan Williams's hand.[20] In the published edition of this song, this date, including the question mark, is printed underneath the title. As the letter from Vaughan Williams to Keith Falkner dated 7 March 1955 indicates, this song was composed earlier than 1956.[21] Indeed, Falkner claims, both in his text to accompany the recording session (printed above) as well as in his own copy of the published *Four Last Songs*, that 'Hands, Eyes and Heart' was written in 1954 while Vaughan Williams was still at Cornell.[22] The letter, however, was sent to Falkner from 10 Hanover Terrace, Vaughan Williams's address in London. (Of course, it is possible that Vaughan Williams set the text earlier, while he was at Cornell, and only thought to send it to Falkner after he had returned to England.)

Vaughan Williams was acutely aware of the poetry that he set, regardless of who wrote it, and many of the alterations that appear throughout the drafts of 'Hands, Eyes and Heart' can be connected in some way to the text, either through his interest in expression or his concern with the clarity of presentation. Because there are no extant sketches for this song, the changes that appear through the series of drafts are relatively small, falling into three basic categories: convenience for the performer, small harmonic changes, and changes in melodic direction.

The line that seemed to cause the most difficulty is that which corresponds to the text at the end of the second sentence of the poem, going on to the third (measures 10–13 in the published edition, 'a thought more whole than constancy/Heart, in his keeping be at rest'). This difficulty is particularly noticeable in the earliest extant draft of the song, BL Add. MS 65088, ff. 31r–2r. In this draft Vaughan Williams uses 12-stave manuscript paper and black ink. Only two sets of three lines (one for voice and two for piano) are used on the first folio of this draft (f. 31r), but he uses all 12 staves on the remaining two folios of this draft, often using a set of staves to rewrite a section of the song. This represents a working draft, and large sections are marked out, primarily with blue pencil, but occasionally with graphite pencil. In the section that corresponds to the printed measure 10 in the draft, Vaughan Williams altered the accompaniment so that the upper notes in the right hand double the vocal melody. This change clarified the vocal melody, making it more prominent, and made it easier for the performer to find his (or her) note (Example 8.1b). A similar occurrence is found further on in the draft in the measures that correspond to published measure 12. In the printed version, the accompaniment leads up to the E♭5 on which the voice enters to sing the word 'heart' (the highest note of the song, incidentally).[23] In two of the three sketches of this section that appear in the draft, the voice enters on that same note in the same place in the measure, but the accompaniment does not double the voice until one beat later. While refining this passage, Vaughan Williams evidently decided that this particular word in the text was of utmost importance and required greater clarity. The performer is better served by the printed version, which corresponds to the second sketch, as the top notes of the accompaniment lead up to the E♭5, rather than having the performer jump from the G4 to an E♭5 above without any accompanying support (Example 8.1c). This spot is compelling for a number of reasons. Vaughan Williams undoubtedly realized that this section was crucial place in the text (the beginning of the last couplet of the poem), and that 'heart' was the most important word in the poem.[24] In the published version, this word is articulated by being set to the highest note in the song, by the accompaniment leading up to the high E flat (C, D, then E♭), and by both the voice and the piano holding that note/chord for a full minim with no other movement. (In his working out of this measure in the draft, the accompaniment continues moving in quavers, then a crotchet, which is not as effective.)

The two remaining sources at the British Library (ff. 62–3 and 64–5) are fair copies of the song, copied by Gustav de Mauny.[25] In these manuscripts the song appears almost exactly as in the published version, with only occasional annotations by Vaughan Williams. These annotations, though, merely clarify a note or the prosody. The holograph draft at Cornell seems to fit chronologically between the two earliest extant drafts, mentioned above, and the two fair copies by de Mauny. This draft retains the descent from B3 to A3 in the left hand of the piano accompaniment in measure 2, as well as the C5 in measure 14 ('... lives ...'). These spots are not altered until the de Mauny fair copy.

'Tired'

Sleep, and I'll be still as another sleeper
holding you in my arms, glad that you lie
so near at last.
This sheltering midnight is our meeting place,
no passion or despair, or hope divide
me from your side.
I shall remember firelight on your sleeping face,
I shall remember shadows growing deeper
as the fire fell to ashes and the minutes passed.

The text for 'Tired' was originally published in 1943 as part of Ursula Vaughan Williams's collection of poetry entitled *Fall of Leaf*. Three manuscript sources for 'Tired' are available in the British Library: a sketch, a complete draft, and a fair copy prepared by Gustav de Mauny with annotations and revisions at least partly in Vaughan Williams's hand (BL Add. MS 65088, ff. 40–3v, 54–5v, and 66–7 respectively). The sketches and drafts for 'Tired' are bound together with those for 'Procris' in a 12-stave hard-paper manuscript book.

The British Library catalogue labels folios 40r–3v of Add. MS 65088 as a sketch of 'Tired'. However, included in these pages are three partial sketches for the song. The initial sketch (f. 40r) is in black ink, with a graphite pencil used to cross out various sections. This sketch contains 20 measures of both melody and partial accompaniment figures. The accompaniment is not written out in a consistent manner and includes only a two-measure introduction and a total of five other measures with accompaniment. In the second sketch (f. 42r), which is approximately fifteen measures in length, the composer had concerned himself solely with the vocal melody. The third sketch, which is slightly longer (24 measures, ff. 42v–3v), also consists primarily of the vocal melody. It does, however, include a one-measure piano introduction and a few chords and accompanimental figures.

The tonal center is consistent in the three sketches and in the portion of text with which Vaughan Williams is working. The changes that take place over the course of the sketches mainly deal with the choice of notes or note values in the vocal melody, but the key center is not altered.

A complete draft of the song appears in folios 54v–5v. This draft is 32 measures long, two measures longer than the published version. This draft is quite different from both the previous sketches and the final version. It begins in common time, then proceeds through 11 time-signature changes before the end of the piece. The published version only has six. In the final version of the song, the vocal melody remains clustered around D♭4, never moving higher than a fifth above (A♭) or a third below (B♭) for all but two measures of the piece. Only in those measures corresponding to the lines 'no passion or despair or hope/divide me from your side' does the melody extend beyond the usual range. Here, in a manner similar to 'Hands, Eyes and Heart', Vaughan Williams uses the highest note of the piece to articulate the climax of the text. He expands the range of the voice, and the D♭5, the highest note of the piece, is used to articulate 'despair'. The draft does not display this same concision and continuity. The tonal center is still D♭, but the vocal range is a bit wider (B♭3 to D♭5).

The earliest source, the sketch, is cast in piano–vocal format; the bottom two staves are not used at all with the exception of the first two measures. At this early stage, Vaughan Williams was primarily concerned with the vocal melody. There are four obvious differences between the sketch and draft: the setting of the text, the rhythm and melodic contour of the vocal line, the character of the accompaniment, and the tonal center.

With the exception of three instances, the text of 'Tired' is set syllabically. However, these instances (the words 'and', 'I'll' and 'near' from the first sentence of the poem), combined with the piano accompaniment, help define the nature of the song. In the draft, the fair copy, and in the published version, the alternating open fifths of the left hand create a static effect. The three words given melismas serve to retard the articulation of the text and to emphasize the crotchet rhythm of the fifths: this enhances the idea of stasis present in the text.

The revisions of the rhythm and contour of the melodic line fulfill three basic functions: to enhance the tonal center, to clarify melodic direction, and to emphasize the natural rhythm of the text. In this song Vaughan Williams establishes the tonal center of the song in the vocal line, more so than in the accompaniment. For Vaughan Williams, melody was clearly the most important aspect of a song. His accompaniments often function primarily to support the voice, then as atmospheric enhancement, and finally as a buttress for the tonal center. Rhythmic alterations were made to the melodic line in order to put emphasis on particular words, thus making a difference to the shade of meaning or the level of importance of the words that would be imparted to the listener. Take, for example, the melody that corresponds to the phrase 'glad that you lie/so near at last'. In the sketch (measures 9–11) and in the draft (measures 8–10) the words emphasized (by longer note values) are 'glad' and 'lie'. In the published version, this emphasis is altered slightly. 'Glad' remains, but 'lie' is articulated with merely a crotchet while 'near' gains greater emphasis as it is held for the duration of three beats (Example 8.1d). This, of course, creates a slight alteration in the reading of the text.

'Procris'

Procris is lying at the waterside,
the yellow flowers show spring, the grass is green,
before a gentle wind the thin trees lean
towards the rushes, the rushes to the tide.
She will not see
the green spring turn to summer, summer go
in a long golden dusk towards the snow,
with eyes so lit by love that everything
burned, flowed, grew, blossomed, moved on foot or wing
with the guessed rhythm of eternity.
All the hope and will
flowed from her unavailing
and she knew darkness, as her eyes know now
shut to the daylight, and despair prevailing
she saw no way to go.

The text for 'Procris' was originally published in 1943 in Ursula Vaughan Williams's collection of poetry entitled *Fall of Leaf*. As her note to Chapman indicates, her text was inspired by a painting in the National Gallery by Piero di Cosimo, *A Satyr mourning over a Nymph* (*c.* 1495). During an interview with Mrs Vaughan Williams (on 15 June 1995), I showed her a postcard reproduction of Piero's painting. She confirmed that it was indeed the painting that had inspired her. But she was unfamiliar with the title of the work and thought that perhaps it had been changed (possibly from *Procris*) in the years since she viewed the work. In the information provided by the National Gallery's Micro Gallery computer system, we are told that the subject of the painting could indeed be the death of Procris. Both the *Encyclopedia of World Art* and *The Dictionary of Art* list the title of the work as *Death of Procris* (see plate 5).[26]

The story of Procris is found in the seventh book of Ovid's *Metamorphoses* and in Book 3 of 'The Art of Love' in his *Erotic Poems*. By Ovid's account, Procris and Cephalus had an interesting (and occasionally interrupted) married life. After settling into domesticity, Cephalus would often go hunting, armed only with his javelin, a gift from his wife. When he grew tired, he would rest in the shade and call on the zephyrs that blew from the chill depths of the valleys. Someone overheard him, mistook 'zephyr' for a 'nymph' assumed Cephalus was having an affair, and immediately hurried to Procris to tell her of her husband's putative unfaithfulness. Distraught, Procris followed him the next day. Upon hearing his call, she realized the mistake that had been made and went running toward him to tell him. Cephalus, hearing the rustle in the bushes, mistook her for a wild animal and hurled his javelin. He struck Procris in the breast. Piero's painting depicts a pregnant Procris lying on the ground with her head cradled by a satyr and watched over by a mournful dog.[27]

There are four extant manuscript sources for 'Procris', all held in the British Library's collection of Vaughan Williams's manuscripts (BL Add. MS 65088, ff. 37–9v, 44–51v, 56–61v, and 68–70v). The latest, BL Add. MS 65088 ff. 68–70v is a fair copy made by Dame Elizabeth Maconchy in 1959 from Vaughan Williams's manuscript.[28]

'Procris' was the last poem set by Vaughan Williams, even though it appears first in the published score. The earliest manuscript source for this song is a holograph sketch, and it is found in a hard-paper 12-stave manuscript music book with sketches and drafts of 'Tired', as well as an additional draft of 'Procris'. The initial sketch in black ink is virtually illegible, but it seems that, as with 'Tired', Vaughan Williams began working by concentrating on the vocal melody, adding only the occasional harmonic and accompanimental figures. Also like 'Tired', the changes made between the sketches, drafts and the published version reflect Vaughan Williams's preoccupation with the melodic line as well as his concern about an expressive rendering of the text. An instance of the composer's care for correct prosody is found in his setting of the first two lines of text. In the final version, the first line is articulated by a stepwise descent from B♭4 above to C4, with the exception of two notes that are used to set the two syllables of the word 'lying'. This initial vocal descent sets the mood of the song and suggests that Procris is not merely 'lying' (that is, resting) at the waterside, but is in fact lying dead at the waterside. Vaughan Williams cleverly begins and ends this line with the descending stepwise articulation of a minor third. (The notes corresponding to the word 'lying' outline the initial minor third.) While the sketch of the vocal line beginning on folio 39v shows a general descent, the outlying minor thirds are not present, and the descent is not as dramatic (the sketch descends from a B♭ to an F, or possibly an E, while the later version, as stated above, descends from the B♭4 above to the C4 below). His treatment of the second line of text and its corresponding stages of revision is much the same. The second line, rather than reflecting death, represents life with a gentle irony ('the yellow flowers show spring, the grass is green'). Consequently, the final setting of this line is almost a mirror image of the previous line, ascending from the lowest notes of the line to the highest. The initial sketch of this section, like the sketch of this first line, is not as effective and does not exhibit the melodic cohesiveness as the final version.

These four songs, composed toward the end of a long and fruitful career, are indicative of the many and varied aspects of the composer's life. Vaughan Williams grew up in a household that was fond of reading in general, and reading aloud in particular. His childhood books included those by Thackeray, Ruskin, de la Motte Fouquet, Lamb and Grimm, and the family spent the evenings of long winters reading aloud from Scott, Shakespeare, Henty and Ballantyne.[29] The composer continued the practice of reading aloud for the rest of his life, and it seems quite appropriate that the idea for Ursula Vaughan Williams's poem 'Menelaus' was sparked by each reading from Homer.

Early premières of many of Vaughan Williams's large-scale works took place in semi-private settings (for example, Michael Mullinar's play-throughs of various drafts of Vaughan Williams's symphonies for an audience of twenty). This common practice of Vaughan Williams's compositional life also occurred in the case of the *Four Last Songs*. 'Menelaus', in manuscript draft, was first performed in a semi-private setting at the 'words and music' recital at Cornell mentioned above.

Throughout his life Vaughan Williams collaborated with a variety of contemporary poets and writers, yet none were as successful, either personally or professionally, as his collaboration with his wife Ursula. Ursula Vaughan Williams was a professional poet who was used to writing words for music. She did not share A.E. Housman's pained and indignant aversion to the omission of lines that were found to be unsuitable, nor was she surprised or offended by the idea of a composer amending or altering words to suit his or her purpose. Indeed, she explains in her article 'Writing for Musicians' that when writing words for music, music invariably comes first.[30] As it happens, Vaughan Williams did not cut, alter, or amend any of the poems discussed above.[31]

In addition to Mrs Vaughan Williams's willingness to allow the music to come before her words, the success of the collaboration was due to other aspects of her work. The classical subject matter of 'Procris' and 'Menelaus' appealed to a composer trained in the classics, for he spent years at Charterhouse studying Latin, Greek and the stories of the ancient writers. The symbolism of 'Menelaus' in particular did not escape his notice. This is made obvious by the dedication to Keith Falkner, a friend who was at the time residing in the United States – not at home in England.[32] With this in mind, it is possible to infer a similar meaning in his initial dedication to his wife. When they wrote this work (she the poem, he the music), they had barely been married a year after an intimate friendship of some twenty years' duration. Perhaps he viewed the marriage as a 'coming home', that is, a natural progression of their friendship, yet something different from the relationship they had experienced previously ('not to the home you know ...').

In addition to the personal elements, there are other aspects of Ursula Vaughan Williams's poetry that contribute to the success of these songs. Her adherence to clear formal structures and her vivid language make the poems easy to articulate musically, a quality that Vaughan Williams failed to find in certain works of other contemporary poets. Take, for example, the *Four Poems of Fredegond Shove*. He found these hermetic poems incredibly difficult to set, primarily because they did not possess any of the elements mentioned above.[33]

His collaborations with Harold Child on *Hugh the Drover* and with Evelyn Sharp on *The Poisoned Kiss* were equally difficult. Both Child and Sharp were professional journalists and critics, but neither had written a libretto before and were unused to writing words that would be articulated in a musical setting; they were unprepared for the idea of the primary importance of the music, rather than the text.[34] In *The Poisoned Kiss* there was the additional problem that the libretto ended up being a different kind of story than the composer wanted or expected.[35]

We may never know, precisely, whether or not the *Four Last Songs* are indeed fragments of two projected song cycles, with 'Procris' and 'Menelaus' included in one cycle and 'Tired' and 'Hands, Eyes and Heart' in another, as suggested by Mrs Vaughan Williams. The existing evidence, presented here, provides an alternative view of the composer's intentions. His letter to Falkner suggests strongly that 'Menelaus' and 'Hands, Eyes and Heart' were meant to be performed together. The inclusion of a sketch of an unidentified song in the manuscript notebook with 'Menelaus' (BL Add. MS 65088, ff. 12v–13) and the inclusion of the incomplete draft of a setting of 'The Romantic' in another manuscript notebook, combined with 'Procris' and 'Tired' (BL Add. MS 65088, ff. 36–53) suggests other possibilities. 'The Romantic', as the title appears in black ink on the top middle of folio 52r, is part II of 'Valentines', a poem that is, along with 'Procris' and 'Tired', included in *Fall of Leaf*. This evidence allows for the distinct possibility that Vaughan Williams was working on a cycle of songs from that collection.

Setting aside the questions that arise from such contradictory evidence, it is perhaps more important to regard this group of songs as the synthesis of literature, poetry, visual art, and music that informs and enriches so many of Vaughan Williams's works.

Acknowledgements

I would like to thank the Carthusian Trust for their support during this project and Mrs Vaughan Williams for the information she provided, the permission she gave to quote from various letters, poems, and manuscripts, and for her unending kindness. I would also like to thank Byron Adams for pointing out the existence of the material at Cornell University to me, and also the Sydney T. Cox Library of Music and Dance, Cornell University Library for permission to publish from this material.

Notes

1　Michael Kennedy, *Works of Ralph Vaughan Williams* (Oxford: Oxford University Press, 1964), 368.

2　James Day, *Vaughan Williams* (Oxford: Oxford University Press, 1998), 117.

3　Here I am paraphrasing from letters that appear in BL Add. MS 62949 ff. 191 and 193. I omit material that is not pertinent to my argument. At the present time I have been unable to obtain permission from the Chapman Estate to publish these letters.

4　Ibid. ff. 194.

5　Ibid. ff. 195. The pencil markings on the typed programme note indicate that the order of the songs as they would presumably be sung on the night was the following: 1. Menelaus, 2. Tired, 3. Procris (the chronological order of composition, incidentally). These markings also indicate that the last sentence should appear directly after the first, with the words 'of them' replacing 'the songs'. It is unclear as to whose marks these are. Most likely these were editorial marks used for the printing of the programme.

6　See, for example, Kennedy *A catalogue of the works of Ralph Vaughan Williams* (Oxford: Oxford University Press, 1982), 233–4 and 254, and Day, *Vaughan Williams*, 116, in particular the passage beginning 'Towards the end of his life...'.

7   Ursula Vaughan Williams, *R.V.W.: A Biography of Ralph Vaughan Williams* (Oxford: Oxford University Press, 1982), 354.

8   This letter is enclosed in the Locked Press ++M1621.2V37 in the Music Library of Cornell University. In the letter, which is typescript, Vaughan William's pen indicated that the last sentence should appear at the end of the previous paragraph.

9   Kennedy, 227. The BBC has a record of Keith Falkner recording songs of Vaughan Williams on 17 July 1955, but unfortunately, the specific songs are not listed. I would like to thank Ms Susan Knowles, Senior Document Assistant at the BBC Written Archives Centre for her assistance and for answering my queries.

10   In fact, in so far as I can ascertain, Vaughan Williams himself never indicates otherwise. Of course, it is possible that he discussed a change verbally and never put it in writing. It is also possible that a change was put in writing and is either not available or no longer exists.

11   In the following discussion, it might prove helpful if the reader has access to the published score of *Four Last Songs*.

12   Mrs Vaughan Williams has published under the names Ursula Wood and Ursula Vaughan Williams. For the sake of clarity, I will always refer to her as Ursula Vaughan Williams even though *No Other Choice*, *Fall of Leaf*, and *Silence and Music*, the collections discussed here, were all originally published under the name Ursula Wood. In 1996 there were all reprinted in a complete edition of her poetry under the name Ursula Vaughan Williams.

13   See above.

14   Ursula Vaughan Williams, ibid., 354.

15   Quoted in ibid., 354, and comes from Book Four of T.E. Lawrence's translation of *The Odyssey*, 48. In Lawrence's translation, there is a full stop after 'souls of men', and 'There you will have Helen ...' begins a new sentence.

16   Roy Douglas, *Working with Vaughan Williams* (London: British Library, 1988).

17   Cornell University Music Library Locked Press ++M1621.2V37, folder 2.

18   This is the schedule for the first performance mentioned in Kennedy's *Catalogue*.

19   Ibid. The date given to the songs is rather misleading. It suggests that both 'Menelaus' and 'Hands, Eyes and Heart' were composed in 1954. However, the letter printed earlier in this essay from Vaughan Williams to Falkner indicates that 'Hands, Eyes and Heart' was composed later than 'Menelaus', that is to say, perhaps 1955. It is possible, however, that it was composed in 1954, and Vaughan Williams did not get around to sending it to Falkner until 1955.

20   This is perhaps Ursula Vaughan Williams's handwriting.

21   This is also noted by Kennedy, *Catalogue*, 1982, 242.

22   Falkner, in his own copy of the published set which is now part of Cornell University Music Library Locked Press ++M1621.2V37, crossed out the date 1956 which is printed, and wrote 1954.

23   I am using the Helmholtz system of octave position identification. Middle C = C4.

24   The poem consists of three sentences, each of which begins with the name of a part of the human body. The order that they appear in the text, hands, eyes and heart, is seemingly mentioned in the order of least to most important, both to life as well as to romantic love. That is to say, it is possible to live without hands and eyes, but not possible to live without a heart. In addition, the hands and eyes can be seen to be on opposite sides of the heart, or, to express it another way, as surrounding the heart (acting as a buttress, giving it support). Thus the hands and eyes would encompass the central feature of both the physical body as well as love: the heart being the center of life as well as the center of a person's thought or emotions, in particular love and/or compassion.

25   We know this because de Mauny has signed both copies at the end of each setting and the handwriting is the same as that which appears above it.

26   Chiarini p.355 and Griswold, 770.
27   In Ovid's account, Procris is not pregnant, nor is her head cradled by a satyr, nor is she guarded by a dog. However, according to the *Oxford Classical Dictionary*, these details are completely in keeping with the Procris myth. The dog is presumably Laelaps, given to her by the goddess Diana, or it could be the dog given to her by Minos of Crete. Also, dogs were often used to guide souls from one world to the next, so its appearance here could be, in part, to serve that purpose. Griswold explains the presence of the satyr as indicative that Piero's work was inspired more directly by Niccolò da Correggia's *Fabula di Caephalo* rather than Ovid's account (770). This may, in fact, be the case, but the painting reminded Mrs Vaughan Williams of Ovid's rendering of the tale, as she explained in her interview.
28   At the end of the copy, Maconchy has written 'copy made from R.V.W.'s Ms. Feb. 1959', then she signed 'Elizabeth Maconchy'.
29   Ursula Vaughan Williams, *R.V.W.*, ibid., 20.
30   Ursula Vaughan Williams, *R.V.W.*, ibid., 6.
31   As I mentioned earlier, there are two typescript copies of the text of 'Menelaus' that are slightly different from the published version. It is not clear, however, whether the small changes that were made were instigated by the composer or whether they were simply natural changes made by the author during her own writing and editing process.
32   Ursula Vaughan Williams, *R.V.W.*, ibid.
33   Both Kennedy, *Works*, 1964 and Day, *Vaughan Williams* claim that since Fredegond Shove was his first wife's niece, Vaughan Williams may have felt prompted by family loyalty to set them.
34   This is alluded to both by Mrs Vaughan Williams and James Day in their biographies of the composer.
35   Ursula Vaughan Williams, *R.V.W.*, ibid., 209.

Chapter 9

'Words and music that are forever England': *The Pilgrim's Progress* and the pitfalls of nostalgia

Nathaniel G. Lew

On 8 March 1877 the children of George MacDonald, the Scottish Nonconformist minister famous for his children's books, gave the first public performance of their family's dramatic production of John Bunyan's Puritan allegory *The Pilgrim's Progress*.[1] Almost three-quarters of a century later, on Thursday 26 April 1951, a distinguished audience containing numerous prominent clergymen from both the Established and Nonconformist Churches attended the première of the opera *The Pilgrim's Progress* by the 78-year-old Ralph Vaughan Williams, then regarded as the dean of English composers. No one in the Covent Garden audience that evening is likely to have remembered the MacDonald family's amateur theatricals, nor to have made a connection between that production and the spectacle unfolding before their eyes, yet not only a chain of circumstances but a profound sympathy of spirit exists between the High Victorian devotional–pedagogical exercise and the postwar opera performed to usher in the Festival of Britain 1951, a festival season thoroughly modern in design and orientation.

We know little about the MacDonalds' *Pilgrim's Progress*. Bunyan's book was one of George MacDonald's favorites; it is widely cited as an influence on his works. In the early or mid-1870s his wife Louisa prepared a dramatic adaptation of Part Two of the book for private performance at the family's Hammersmith home. After settling in Italy in 1877, the large family financed their summer trips back to England by touring with the production as a family acting troupe (Wolff, 1961, 111). These very successful annual tours lasted until 1887. A young woman, later Mrs Walter Ouless, attended one of the performances and the memory of the event stayed with her. Decades later she persuaded her daughter Evelyn to suggest to a friend, Joanna Hadley, who managed theatrical entertainments in Reigate, Surrey, that the Bunyan text might serve as the source for a community project.[2] In 1905 or 1906, as the plans for the production developed, Hadley invited Lucy Broadwood, the folk-song collector and editor, who had local ties, to provide the incidental music. Broadwood declined but suggested instead her neighbor, the 32-year-old Ralph Vaughan Williams, who was just beginning to gain renown as a composer.

The Reigate *Pilgrim's Progress* was to prove as profoundly influential on Vaughan Williams's imagination as Louisa MacDonald's production had been on Mrs Ouless's. Indeed it was even more influential, for out of this initial stimulus were to arise a series of three other major dramatic works: the 'pastoral episode' *The*

Shepherds of the Delectable Mountains of 1922, the incidental music for Edward Sackville-West's BBC radio version of *The Pilgrim's Progress* of 1942, and the full-length opera, or 'morality', of 1951 (as well, indirectly, as the Fifth Symphony of 1943). Although none of these Bunyan-related dramatic works has achieved a permanent place in the repertory, they span a 45-year period covering the middle of Vaughan Williams's career.

Vaughan Williams's periodic returns to this subject demonstrate both its importance to him and its congruity with certain of his musical aims: he retained certain elements from work to work despite changing times and performance opportunities and even as his own musical and aesthetic ideals varied. His compulsion to revisit Bunyan's text also suggests that it was an important link in a strong attachment that Vaughan Williams felt to his personal and cultural past. As a result the 1951 opera has a double significance. It is his final and grandest operatic statement, the culmination and consummation both of his operatic ambitions and of his life-long fascination with Bunyan's text. The score draws together themes from much of his career and provides a synopsis of his musical concerns. But at the same time it is an exercise in nostalgia, an attempt to preserve or recreate an earlier work from an earlier period of his life. The work memorializes both a specific musical and theatrical past and vanishing aestheticizations of religious and national expression.

Bunyan's book was an obvious choice for a company seeking a suitable basis for a religious dramatic production, because the book has a unique place in the English literary canon. The Baptist preacher John Bunyan (1628–88) produced the first part of his most famous work, *The Pilgrim's Progress from This world to That which is to come Delivered under the Similitude of a Dream*, while serving a 12-year jail term during the Restoration due to his public preaching of his Puritan religious beliefs. The book was published in 1678, after Bunyan's release, and a second part appeared in 1684. Immediately upon its publication *The Pilgrim's Progress* attracted enormous and lasting popularity with a wide audience (see Owens, 1990). As the book entered the literary canon Bunyan's central images insinuated themselves into the consciousness of the English reading public, where they evoked a more general Englishness, both religious and cultural, than Bunyan probably intended. Although sharply critical of the formalism of the Anglican Church, the book was adopted (at least by the laity) as a key to the simpler side of the Christian faith and became universal childhood reading (Chadwick, 1970, 467). Even to nineteenth-century readers with little sympathy for a narrative of salvation and the triumph over sin the book offered a nostalgic picture of English country life of the seventeenth century and was an accessible literary link to the tradition of religiosity which so many otherwise secular Britons (still) hold dear.

Part One of the book, on which the Reigate production was based, has a more focused and intense narrative than Part Two, and limits the number of central relationships to two. In it the protagonist, Christian, sets out for the Celestial City alone and, although heavenly messengers and guides aid him along the way, he proceeds alone until, after battle with the demon Apollyon and passage through the Valleys of Humiliation and the Shadow of Death, he at last overtakes another pilgrim, Faithful. Their friendship, though brief, forms the central relationship of the book. In light of their affection and support for one another, their trial at Vanity Fair and Faithful's martyrdom are truly climactic events. Commentators have pointed out that the literal death of Faithful violates the allegory (Nellist, 1980) but perhaps for this very reason the sequence leading up to this point is the most novelistic and dramatic. By contrast Christian's relationship with his second companion, Hopeful, who accompanies Christian for longer than Faithful, doesn't achieve quite the same intensity. But the quick replacement of Faithful with Hopeful reveals Bunyan's decision to maintain at the center of the narrative a pair of travelers who reveal their personalities through their conversations, disagreements, and support for one another in adversity.

Because Evelyn Ouless's name alone appears on the version of the script published after the successful run (Ouless, n.d.),[3] it appears that she took the lead in adapting Bunyan's text for the Reigate production. She created an elaborate entertainment with a plan of twelve scenes (see Table 9.1) and more than forty

Table 9.1   Order of scenes in the Reigate *Pilgrim's Progress*

Prologue	Bunyan in prison
Scene I	Christian sets out from the City of Destruction
Scene II	The Wicket Gate (*tableau*)
Scene III	Christian losing his burden at the Cross (*tableau*)
Scene IV	The House Beautiful: Piety, Prudence and Charity arming Christian (*tableau*)
Scene V	Christian meets Apollyon in the Valley of Humiliation. [This sequence added for the 1907 Imperial Theatre and 1908 Lincoln's Inn performances.] Christian meets Faithful. Evangelist's Warning to Christian and Faithful
Scene VI	Vanity Fair
Scene VII	Faithful at the Stake (*tableau*)
	[Interval]
Scene VIII	Christian and Hopeful meet Mr By-Ends and the Shepherds of the Delectable Mountains
Scene IX	The River of Death (*tableau*)
Scene X	The Celestial City (*tableau*)
Epilogue	Bunyan in prison

Source: adapted from BL Add. MS 70935.

characters (allowing for extensive doubling of roles). The framing prologue and epilogue for Bunyan himself, their texts drawn largely from 'The Author's Apology for his Book', parallel, at least at the margins, the authorial voice which constantly intrudes upon the book's narrative ('Then I saw in my dream ...') and lend the proceedings gravity, reminding the viewer with the words of the author himself (and those from prison) that the story is not just a good adventure tale but a profound moral lesson.

Ouless's script fundamentally restructures Bunyan's narrative. The early part of the book, Christian's preparation for the pilgrimage, is well represented in the first four scenes. But the elimination of the trials that Christian undergoes between these scenes in the book – his initial doubts and fears and the celebrated Slough of Despond – renders this preparatory stage more unified and heroic than it is in Bunyan. The picaresque events of the pilgrimage are then represented by three scenes depicting the set of episodes surrounding the figure of Faithful, from Christian's fight with Apollyon to Faithful's martyrdom at Vanity Fair. This section of the book is particularly apt for dramatic treatment. It contains an exciting battle and a crowd scene, maintains a continuity of character which is lacking in the work as a whole, and it is centered on a relationship which allows for dialogue and character development.

A single scene then combines a number of other elements of the book: Hopeful is introduced, a single representative 'unworthy pilgrim' (Mr By-Ends) provides a comic interlude, and the pilgrims arrive at the outskirts of their final destination. The significance of this last part of the scene, the Shepherds of the Delectable Mountains, is different from that of the equivalent scene in the book. The simplification of the end of the story parallels that of the beginning: in the script the arrival at the Delectable Mountains effectively marks the end of the pilgrimage, just as the House Beautiful served as the final preparation for pilgrimage. In the book, by contrast, Christian has a number of significant adventures and reverses before arriving at the House Beautiful, and the Delectable Mountains are only a temporary point of rest from which one may gain the first glimpse of salvation. Ouless's shepherds inform Christian and Hopeful of the territory that they must still cross but we see nothing except the crossing of the River of Death and triumphal entry into the Celestial City.

Undoubtedly the full panoply of Bunyan's multifarious allegorical characters and situations could never be adequately portrayed on the stage – at least not in a single evening's entertainment. The Reigate script represents a successful compression of *The Pilgrim's Progress* down to a reasonable length but this compression profoundly changes the work's tone. This streamlined version, imposing formal clarity on Bunyan's deliberately picaresque and at times chaotic plot, gives a very different picture of the path to salvation, making it easier and more direct. Similarly the elimination of most of the unworthy pilgrims with their various flaws encourages a more sanguine outlook on the chances of salvation. These changes can be attributed to the different conventions that governed the Edwardian stage as compared with the Puritan religious allegory but they also reflect the more self-congratulatory side of late Victorian Christianity, the tendency to de-emphasize the ideas of judgement and damnation in favor of the positive messages of self-improvement and salvation (Davies, 1962, 290ff.).

This change in aesthetic was further intensified by what we can recover of the staging techniques used in the production. Of the twelve scenes half are *tableaux vivants*. Although tableaux are as old as the theatre itself, *tableaux vivants* became a favorite theatrical device in the nineteenth century, often used for large-scale public events. Since the actors did not have to memorize and recite lines – or even move much – this style permitted the use of amateurs with limited acting ability and the inclusion of a great many people. It was therefore well suited to a community theatrical project such as the Reigate *Pilgrim's Progress*. If followed literally, however, the text allowed a very limited application of *tableaux*, at least of the grand variety. Bunyan's text contains no crowd scenes other than Vanity Fair. At the House Beautiful, according to Bunyan, Christian meets only five people in all and at the very end there are only vague references to the Host of Heaven, men with harps, and 'winged ones' who call out acclamations. At other points, when Christian receives aid from heavenly beings, they tend to arrive alone or in small groups. The importing of the *tableau* technique necessarily shifts Bunyan's homely tale on to a more formal plane. When, as in Ouless's play, we see three maidens presenting shield, sword and breastplate to a Christian frozen in a properly reverential attitude, all accompanied by the singing of an invisible choir, the House Beautiful easily loses its identity as a roadside way-station for travelers – a sort of blessèd public house – and becomes a solemn abode of heavenly beings. Such a retreat towards the safely otherworldly fits the Victorian squeamishness about the earthier elements of Bunyan's story. (Forrest and Greaves, 1982, lists numerous Victorian bowdlerizations of Bunyan in which the rougher elements, considered inappropriate for children or ladies, were eliminated.[4])

Vaughan Williams had little say in the overall dramatic structure of the work although he made a number of crucial smaller suggestions. Nonetheless details of the script and tone of the Reigate production made a great impression on him and turn up again in his later Bunyan works. Among these was the most significant change made when the production transferred to London: the addition of the battle with the demon Apollyon. Ouless and Hadley devised a highly stylized way of representing this climactic sequence. The script (in BL Add. MS 70936) reads:

CHRISTIAN (drawing his sword) Apollyon, beware of what you do; for I am in the King's highway, the way of holiness, therefore take heed of yourself!

APOLLYON I am void of fear in this matter. Prepare thyself to die, for I swear by my infernal den that thou shalt go no farther. Here will I spill thy soul!

MUSIC As they rush upon each other, there is total darkness. Clashing of Xtian [*sic*] and Apollyon's weapons is heard.

APOLLYON I am sure of thee now.
Christian groans. A shaft of dim light shows. TABLEAU: APOLLYON lifting his spear to strike CHRISTIAN, who has sunk on one knee. CHRISTIAN's sword lies on ground. Total darkness again. Clashing of Xtian and Apollyon's weapons and CHRISTIAN's voice is heard crying out in the darkness:

CHRISTIAN Rejoice not against me, O mine enemy. When I fall, I shall arise.
Shaft of dim red light once more falls upon CHRISTIAN and APOLLYON. TABLEAU: CHRISTIAN in the attitude of picking up his sword, lifts it up over his head ready to strike APOLLYON. APOLLYON draws back and retreats into the darkness and disappears. CHRISTIAN sinks down – resting.

In an elaboration of the *tableau vivant* concept each of the two blackouts interrupting the scene 'catches' a visually striking and highly dramatic moment, the spectators' imagination supplying the gaps in the encounter. The blackouts obviate the need for an elaborately choreographed battle scene, which, given the inexperience of some of the performers, might have been unsatisfactory.[5]

Vaughan Williams's contribution to the production was modest but concentrated on the most effective moments for music. In addition to several members of the cast who could sing, Vaughan Williams had at his disposal a choir and a small string orchestra made up largely of amateurs. (The local parish church choir sang in Reigate, and the Southwark Cathedral choir sang at the London performances.) Much of the musical score can be assembled from surviving documents, which include a note on the music's sources that Vaughan Williams wrote for the programme: fifteen numbers either survive in manuscript or are referred to unambiguously. These are listed in Table 9.2.[6]

The use of the hymn 'York' at the opening and close of the play (nos. 1 and 15), where Bunyan himself appears in prison, creates an association with the author and the dramatic frame appropriate to the tune's genuine seventeenth-century Calvinist pedigree: it is a metrical psalm tune from Hart's Scottish Psalter of 1615 and was associated with the Roundheads during the Civil War (Kennedy 1980, 353). Vaughan Williams also exploits the *gravitas* of the tune's solemn half notes for the climactic scene of Pilgrim's entry into the Celestial City (no. 14), one of only two substantial original composed sections of the score. It begins with rustling arpeggios building up from the lower strings which, when they reach the top of the violins, are interrupted by several choral outbursts of 'Holy, holy, holy is the Lord'.[7] The strings then play the hymn, preceding each phrase with several more bars of the rustling arpeggios, while the chorus chant 'Holy, holy, holy is the Lord' in descant to the tune, and then the rustling and the choral interjections fade away. After a contrasting passage based on different material, discussed below, this entire first section is recapitulated. Vaughan Williams later used this movement as the model for the choral finales of both the 1942 radio incidental music and the 1951 opera.

The hymn 'Monks Gate' was one of Vaughan Williams's original additions to *The English Hymnal*, adapted from the folk-song 'Our Captain calls' to fit an altered version of Mr Valiant-for-Truth's song from Part Two of *The Pilgrim's Progress*, 'Who would true valour see' (Bunyan, 1984, 247; Kennedy, 1980, 75). Vaughan Williams himself suggested that 'Monks Gate' be used in the play, where it is associated with Christian in his capacity as a warrior for God. It is first sung (to Bunyan's original words) when he is armed at the House Beautiful (no. 5). When he enters in the next scene (no. 6) the strings begin the tune but break off hesitantly when Apollyon challenges Christian. The music to the battle scene (no. 7) mirrors its stops and starts – the blackouts devised by Ouless and Hadley. The substance of the music is thin, consisting of repetitions of two melodic motives in octaves or parallel first- and second-inversion triads often with either the upper or lower strings maintaining a *tremolando* pedal E. At the two blackouts where Apollyon appears to be overpowering Christian the upper strings drop out suddenly, leaving the cellos and basses rumbling away on their 'infernal' *tremolo* for a whole measure marked with a fermata. Finally, at the conclusion of the battle, to mark Christian's victory the lower strings drop out and the violins have the now 'celestial' *tremolo*. Upon the successful conclusion of the battle the entire band plays 'Monks Gate' triumphantly but evades the final cadence, continuing the melodic line down through several bars and into a modulation which prepares the song of the Angel who heals the wounded hero (no. 8).

This Angel's Song, which served as the model for the opening pages of *The Shepherds of the Delectable Mountains*, is the best crafted movement in the score, revealing Vaughan Williams's talent for modal harmonization and sensitive writing for strings. The Angel was an innovation of Ouless's, with no source in Bunyan. In

Table 9.2   Musical numbers from the Reigate *Pilgrim's Progress*

	Siglum in Kennedy (1996)	
1.	1906–5a	Prelude, based on the hymn 'York': three verses with different harmonizations arranged for strings.
2.		Opening dance, based on the folk-songs 'Sellinger's Round' and 'Lost Lady': a straightforward presentation of the two tunes with repeats *ad libitum*. Only a piano score survives but this was played by strings.
3.		Flower Girl's song. No score survives but Vaughan Williams's programme note identifies this as the unaccompanied folk-song ''Tis young men and maidens all' from 'English Country Songs'.
4.		Entry of Christian: a lost movement (presumably for strings) based on Thomas Tallis's 'Third Mode Melody'. (See discussion in text.)
5.	1906–5b	The Arming of Christian: the hymn 'Monks Gate' with Bunyan's original words, not the version used in *The English Hymnal*, arranged for chorus and strings.
6.	1906–5c	Apollyon: entrance of Christian: a very brief movement for strings (12 measures) consisting of a simple tune and a fragment of 'Monks Gate'.
7.	1906–5d	Christian and Apollyon fight: a short movement for strings based on the melody in no. 6 and 'Monks Gate' which segues into ...
8.	(1906–5d)	The Angel's song, 'Whoso dwelleth under the defence of the Most High', for alto and strings, marked 'very quietly and impersonally'. The text is composed of verses from Psalm 91.
9.	1906–5e	Vanity Fair: men's quartet: an arrangement of the folk-song 'Down among the deadmen' for four unaccompanied male voices. This item was published in 1912 (Kennedy, 1996, 59).
10.		Vanity Fair: Strolling musician's song: a folk ballad about Robin Hood, changed in later performances to a love song. There is nothing in the performance materials that identifies the song(s) used.
11.		Vanity Fair: End of scene: a very brief and simple movement (13 measures) for strings.
12.	1906–5f	Death of Faithful, based on an anthem by Farrant, arranged for chorus and strings.
13.		Shepherd's song. The text is a metrical version of Psalm 23 and Vaughan Williams identifies the tune as a Northumbrian folk-song. A piano accompaniment survives but Vaughan Williams's notes make it clear that this was for rehearsal only and that the song was to be unaccompanied. (Ouless's original script had called for the use of Bunyan's 'He that is down need fear no fall' at this moment but Vaughan Williams in a letter suggested the use of 'a real folk-song' [BL Add. MS 70935].)
14.	1906–5g	Final chorus: a movement for soloists, chorus and strings, based on 'York', a harmonized psalm tone, and Tallis's 'Third Mode Melody'. The text consists of 'Holy is the Lord', two biblical verses drawn from Bunyan, and alleluias.
15.	1906–5h	Epilogue: one verse of 'York' arranged for strings.

Source: adapted from BL Add. MSS 70934–36 and 50418 A.

the earliest script it had no text but at some point the collaborators decided to use a singer in the role. Vaughan Williams's first letter to Hadley requests 'a few words – just a sentence or two for the singing of the Angel – something that can be repeated often, like "alleluia"' (BL Add. MS 70935). Bunyan's text contains a number of songs, almost all of which are sung by the pilgrims themselves. Instead of using one of these, however, the Reigate collaborators chose to insert verses from Psalm 91, establishing an important precedent for Vaughan Williams's later Bunyan adaptations. It is a curious decision because, although Bunyan himself incorporates phrases from the Psalms into his narrative, he never once places a substantial excerpt from that book of the Bible in the mouth of one of his characters.

In his note in the programme, between the comments on the Flower Girl's song (no. 3) and the Arming of Christian (no. 5), Vaughan Williams writes 'The entry of Christian is founded on a melody of Tallis (1515–85).' The movement in the score headed 'Apollyon: Entrance of Christian' (no. 6) cannot correspond to Vaughan Williams's note: it is thin in melodic content, using only a few bars of a rather uninteresting tune apart from some colouristic devices and a fragment of 'Monks Gate'. There is, however, a cue for music in the script at the moment when Christian enters at the Wicket Gate. This could correspond to the movement described in the programme note – it comes between the other two movements mentioned – but no such movement survives in the score. Foraud (1975) notes this discrepancy and surmises that there was an additional 'Entry of Christian' movement based on a Tallis tune, now lost (no. 4). Based on the memories related to her by participants in the production, Foraud concludes that the melody in question was the Third Mode Melody from Archbishop Parker's *Psalter*, the theme of Vaughan Williams's 1910 *Fantasia on a Theme of Thomas Tallis*. She reports that during the rehearsal period, 'One memorable occasion was the first time [Vaughan Williams] played the Tallis melody to [the Hadleys and their London friends].'

Despite the lack of documentary evidence, Foraud's conclusion seems likely. Tallis's Third Mode Melody was certainly in Vaughan Williams's ear while he was writing the Reigate score, for he adapted it in the central section of the final chorus. A baritone solo chants a verse drawn from Bunyan to a rhythmicized psalm tone, echoed by the chorus in full harmony. Then a solo soprano chants another biblical verse, answered by a threefold alleluia. Although Kennedy (1996, 36) claims that the alleluias derive from those in Vaughan Williams's hymn 'Sine Nomine', they bear no resemblance to that melody. In fact the soprano solo and alleluias are a conspectus of the last three phrases of Tallis's Third Mode Melody. The rhythm is altered to fit the new text and one chord progression is condensed with the vocal lines interchanged but almost every harmonic detail derives from the Tallis hymn. This partial use of Tallis's melody at the end of the work makes more credible the conjecture that an earlier instrumental movement employed the melody more fully. There would then be a parallel with the dramatic return of 'York' and 'Monks Gate'.

If Vaughan Williams went beyond simple statements of the Tallis melody in the proposed lost movement and developed its motivic material, the exercise may have sparked his interest in composing a longer work. The absence among the Reigate manuscripts of such a movement could then be significant: setting to work on the *Tallis Fantasia* Vaughan Williams may have separated the movement from the rest of the Reigate score. This is precisely what happened later with the Angel's Song. In a 14 August 1921 letter preserved in BL Add. MS 70935, Vaughan Williams asks Hadley to send him the score of the Angel's Song; he was setting to work on *The Shepherds of the Delectable Mountains* and wanted to adapt the song as the opening of the new opera. (Luckily the full score was preserved in BL Add. MS 50418 A and Hadley kept the vocal score, which is now in BL Add. MS 70934.) Thus the Reigate *Pilgrim's Progress* may have contained the original source of the *Tallis Fantasia*.

We do not know if the musical forces – chorus and string orchestra – were already fixed before Vaughan Williams was commissioned to supply music for the Reigate production. Like the use of *tableaux vivants* the use of the chorus in a dramatization of Bunyan is problematic if faithfulness to Bunyan's own religious spirit is intended. Bunyan was a strict Baptist and disapproved strongly of all church 'formalism', a category that included the use of choirs and anthems. In *The Pilgrim's Progress* the only songs are those the travellers and their companions sing to pass the time or comment on their experiences. Even in the Celestial City there is only the slightest indication of singing; Bunyan's description focuses more on trumpets and bells.[8] The use of a choir in the project was inevitable, however. The common nineteenth-century practice of supplying plays with elaborate incidental music containing choruses, inserting texts for them if necessary, lies behind this aspect even of an amateur production such as the Reigate *Pilgrim's Progress*. The practice also has roots in the English oratorio tradition: the theatrical treatment of a religious subject in England in 1906 is scarcely imaginable without the use of the chorus since large-scale religious choral singing was one area of musical activity in which the English could claim uncontested superiority.

Vaughan Williams took care not to overload the story with extraneous choruses; he reserves them for only three scenes: the Arming of Christian at the House Beautiful (no. 5), the Death of Faithful (no. 12) and the Celestial City (no. 14). The use of the chorus in the last two scenes is conventional; its origins lying in the long literary tradition of heavenly choirs. In the first scene the chorus is more incongruous as there is no indication in Bunyan that there is anything particularly supernal about the House Beautiful. But the choruses in the 1906 *Pilgrim's Progress* are simple; by adapting old music and avoiding learned devices Vaughan Williams partially resists the Victorian oratorio tradition even as certain of its conventions inform his work.

The first performances of the Reigate production of *The Pilgrim's Progress* took place in the Holbein Hall of Reigate Priory, a large country house, at 3:00 p.m. and 8:00 p.m. on Saturday 1 December 1906. The initial production was such a great success that its sponsors decided to repeat it in London. Thus at 2:30 p.m. and 8:30 p.m. on Saturday 16 March 1907, two further (expanded) performances were given at the Imperial Theatre. The following year the production was revived with performances from 12 to 14 March in the Hall of Lincoln's Inn.[9] Critical reaction to the production was positive. In Reigate the people naturally took great pride in such an elaborate presentation. But even in London the edifying spectacle of Joanna Hadley's London friends along with a generous selection of the good people of Reigate, dressed in their simple robes, striking stylized *tableaux* and enacting the drama of salvation, attracted some notice and critical comment. For the most part the reviews are glowing, in keeping with the usual tone with which such pious amateur efforts were reviewed at the time.[10] But even so, a certain inadequacy was noted:

Bunyan's vision, in which the allegorical figures are always vividly concrete, lends itself well to spectacular representation; and the adapters, Mrs W. Hadley and Miss E. Ouless, have done their work admirably. They have preserved just enough of the theological exhortation and disputation to keep that element in the mingled flavour of the story. The element that suffers most is Bunyan's ironic humour, the humour which makes, for instance, the trial in the town of Vanity so pungent a comment on his own experiences before the magistrates of Charles II's day (*The Times*, 13 March 1908, in BL Add. MS 70937 A).

Similar complaints have been leveled against all of Vaughan Williams's Bunyan settings. But because in this production others had compiled the script and devised the staging, no one held Vaughan Williams responsible.

Vaughan Williams's original impetus to adapt *The Pilgrim's Progress* as a full-length operatic work may simply have been his ongoing love of the book and the positive reception of both the Reigate production and *The Shepherds of the Delectable Mountains* of 1922.[11] Vaughan Williams began to make sketches for a larger-scale version as early as the 1920s. Kennedy (1996, 192) claims that between 1925 and 1936 he completed 'considerable parts of Acts I and II'. At this point, however, work seems to have halted. The modest and evanescent success of Vaughan Williams's previous operatic works may have discouraged him from the project. Then, possibly as a result of the outbreak of the Second World War and the consequent reduction in opportunities for performances of operas in Britain, he decided to use some of the material from the opera in his Fifth Symphony, composed 1938–43.[12] Ursula Vaughan Williams (1964, 216) claims that at this period he suspected that he would never finish the opera; work on the score came to a standstill.

The matter might have rested there had not the BBC commissioned Vaughan Williams in 1942 to provide incidental music for a two-part radio version of *The Pilgrim's Progress* with a script by Edward Sackville-West. Vaughan Williams seized the opportunity and incorporated into the score much of the music of the unfinished opera. Without the need for sets, costumes and visual illusion, Sackville-West could follow the picaresque details of Bunyan's plot more closely, and include a greater variety of Bunyan's characters and incidents than Ouless did. Consequently the BBC score far outstrips both the Reigate score and *The Shepherds of the Delectable Mountains* in dramatic intensity and scope.

Preparation of the BBC score once again immersed Vaughan Williams in Bunyan and stimulated him to resume composition of the opera. Almost certainly he had substantially worked out the scenario, if not the actual libretto, by 1942 and – although Kennedy (1980, 309) mentions that Sackville-West's fuller adaptation also stimulated a revision of the libretto – he was apparently not inspired by working on the radio score to reconsider his radical condensation of the plot. But most of the additional music that he composed for the additional characters and situations eventually found places in the opera. Vaughan Williams may have worked further on Act Two of the opera in 1943. Work then proceeded steadily alongside other pieces from 1944. Conveniently 1945–46 saw the première of *Peter Grimes* and the resultant interest in new British opera, which must have encouraged Vaughan Williams. He completed the score in the years 1947–48, except for the kind of adjustments he habitually made to scores once they had been tried out. (Kennedy

[1980, 353] lists Act Two as having been completed in 1947–48 and Acts Three and Four in the 1940s.)

Most of the literature on the 1951 opera mentions that Vaughan Williams himself was solely responsible for the libretto of the opera, that is, the specific words sung. It has not been noted, however, that the dramatic plan of the opera relies fundamentally upon that of Evelyn Ouless's 1906 play. Table 9.3 shows a scene-by-

Table 9.3   Order of scenes in the 1906 Reigate and the 1951 opera versions of *The Pilgrim's Progress*

	1906 – Order of scenes as designated in the programme		*1951 – Order of scenes* as designated in the vocal score (Additional episodes included in the scenes are given in brackets.)
Prol.	Bunyan in prison	Prol.	Bunyan in prison
i	Christian sets out	I/i	The Pilgrim [sets out,] meets Evangelist
ii	The Wicket Gate		[The Wicket Gate]
iii	Christian loses his burden		[The Pilgrim loses his burden]
iv	The House Beautiful		The House Beautiful
	The Arming of Christian	II/i	The Arming of the Pilgrim
v	Christian meets Apollyon Christian meets Faithful Evangelist's warning	II/ii	The Pilgrim meets Apollyon
vi	Vanity Fair	III/i	Vanity Fair
vii	Faithful at the stake		
		III/ii	Pilgrim in prison
viii	Christian and Hopeful meet Mr By-Ends	IV/i	The Pilgrim meets Mister By-Ends
	The Shepherds of the Delectable Mountains	IV/i	The Delectable Mountains
ix	The River of Death		[The River of Death]
x	The Celestial City	IV/iii	The Pilgrim reaches the End of his Journey
Epil.	Bunyan in Prison	Epil.	Bunyan in Prison

Source: adapted from BL Add. MS 70935 and Vaughan Williams (1974).

scene comparison of the two scenarios. The opera follows the same overall form as the Reigate production, tightening the action into a single arc framed by a prologue and epilogue for Bunyan himself.[13] Furthermore, with only a few additions and subtractions the selection and order of incidental scenes are identical, as is the selection of the one dubious fellow pilgrim, Mr By-Ends, whom Vaughan Williams provides with a simpering wife not found in Bunyan.

Reliance on the Reigate outline helps explain some apparent anomalies in the opera libretto. About 'The Arming of the Pilgrim' Vaughan Williams wrote in his programme note for the 1954 Cambridge production, 'In Act II, the House Beautiful and the House of the Interpreter have been merged into one, and an elaborate scene of initiation is built up from Bunyan's few hints' (Kennedy 1996, 195). Bunyan's hints for such a scene are few indeed. He writes only two sentences about the Armoury of the House Beautiful when the keepers first show it to Christian (Bunyan 1984, 46) and then, when Christian is about to leave, Bunyan writes:

> Now he bethought himself of setting forward, and they were willing he should: but first, said they, let us go again into the Armoury, so they did; and when he came there, they harnessed him from head to foot, with what was of proof, lest perhaps he should meet with assaults in the way. (Bunyan, 1984, 47)

This is only one of many incidents at the House Beautiful (the whole episode takes up nine pages in the Oxford edition) and there is no explanation of why it should have merited selection at all were it not that Vaughan Williams was working from the outline already developed for the Reigate production. He took the scene, which Ouless had chosen as one of the *tableaux*, and expanded it into an elaborate ten-minute choral sequence.

In preparing the scenario for the opera Vaughan Williams made only two major changes to Ouless's adaptation. First, he completely eliminated Christian's travelling companions, Faithful and Hopeful, and thus their meetings with Christian as well as Faithful's martyrdom. Then, to fill the gap after Vanity Fair, he added the scene of the Pilgrim's escape from prison (which he borrowed for the purpose from the Doubting Castle episode that occurs in Bunyan after Vanity Fair). In a few places, while preserving an incident from the 1906 model, Vaughan Williams gave it greater or less weight. In the case of 'The Arming of the Pilgrim' the model was expanded. But the comparison of the two scenarios also reveals Vaughan Williams's interest in compressing and clarifying Ouless's already scaled-down version of Bunyan's involved plot. The elimination of both travelling companions obviates the need for much of the dialogue. Vaughan Williams also condensed the early scenes chosen by Ouless: where in the Reigate version Christian's passage through the Wicket Gate, the loss of his burden at the cross, and his arrival at the House Beautiful were all separate scenes and therefore could at least be imagined as separated by other adventures (as indeed they are in Bunyan), Vaughan Williams combined all of this into one scene. Similarly he borrowed the telescoped version of the end of the plot that he had worked out in *The Shepherds of the Delectable Mountains*: Act Four, Scene Two of the opera takes over the 1922 score almost in its entirety.[14]

Vaughan Williams borrowed more than just the plot outline from the Reigate *Pilgrim's Progress*; details of the opera's staging and action have origins in the earlier work. The most notable of these is also the most controversial of Vaughan Williams's stage directions in the opera: the fight with Apollyon. For the opera Vaughan Williams conceived of Apollyon as being seen only as a shadow cast on the backdrop while his voice was sung offstage through a megaphone.[15] The stage directions in the opera score for the fight then read as follows:

Apollyon: Here will I spill thy soul.
(*Blackout.*)
(*Lights up.*)
The Pilgrim and Apollyon's shadows seen in close combat. (Tableau)
(*Blackout.*)
Apollyon: Surely I have thee now.
(*Lights up*)
The Pilgrim is forced back on one knee, Apollyon's shadow stands over him. (Tableau)
(*Blackout.*)
Pilgrim: Rejoice not against me, O mine enemy: When I fall, I shall arise.
(*Lights up.*)
Pilgrim stands over Apollyon with his sword at Apollyon's heart (Tableau)
The vision of Apollyon fades out. The Pilgrim stands alone with full light on him
    (Vaughan Williams, 1974, 82–4)

Vaughan Williams had obviously been impressed by Ouless and Hadley's staging in London in 1907–8 and derived this concept, frozen *tableaux* separated by three blackouts, from the earlier production. Again his decision reveals an interest in simplifying the stage action of the drama by avoiding the graphic portrayal of incident.

Although Vaughan Williams had been engaged with Bunyan on and off for over forty years and had worked on the score of the opera for as long as a quarter of a century, upon its completion (or at least completion of a presentable form of the whole) in 1948 he had no obvious opportunities for performance of such a large work. Only after some negotiation did the Royal Opera House agree in late 1949 to undertake the première of the opera. Correspondence in the Opera House archives shows that it took a long time for David Webster, the General Administrator of the Royal Opera House, and Vaughan Williams to settle on a producer (stage director). Finally in November 1950, five months before the première, Webster invited Nevill Coghill, a Fellow and Lecturer in English literature at Exeter College, Oxford, and an amateur theatrical director, to direct *The Pilgrim's Progress*.

Coghill had worked mainly on regional and student productions (particularly of Shakespeare) and had never directed at the Royal Opera House. This lack of experience was a distinct liability, especially considering the short time he had to prepare the entire production. Compounding matters was a noticeable lack of enthusiasm from the administration of Covent Garden. In the end, because the preparation of the score and the details of the production were left unfinished for so long, the rehearsal period was rushed and by some accounts unsatisfactory, with predictably deleterious results for the performances (Ursula Vaughan Williams, 1964, 306).

Despite the short preparation time, Coghill leapt at the chance to direct, inviting a colleague, Hal Burton, to design the sets and costumes. All of Coghill's correspondence to Burton over the ensuing months is preserved in the British Library (Add. MS 69448 A), so we have an unusually clear picture of how the production was mounted. In December 1950, before he even had a good idea of the score, he sent Burton a series of letters giving a full outline of his concepts for blocking, lighting, sets and costumes, based only on the synopsis, a rereading of Bunyan, and a recording of Vaughan Williams's Fifth Symphony. Early on Burton proposed using projections and a fluid, abstract design, but Coghill rejected this proposal by deferring to Bunyan and *The Vision of Piers Plowman:* 'The English peasant–mystical tradition is earthy, realist, and exact.' Coghill's guiding design principles were concreteness and historical specificity. To explain his production he wrote a note for the programme book:

> Whoever reads *The Pilgrim's Progress* feels himself to be moving through a clear, natural landscape and meeting with actual people whose natures are precisely indicated by their names. This is what one might expect from 'The Author's Apology for his Book' in which Bunyan says:
>
> > Solidity indeed becomes the Pen
> > of him that writeth things Divine to men.
>
> He approaches the Unknown through the Familiar and his Dream, in this respect, is in line with the great English mystical tradition that stretches from *The Dream of the Rood* of Anglo-Saxon times through *Piers Plowman* in the fourteenth to *The Pilgrim's Progress* in the seventeenth century and beyond. ... I have sought in this production, therefore, to be faithful to the conceptions of the Author and Composer as well as to the great tradition and have aimed at creating a sense of the holy, as well as of the unholy, by a clear naturalism and beauty, avoiding surrealist fantasy, symbolist vagueness and other stylistic freaks of suggestion, whether in action, costume, or decor, because I believe such things are hostile to the immediate sincerity and style of the work. (BL Add. MS 69448 A)

Sets and costumes were to be based on particular historical models from art history and local architecture, preferably of types that would have been familiar in Bunyan's time. 'Tradition has it', Coghill wrote later, 'that Bunyan's idea of "The House Beautiful" came from a great classical mansion that still stands at Ampthill. It was no vague and visionary affair, but something solid that he knew ...' ('Did you hear that?' 1951). He sent Burton images of medieval chantries as inspiration for the Celestial City and Samuel Palmer landscapes for the Delectable Mountains. Bosch and Grünewald would supply the models for the Doleful Creatures attending Apollyon.

This initial dedication to historical specificity, however, was not always borne out by the sets and costumes in their final form. Nor did it conform to Vaughan Williams's own staging ideas, which, as Ursula Vaughan Williams describes in her biography, admitted a greater measure of abstraction:

> Ralph was very positive about some aspects of the staging, vague about others. His idea was that as much as possible should be done by lighting, and that the celestial beings should be radiant and undated ... His idea was for historical clothes for the real people, Bunyan, and Pilgrim, the neighbours, the By Ends couple, the woodcutter's boy, and the shepherds; a dazzling confusion of times and places for Vanity Fair ... while those for the people in the House Beautiful should be hieratic, as should those of the branch bearer and the cupbearer and the people of the Celestial City. (Ursula Vaughan Williams, 1964, 306)

Records of the sets, costumes, and some of the basic stage pictures exist but from photographs and reports of the audience it is difficult to reconstruct the movement and blocking. Since Vaughan Williams was involved in most of the planning decisions one cannot always determine who originated a particular element of the production but it is reasonable to assume that his stage directions were followed where possible.[16]

From the evidence of his letters to Burton, Coghill's imagination was most captured by the two most dramatic scenes, the fight with Apollyon and Vanity Fair. Coghill was unimpressed with Vaughan Williams's stage directions for the former scene and expressed his intention of having a solid figure in a papier-mâché headdress instead of the shadow figure called for in the score. Although Vaughan Williams never agreed with the decision to show Apollyon on stage, by February, in keeping with the Doleful Creatures and the rest of his designs, Coghill's Apollyon (Plate 6) was a concrete devil based on Bunyan's description: 'He was cloathed in scales like a Fish ... he had Wings like a Dragon, feet like a Bear, and out of his belly came Fire and Smoak, and his mouth was as the mouth of a Lion' (Bunyan, 1984, 47).[17] Vaughan Williams's blackouts in the fight also worried Coghill. In December he wrote to Burton: 'This is the first scene in which violence is possible, and I think it is *necessary* because up to this the whole opera has been so ceremonial and liturgical' (emphasis in original). Although he acquiesced to Vaughan Williams's lighting directions in the end, he was still concerned about the blackouts in late February, worrying that the audience might believe them to be power failures.[18] Indeed, whereas in the Reigate production the blackouts and frozen *tableaux* probably came off as a highly dramatic and original solution to the problem of staging a battle, in a full-scale professional opera production it may have come off as avoidance of a scene of action. The problem was not merely one of staging; Vaughan Williams wrote music specifically to his concept. Thus even if the fight had been fully staged the music would not have matched it and, with its slow grinding syncopated dissonances, its stops and starts keyed to the blackouts, and its long *tremolando* open fifths, the music would have undercut the fight dramatically.

Coghill saw Vanity Fair similarly as a necessary release both from the uplifting tone and the dramatic uniformity of the rest of the opera. He wanted to have the crowd engaged in all kinds of commerce and amusements but recognized that 'The danger is lest Vanity Fair seems [*sic*] *gay* and *innocent*. We must make it *cruel* and *sinister*' (emphasis in original). Unfortunately, although the set and costumes for this scene were the most varied and flamboyant in the production, the designers' amateurish decision to light the scene entirely in red (a rather blunt departure from 'naturalism') detracted from its dramatic impact.

Coghill's principles seem to have provided little inspiration for the ritualistic choral scenes 'The House Beautiful', 'The Arming of the Pilgrim' and 'The Pilgrim reaches the End of his Journey', or for the long stationary sequences that end 'The Pilgrim meets Apollyon' and 'The Pilgrim in Prison'. Although based on historical models, the sets he commissioned from Burton for these scenes seem unfortunately remote from the world of either Bunyan's or Vaughan Williams's work. Also unfortunate was Coghill's decision to have the chorus stand still in ether straight lines or homogeneous groupings. Plate 7 shows a *tableau* from the last scene of the opera, with Coghill's interpretation of a seventeenth-century conception of Heaven, the choir of angels complete with crowns, haloes, laurels and harps. In Plate 8, a still from 'The House Beautiful', the House itself looks like an ill-proportioned Italian Renaissance basilica; the chorus, dressed in abstracted historical garb, are ranged unimaginatively in two straight lines – hardly a picture of a 'clear natural landscape' inhabited by 'actual people'.

A letter from Coghill to Vaughan Williams makes it clear that when in February the two met to look over the designs, Vaughan Williams objected to their liturgical nature and churchiness, especially in the House Beautiful scene. Although Coghill's concept was static and hieratic and Vaughan Williams's disappointment was undoubtedly genuine, Coghill was not entirely to blame. Especially with the ritual scenes it is difficult to separate the contribution of Coghill from that of Vaughan Williams himself, who wrote the long stretches of music and described his own ideas for stage pictures with detailed directions in the score. In staging a scene such as 'The House Beautiful' Coghill was acting on hints gleaned from Vaughan Williams's own stage directions:

> Here the great doors open and within is seen a vista of colonnades and arches. A white procession is dimly seen approaching the doors – it is seen to be a body of assistants carrying a white robe. The Three Shining Ones take it and approach the Pilgrim. (Vaughan Williams, 1974, 34)

Thus, although undoubtedly many of Coghill and Burton's design and directorial decisions, especially the concretizing of so much ritual action in specific historical terms, were poor, some of the responsibility for the (ultimately unsuccessful) visual element of the production must be ascribed to Vaughan Williams's own lack of imagination in this regard.

The first performance of *The Pilgrim's Progress* was set for Thursday 26 April 1951, exactly a week before the official opening of the new Royal Festival Hall, itself a week before the opening concert of the Festival of Britain 1951 London Season of the Arts.[19] The première of an opera by Vaughan Williams constituted a major national musical event, but the national and international spotlight provided by the Festival context lent it even greater importance. Furthermore (and surprisingly), *The Pilgrim's Progress* was the only English work presented in Covent Garden's Festival of Britain season, which otherwise consisted of the complete *Ring, Tristan und Isolde, Die Meistersinger* and *Parsifal*, along with *Fidelio, Salome, Rigoletto, Madama Butterfly* and *Tosca*. Because of the opera's subject, the première became something of a religious event as well; some Christian periodicals announced or reviewed the work and the first performance was attended by the Archbishops of both Canterbury and York and several other Anglican dignitaries as well as a number of highly placed ministers of Nonconformist churches. Both the first performance and the second one, on Sunday April 30, were broadcast live over the BBC.

On the night of the première the work was greeted with sustained attention and rapturous applause, Vaughan Williams receiving a lengthy ovation. In a 'post mortem' letter to Vaughan Williams the next day (quoted in Kennedy, 1980, 196) Edward J. Dent commented on the rapt attention that both the audience and the performers had shown. Critical reaction to the opera was, however, mixed. Of the critics who were unreservedly enthusiastic none was more generous in praise than Dent, who took up his pen to declare the opera 'a work of supreme beauty and impressiveness that has lifted English Opera on to a far higher plane than any previous native musical drama' (Dent, 1951, 35) and 'undoubtedly the greatest and the most deeply moving contribution of modern times to the building-up of a national repertory of musical drama' (Dent, 1952, 444). Critics with firmly held religious convictions like Dyneley Hussey (1951) found that the spiritual experience of the work overpowered any possible criticism.

On the whole, though, the tone was skeptical at best, focusing on a series of defects concisely laid out by Mosco Carner in *Time and Tide:*

> the succession of (mostly) static tableaux, the absence of a plot in the dramatic sense, the concentration on a single leading character, essentially passive at that, the predominance of religious allegory over human drama, and, last but not least, the considerable retarding of what little action there is by long stretches of cantata-like choruses. (Carner, 1951)

The most cogent and pointed of the negative reviews was that of Martin Cooper, published in the *Spectator* a week after the première. This review touches on so many of the points made by other reviewers that it is worth quoting almost in full:

> 'In the theatre, where technical knowledge and skill look comic and the most revolting crimes are not without their power of attraction, the love of God is just dull.' Saint-Saëns's comment on Gounod's pious opera *Polyeucte* sprang unbidden to mind as I listened to Vaughan Williams's *Pilgrim's Progress*. Call the piece what you will, morality or opera, nothing will alter the fact that, given at Covent Garden, it must conform to the demands of the theatre or be judged a failure. It might be given at a Three Choirs Festival in cathedral precincts and succeed; but in a theatre it fails for want of variety (both musical and dramatic) and of interest, either in the action or in the psychological development of Pilgrim's character.
>
> Many have blamed Bunyan; but Bunyan wrote a picaresque novel, crowded his canvas with well-observed characters (personifications, but alive) and made his protagonist, for all his theological ranting and unctuously expressed aspirations, a fallible and recognisably human being. Vaughan Williams's selection of scenes never once shows Pilgrim failing. He does not fall into the Slough of Despond, lose his roll or wander off to Doubting Castle. He has no companions, Faithful or Hopeful, but appears as the solitary saint in a world of sinners, a most unattractive predicament calculated to alienate the spectator's sympathy entirely. This circumstance, and the number of psalms he intones during the course of the evening, confirm the popular, though doubtless unjust, impression of the Puritan as a psalm-singing prig.
>
> The vaguely pious symbolism of the production increased the atmosphere of unreality. Who are the crowds at the House Beautiful, stepped straight from the illustrations of a Victorian Bible and moving as in a church pageant? They are not to be found at Bunyan's Interpreter's House or House Beautiful, which Vaughan Williams has combined. What is the solemn oblation of the Key, the Branch of the Tree of Life and the Cup at the end of Act 2? Surely not in Bunyan and quite alien to his un-ritualistic temper. '*La religiosità è vaga, la religione precisa*', wrote Croce; and this production too often substituted vaguely picturesque religiosity for Bunyan's precise imagery – in the manner of costume especially, where, for instance, Watchful was dressed like a bogus archimandrite and the Herald wore a vestment that only escaped popery by being adorned with stars instead of crosses.
>
> The scene at Vanity Fair brought some welcome relief from psalms, hymns and spiritual songs, though Pilgrim made up for it in prison (his escape from which, so dramatically feeble, was effected as Bunyan's hero escaped from Doubting Castle). How welcome were the world, the flesh and the devil after so much pious symbolism! And though Vaughan Williams's music is not well suited to suggest the allurements of the flesh, the chorus of

hatred, malice and all uncharitableness was most effective. Mr and Mrs By-Ends were heavy going, such an easy couple of straw for Pilgrim's pious intransigence to destroy. If only one or two of Bunyan's subsidiary characters could be introduced, surely the subtler figures of Talkative (a patter-singer, obviously) or Ignorance would have been a better choice.

No one will question the solemnity or the ruminative, wholly untheatrical beauty of Vaughan Williams's music. Its temper and its contours are very familiar, and as a vehicle of a specifically English kind of moral earnestness it is unsurpassed. ... One specifically English characteristic marked the whole performance. There is no word in French, German or Italian which expresses quite what the English mean by 'reverent', and this 'reverence' was the note of the whole evening. (Cooper, 1951, 585)[20]

Many critics agreed with Cooper's judgment on the opera's lack of theatricality. This was not necessarily meant as damning criticism; a common observation was that the piece was really a religious pageant more appropriate to cathedral performance than to the opera house.[21] Noting the large role played in many scenes by a chorus lacking any specific character or function in the plot, one critic even designated the work an 'oratorio in fancy dress' ('G.N.S.', 1951).

More cogent than the simple declaration that the opera was unsuited for the opera house were the complaints, also adumbrated by Cooper's review, that the work failed to elicit identification with its central character and that the conflicts and dangers of the journey were not strongly enough portrayed. One such critique was given by Philip Hope-Wallace (1951):

[H]ow fatally easy the progress seems to be; neither in the clutch of Apollyon nor in Despair's dungeon, least of all in the deeps of the last river, is Christian the Pilgrim felt to be in danger. V.W. does not deal in those strokes of artifice which (rightly or wrongly) are the life of the thing theatrical. He feels that for his hero to declaim in the manner of a priest intoning 'I sink, the waves go over me' (followed by choral comment) will make the point well enough. But on a stage this was totally inadequate. Never, indeed, do we 'feel with' the hero as we so easily 'feel with' other, and you may say, more meretricious heroes, *Parsifal*, Berlioz's *Faust* (semi-opera) or Elgar's *Gerontius* (oratorio). Instead of living through the progress of the pilgrim, we sit through a beautiful choral symphony watching by the way some illustrative tableaux from Bunyan.

The most sarcastic such criticism was that of Desmond Shawe-Taylor (1951), who complained that 'There is no chill of terror about Apollyon, and about as much wantonness in Vanity Fair as we might hope to find on a quiet night in the Battersea Pleasure Gardens. ... We seemed to be watching, not so much the spiritual struggles of a sorely tried man, as the illustrious ascent of the best boy in the school from Lower Third to Upper Sixth ... with a dull passing-out ceremony'.[22]

Reaction to the score considered as an entity separate from the stage was more positive. Most critics, even ones utterly unconvinced of the work's stageworthiness, were impressed by the music, albeit often in general terms. The qualities most often praised in the score were serenity and beauty:

The score of *Pilgrim's Progress* – undoubtedly, I should think, the noblest to be made known on any of the world's lyric stages since the end of the war – is beautifully and expertly wrought ... The long melodic lines, with their suggestions of church chant and ancient folk songs, and the subtly shifting modal harmonies in which they are couched, attain genuine and unflawed eloquence, and the syllables of Bunyan's prose and of the Psalms float upon this flowing stream of song with unparalleled serenity and naturalness. (Smith, 1951b)

Although comments like this were common, another view saw the score as suffering (like the stage action) from the superfluity of these very qualities: '[T]he composer has fallen back too readily on his standard formulas for mystic exaltation ... The result, to be frank, is monotonous' (Shawe-Taylor, 1951); '[T]oo often, Vaughan Williams repeats the solemn chords, the trumpet fanfare, the pastoral melodies, until their effect becomes stale' (Jacobs, 1951).

Most critics deplored the visual element of the production. One critic wrote:

All the more painful ... was the crudity of the visual presentation. Hal Burton's settings were, for the most part, of the quality of calendar art. Nevill Coghill, the director, put the crowds either in V-shape or in a solid, undigested mass. He encouraged Mr Matters [the Pilgrim] to use the gestures of a rural vicar, and in general seemed to be drawing on Sunday school picture books for his inspiration. (Smith, 1951a)

The final set (the Celestial City) was variously described as the 'nineteenth-century mock-Gothic of an ambitious station hotel, brightly redecorated to represent something very unlike a Puritan's Heaven' (Blom, 1951) and 'a cross between a Christmas Card and a rather highly coloured stained-glass window'. This last quote comes from the most sustained attack on Coghill (and by extension Burton), Peter Wolfe's article 'Naturalism in opera' in the *Theatre Newsletter*. Wolfe took strong exception to the decor (which he called 'ugly' and 'vulgar') and to Coghill's programme note, especially its last sentence, which struck him as extreme and impassioned – special pleading to justify an unwillingness to address the problems of the stage with creativity and originality. Even supporters of the work's claims to a place in the theatre, such as Hubert Foss, used the 'amateurism' and 'juvenile ineptitudes' of Coghill and the Covent Garden management to explain the production's apparent failure.[23]

Predictably, those with a taste for the 'uplifting solemnity of cathedral ceremonial' (Tarran, 1951) found the opera's religious sensibility mystical and awe-inspiring, but many were troubled by the obvious similarity of much of the opera to High Church ritual, finding it monotonous, unoperatic, or a violation of the spirit of Bunyan: 'I don't think Bunyan, sturdy independent as he was, would have approved of what Vaughan Williams has done with his book' (*Daily Mail*, 1951); 'The extraordinary clarity and vividness of [Bunyan's] original is obscured in heavy-handed ritual that destroys simplicity without adding anything illuminating, and which, with its suggestion of Puseyite fal-lals, would certainly have outraged Bunyan' (*Glasgow Herald*, 1951). (The *Daily Mail* review also sarcastically pointed out that Bunyan would have considered Covent Garden to be the very heart of Vanity Fair.) Several years later another writer, generally sympathetic to Vaughan Williams's work, concurred: 'Is it not a little sad that the Pilgrim (who, presumably, was of Bunyan's puritan and Low Church turn of mind) should cross the river to find himself received into a Heaven so be-vestmented and obviously Anglo-Catholic?' (Pakenham, 1957, 150).

With his great love of Bunyan, and having spent as long as 45 years working on music inspired by Bunyan, Vaughan Williams had great hopes for *The Pilgrim's Progress*, his longest and most complex stage work; it is easy to believe Ursula Vaughan Williams's contention that the work had special meaning for him. Of his reaction to the shoddy production at Covent Garden, Roy Douglas (1988, 27) reports: 'I would say with some confidence that this shabby miscreation of his beloved *Pilgrim's Progress* was the bitterest disappointment of his musical life ....' And although he was prepared for the worst, declaring 'They won't like it, they don't want an opera with no heroine and no love duets – and I don't care, it's what I meant, and there it is' (Ursula Vaughan Williams, 1964, 308), he was also deeply aggrieved by the savaging that the opera received at the hands of the critics. In response to one common criticism he insisted that he had conceived and orchestrated the work for the operatic stage and its resources, even to the point of timing the processionals and interludes (letter to Hubert Foss, quoted in Kennedy, 1980, 312). He declared that it should always be performed in the theatre, not in the concert hall or cathedral (letter to Rutland Boughton, quoted in Kennedy, 1980, 313–14), even though the latter option was perfectly viable and in line with a common English tradition of dramatic-religious works performed in churches.

Although he knew that the production was partly to blame, Vaughan Williams also recognized that there were portions of the opera that needed improvement. Immediately after the first performances E.J. Dent, who as a close colleague of Vaughan Williams with practical experience of supervising operatic productions could be more direct in his criticisms, sent Vaughan Williams several letters laying out his critique of the opera's score and production and his suggestions for their revision. Vaughan Williams had apparently already hinted in a letter that he was prepared to expand the Vanity Fair scene and Dent argued in favor of this plan, suggesting that the bit parts (Demas, Judas Iscariot, Simon Magus and Worldly Glory) be given more stage time and that there be more music to introduce the scene before the Pilgrim's entrance. He also objected to parts of the Apollyon scene, calling for more effective use of the chorus and the Doleful Creatures and in general a more 'impressive' and 'frightening' atmosphere – perhaps a great *crescendo* and *accelerando* up to Apollyon's first challenge. He did not like the fact that Apollyon sang on only a single note and felt that the angelic ministrations at the end of this scene went on too long. Finally, despite his unswerving public support, he opined in private that there was not enough fast music in the score. Of his criticisms of the staging, two stand out. First, he wrote, 'There is far too much self-conscious "reverence" throughout. There must be about three dozen or more "kneel-downs" and two-thirds of them ought to be taken out, as they become horribly *cheap* as the opera goes on' (emphasis in original). (He probably had not realized that in many cases the instructions for characters to kneel originated with Vaughan Williams himself.) Dent also objected on similar grounds to the House Beautiful scene: '[T]he atmosphere required is surely not Priestly Authority, Penance, formal Worship and Reverence, but Kindness and Friendliness, Love and Sympathy, *Helpfulness* on the part of all the heavenly beings' (emphasis in original).

Vaughan Williams's response on 17 May 1951 (also reprinted in Kennedy, 1996, 196–206) is the most revealing and detailed document we have of his attitudes towards the work and his intentions for its performance. He rejected many of Dent's criticisms and strongly defended the score and his own original staging concepts. Although he complained that the staging was not what he had imagined and described in his score, the letter leaves little doubt that the dramatic problems identified by so many critics stemmed as much from his vision as from Coghill's. The House Beautiful, he wrote, was a 'scene of initiation', implying that it required a more formal tone than Dent described, even going so far as to claim that '[The Pilgrim] ought not to be armed by three young women, but by a lot of soldiers.' He also defended the ritualism and repetitive kneeling: 'I agree there is too much kneeling. On the other hand you must remember that the Opera is to be acted almost like a ritual and not in the ordinary dramatic sense.' He expressed regret that the Apollyon scene was not being staged with shadows as he originally conceived it and again defended his conception of the scene as more doleful than frightful.

Vaughan Williams also rejected most of Dent's musical suggestions – the rethinking of the Apollyon scene and the cut in the long static *tableau* following the heavenly ministrations – but revealed that he planned to fix a few small problems (for example, the end of 'The Arming of the Pilgrim') and expand the middle sequence of Vanity Fair. Covent Garden had agreed to take the opera on tour to several provincial centres and to give a few more performances in London the next season, so over the summer Vaughan Williams made several revisions to the score. The major revision was the expansion of the Vanity Fair scene, which, with the addition of the song for Lord Lechery (to words by Ursula Wood) and the trial scene, and some filling out of other material, doubled in length. The following season saw several more performances – the revised version received its first performance on 12 February 1952 – but they attracted little attention or comment and the work fell out of the repertory without further comment from the press.[24]

Although it is hardly the staple of the operatic repertory that Vaughan Williams hoped it would become, *The Pilgrim's Progress* occupies a unique place in his *œuvre*. Because of its unusually long genealogy it offers a rare glimpse at his artistic interactions with the past and at the kinds of cultural memories that fed his creativity. That Vaughan Williams was unable to transform his material into the hoped-for operatic masterpiece makes the result all the more transparent to the influences that lie beneath it.

Chief among these is its 1906 predecessor, to which the 1951 opera owes so much that the later work may be justly called the product of an earlier time and sensibility. Ouless's play is very much a period piece; there is every reason to suppose that a dramatist of a different period and aesthetic adapting Bunyan would have produced something quite different. Yet somehow through all of Vaughan Williams's interactions with the book, its dramatization was linked to the Reigate model. His adherence to the outlines of the Reigate version, to its scenario, to its *tableaux vivants,* so outmoded by the 1950s, even to some of the musical decisions he made for it, suggest a personal nostalgic attachment both to the period of his first youthful encounter with Bunyan and to the particular view of Bunyan and the meaning of his book presented in the 1906 play.

In Bunyan's rugged Calvinism the great majority of the pilgrims are predestined for damnation and Christian himself suffers every imaginable reverse, both internal and external, before his eventual triumph. In her adaptation, Ouless, while bringing Bunyan's picaresque story into tighter focus, still retained a variety of characters and incidents and a fundamentally religious outlook. The changes that she made and that Vaughan Williams inherited from her rejected Bunyan's pessimistic view of the hopes of the majority of humankind and turned the progress of his Christian, full of dire warnings of the difficulty of achieving salvation, into the reassuringly untrammelled success of the Edwardian middle class, attended by a few obstacles but nothing that a mildly proper spiritual exercise and ritual action could not overcome.

The further changes that Vaughan Williams made for the opera complete this process: the remaining obstacles and moments of tension are cleared away almost entirely, the concern with any dogma obliterated, and even the personality of the Pilgrim obscured. Vaughan Williams so simplifies the plot that he makes the process of pilgrimage itself seem rather easy. The elimination of Faithful (and Hopeful and all the Pilgrim's other companions) removes human relationships from the plot and as a result isolates and reduces the humanity of the Pilgrim. His opinions, observations and improving conversations also necessarily disappear, to be replaced by solitary prayers and psalms and by the comforting texts of the greatly expanded corps of heavenly messengers and helpers. None of these interpolations to the libretto have any basis in Bunyan – whose characters tend to speak in a pithy colloquial idiom (full of biblical references but always to the point) – but are rather the logical extension of the Angel's Song in the Reigate script. Even in the scenes where there is action, '[The composer] finds himself reduced to furnishing many singers with adapted scriptural quotations and accessory informative phrases such as "Be thou arrayed in fine linen", "A treasure of joy and gladness be given thee", "I am more than conqueror through him that loveth me"...' (Dickinson, 1963, 359).

Vaughan Williams cannot be criticized *per se* for abandoning Bunyan, but he does not replace Bunyan's vision with a strong vision of his own. He was drawn to Bunyan's book initially, he said, because of its status as a 'universal dramatic allegory' and he said he changed the name of the main character from 'Christian' to 'the Pilgrim' 'because I want the idea to be universal and to apply to anyone who aims at the spiritual life whether he is Christian, Jew, Buddhist, Shintoist, or Fifth Day Adventist' (letter to Rutland Boughton, quoted in Kennedy, 1980, 313).[25] One must conclude that Vaughan Williams was not particularly interested in the struggle for salvation and that he didn't want to project action and conflict but rather a relatively unproblematic process of internal spiritual development. This is a sanguine and universalist view of the road to salvation, one which offers an unsuitably subdued subject for an opera.

Paradoxically the work has at the same time a very specific religious tone. All the scriptural recitation, the robing and disrobing, the hieratic disposition of soloists and choral forces, and the kneeling that Vaughan Williams calls for in the score suggest the High Church Anglicanism that developed during the latter half of the Victorian period, sometimes referred to as 'ritualism' (see Hanson, 1997, 241–63, Davies, 1962, 114–39, Chadwick, 1970, 308–29). In this period the Oxford Movement's claims that the validity of the Church lay in its corporate and historical roots was translated into a revival of the historical trappings and liturgies of medieval Christianity and Roman Catholicism, with its 'emphasis on the element of ritual –

solemn, fully vestmented, often elaborate' (Mitchell, 1988, 361–2). This spirit of ritualism pervades *The Pilgrim's Progress*. It is strongest in 'The House Beautiful' with its orderly disposition of priest (Interpreter), attendants (Shining Ones), penitent/initiate (the Pilgrim), and chorus. In the action of this scene the Pilgrim twice kneels ceremonially, there are two solemn processions, the laying on of hands, the anointing of the Pilgrim's forehead, and a robing ceremony. (Similarly the ministrations of the two Heavenly Beings and priestlike Evangelist after the fight with Apollyon – the leaves of the Tree of Life and the water of the River of Life – echo the bread and wine of the Eucharist.)

Elaborately ritualistic worship could still be found in Britain in 1951, as it can today, but even by then the style was viewed by many as a Victorian throwback; the quasi-liturgical formalism in the opera was at odds both with John Bunyan's Puritanism and with the spirit of the times. No less significantly, it was at odds with Vaughan Williams's own 'cheerful agnosticism' and much of his religious *œuvre*. Vaughan Williams's attitude toward Christianity was ambivalent. Never a traditional believer, he still found life-long inspiration in the language of the Bible, its humane and universal message, and in the liturgy, poetry and hymnody that grew up within English Christianity. He saw these traditions as crucial binding elements in the shared moral culture of the nation. Nonetheless his rejection of Victorian religious sensibilities is evident in his reduction of the poetic and musical excesses of Victorian hymnody the *Hymnal* (1906) as well as in his sensual Debussian *Magnificat* (1932), whose text, he wrote to Gustav Holst, he hoped to 'lift ... out of the smug atmosphere which had settled down on it from being sung at evening service for so long' (letter to Gustav Holst, quoted in Adams 1996, 114). As Byron Adams (ibid.) writes, 'He need not have worried, for not only did he eradicate any lingering whiff of stale ecclesiastical incense, he reinterpreted the text in a manner utterly at variance with its context in the Gospel according to Luke.'

It is therefore surprising to find Vaughan Williams producing in *The Pilgrim's Progress* a work perfumed by this very incense. If the results are for the most part anachronistically Victorian, Vaughan Williams's impulse to universalize the story while embedding it in a High Church context also corresponds to a common twentieth-century English attitude toward religion: the attachment to its picturesque element. The ritualist style of worship, involving 'the wearing of Roman Catholic vestments by a priest or bishop, his assumption of an eastward position during the Holy Communion, auricular confession, sacerdotalism, Marianism, incense, bells, lighted altar candles, and the mixed chalice' (Hanson, 1997, 253), was extremely controversial when first introduced. Associated with progressive social ideas – some of the first experiments with such revivals had the particular intention of attracting the urban poor to church – it attracted the wild condemnation of political conservatives as well as evangelical Christians who saw it as Roman Catholic infiltration.[26] By early in the twentieth century the proponents of ritualism had been widely successful in their goals, but religion as a whole was losing its hold on the English. Ironically, Anglo-Catholicism eventually proved most popular with middle- and upper-class churchgoers, who increasingly attended church for the aesthetic and theatrical qualities of the services and the awe inspired by the buildings rather than out of a sense of personal conviction or the desire for salvation (McLeod, 1974, 205–6).

The Pilgrim's Progress satisfies this same desire for ritual without dogma. The distinction in the Croce quotation in Cooper's review is perfectly apt here: the opera expresses a vague religiosity without presenting any precise religion. For some critics this sensibility was identified as 'mystical'. Properly speaking, in some of Vaughan Williams's religious works such as the *Five Mystical Songs* (1911) and *Sancta Civitas* (1925) there is a strong and contemporary strain of mysticism related to that of Gustav Holst. I would argue, however, for a distinction, even in metaphorical use when discussing music, between *mysticism*, the intuitive and personal experience of the divine, usually apart from liturgy, and *ritualism*, the experience of the divine through systematized action sanctioned by tradition. *The Pilgrim's Progress* shows only a small influence of the former, chiefly in the final scene. Beyond this, as Dickinson (1963, 368–9) points out, what a listener *experiences* as mystical is an entirely personal matter.[27]

Musically and dramatically, too, the opera draws on outmoded models. As countless critics have noted, and despite Vaughan Williams's strenuous insistence that the work was a species of opera, *The Pilgrim's Progress* has much in common with the contemplative oratorio. Although it was becoming old-fashioned as a compositional genre by 1951, the *Messiah–Elijah–Gerontius* tradition of oratorio, which had virtually defined public music-making in England throughout the Victorian and Edwardian periods, still had powerful resonances for Vaughan Williams and his public. The nineteenth-century oratorios popular in England had religious themes, which lent themselves to a leisurely unfolding, and they tended to have little overt incident or character-driven action, substituting instead narration, reflection and commentary. The use of the chorus as a commentator was also characteristic, especially in scenes where specificity of character was submerged in favor of an overarching group expression – such scenes would resemble *tableaux* if they had any visual component. Indeed, although the similarity was not noted at the time, models for Vaughan Williams's mixture of ritual, action and commentary, and of character and impersonal narration, may be Elgar's two later oratorios *The Apostles* and *The Kingdom*.

In comparison with the 1906 incidental music, where he uses the chorus only in the most conventional and unavoidable moments, Vaughan Williams deploys the chorus in the opera frequently and without any specific dramatic motivation. One paradigmatic scene is 'The Arming of the Pilgrim'. In its sheer volume of sound and excitement this scene is impressive, especially with the explosive ending that Vaughan Williams added in the 1951 revision, but almost nothing happens on stage and the composer makes no attempt to differentiate musically between the Herald, the Pilgrim, and the chorus of 'certain persons clothed in gold'. All three share both the fanfare-based music which makes up the first half of the scene and the new melody ('Put on him the whole armour of light') which makes up the second half. The chorus provides a running commentary with the words of Bunyan's hymn, 'Who would true valour see', describing the action as it happens and alternately speaking *about* and *to* the Pilgrim: 'Put on him the whole armour of Light that he may be able to stand in the evil day, the shield of faith, the breastplate of righteousness, the sword of the spirit. God girdeth thee with strength of war and maketh thy way perfect.' The final scene of the opera suggests oratorio in the same fashion, as do some of the non-choral scenes such as 'The Pilgrim in Prison', which is really a setting for baritone and orchestra of Psalms 22 and 139 set in a tenuous narrative context. One could similarly argue that the Apollyon scene is more a choral–orchestral picture of the Valley of Humiliation than a scene of action and conflict. It is these very scenes, the ones most redolent of the oratorio, that have stymied directors and were the source of many of the problems of Nevill Coghill's original production.

All these elements – nineteenth-century theatrical techniques, ecclesiastical ritualism, the oratorio tradition – are not only historically retrospective but specifically national. Taken together they form a powerful nexus of markers that, intentionally or not, render *The Pilgrim's Progress* paradigmatically national in subject-matter and treatment. The source of the opera is a book central to a specifically English literary canon and one which exerted a profound influence on spoken English. The landscapes and characters are (at least presumably) historical English types. Vaughan Williams's characteristic stylistic traits were familiar to audiences throughout Great Britain and carried strong associations of essential Englishness (see Frogley, 1996). In the opera he concentrated on just these elements and capitalized on these associations, employing a straightforward 'English' modal style, almost an apotheosis of this side of his art. Even the watering-down of Bunyan's sterner vision aids this construction, as the salvation enacted becomes one that the entire nation can share without religious (or even moral) distinction. The work thus exploits the native audience's pride in its cultural past and unique religious and historical identity, an effect which resonated with certain sympathetic critics even to the point of justifying the abandonment of judgment altogether in favor of celebration. The enthusiastic critic for the *Evening News* wrote 'I don't want to analyse or criticise this work. My heart is too full. I just want to give thanks to John Bunyan and Vaughan Williams for words and music that are forever England' (Williams, 1951).

If the opera is indeed a musical–dramatic representation of England, it is a rosy prelapsarian England irretrievably at odds with social and economic reality; in this regard the opera again focuses single-mindedly on the past. Ironically, not only the England invoked but the very project of invoking it was outdated by 1951. Constructions of rural England are common in English music in the period immediately following the First World War, when in part in reaction to the war pastoralism coalesced into a recognizable cultural movement (Howkins, 1986, 80–84).[28] *The Shepherds of the Delectable Mountains*, with its elegiac tone and controlled bitonal harmonies, is one of Vaughan Williams's finest contributions to the spirit of those times.[29] *The Pilgrim's Progress* was first conceived in the same period and is an attempt to expand on the sentiments evoked by the earlier work by enlarging a brief intimate one-act opera into a grand choral public statement. But the opera's completion came in a period of vastly different national preoccupations forged by a different war and its première marked the opening of a festival dedicated to the celebration of a forward-looking, industrial, classless Britain. The type of national nostalgia in which the opera trafficked in was itself of the past.

John Bunyan's book carried associations for Vaughan Williams dating probably from his nursery days, and continuing through all his musical reactions to it, large and small, especially the seminal Reigate version. In fashioning the opera Vaughan Williams simply failed to overcome or assimilate the influence of all this earlier experience. Instead it drew him back to a vanished or vanishing aesthetic associated with earlier eras: outmoded styles of theatrical presentation, religious worship, musical expression, and national self-definition. Although there are critics who see Vaughan Williams in an exclusively nationalist and pastoralist light, these elements of *The Pilgrim's Progress* are in large part the cultural paraphernalia of the world of George MacDonald, not the materials we find in Vaughan Williams's other mature works – the grim and powerful *Sinfonia Antartica* was his next major work after the opera. One can only speculate on the reasons why these associations so dominated Vaughan Williams's work on the opera. Perhaps he was too close to the book and as he grew older, it and his earlier music for it became a means of revisiting his own personal past in a way that overwhelmed his more contemporary creative impulses. Despite his high hopes for the work, by 1951 *The Pilgrim's Progress* was something of an anachronism, even within his own *oeuvre*. The work attempts to be affirmative, but the pleasure and pride Vaughan Williams took in the score and the virtues that its proponents found in it were those of the backward glance. In Vaughan Williams's own considerable 'progress' *The Pilgrim's Progress* represents a danger not identified by Bunyan: the pitfalls of nostalgia.

Notes

1   This essay is a version of a chapter in my dissertation, *A New and Glorious Age: Constructions of National Opera in Britain 1945–1951*. I am grateful to the Carthusian Trust and the University of California at Berkeley for grants which enabled me to research this material.

2   In 1972–73 Daphne Foraud, a music teacher at Reigate Priory County Secondary School, interviewed and corresponded with the surviving members of the cast of the Reigate *Pilgrim's Progress*, uncovering the connection with the MacDonalds. Her published article (Foraud, 1975) and the fragmentary related correspondence, now part of BL Add. MS 70935, provide invaluable and neglected material on the Reigate production.

3   This later script, probably from the 1910s, contains a list of music cues which derives from the music used in the Reigate version. It includes the published materials (folk-songs and hymns) and substitutes further such material for everything composed or arranged by Vaughan Williams.

4   Another contemporary aspect of the staging was the choice of Joanna Hadley's two adolescent daughters, Ruth and Rachel Charrington, to play Faithful and Hopeful as trouser roles. Paired as these characters are with Christian, this casting must have lent a sexual *frisson* to the proceedings and at least one reviewer objected (*British Weekly*, 19 March 1908, in BL Add. MS 70937 A). Publicity photos of the Charrington sisters in the plain shifts they wore (in BL Add. MS 70937 B) suggest a Pre-Raphaelite sensibility in the design; the parallel with D'Annunzio's casting of Ida Rubinstein as St Sebastian five years later is striking.

5   The fight with Apollyon in the Village Drama Society version of Ouless's script (Ouless, N.d.) does not contain these two blackouts but occurs instead more conventionally 'in semidarkness'.

6   In addition to the numbers listed in Table 9.2 the scripts contain numerous vague indications of music to open and close scenes and to bridge scene-changes but almost no such numbers survive and there is no mention of them in the correspondence or in Vaughan Williams's programme note. Furthermore Foraud (1975, 17) claims that 'The play was greatly expanded for the London audience, not only in production, but also in music'. From the surviving manuscripts it is difficult to assess this claim. The scripts from Reigate and London reveal where additions were made to scenes but we do not

have separate lists of music cues from the different venues that would constitute definite evidence of musical changes.

7   These rustling string passages appear to represent the River of Death, the music for which one reviewer found 'beautiful in the extreme' (*Queen*, 21 March 1908, in BL Add. MS 70937 A). Although the script lists the River of Death and the Celestial City as two separate *tableaux*, the former was performed before drawn middle curtains so that the latter could already be prepared upstage. The music of the final chorus is continuous, the two scenes separated by only a brief fall of the main curtain.

8   For a discussion of scenes of music-making in Bunyan's *Pilgrim's Progress*, see Arleane Ralph 1994, 59–62.

9   Programmes from the productions and several versions of the script survive in the British Library (BL Add. MSS 70936 and 70937). In addition Foraud (1975) gives a detailed account of the planning of the Reigate production and discusses the choice of venues.

10 Clippings of advance publicity and reviews are in BL Add. MS 70937 A.

11 This one-act opera covers in a single span the same material as the last three scenes of Ouless's play. Since the action is continuous there can be no question of further trials between Christian's arrival at the Delectable Mountains and his passage through the River of Death and eventual salvation. For this reason all mention of such trials is eliminated and the Mountains are geographically relocated to the shores of the River. Ouless's published version of the Reigate play (Ouless, n.d.) adopts this same tidy compression of the end of the story.

12 Most of the musical connections in the symphony are with passages in Act One of the opera, which suggests that Vaughan Williams had worked principally on this act through the late 1930s. For a list of the passages of the opera used in the symphony see Kennedy (1996, 206). For a more thorough discussion of these borrowings see Ottaway (1953).

13 Although Kennedy (1980, 353) says that the prologue to the opera was added to the score in the 1940s (Act One having otherwise been completed by the late 1930s) and was conceived as a response to similar scenes in the BBC version, both the prologue and epilogue have more exact musical and dramatic ancestors in the Reigate production. The existence of a sketch of the opening of the opera missing both the prologue and the hymn tune 'York', mentioned in Kennedy (1996, 196), is surprising given the centrality of both of these elements to all of the versions. It may be very early, dating from a period when Vaughan Williams had not decided to adopt so much of the Reigate production, but more likely this is a sketch of the main part of the act and was intended to be combined with a prologue that was separately sketched.

14 The inclusion of *The Shepherds of the Delectable Mountains* within *The Pilgrim's Progress* creates a certain stylistic inconsistency since the music of the former work is smoother in texture, rhythmically freer, and more dissonant than the bulk of the newer music that surrounds it.

15 According to Ursula Vaughan Williams (1964, 260), the staging of the Boyg scene in a 1944 production of Peer Gynt at the Old Vic gave Vaughan Williams the idea for representing Apollyon as only a shadow.

16 Evidence that Vaughan Williams played a part in the production comes from Coghill's account of the collaboration: 'When I was asked to produce "The Pilgrim's Progress" and introduced to Dr. Vaughan Williams ... almost the first question he asked was "Will you allow me to attend rehearsals?" Nothing could have pleased me more than to have his presence; and in fact he came to almost every one, and was a mainly silent tower of strength to me, never interrupting, but often suggesting touches of the most effective kind during pauses. It turned out that the main of my ideas had his approval. Sometimes, however, when I would suggest something, he would say, "Don't like it"; then he would

pause quickly and add "But don't alter it, I may come to like it!" His ideas about the work had a welcome mixture of definiteness and elasticity' ('Did You Hear That?', 1951).

17   Coghill wisely skipped the 'Fire and Smoak'; see Wolfe (1951) for a critical reaction to this costume. Ursula Vaughan Williams (1964, 316) reports Vaughan Williams's dissatisfaction with this 'large and ridiculous Apollyon which looked like a cross between an Assyrian figure and the Michelin tyre advertisement'. See also Vaughan Williams's 17 May 1951 letter to Hubert Foss quoted in Kennedy (1980, 312).

18   A 6 May 1951 letter from E.J. Dent to Vaughan Williams (quoted in Kennedy, 1996, 202) states that much of the music that Vaughan Williams composed for the Apollyon scene was cut in the initial performances. I have found no confirmation of this contention.

19   Kennedy (1996, 193–4) gives a complete list of the cast of the first performances.

20   Reprinted with permission from *The Spectator* Magazine Limited.

21   It is not entirely clear what the critics were referring to when they argued that the opera was or was not essentially a 'pageant'. Some oppose 'pageant' to 'stage work' (as if pageants were not staged), some to 'opera'; sometimes it is a term of abuse, sometimes of praise. For most writers one element that makes a work pageant-like is the use of *tableaux*.

22   These criticisms are echoed strikingly in Furbank's (1991, 95) more general discussion of theatrical versions of Bunyan: 'In any adaptation of *The Pilgrim's Progress* ... enormously much turns, or should turn, on the handling of Christian; and this is where they mostly fall down. Something seems, fatally, to suggest to adaptors that Christian should be naive and just a shade gormless and unintelligent – the salt of the earth, of course, but dim. We look at him kindly but patronisingly, as if his problems were not our own.'

23   The 'notes on production' in the letter 6 May 1951 from E.J. Dent to Vaughan Williams after the première, quoted in Kennedy (1980, 201–2), list numerous unsuccessful and troubling details of the production, some of which indeed sound ludicrous from Dent's (admittedly partisan) description.

24   A student production was mounted in Cambridge in 1954 but, although better received in the press, it did little to stimulate renewed interest in the work. Adrian Boult recorded the work in 1970–71. The opera was first revived by the Royal Opera for several semi-staged performances and a recording in 1997.

25   Vaughan Williams's objection to cathedral performances of *The Pilgrim's Progress* may have derived in part from his desire to avoid association with any one sect or religious tradition, but in other guises, for example, as the site of the Three Choirs Festival, cathedrals seem to have been for him less sectarian houses of worship than historical meeting-places for the English nation – ideal venues, one would have thought, for a work like *The Pilgrim's Progress*.

26   In his excellent discussion of ritualism and the attacks upon it, Hanson (1997, 241–63) points out that in addition to the perceived threat of 'Popery' the movement attracted violent opposition through its associations with dandyism and decadence.

27   Several of the early reviewers claimed to see a similarity between *The Pilgrim's Progress* and *Parsifal* or claimed Wagner's work as a precedent or even a justification for Vaughan Williams's infusion of opera with ritualism. While the comparison is apt as far as scenes of ritual go, once any other dramatic element of *Parsifal* is considered – say, its elaborate musical-philosophical system of reference, or the complex psychology of its characters – the comparison begins to look a bit strained.

28   Harrington (1989), by contrast, argues that socialist politics lay behind the pastoralism of the main musical figures of this period.

29   *The Shepherds of the Delectable Mountains* is also, like the *Pastoral* Symphony, an elegy for the dead of the First World War. Paul Fussell (1975, 137–44) describes the

universal knowledge of Bunyan's book among soldiers at the front and how they drew on its geography and plot to communicate and make sense of their horrific situation. Vaughan Williams's own wartime experiences in a field ambulance unit in France probably brought him into contact with this practice. Thus there may be an additional depth of meaning to his attachment to the book after the war.

Select Bibliography

Archival Sources

Archive of the Royal Opera House, Covent Garden.
British Library Manuscript Collection.

Published Sources

Adams, Byron, 'Scripture, Church, and Culture: biblical texts in the works of Ralph Vaughan Williams', in Frogley, *Vaughan Williams Studies*, 1996a, 99–117, 1996.
Blom, Eric, [Review of *The Pilgrim's Progress.*] *Observer* (London), 29 April, 1951.
Bunyan, John, *The Pilgrim's Progress*, edited with an introduction by N.H. Keeble. Oxford: Oxford University Press, 1984.
Carner, Mosco, [Review of *The Pilgrim's Progress*] *Time and Tide*, 5 May, 1951.
Chadwick, Owen, *The Victorian church*, Part II: 1860–1901, London: Adam and Charles Black, 1970.
Cooper, Martin, 'Contemporary arts – music', *Spectator*, 585, 4 May, 1951.
Daily Mail (London), [Review of *The Pilgrim's Progress*] 27 April, 1951.
Davies, Horton, *Worship and theology in England*, Vol. 4: From Newman to Martineau, 1850–1900, Princeton: Princeton University Press, 1962.
Dent, Edward J., 'A history of English opera [Eric Walter White]', book review, *Tempo* 20 (Summer 1951), 35–6, 1951.
Dent, Edward J., 'Ralph Vaughan Williams', *Musical Times*, October 1952, 443–4, 1952.
Dickinson, Alan Edgar Frederic, *Vaughan Williams*, London: Faber and Faber, 1963.
'Did you hear that?', *Listener*, 21 June, 987, 1951.
Douglas, Roy, *Working with Vaughan Williams: The correspondence of Ralph Vaughan Williams and Roy Douglas*. London: The British Library, 1988.
Evening News (London), [Preview of *The Pilgrim's Progress*] 20 April, 1951.
Foraud, Daphne M. 'Vaughan Williams at Reigate Priory', *Composer* 43 (Spring), 15–18, 1975.
Forrest, James F. and Richard Lee Greaves, *John Bunyan: a reference guide*, Boston: G.K. Hall and Co., 1982.
Foss, Hubert James, '"The Pilgrim's Progress"', *Musical Times* (June), 274–5, 1951.
Frogley, Alain (ed.), *Vaughan Williams Studies*, Cambridge: Cambridge University Press, 1966a.
Frogley, Alain, 'Constructing Englishness in music: national character and the reception of Ralph Vaughan Williams', in Frogley, *Vaughan Williams Studies*, 1996, 1–46.

Furbank, P.N., 'Review article: Pilgrim's Progress on the stage', *Bunyan Studies* 4 (Spring), 92–5, 1991.

Fussell, Paul, *The Great War and modern memory,* London: Oxford University Press, 1975.

Glasgow Herald, [Review of *The Pilgrim's Progress*] 30 April, 1951.

'G.N.S.', 'Covent Garden. *The Pilgrim's Progress:* 26th April. Oratorio in fancy dress', *Music Review* 12/2 (May), 160, 1951.

Hanson, Ellis, *Decadence and Catholicism*, Cambridge, MA: Harvard University Press, 1997.

Harrington, Paul, 'Holst and Vaughan Williams: radical pastoral', in Christopher Norris, (ed.), *Music and the politics of culture,* London: Lawrence and Wishart, 1989.

Hope-Wallace, Philip, 'Opera: "The Pilgrim's Progress" ', *Public Opinion*, 4 May, 1951.

Howkins, Alun, 'The discovery of rural England', in Colls, Robert, and Philip Dodd, eds, *Englishness: politics and culture 1880–1920*, London: Croom Helm, 1986.

Hussey, Dyneley, 'Broadcast music: The Pilgrim's Progress', *Listener*, 3 May, 731–2, 1951.

Jacobs, Arthur, [Review of *The Pilgrim's Progress*] *Daily Express* (London), 27 April, 1951.

Kennedy, Michael, *The works of Ralph Vaughan Williams*, Second edition. Oxford: Oxford University Press, 1980.

Kennedy, Michael, *A Catalogue of the Works of Ralph Vaughan Williams*, Oxford: Oxford University Press, 1996.

McLeod, Hugh, *Class and religion in the late Victorian city*, London: Croom Helm, 1974.

Mitchell, Sally (ed.), *Victorian Britain: an encyclopedia*, New York and London: Garland Publishing, Inc., 1988.

Nellist, Brian, '*The Pilgrim's Progress* and allegory', in Vincent Newey, ed., *The Pilgrim's Progress: critical and historical views*, Liverpool: Liverpool University Press, 132–53, 1980.

Ottaway, D. Hugh, 'Vaughan Williams: Symphony in D and "The Pilgrim's Progress". A comparative note', *Musical Times* 94-1328 (October), 456–8, 1953.

Ouless, E[velyn] U. N.d. *Scenes dramatised from Bunyan's* Pilgrim's Progress, in the series 'Plays for Villages' Kelly, Lifton, North Devon: Village Drama Society, A copy of this publication is BL Add. MS 70936 C.

Owens, W.R., 'The reception of *The Pilgrim's Progress* in England', in M. van Os and G.J. Schutte (eds), *Bunyan in England and abroad: Papers delivered at the John Bunyan Tercentenary Symposium, Vrije Universiteit Amsterdam, 1988*, Amsterdam: VU University Press, 1990.

Pakenham, Simona, *Ralph Vaughan Williams: A discovery of his music*, New York: St Martin's Press, 1957.

Ralph, Arleane, '"They do such Musick make": *The Pilgrim's Progress* and textually inspired music', *Bunyan Studies* 5 (Autumn), 58–67, 1994.

Shawe-Taylor, Desmond, [Review of *The Pilgrim's Progress*] *New Statesman*, 5 May, 1951.

Smith, Cecil, [Review of *The Pilgrim's Progress*] *Daily Express* (London) [April], 1951a.

Smith, Cecil, [Review of *The Pilgrim's Progress*] *Musical America*, May, 1951b.

Tarran, Geoffrey, 'Bunyan's classic becomes a major musical event', *Morning Advertiser* (London), 1 May, 1951.

Vaughan Williams, Ralph, *The shepherds of the Delectable Mountains: a pastoral episode founded upon Bunyan's 'Pilgrim's Progress'*, completed 1922, Oxford: Oxford University Press, 1925.

Vaughan Williams, Ralph, *The Pilgrim's Progress: a morality in a prologue, four acts and an epilogue founded on Bunyan's allegory of the same name*, completed 1951, revised 1952. Piano vocal score. London: Oxford University Press, 1974.

Vaughan Williams, Ralph, Symphony No. 5 in D Major, completed 1943, music copyright Oxford University Press 1946, Miniature Score. London: Eulenberg, 1982.

Vaughan Williams, Ursula, *R.V.W.: A Biography of Ralph Vaughan Williams*, Oxford: Oxford University Press, 1964.

Williams, Stephen, [Review of *The Pilgrim's Progress*] *Evening News* (London), 27 April, 1951.

Wolfe, Peter, 'Naturalism in opera', *Theatre Newsletter*, 5/122 (12 May), 6, 1951.

Wolff, Robert Lee, *The golden key: a study of the fiction of George MacDonald*, New Haven: Yale University Press, 1961.

Chapter 10

Music, Film and Vaughan Williams[1]

Daniel Goldmark

Until recently, the least-discussed works of Ralph Vaughan Williams's musical output were his film scores, with the exception of a monograph on British film music by John Huntley and passing remarks by other critics in discussions of scores by English composers such as Walton and Britten. Jeffrey Richards's recent essay presented valuable documentation on the genesis and historical context for Vaughan Williams's wartime films.[2] His explication of the composer's film-music *œuvre* takes special account of the propagandist agenda of the pseudo-documentary films that Vaughan Williams scored, as well as how all these films fit into the general output of English film studios in the 1940s and 1950s. Yet within this account there is scant commentary on how the scores interact with and colour their narratives. For instance, Richards refers to the music for one film in the following generalized terms: 'Throughout the music is either functional or atmospheric, heightening emotion or scene-setting. It is mostly competent rather than outstanding.'[3]

This dismissal of the narratological potency in Vaughan Williams's film music is both regrettable and all too common; in fact, few critics seem willing to come to terms with the notion that the composer would write music of such limited practical value as being destined *only* for the screen, buried beneath a soundtrack dominated by dialogue and sound effects. Instead, the writers heap praise on the conversion of the scores into concert suites, dissecting how the scores became the starting-point for larger and greater (and more utilitarian) chamber and orchestral pieces.[4] Several of Vaughan Williams's later works do indeed draw upon, either explicitly or more indirectly, musical themes first created in his film scores. While this discussion touches upon the reactions of certain of the composer's contemporaries to these cinema-inspired concert works, most of this essay will investigate exactly how Vaughan Williams's music interacts with the visual imagery and the dramatic narrative contained in the films he scored. Since two of these films have received a disproportionate amount of criticism – also the same film scores from which the composer created new and successful symphonic works – they seem the most appropriate for scrutiny: *49th Parallel* and *Scott of the Antarctic*. Looking at these two feature films from the opposite ends of Vaughan Williams's film music career will allow us to see not only how his abilities and attitudes as a film composer developed over the years, but will also let us compare how his music evolved from being largely effective – music appropriate only to specific scenes in a certain film – to evoking more of an affective atmosphere.

208 *Vaughan Williams Essays*

Vaughan Williams on Film

> Ralph had been a fairly regular cinema goer ... He enjoyed films, though he maintained that
> the cinema had never been fantastic enough, and that no one had explored the possibilities
> of the medium. Disney, he said, had paved the way for an El Greco, who had not yet arisen,
> and he would have liked to work with Disney in a cartoon film. He was delighted when, in
> 1940, he was asked to write music for an exciting spy-adventure story, with an excellent
> cast, called *49th Parallel* – an ex-pupil of his, Muir Mathieson, was the director of music
> for London Films, and it was to his suggestion that Ralph owed this invitation. He was
> rather dismayed to find that he had to write very fast: the first lot of material was wanted
> almost at once, but his ideas flowed, and there was no limitation on the size or composition
> of the orchestra. He became fascinated too by the split-hair timings: a second of music
> meant *exactly* a second of music and this was quite a new frame to musical thought. He
> liked the people at the studio and he thoroughly enjoyed having a musical job to do.[5]

Vaughan Williams was 68 years old when Muir Mathieson, the musical director for
the Crown Film Unit, first approached him and asked if he would be interested in
writing an original score for a motion picture.[6] With four symphonies, several stage
works, dozens of chamber pieces, and countless folk song transcriptions already to
his credit, Vaughan Williams made the unexpected foray into one of the few areas of
musical exploration he had yet to investigate. He could not have taken on the new
task for the prestige value, as he was one of the pre-eminent composers of concert
music in Britain. Money – had an amount of any significance been available – would
not have influenced him either. As the above recollection from Ursula Vaughan
Williams indicates, the composer had already given some thought to the art of
film-making, and most likely harboured a hitherto unacknowledged desire to be
involved with a project of some sort. The outbreak of war compounded his longing
for some task by which a musician – especially an older composer – could serve his
country in a time of need. Mathieson recalled recruiting Vaughan Williams as follows:

> 'When I went to see Vaughan Williams at his country home in the spring of 1940,' says
> Muir, 'I found him strangely depressed at his inability to play a fuller part in the war. He
> felt that the musician had done little to express the spirit and resolve of the British people.
> At that time he was 'doing his bit' by driving a cart round the village and countryside,
> collecting scrap metal and salvage. (Vaughan Williams was then over 70 years [*sic*] of
> age). I told him the story of *49th Parallel* and tried to show how the cinema could help to
> achieve those objects for which he was striving. His enthusiasm was wonderful. He set to
> work right away – and remember this was the first time he had ever consented to write for
> the screen.'[7]

Vaughan Williams eventually wrote his first score, for *49th Parallel*, without any
apparent training or instruction in the nuances of film composition. Not until he
had worked on several films did he seek any formal advice, in the guise of some
helpful hints from Roy Douglas, the composer and copyist who would eventually
come to work with Vaughan Williams, copying and otherwise preparing most of
his later large scores for publication. Douglas recalled:

> In this instance he had been told that I might be able to give him information about certain
> 'tricks of the trade' in connection with scoring music for film sound tracks; in those days

some combinations of instruments were more effective than others for recordings purposes, and it was useful for a composer to know about such refinements of technique ... Then he showed me the scores which he had written for his next film (this was either *The People's Land* [1942] or *Flemish Farm* [1943]), and I suggested a few minor alterations here and there to improve the clarity of texture for the sound track.[8]

It seems unlikely that Vaughan Williams, who studied orchestration with Ravel, would have needed any advice in that area, but, as Douglas mentioned, certain timbral combinations did indeed (and still do) come across better than others in the film soundtrack. Considering the still somewhat primitive state of sound-recording technology at the time, the film composer needed to use all the skill at his disposal if the melody was to be projected clearly through a lattice of effects and dialogue. Hints such as these no doubt encouraged Vaughan Williams when composing for future films; by the time he finished the score for *The Loves of Joanna Godden* (1947), for example, he so surpassed the production curve that he sent the musical director the score before the film's completion![9]

The same year that Vaughan Williams wrote the score for the film *Stricken Peninsula* (1945), his essay 'Composing for the Films' appeared in *The R.C.M. Magazine*, presenting his ideas about the role of music in film, the kinds of film-music he believed to be useful, as well as his recommendations as to how an effective and compelling score might be written.[10] He regards wryly the time limits put on film music composers – mentioning that he was once given a score assignment to be completed in four days' time – and speaks from the point of view of an experienced teacher when he calls film composing a 'splendid discipline' for those young composers with a tendency toward procrastination or taking their own music too seriously. Acknowledging the *least* appealing aspect of film music – dealing with the producer – Vaughan Williams delineates two approaches. The first, 'in which every action, word, gesture or incident is punctuated in sound', leans toward the effective side of composing; this practice typically involves, just as Vaughan Williams describes, writing musical cues for a film that musically emphasize or even mimic the action on screen. The 'other method of writing film music, which personally I favour, partly because I am quite incapable of doing the first, is to ignore the details and to intensify the spirit of the whole situation by a continuous stream of music. This stream can be modified (often at rehearsal!) by points of colour superimposed on the flow.'[11] By the time he wrote this essay, Vaughan Williams had already written music for five of the ten films to which he would contribute original scores, and thus had already come quite far in his transition from composing in the first style. Whether he acknowledged it or not, however, he did occasionally practice the first method, particularly in his earliest films, such as *Coastal Command* and *49th Parallel*, which I will discuss presently.

His reference to the stream of music changing during rehearsal reveals that Vaughan Williams showed an acute awareness of perhaps the greatest challenge the composer faces when working in the film industry: the constant production changes, often made up to the very day of a film's release. Scenes may appear on or disappear from the working print of a film with amazing celerity, and since the score usually does not come into consideration until late in the production schedule, the composer may face an entirely different turn of cinematic events when he goes to write his music and looks at the film's *original* manifest. While a spotting session – the meeting at which the composer, director and music editor gather to watch a rough cut of the film and determine for what scenes music should be composed – gives the director the opportunity to make specific requests for the music, no promises or guarantees are made that the director will keep any or all of the music once it has been completed.[12] Composers must therefore be willing to shorten, lengthen, or otherwise alter their original music until it fits both the film's needs and the director's capricious whims. Vaughan Williams obviously understood the desires of the directors he worked with, and apparently was quite willing to let them manipulate his scores; in 'Composing for the Films' he mentions: 'I need hardly say that the same give-and-take would be necessary here, that is, that the composer must be ready occasionally to modify his music to fit the action and dialogue.'[13] Jeffrey Dell, the writer and director of *Flemish Farm*, commented that, 'He was quite wonderful at recording sessions, inviting criticism and making alterations to the score on the spot to meet our ideas. I blush at the memory of our effrontery!'[14] Michael Kennedy also mentions that Vaughan Williams trusted Ernest Irving, musical director of *Flemish Farm* (and all of Vaughan Williams's Ealing films) with the great responsibility of faithfully manipulating the composer's completed score for the sake of its continuity and efficacy in the film. We will see just how dedicated Irving was to preserving Vaughan Williams's artistic integrity when we look at *Scott of the Antarctic*.

Not surprisingly, Vaughan Williams also disagrees with the usual point at which the discussion and creation of music should begin in the production process. Although he offers no real solution, we can sense his frustration with how little regard film music receives from producers and directors alike, realizing that the music can become an easy target for criticism, especially when a score aspires to weave itself into the consciousness of the viewer. Even the composer rarely has much invested in the music other than seeing it as a source of financial gain:

> So the music only comes in when all the photography is done and the actors dispersed to their homes or to their next job. Perhaps the composer has (unwisely from the practical point of view) already read the script and devised music for certain situations as he has imagined them before seeing the pictures, but what can he do about it? The photograph is already there, the timing is rigidly fixed and if the composer's musical ideas are too long or too short they must be cut or repeated, or worse still, hurried or slowed down, because, the photograph once taken, there can be no re-timing.[15]

Despite the risky nature of composing in advance of the film's completion, as he outlines above, Vaughan Williams became known for working from the most basic story elements available, possibly to compel himself to compose not to the action of the film, but rather to the emotional undercurrents throughout the story. As noted above, an example of Vaughan Williams's promptness may be found in the history of his work on *The Loves of Joanna Godden* (1947): Ernest Irving's letter to Vaughan Williams indicating his receipt of the score read, in part, 'Never in the history of Ealing, or for that matter of the world, has the score been finished before the film, and I am carefully concealing it from the directors, who must not be approached from windward.' Perhaps Vaughan Williams's zeal betrayed his interest in creating a film in which the score comes first, the film therefore being shot and edited to correspond with the score. In his own way he tried to change the dominant system in the industry with his industrious composing.

Critical Responses to Vaughan Williams's Film Music

By the time Vaughan Williams entered the world of film music, established composers of concert music had already been working in cinema for some thirty years, beginning with Camille Saint-Saëns's original music to accompany the pre-sound film *L'Assassinat du duc de Guise* (1908). In England, Bliss, Britten and Walton already had much experience scoring films by the late 1930s, and thus Vaughan Williams began his career as a film composer quite late, not only for his age, but also compared to the precedent set by younger colleagues.

Few critics understood film composing the same way the composers did; the latter saw exciting opportunities for creativity and involvement in a burgeoning industry, along with a new, previously unheard-of manner of getting one's music to tremendous numbers of people at once, especially people who had little or no interest in classical music. As Ernest Irving put it, 'There is one advantage in writing film music; millions of people have to listen to it whether they like it or not'.[16]

From the perspective of those critics intimately involved with film music, Vaughan Williams was not only a capable composer, but one whose pedigree as a famous 'classical' composer, like Walton and others, might have compelled directors to give him work on more important film projects. As English critic John Huntley put it in 1946:

> Once the names of Arthur Bliss, William Walton, and Ralph Vaughan Williams meant little to the publicity offices of the British film distributors. Music was not worth bothering about; who cared if the London Symphony Orchestra was playing the background music in 'Passion Dust'? Today we are delighted to find that the film companies are beginning to realize that music is an important component in modern motion pictures, that here the foremost composers of today are expending their talents to give added punch to pictures.[17]

Of course, Huntley does not clarify whether the 'added punch' in modern pictures came from the general increase in skilled writing by film composers, or from the years of experience possessed only by those musicians with name recognition before working in films. Either way, he and others interested in film music seemed genuinely glad to have a man of such fame and stature as Vaughan Williams working in films; perhaps they believed if enough established composers wrote for films, listeners, including critics, would take the music more seriously.

Unfortunately, not all of Vaughan Williams's associates and admirers regarded his foray into film quite so positively. Hubert Foss, Vaughan Williams's original publisher at Oxford University Press and also one of his earliest biographers, was rather dismissive of film music; perhaps he was upset because the film scores seemingly had little or no potential for further publication as symphonic scores.[18] Foss finds so little value in film music, even that composed by Vaughan Williams, that he reassures his readers that the main title music for *49th Parallel* eventually found a more accessible – and even *more* commercial – format: 'The first tune – across the "credits" – of *49th Parallel* was splendid, and I am glad to record that this tune is available in print to all under the guise of *The New Commonwealth*, with admirable words by Harold Child.'[19] Foss further delivers a backhanded compliment when he lauds Vaughan Williams's abilities as a film composer while simultaneously revealing that he knows nothing about film music: 'For myself, I am incapable of judging film music without extra-musical information. Of Vaughan Williams's technical skill there could be no longer any doubt.'[20] While Foss would not have dared to characterize Vaughan Williams's film music as pandering to the public taste, he can still only offer his friend's work qualified praise.

Foss's stature in the English musical and critical establishment clearly influenced other critics. One of these was Frank Howes, who takes the disapprobation leveled at Vaughan Williams and brings it up to date with the score for *Scott of the Antarctic*: 'the inevitable scrappiness of the completed film score ensures that such music will rarely achieve any independent life of its own; it will not be published, and as Hubert Foss says, it can hardly be criticized without seeing the film concurrently with the hearing of its soundtrack.'[21] Howes takes Foss's argument even further, however, by stating that the music created for a film cannot stand on its own merits without the film to support it:

> The other subjects show how it is possible in a few bars to set a scene, depict a mood, sketch an episode, and also how such vignettes, vivid and even perfect as they may be, are useless for any other purpose as they stand. The *Sinfonia Antartica* however shows that regarded as raw material they can be recomposed into an expanded composition. But this is a supreme exception to a general rule that such episodic music has no inner vitality of its own and, owing to formal restriction that precludes repetition and development, is incapable of achieving independence of the film.[22]

Yet another contemporaneous critic, Simona Pakenham, sees only in Vaughan Williams's scores the seeds of future concert works unfettered by the visual handicap of film:

> His scores were masterly, in one or two cases lifting a mediocre script into distinction, only occasionally overpowering the film altogether. Finally in 1948 the score commissioned by Ealing Studios for *Scott of the Antarctic* started something in his mind that would not let him rest until, in 1952, it emerged as the colossal 'Sinfonia Antartica'. I listened to these film scores, I have to admit, with my eyes occasionally shut in case the film for which they were supposed merely to be the background might detract from my enjoyment of the music. I was deeply suspicious of my favourite composer's new-found enthusiasm, fearing for all the music that might be lost for ever. I need not have worried. Vaughan Williams is no more willing than his hearers to lose sight of a good idea.[23]

It would be fascinating to know if Vaughan Williams ever saw this review and had any opinion of it; Pakenham, in her reverence for Vaughan Williams's music, did not realize that by genuflecting in the theater every time the music played, she robbed herself of the pleasure of seeing how well the music illustrated the images on screen, leaving it instead to her own imagination. Like the other critics,

Pakenham tries to convince the reader that the musical ideas contained within the *Sinfonia Antartica* merely appeared in the score for *Scott* in an embryonic or imperfect state, as if the composer wished to experiment with some new ideas in a less serious medium, and thus could use the film as a testing ground for his ideas.

Vaughan Williams apparently foresaw the possibility that commentators would make comparisons between the film and orchestral scores of *Scott* and the *Sinfonia*, which the following letter, dated only 'October 26', from Muir Mathieson's brother to the Head of the Music Library of the British Museum attests:

> At the time that V.W. wrote the music
> to the film 'Scott of the Antarctic', he was insistent that
> his score should not be available for comparison
> with that of the Antarctic Symphony, a responsibility I
> accepted when I became Music Director at Ealing Studios, but
> without much confidence as the score had been duplicated
> in the first place. The Main Title music and Prologue were put
> on exhibition at one time and never returned to me, but
> pages 11–145 and the alternative march that V.W. wrote
> during the recording are still with me and have been
> seen by no one else except James McKay Martin
> who knew V.W. well ...[24]

His vehement opposition to comparing the two works reveals that Vaughan Williams *did* see them as separate entities, and that the film score was not an early sketch whose ideas were eventually worked out and perfected in the *Sinfonia*, as his critics are wont to suggest. Unfortunately, Vaughan Williams's desires went unheeded; as recently as 1970 his biographers still took a dim view of the music for *Scott*, in this case as a detracting element to the *Sinfonia*: 'Despite moments of grandeur and great beauty, the [*Sinfonia Antartica*] has never been wholly accepted. Perhaps its connection with the film world is a little too obvious.'[25]

Throughout his life, music critics constantly reminded Vaughan Williams that music composed for use in films would *never* attain the status of a piece written for its aesthetic value alone; this critical assault persisted long after the composer's death. The 'lowbrow' position to which film music was relegated by such commentators, because of its association with cinema, an art form still struggling for acceptance as a fine art, comes not only from the mistaken notion that films pander to audiences, but also from the similarly misguided idea that a score serves no other purpose than to provide musical clichés and evoke the proper sentiment at the appropriate moment. Arguments such as these – perhaps articulated most notoriously in Hanns Eisler and Theodor Adorno's Marxist text (coincidentally titled) *Composing for the Films* – refer usually to the films produced by the Hollywood studio system, where mass production was widely perceived as its *raison d'être*. Criticism of this sort aimed at film composers who worked outside of Hollywood comes more from a lack of knowledge on the authors' part of the methods employed by independent film companies. Yet even film historian Jeffrey Richards, whose essay on Vaughan Williams's film scores thoughtfully accounts for his interactions with the studios, still finds no fault with previous critics' dismissal of Vaughan Williams's scores:

But Vaughan Williams was well aware of what elements within the score could be retrieved. A suite was prepared from the music [to *49th Parallel*] and played at a festival of British film music in Prague in 1946 but this was subsequently suppressed by the composer. [The prelude] was set to words as an anthem *The New Commonwealth* by Harold Child, librettist of [Vaughan Williams's] opera *Hugh the Drover*, for unison voices with piano or orchestral accompaniment.[26]

Like Hubert Foss above, Richards immediately directs the reader to the rearrangement of the music from *49th Parallel* rather than discussing the score or bringing any of its numerous high points to the attention of his readers. Although he has less invested in Vaughan Williams's collected works than did Foss, Richards still fails to find any intrinsic merit in the music for its contributions to the film, valuing it only as a stepping-stone to a new concert work.

49th Parallel

The *49th Parallel* recordings were most exciting – the London Symphony Orchestra, led by George Stratton, enjoyed themselves, the tunes seemed to fit well to the film sequences, Ralph did not appear to be at all nervous, he was prepared to cut, enlarge, alter, adapt – in fact he had begun to realize that, as he said later, you could use the same music for a landscape, a car crash, or a love scene; it would sound different if it looked different ... We saw the film in the autumn and it had a great success.[27]

For most composers, inexperienced or seasoned, *49th Parallel* would have been an overwhelming assignment: its story embodied elements of a war picture, an action film and a travelogue, all of which needed to satisfy the requirements of the government bureau that produced the film, the Ministry of Information (MoI). Anthony Aldgate discusses that the propagandist nature of *49th Parallel* meant emphasizing the intelligence, strength, and willpower of the Canadians, while simultaneously undercutting the Nazis at every turn by portraying them as petty, sadistic, and 'making absurd errors of judgement'.[28] Vaughan Williams was undeterred by the complexity of the film, and understood what the score needed to be successful: first, music that would evoke the beauty and splendor of the Canadian countryside, panoramic shots of which featured largely in the film; next, music specific to the individual episodes or incidents involving the Nazis and the Canadians whom they encountered; and, finally, music for the Nazis themselves, probably the most difficult task, as giving the protagonists their own theme or motive, quite a common practice in most films (and operas before them), might have the undesired effect of prompting the audience to sympathize with their position, as opposed to regarding the Germans as ruthless, cut-throat villains.

Briefly, the film follows members of a Nazi submarine crew who, their sub having been destroyed by the Canadian Royal Air Force not long after they left it to forage for supplies, must make their way to freedom through enemy (that is, to the Nazis) territory. Each encounter they have with Canadians – an incident at a trading post, a brief stay at a Hutterite settlement, an Indian Day celebration, a battle (verbal and physical) of aesthetics in the forest, and, finally, with a Canadian soldier on the US/Canada border – would be, as Aldgate says, 'a thoroughly schematic and heavily programmed attempt to fulfil all the criteria of excellence for film propaganda laid down by the Films Division of the MoI. It addressed the larger question of "what we are fighting for" and in so doing very carefully and conscientiously set out the advantages of adhering to democratic ideals ...'.[29]

In his desire to portray the fugitive Nazis in the least favorable light possible, Vaughan Williams consequently denied them any extensive thematic development. Because the story progresses as we watch the Nazis work their way slowly to the forty-ninth parallel and freedom, and as the members of the submarine crew yield to one domineering force or another, picked off one by one like weak animals, the composer provided music (although not nearly as much for the Nazis' sake) for the dramatic moments in the film in which their path intersects the lives of the unsuspecting – although certainly not helpless – Canadians.

Lieutenant Hirth (Eric Portman) wins the prize as the Nazi most unwilling to keep his political views to himself, even when he faces imminent danger. A true zealot, Hirth goes through the entire film without showing a shred of compassion or emotion – other than what he displays during his vitriolic speechifying – and thus receives absolutely no music of his own. Leaving all the Nazis totally without music would have been jarring, however, as they do occupy the majority of the narrative, and so Vaughan Williams uses cues for the Nazis that give them a menacing aura, without romanticizing their situation; in fact, practically all of their cues come at moments of desperation or simply abject villainy.

Witness their initial appearance: disturbing the peaceful waters off Port Lawrence, the Nazi submarine surfaces, bringing the front lines of the Second World War uncomfortably close to Canadian soil. The manner in which Vaughan Williams signifies the Germans musically would become typical in his future film projects, for he employed a traditional religious (or folk) melody that the audience could identify with the characters. In this case, Vaughan Williams distorts the Lutheran chorale 'Ein feste Burg ist unser Gott', which, Richards points out, is 'an ironic comment, surely, on the perversion of German faith by the Nazis'.[30] The melody – rather, its initial motive, the three repeated notes and then the leap of a fourth downward, played on the low brass – suddenly disrupts the quiet mood of the seascape as the submarine breaks the surface. Moving inside the vessel, we hear an entire statement of the first phrase of the melody, followed by two repetitions of the last four notes of the theme, a four-note descending scale with denser orchestration. Vaughan Williams will bring back this descending line, along with the opening motive of the hymn, to use for the Nazis in later scenes. To finish off this scene, however, he continues with parts of 'Ein feste Burg' on various instruments as the U-boat surveys the damage it has inflicted on a Canadian oil tanker; as one of the officers walks across the surfaced submarine's deck, for instance, high, muted trumpets play quickly through the full melody, conjuring a militaristic sound.

The next time we hear these motives it is just after the Nazis' stolen plane runs out of fuel and crashes, killing Lieutenant Kuhnecke, the pilot and second in command under Hirth, with whom the latter had disagreed over leadership. A somber string cue plays as the soldiers inform Hirth of Kuhnecke's death; 'Ein feste Burg' does not come in until one of the soldiers, Vogel, crosses himself in plain sight, to Hirth's evident displeasure. As Vogel mourns, the light pizzicato theme shifts suddenly to three slowly repeated notes on trombones, growing in intensity, and punctuated with a final and quite loud chord – an A minor ninth missing the seventh of the chord. The sudden *sforzando*, referred to in film-music parlance as a *stinger*, assures the audience that Vogel's overt display of piety foreshadows his unhappy fate, especially with Hirth watching him constantly. We also hear hints of the motive from the film's opening during the scene in which Hirth and the remaining two soldiers assault a traveling salesman on the road. Here, a sequence of chords, again played in the brass, builds in strength as the impending danger to the salesman increases. Later, when Hirth's henchman Lohrmann (John Chandos) faces an irate Philip Armstrong Scott (Leslie Howard) one on one, 'armed superman' against 'decadent democrat', the music does not appear. We should not be surprised by this, however, for without his fanatical leader there to urge him on, Lohrmann's anger and strength abate; Vaughan Williams lets the viewer know that the Nazi will lose the battle by not allowing him any music.

Vaughan Williams's atmospheric music also figures in several recurring scenes; in this case, since much of the film involves traveling throughout the countryside, many opportunities arise to provide music for montages that feature footage of various Canadian landscapes. The first of these immediately follows the film's opening prologue, with the narrator's description of the 'only undefended frontier in the world'. The theme, at first stately and solemn with a sustained high note on strings and melody in the woodwinds as we view Canadian plains and wheat fields, soon erupts into a brass fanfare to accompany an overhead shot of an urban manufacturing site, then quickly transforms into the opening chords of 'O Canada!' Similar montage scenes occur when the three Nazis walk through the Canadian countryside in search of transportation, accompanied by a new theme led by a bassoon.

For Hirth and Lohrmann's encounter with the aesthete Philip Armstrong Scott, Vaughan Williams employs some of his most impressionistic sonorities. The image is of Scott sitting in a canoe, fishing on a serene lake in the middle of the mountains; since neither the Nazis nor the audience know exactly what to think of or expect from this new personage, the composer fills in the blanks. The gentle, slowly unfolding melodic line played on solo piano offers a welcome contrast to the often harsh sounds that have accompanied the Nazis' path of mayhem through the previous scenes, and gives us adequate insight into Scott's artistic and peaceful psyche.[31]

Vaughan Williams's understanding of the powerful narrative role the score for *49th Parallel* possessed becomes most clear in his music for the encounters with various Canadians. A good example is the episode that takes place at a settlement of Hutterites (a sect of Mennonites). Walking through the woods (underscored by pizzicato strings), the remaining Nazis – now numbering four, including Hirth and the sympathetic Vogel – come upon a large expanse of waving wheat. A folk-like melody on oboe immediately begins to play, with other woodwinds harmonizing behind it. Seeing a young girl, Anna (Glynis Johns), building a scarecrow, the Nazis hide. The camera moves closer into Anna's space, where we see the scarecrow she builds while humming a melody to herself. As the point of view switches back to the Nazis spying on her with binoculars, her song's melody continues – having been assumed by a lone clarinet in the underscore – beneath her observers' scheming conversation. The score thus bridges the visual gap between Anna and those spying on her by allowing her melody to underscore their conversation.[32]

Incidentally, the melody introduced by Anna in this theme, referred to in the original manuscript both by its opening line, 'Lasst uns das Kindlein wiegen', and by the title 'Anna's *Volkslied*', becomes the dominant theme for the Hutterite portion of the film. Vaughan Williams wrote a harmonized version of the theme (in G major, the same key it is originally sung in) alongside the score indication, 'Dinner time. The head of the settlement enters and greets them.' In fact, the music does not actually appear until the end of the dinner scene, as the Hutterites exit the dining hall and sing the *Volkslied* again, further identifying that particular melody with the settlement as a whole (Example 10.1). Vaughan Williams's

Example 10.1   Add. MS 50422 D, f. 14v; five measures, piano score

setting, obviously influenced by years of writing new folk-song harmonizations, creates the perfect balance between religious piety and a simple, meaningful purity that these immigrant settlers are meant to evoke. The Nazis clearly have no chance in this clash of ideologies: as the Hutterite leader Peter reminds Hirth, who unsuccessfully addressed the settlement on the superiority of the Aryan people, the Hutterites left their native Germany to escape the mentality that the Nazis espouse. Since the Nazis never get a solid footing in the settlement, their music does not dominate any of the scenes in this portion of the film; it's the Nazis who have crossed into the settlement, therefore the music they (and we) hear belongs to the Hutterites.

In an apparent desire to get a jump on the writing process – clearly a necessity judging by the 'Till Wednesday' quotation often attached to the length of time he was given to write this score[33] – Vaughan Williams devised several themes that did not end up in the film's final soundtrack, most likely because the scenes for which they were written seem to have been excised from the film's final cut. In the set of music manuscript books labeled '49th ||ᵇ', we find that Vaughan Williams titled each section of his manuscript according to the story being acted out – a common technique among film composers for keeping track of the narrative.[34] In several of the notebooks, however, the words to what is presumably voice-over dialogue for the opening of the film that went unused can be found throughout the score. For instance, in one sketchbook the text begins, 'Canada! A country of homely people, bound by strong ties of sentiment to the mother country.' The description later goes on to read, with the music for the first shot of the Nazi submarine, 'But suddenly there appears on the horizon a new element. The Nazi with his creed "Ein Feste Burg ist unser – Führer"!' While this dialogue – presumably edited in parts by the composer – did not make it into the film, the music Vaughan Williams wrote did; these early two-stave sketches include the use of a menacing harmonization of 'Ein feste Burg' for the Nazis' introductory theme (Example 10.2).[35]

Example 10.2   Add. MS 50422 A, f. 12v ; two measures, single stave

One theme that did *not* make the film, however, appeared in a scene omitted from the introduction: the manuscript indicates that panoramic shots of several cities were to be shown, presumably during the opening montage sequence, including Ottawa, Montreal, Quebec and Vancouver. The text for this final city reads, 'To Vancouver – In a dance hall a (german) band is playing a (german) valse. The dance is interrupted while the news is announced. The Dance starts again – at first slowly – But soon spirits rise and the news is forgotten.' (The 'news' refers to the presence of the Nazi submarine in Canadian waters.) Vaughan Williams had written a waltz melody to accompany this scene (Example 10.3). This music does not appear

Example 10.3   Add. MS 50422 D, f. 1r; three measures, piano score

anywhere in the film, since the final story did not include any scenes of dancing or merry-making; in fact, with the exception of a few scenes of playful banter between Johnnie the trapper (Laurence Olivier) and his friend the factor (Finlay Currie), and Anna the Hutterite's cheerful singing, very little about this film evokes feelings of happiness or merriment. Yet in spite of the cloud of fascism that hangs over the story – constantly reminding us of the evils of Nazism – Vaughan Williams's score varies greatly in mood, moving from jarring, violent chords – when the Nazis attack a motorist and steal his possessions – to the highly impressionistic piano music used for Scott's backwoods retreat.

Just as important as the scenes with music are those that went unscored. The bombing of the Nazi submarine by the Air Force goes on for quite some time, and has no underscore whatsoever. Likewise, no music colors the entire sequence beginning with Johnnie's shooting at the Nazis' hands and continuing on with the looting of the trading post, the mass shooting of the Eskimos on the beach, and the

Nazis' subsequent escape by plane and eventual crash landing. According to Vaughan Williams's sketchbooks, he did write music for the looting and for the frantic plane trip, but somewhere during the production process these cues must have been cut. The entire final scene set in the train bound for America has no music, although the film ends with a complete restatement of the music for the main titles. In this case, we can assume Vaughan Williams may have had ideas about scoring these scenes – judging from the remaining sketches he obviously had more than just ideas about some of them – but the film's director or musical director decided that those scenes would be best served without music. Perhaps the director felt that too much dramatic underscoring might detract from the hyper-realistic manner in which the Nazis' evil was made manifest; on the other hand, some truly pathetic music for the beach shooting or Johnnie's death would have served to vilify further the Nazis.

The music in *49th Parallel* strikes a careful balance between atmospheric cues representing the Canadian setting and specific cues meant to enhance the action or understanding of a particular scene. This latter form, referred to in Vaughan Williams's essay above as the lesser form of film composing, cannot help but dominate the score, as action-adventure films usually demand that a great deal of the actual storytelling is found in the score, simultaneously enhancing the general mood of the narrative. While such scene-painting was a requirement for wartime action films (including his next film, *Coastal Command*), Vaughan Williams quickly moved to working almost exclusively in the second mode, in which the score both draws from and nourishes the underlying emotions and mood of the narrative. This is the style that he experimented with in *Flemish Farm* and *The Loves of Joanna Godden*, and finally perfected in *Scott of the Antarctic*.

Scott of the Antarctic

> In the pantheon of British polar failures, no one could be more romantic than the man Amundsen beat, Sir Robert Falcon Scott ...
>
> – Anne Fadiman[36]

Like *49th Parallel*, *Scott of the Antarctic*'s narrative involves individuals traversing a hostile environment. For the Nazis in *49th Parallel*, their presence in Canada immediately turned them into enemies of practically everyone whom they encountered, as their ideological views (and desire for world domination) were in sharp conflict with the ideals of the democratic Canadian citizens. *Scott of the Antarctic*, however, deals with an alienation rooted slightly more in terra firma: the long-awaited conquest of the Antarctic, to be achieved by whomever was the first to reach the South Pole.

Ealing Studios produced *Scott* in 1948, some three dozen years after Scott and his quartet of ill-fated traveling companions had perished in the Arctic wastes. Scott's story continued to resonate as a national tragedy in England. To succeed in 1948, however, the film could not just draw on the general public's knowledge of what Scott and his men had attempted to achieve; the film-makers had to create a truly vibrant and compelling depiction of the expedition. The film's setting was potentially both an advantage and a drawback: while few people had ever been to the Antarctic, just as few might have had any interest in the snowy wasteland. Director Charles Frend's decision to produce portions of the film in the Antarctic must have seemed like a surefire way to interest audiences in the production. George Perry also points out that the 'beautiful documentary footage shot on the original expedition on black-and-white nitrate stock by Herbert Ponting was studied closely and some shots were even accurately duplicated'.[37] A technical innovation also set *Scott* apart for the studio, for this was only Ealing's second film shot in color. While much of the landscape would be monochromatic, the thrill of seeing such a strange and forbidding place in true-to-life color added another level of visual intensity and vibrancy to the film.[38]

Meanwhile, in Dorking:

> Earlier in the year Ernest Irving had written to ask Ralph to write music for the film about Scott's expedition to the South Pole. He was at first reluctant to commit so much time – but Irving was persuasive, and the idea of the strange world of ice and storm began to fascinate him. The film studio provided books, and *The Worst Journey in the World* joined *Jane Eyre, Pendennis, The Way of all Flesh*, and *Far From the Madding Crowd* as general reading. Pictures of the Scott expedition lay about the house and work was begun. Ralph became more and more upset as he read about the inefficiencies of the organization; he despised heroism that risked lives unnecessarily, and such things as allowing five to travel on rations for four filled him with fury.[39]

While the film-makers strove for realistic footage of the Antarctic landscape, adding Vaughan Williams's name to the production increased the prestige surrounding the film. Vaughan Williams had worked with Ernest Irving, the musical director at Ealing, once before, while writing his first score for the studio, *The Loves of Joanna Godden*. Irving received his early training in dramatic music – as did many film composers of the time – as a theater musician. He worked as a conductor and composer in West End theaters for many years before beginning his tenure at Ealing. Irving's long experience in the theater world, as well as his work composing music for silent films and conducting the film scores of others, made him somewhat cynical – or perhaps simply realistic – when discussing the place of the musician within the motion picture industry. In a 1943 article in *Music and Letters* Irving asserted that music in films 'is more frequently used to intensify, underline, accelerate or aggrandize, to cause excitement and to affect the subconsciousness of the audience. Its appeal must be eighty per cent. subconscious because it has to operate upon a large body of people of whom at least eighty per cent. are non-musical.'[40] Irving understood that the audience could not be expected to pay conscious attention to the music; he accordingly directed the composers he commissioned to write Ealing scores to create music that would heighten the emotional level of a scene and therefore 'affect the subconsiousness of the audience'.

Vaughan Williams was Irving's original choice as the composer for *Scott*. Irving recalled that 'everybody [at Ealing Studios] agreed that, if Dr Vaughan Williams could be interested, he was the one man in the world to write the score. I rang him up; he liked the idea ... and we had a big round-table conference at which he told us all his plans which were agreed enthusiastically and unanimously.'[41] As Ursula

Vaughan Williams documents, Vaughan Williams threw himself into the task of composing a score for *Scott* with great gusto, so much so that he decided to forgo the traditional – and practical – process of seeing a rough cut of the film before writing the score.[42] While we can admire his enthusiasm, composing the cues in advance meant that Vaughan Williams relied upon the film's script, as well as written accounts of the journey as it was described in books like *The Worst Journey in the World*, not knowing how the story might be altered or embellished in production. This explains why so many of the cues expressly establish mood and setting of the story, rather than describing specific moments of action, as in *49th Parallel*.[43] Rather, the near-crepuscular skies, with the light staying at the same level for days on end (an annual event in the extreme latitudes, referred to as the 'midnight sun'), in addition to the ice floes and polar winds mentioned above, offered several (more conceptual) idiosyncrasies of the polar region that might benefit from a musical analogue. By concentrating on describing images of 'the physical sensations of ice, of wind blowing over the great, uninhabited desolation, of stubborn and impassable ridges of black and ice-covered rock', as well as trying 'to suggest man's endeavour to overcome the rigours of this bleak land and to match mortal spirit against elements...', Vaughan Williams may have felt that he could write the score without seeing actual scenes from the film.[44]

Irving's reaction to Vaughan Williams's speedy output shows how unprepared the studio was for the composer's work ethic:

> Vaughan Williams proceeded to sketch the entire music of the film, which we received within a fortnight, including many of the important numbers in full score! As we had not yet taken the floor at Ealing, and the script was in a state of flux – not to say metamorphosis – nearly all the music had to be re-shaped after the location and studio shots had been cut together and the editorial department had done its work.[45]

Reshaping the music inevitably meant using cues in certain moments of the narrative Vaughan Williams had not foreseen. As with *49th Parallel*, some of Vaughan Williams's music had to be cut from the final soundtrack. The wives of the two main characters, Scott and Dr Wilson, were the biggest casualties; the theme for Kathleen Scott plays only briefly and almost inaudibly in the final cut, in the furthest reaches of the soundtrack, as she sculpts her husband's likeness, while Oriana Wilson's theme was cut altogether.[46]

In some cases 're-shaping' also meant reusing a cue for more than one scene, depending on how well Irving felt it illustrated and underscored the story. The most noticeable example of this kind of repetition occurs during the scene in which the polar party climbs Beardmore Glacier, which Irving underscored with the music for the main titles. The opening music, from which Vaughan Williams derived all of the score's significant themes, was originally conceived of as an 'orchestral "prelude" ' of the composer's own devising; Irving reports having to convince the film's directors that such an opening would work at all.[47] The prelude begins subdued at first, with the melody played by the woodwinds and then strings, but inevitably builds in emotional intensity, reaching a peak just as the dedication to the survivors of the expedition appears on screen. Irving explained his decision to reuse cues in the film as follows:

> [The music] was all so akin to the thoughts and emotions that stirred that devoted little party of explorers that I was often able to move it about inside the film, applying some of it to incidents for which it was not designed. For instance, the music composed for the main titles – or overture – to the film, exactly fitted the climbing of the Glacier and stopped with a shuddering roll on the bass drum as the party reached the very edge of a fathomless crevasse ....[48]

Indeed, the cue seems to fit as if it had been written for the sequence, with an especially appropriate dramatic swell from the brass and timpani when it seems as if a sledge is about to tumble down the glacier. Appearing at this juncture in the film, this cue also provides an impression that the story has reached an important plateau; while the full theme at the beginning of the film is heard, only shorter pieces of the melody are presented in the following scenes until the party reaches the glacier. By bringing back the full theme as the men climb the glacier, the melody unifies the entire score, and comes to represent the perseverance and determination of the polar party.

An important practical component of *Scott*'s score is its actual sound. Part of the 'grandeur of the main theme', as Irving described it, comes from Vaughan Williams's choice to score for a large ensemble, which allowed him to create a dense, rich texture with ease.[49] In the late 1940s, however, an ensemble of this size posed certain technical difficulties, as Irving discovered:

> Vaughan Williams' sound picture is painted on a large canvas and calls for seventy-five players – twelve wood-wind, four horns, seven brass, five percussion, forty-five strings, pianoforte, xylophone, and harp. It is difficult to record sound of this volume and intensity upon a film-track as it represents at its peak about ninety 'decibels' of which the track can take just over fifty. The composer cannot use a cumulative crescendo as he does so effectively in the concert hall, and a certain amount of mechanical compromise is therefore necessary.[50]

Another of Irving's responsibilities in the creation of this score thus involved balancing the capabilities of the sound equipment with the demands of Vaughan Williams's complex orchestration.

Following the initial shots of polar landscape, a full 35 minutes of the film pass before the expedition arrives in Antarctica and the polar party sets off. The most dramatic moments during Scott's journey do not take place on the way to the Pole, however, but on the doomed march back. Not even the discovery of the Pole itself is especially dramatic; if anything it is anticlimactic, as the Norwegian team led by Roald Amundsen forestalls Scott as the first to the Pole. The only music for the arrival of Scott's team on the scene at the Pole – an extended sequence of stinger chords in the brass and low bass – comes at the sighting of Amundsen's flag (and abandoned campsite) on the horizon. The remainder of this sequence is deathly silent, as the group's disappointment at being second to the Pole overshadows their achievement.

The death of Evans occurs not long into the return march from the Pole. Evans's health deteriorates quickly due to the oppressive cold and the cut on his hand that refuses to heal. Probably the most visually disturbing scene occurs when we finally see *what* Evans's hand has mutated into due to frostbite and gangrene. Since

Vaughan Williams did not know such a scene occurred in the screenplay, he wrote nothing to accompany a moment that might have worked well with a stinger chord of some sort, helping to emphasize the shock on Scott and the other men's faces at seeing Evans's fingers. Irving obviously did not feel any of the music written for other parts of the film would fit properly, and thus left the scene silent. The poor man's visible deterioration – as well as that of the entire quintet – progresses through the next two scenes of marching through the snow, both of which have the same cue: an inexorably slow marching rhythm set up in the low brass and percussion, emphasizing the heavy footstep of the weary men on each off-beat, all of which plays under a string motive based on the main theme of the overture.

Evans's health finally fails altogether, and his passing provides one of the most dramatic scenes, both musically and within the narrative, of the entire story. With the cue titled 'Death of Evans', Vaughan Williams combines another motive from the main theme, a melody of four notes rising and falling, with a new theme used only for Evans's death. With a close-up of Evans and the wild, frightening look in his eyes, the new theme suddenly appears on oboe, twice outlining a tritone in a single phrase (Example 10.4). As his condition worsens further before our eyes,

Example 10.4   Add. MS 59537, f. 81r; four measures, single stave

Vaughan Williams continues with a pedal under the four-note theme until, as Scott turns back to see Evans fall over, the soundtrack suddenly goes silent.

Evans's death greatly demoralizes the rest of the team, adding another defeat to their ongoing list of misfortunes.[51] The lack of music for this scene actually forces the harsh reality of the team's position on to the viewer; immediately following Evans's death the film cuts to Scott standing over the dead man's grave with a voice-over of the leader briefly eulogizing his companion. No heroic fanfares, no funereal themes, not even a stereotypical solo melody on a trumpet colors this scene, adding to the sense of loss rather than making the shot feel bare. The discovery not long after this of Oates's gangrenous feet and the shortage of heating oil go silent as well. The music finally returns at the moment of Oates's imminent death. With his poor physical state slowing the team's progress, Oates decides that the most valorous action would be to die quietly and bravely. The 'night' of his fateful decision, we see the tent, dark on the inside with light on the outside, accompanied by the sound of screaming winds and, briefly, a women's choir as well. The camera shows us Oates's perspective of the tent roof as he closes his eyes, hoping never to wake. When he does awaken again, he has a fevered look in his eyes; the score creeps in with a short, knell-like chimes sequence. Having established a sense of foreboding, the music further intensifies the scene with an altered motive from the main title, complete with high tremolo violins to heighten the dramatic effect, while Oates gets up and says, in Anne Fadiman's description, 'the most famous and gallant words in the history of polar exploration: "I am just going outside and may be some time."'[52] As he quickly darts through the tent flap, the fierce blizzard fills the tent with a scream; this time, however, the wailing comes from the wordless soprano soloist and choir heard earlier in the film.

Vaughan Williams's final task involved depicting the final trio's ever-decreasing rate of movement through the early winter conditions. The slow marching theme returns, as well as another melody derived from the main title, heard already during the beginning of the journey (Example 10.5). When the end finally arrives,

Example 10.5   Add. MS 59537, f. 77r; four measures, single stave

Vaughan Williams (and Irving) chose *not* to score the final scene of letter-writing in the tent, letting the stark reality of Scott, Bowers and Wilson's plight sink in fully upon the spectator. Especially moving are the brief flashbacks Wilson and Scott have of the places precious to them and their wives; the lack of music for these brief images once again indicates implicitly to the viewer the utter hopelessness of the men's situation. Perhaps if the themes for Mrs Scott and Mrs Wilson had not been cut from the earlier sections in the film they would have made appropriate reprises during the final moments of their husbands' lives. Instead, Scott and Wilson die in silence, and only the dedication of a monument to their memories brings about a final heroic fanfare in the last seconds of the score.

We have seen that the unfathomable landscape of the Antarctic evoked from Vaughan Williams a score that not only conveys the emotions of the expedition, but also elicits a feeling of the wild unknown that lay ahead of Scott and his men. With his use of a soprano soloist and choir singing textless phrases, Vaughan Williams was clearly influenced by an earlier mentor, Maurice Ravel.

Vaughan Williams went to Paris in December of 1907 for a three-month stay, crossing the Channel to work with a composer almost three years his junior. At the time, Ravel was about to begin writing his ballet *Daphnis et Chloé*.[53] A letter from Vaughan Williams shows some of the ideas the younger man tried to impress upon his student:

> For example, [I learned] that the heavy contrapuntal Teutonic manner was not necessary. '*Complexe mais pas compliqué*' was his motto. He showed me how to orchestrate in points of colour rather than in lines. It was an invigorating experience to find all artistic problems looked at from what was to me an entirely new angle.[54]

While the technique of orchestrating to evoke particular harmonic colors affected virtually all of Vaughan Williams's future works, a certain aspect of the Frenchman's instrumental palette seemed to capture the Englishman's fancy. Previously introduced in the 'Sirènes' movement of Debussy's *Nocturnes* for orchestra (1897–9), the 'textless' chorus – in which singers, either on or off stage, vocalize using vowel sounds rather than articulating a text – became an essential storytelling element in *Daphnis et Chloé*, which features an off-stage choir singing textless phrases as a means of enhancing the ballet's narrative without the explicit use of a text.[55] For Ravel, the choir supplements the eroticism of the Attic myth of love between two shepherds by adding a further sensual dimension to the overall sonorous profile. Through *Daphnis*, Ravel demonstrated the broad range of effects that the human voice could achieve, made more immediate and telling through an *absence* of words.[56]

Vaughan Williams originally used a wordless chamber chorus in the overtly erotic *Flos Campi*, for chamber orchestra, chorus and solo viola, in 1925. Kennedy points out that this 'was the first of his works to show, foremost of its qualities, a preoccupation with sonorities'. Vaughan Williams's familiarity and love of the choral idiom surely gave him added insight as to how best to employ the aural characteristics of the chorus at crucial moments throughout the score. Rather than leave the chorus completely without a storytelling voice, however, Vaughan Williams articulated an implied narrative by marking each of the score's five sections with a quotation from the Song of Solomon. A dozen years later he used textless voices again, this time in a more explicitly dramatic idiom: his one-act opera *Riders to the Sea* (1937). In this instance Vaughan Williams combined both Debussy's use of a textless *women's* choir in a concert piece, evoking ideas of the untamed ocean, with Ravel's later use of an off-stage choir in a staged dramatic work, to add another level of intensity to the music. As in *Flos Campi* (and *Daphnis*), the choral parts in *Riders* used the same idea of creating a sense of undulation between the voices through the movement among the vocal parts of seconds and thirds; a sense of despair also seems implicit in the voices, however, much like the mournful sound of keening, in this case over the men's deaths around which the opera's plot revolves.

Vaughan Williams next used textless voices for a film score, *The Loves of Joanna Godden* – the score that immediately preceded *Scott*.[57] The unseen voices in *Joanna Godden* surface during one scene alone: the macabre drowning of Joanna's fiancé, Martin, during a visit to Dungeness. The build-up to the climactic scene has some wonderfully dramatic moments, the most interesting of which occurs when Joanna says to Martin, 'Perhaps it's the place, but I feel frightened.' Martin then kisses her, accompanied by no music whatsoever. The lack of Joanna's theme during this moment of passion foreshadows the approaching tragedy. While the choir has only a brief appearance in the film – first creeping into the soundtrack in thirds, with the trumpets, as Joanna lies down on the beach and Martin goes swimming – their remarkably unusual affect compelled Vaughan Williams to use them again in his very next assignment from Ealing. Associated with the water that kills Martin, like the sea that destroys Maurya's husband and sons in *Riders to the Sea*, we can see that the wordless choir has become a trope for the composer, representing the idea of 'man against nature' which comes up repeatedly in Vaughan Williams's works, and which would be a central theme of *Scott*.

Part of Vaughan Williams's provisos to Irving over how the music should work in *Scott* regarded *how* he wanted the choir to be heard.[58] For Irving, however, using a choir meant something altogether different from just an additional sonority in the score; a choir involved extra time and extra money, two rare commodities in Ealing productions. In his communications with the composer, Irving clarified a logistical concern:

> There is no objection *per se* to the use of a vocal theme; it is purely a technical difficulty which has been empirically found to be insoluble ... We *did* have some singing, and very effective it was, in the Dungeness scene [in *The Loves of Joanna Godden*] but there was no conversational dialogue. You may be sure that we shall do our best to bring the thing off, and if it fails it will be for the same reason that Scott failed![59]

The vocal parts did not make it into the score without some additional wrangling, as Ursula Vaughan Williams recalled, 'The film work, with consultations and visits to the studio to see the pictures, went on all through the year [1947] at irregular intervals, enlivened by letters from Ernest Irving, sometimes in verse, as one that came in answer to Ralph's suggestion for the use of voices singing wordlessly.'[60] A later memory informs us of how the composer wished the voices to be understood: 'During the autumn he was still working on his Scott music; he had won his point about the use of voices to suggest desolation and icy winds....'[61] Once Irving began the recording sessions for the score, Vaughan Williams's insistence immediately paid off; Irving commented to the composer in a letter: '"The Antarctic Prologue with the voices comes out very well indeed, and I think we may be able to get away with the voice in the footstep scene ... The vocal effect is sufficiently disembodied to make it usable as a background even behind dialogue." '[62]

For Vaughan Williams, the use of the human voice in *Scott*'s score is used paradoxically to paint a landscape devoid of humanity and indifferent to human suffering through the use of an instrument that implies vitality. Vaughan Williams sought to elicit two separate reactions from the same sound: at first, Margaret Ritchie's solo melody characterizes the desperately barren and lonely Antarctic landscape. In this context – the sequence following the main titles – the voices seem to represent the frozen winds shown rushing over the ice, winds that seem just as cold and lifeless as the snowbound wastes. Later on, however, the same vocal and choral themes convey the sense of diminishing hope as the quintet's trek back from the Pole grinds to an excruciating halt and the men die one by one. Since the self-consciously British and 'heroic' explorers do not describe their feelings directly, as they all feel the need to act unremittingly noble and manly – exploring the unknown, enduring unthinkable hardships, risking death for the glory of the Empire – and thus will not discuss their inner thoughts, the solo soprano and choir evoke the inexpressible: fear and anguish for the men's struggle with nature combined with the lifeless void of their surroundings. Even the voice-over of Scott's diary entries informs the viewer only of the group's progress, and seldom keys into the emotional distress of Scott himself and his companions. John Huntley and Roger Manvell read the voices as anthropomorphizing the frigid arctic wind, especially on the trek back from the Pole, where the choral sound 'returns to imitate the tearing wind which rages round the isolated tent where Scott and his companions write with frost-bitten fingers their last letters to their families'.[63] From this perspective, we might hear the voices that accompany Oates's death as an ironic lament on his noble but pointless demise – similar to the despairing tone the voices elicited in both *Riders to the Sea* and *The Loves of Joanna Godden*, which, along with *Scott*, all involve death by (some form of) water – with nature having once again defeated human hopes and aspirations. The absence of words only strengthens the emotional power of the women's voices (Example 10.6).

Example 10.6   Add. MS 59537, f. 84r; three measures, piano score

Epilogue

Vaughan Williams had several more opportunities to write music for films, the last being the original songs he wrote for the British Council film *The Vision of William Blake*. However, *Scott of the Antarctic* was the last feature film Vaughan Williams would score completely on his own, as Irving would write a significant portion of the 1950 Ealing film *Bitter Springs*.[64] Had he continued in this medium, he might have reached the idealistic method he described in 'Composing For the Films':

> Perhaps one day a great film will be built up on the basis of music. The music will be written first and the film devised to accompany it, or the film will be written to music already composed. Walt Disney has pointed the way, with his *Fantasia*. But must it always be a cartoon film? Could not the same idea be applied to the photographic film? Can music only suggest the fantastic and grotesque creations of an artist's pencil? May it not also shed light on real people?[65]

We have seen the clear development in Vaughan Williams's style and ability as a composer for film, moving from writing music distinct to a single scene to writing cues that musically describe less tangible concepts and moods. The reason the struggles and triumphs in *49th Parallel* and *Scott of the Antarctic* affect us so strongly is because we sympathize with the characters' trials as 'real people'. Vaughan Williams's contribution to these and the other films he scored was to help us understand clearly what was at stake in each story, and thus to shed light on human nature.

Notes

1   I would like to thank the following for their assistance in this paper's creation: David and Irene Wright; Robin Wells; the staff at the British Library Manuscript Reading Room; the British Film Institute; John Hodgson and the reference staff at the John Rylands Library, Manchester; John Huntley; Vanessa Atkins; Mitchell Morris; Sarah Randall; Mai Kawabata; Byron Adams; and of course, the Carthusian Trust, for providing the fellowship that made my research in England possible.
2   Richards's essay first appeared in *Vaughan Williams Studies* under the title 'Vaughan Williams and British Wartime Cinema', and later in a lengthier version entitled 'Vaughan Williams, the Cinema and England', in *Films and British National Identity*.

3   Richards, *Films and British National Identity: From Dickens to* Dad's Army (Manchester and New York: Manchester University Press, 1997), 293. The score in question is *49th Parallel*.

4   Richards makes a point of this early on in his essay: 'His film music cannot be isolated from his other music ... the film scores relate to the main body of his work, on several occasions inspiring and generating new work....' Richards, *Films and British National Identity*, 290.

5   Ursula Vaughan Williams, *R.V.W.: A Biography of Ralph Vaughan Williams* (London: Oxford University Press, 1964), 239.

6   John Huntley, *British Film Music* (London: Skelton Robinson, 1947), 56.

7   Quoted in Huntley, *British Film Music*, 56–7.

8   Roy Douglas, *Working With Vaughan Williams* (London: The British Library, 1988), 5–6.

9   Ursula Vaughan Williams, *R.V.W.*, 271.

10   Director Hans Nieter described Vaughan Williams's involvement with the film *Stricken Peninsula* as follows: 'Dr. Vaughan Williams only received nominal fee – was part of his war effort. Muir Mathieson interested the old man for the film. In his composition for the film Italian folk music was interwoven and used merrily in an Italian brass band which appeared in the film. Including flat notes and all. When the music was recorded by Ken Cameron Dr. Vaughan Williams was present but talked mostly about gardening.' Letter from Hans Nieter to Michael Kennedy, dated 19 January 1964. From the Michael Kennedy Collection (KEN/3/1/96/2), John Rylands Library, Manchester.

11   Vaughan Williams, 'Composing for the Films', *National Music and Other Essays* (Oxford: Clarendon Press, 1996), 161.

12   Of course, the infamous story involving Stanley Kubrick and Alex North immediately springs to mind: North composed an original score for Kubrick's *2001: A Space Odyssey*. Kubrick had used classical favourites as a temporary or 'temp' track for the film, and eventually decided that he would keep those pieces and forgo North's already completed score.

13   Vaughan Williams, 'Composing for the Films', 164.

14   Letter from Jeffrey Dell to Michael Kennedy, dated 18 February 1964. From the Michael Kennedy papers, John Rylands Library, Manchester. Dell felt justifiably mortified at the mere idea of making musical suggestions to a composer of Vaughan Williams's stature.

15   Vaughan Williams, 'Composing for the Films', 163.

16   Ernest Irving, *Cue For Music* (London: Dennis Dobson, 1959), 161.

17   Stanlie McConnell, 'Items and Comments: News from John Huntley', *Film Music Notes* VI/1 (September–October 1946), 5. Huntley was clearly referring here to the hiring practices of such studios as Ealing, which I discuss below.

18   Unfortunately, Foss's death on 26 May 1953 prevented him from knowing just how successful – with audiences and on a financial level – a film score could be: the *Sinfonia Antartica*, adapted from the music for *Scott of the Antarctic*, premièred four months before Foss died, eventually becoming one of Vaughan Williams's most popular symphonies, and a significant money-maker for Oxford University Press.

19   Foss, *Ralph Vaughan Williams*, 186–7.

20   Ibid., 187.

21   Frank Howes, *The Music of Ralph Vaughan Williams* (London: Oxford University Press, 1954), 362.

22   Ibid., 363–4.

23   Simona Pakenham, *Ralph Vaughan Williams: A Discovery of his Music* (London: Macmillan & Co. Limited, 1957), 126–7.

24   This letter from J.D. Mathieson can be found in the full original manuscript for *Scott of the Antarctic*, British Library Add. MS 59537. A curious feature of this undated letter is

that the writer seems to conflate the composition of the film music (1948) with that of the later symphony (1949–52).

25 Michael Hurd, *The Great Composers: Vaughan Williams* (New York: Thomas Y. Crowell Company, 1970), 53.

26 Richards, *Films and British National Identity*, 293.

27 Ursula Vaughan Williams, *R.V.W.*, 245.

28 Anthony Aldgate and Jeffrey Richards, *Britain Can Take It: The British Cinema in the Second World War* (Edinburgh: Edinburgh University Press, 1994), 26–7.

29 Ibid., 37.

30 Richards, *Films and British National Identity*, 292–3. Vaughan Williams was apparently quite conscious of the association of 'Ein feste Burg' with the Nazi Party; in a letter reprinted from 1944 in *R.V.W.*, the composer discusses a church service that took place on the day of the Normandy invasion, stating: 'The hymn chosen after the 7.55 a.m. sermon on that day was not played through as usual but was sung with great pomp by a full choir and the hymn sung was "Ein' feste Burg". I could hardly believe my ears!' Ursula Vaughan Williams, *R.V.W.*, 261.

31 This cue was published in 1947 as a work for solo piano entitled, not surprisingly, *The Lake in the Mountains*.

32 In *R.V.W.*, Ursula Vaughan Williams relates an interesting anecdote about this scene, explaining why we don't actually get to hear the *words* to the *Volkslied* during its first appearance: 'But there seemed to be very little that needed changing, except for the short Austrian folk song he had put in for Glynis Johns to sing in the Hutterite settlement. She was very young, very frightened of the orchestra, and quite unable to sing it in the key in which it had been written – sing it as you like, said Ralph, and I'll change the key. But it was no good, so eventually George Stratton more or less played it into her ear, and she managed a husky hum, while Muir Mathieson whistled the second verse – and so after a delay of an hour or so the half minute was recorded.' *R.V.W.*, 245.

33 I refer here to the first paragraph of 'Composing for the Films'.

34 British Library Add. MS 50422 A–I.

35 Add. 50422 A, 12v.

36 Anne Fadiman, *Ex Libris: Confessions of a Common Reader* (New York: Farrar, Straus and Giroux, 1998), 25.

37 George Perry, *Forever Ealing: A Celebration of the Great British Film Studio* (London: Pavilion Books, 1981), 107–9. That is not to say, of course, that there weren't scenes shot in the studio with fake snow; scenes were shot primarily in three locations: at the London studio, in Switzerland, and in Norway. The shooting in Antarctica was meant to serve as location footage alone, shot without the actors present.

38 Charles Barr, *Ealing Studios*, 3rd edn (Berkeley: University of California Press, 1998), 198–9.

39 Ursula Vaughan Williams, *R.V.W.*, 279.

40 Ernest Irving, 'Music in Films', *Music and Letters* XXIV/4 (1943), 227.

41 Irving, *Cue For Music*, 175–6. Although Irving did consider hiring a composer of Vaughan Williams's stature a coup, he also believed (in contrast to John Huntley, whom I quoted earlier) that composers of traditional 'concert' music had no more ability necessarily than composers who dedicated themselves solely to film – yet the scores of the former still, somehow, seemed better. In *Music and Letters* he stated: 'Recently there has been a welcome tendency on the part of film "magnates" to commission musicians of repute to provide scores for the films. Notably Bax, Bliss, Vaughan Williams and Walton have turned their hands to this with great profit to all concerned ... There is not reason why a master *should* write more effective film music than a hack, for artistic merit and authenticity of style have no "film value" *per se*, but it is pleasing to record that in

point of fact they do. They cannot use their ordinary methods of symphonic expression, but there is no reason why they should not slip in a little counterpoint, so long as it doesn't get in the way of the film ... Dr. Vaughan Williams' score for "Coastal Command" was perhaps not quite up to his best standard; neither was it particularly good film music. Solid, musicianly and melodious, of course ....' Irving, 'Music in Films', 229. This does not mean that he didn't hire renowned concert composers as often as possible, however; other composers who scored Ealing productions under Irving's direction included Georges Auric and William Walton.

42   In fact, as Irving recalled, the composer did not even wait to see the film's script, let alone a rough cut of the film: 'I received a holograph letter, about as legible as the Rosetta stone, thanking me for the timings which he said were a little late to be of use. He had that morning posted to me full score of the whole work, including a pianoforte sketch for use at rehearsals!' Irving, *Cue For Music*, 176.

43   The only obvious scene of direct synchronization occurs in the short penguin sequence, a scene that seems to satisfy an unwritten rule that all films about the South Pole must include footage of penguins. What the film does not address is the tremendous amount of scientific research performed during the trip, including the data collected by those members of the expedition who did *not* make up the Polar party, but stayed back at the main hut. The second volume of *Scott's Last Expedition* describes their findings in great detail.

44   Ursula Vaughan Williams, *R.V.W.*, 279–80. The non-specific nature of the music must have also been instrumental in Vaughan Williams's decision to adapt the cues for use in his new symphony; he obviously felt that the music could stand on its own and was not so invested in the film's narrative that it would seem out of place in the concert hall. The composer actually provided notes for the symphony's première that included, among other things, specific references to moments in the story of Scott's exhibition, such as 'Towards the end of the movement the bell passage reappears followed by some very soft music connected in the film with the death of Oates.' Kennedy, *A Catalogue of the Works of Ralph Vaughan Williams* (London: Oxford University Press, 1996), 212.

Irving did not feel that the music was any less effective, in spite of the lack of cues specific to certain scenes: 'There is no doubt at all that all the main themes were composed *ad hoc* and inspired by the history of the expedition on which the film was strictly based. They spring from the deep wells of the composer's mind, from which he draws his ideas ... Desolation is the same thing spiritually if expressed by the South Pole, the battlefield or the Elysian Fields. The relations between his musical forms are therefore very deep down, and may not produce any similarity in musical notes, but only a similar trend in musical thought'. Vaughan Williams, 'Ernest Irving', 18.

45   James, *Scott of the Antarctic*, 145. John Huntley recalls, however, that director Charles Frend wanted to scrap the opening montage without first hearing the music that Vaughan Williams wrote to accompany it. On Irving's suggestion, Frend listened to the music, and then went back and re-cut the montage to match the music, getting, as Huntley put it, 'every spare scrap of landscape shots we could find'. These comments are taken from John Huntley's talk at the Vaughan Williams Symposium at Charterhouse, 26 July 2000.

46   British Library Add. MS 52289 A. The manuscript also indicates a return of the 'Kathleen' cue not long before the group reach the Pole.

47   Ursula Vaughan Williams, *R.V.W.*, 298.

48   Irving, *Cue For Music*, 176.

49   James, *Scott of the Antarctic*, 144.

50   Ibid., 146.

51   On Saturday 17 February, 1912, the day Evans died, Scott began his journal entry with the words 'A very terrible day'. He described Evans's death, concluding (in part) with,

'It is a terrible thing to lose a companion in this way, but calm reflection shows that there could not have been a better ending to the terrible anxieties of the past week.' This passage, and many more from Scott's and Wilson's journals up to the last days, were reprinted in *The Worst Journey in the World*. Apsley Cherry-Garrard, *The Worst Journey in the World: Antarctic 1910–1913* (London: Chatto & Windus, 1965), 525–6.

52 Fadiman, 27. The line actually spoken in the film is: 'I'm just going outside. I may be away some time.'

53 Arbie Orenstein, ed., *A Ravel Reader: Correspondence, Articles, Interviews* (New York: Columbia University Press, 1990), 36. Orenstein points out in a footnote to a short autobiographical 'sketch' by Ravel that the exact date the composer received the commission for *Daphnis et Chloé* remains in dispute: the composer himself says in that he first sketched the ballet in 1907, but several contemporaries, such as Roland-Manuel and M.D. Calvocoressi, maintain that he did not receive the commission at least until 1908 or 1909.

54 Ursula Vaughan Williams, *R.V.W.*, 79.

55 Debussy's first experiment with textless voices was in *Printemps*, written in Rome in early 1887. Required by the Académie des Beaux Arts to submit several *envoi* or proofs of his work (as part of winning the Prix de Rome in 1885 for the cantata *L'enfant prodigue*), Debussy included in *Printemps*, a symphonic suite, parts for a female chorus singing without a text. The Académie reproached Debussy's 'vague impressionism' in *Printemps*. Strangely enough, the original full score supposedly burned in a fire, and was reorchestrated without the vocal parts from the piano score and performed in 1912. Vaughan Williams had previously used a women's chorus *ad lib* in the revised 1908 version of the cantata *Willow-Wood*, and full chorus *ad lib* in the 1923 ballet for chorus and orchestra, *Old King Cole*. My thanks to Alain Frogley and Byron Adams for bringing this to my attention.

56 Ravel wrote only a smaller amount of music for choirs in his lifetime. Besides the choral parts in *Daphnis et Chloé*, Ravel's choral writing was limited to the *Trois Chansons* (1914–15), occasional ensemble vocal parts in his two operas, *L'Heure espagnole* (1907–9) and *L'Enfant et les sortilèges* (1920–25), and the five choral works he wrote as part of the requirements for the Prix de Rome competition: *Les bayadères* (1900), *Tout est lumière* (1901) *La nuit* (1902), *Matiné de Provence* (1903), and *L'aurore* (1905).

57 Both Kennedy in his *Catalogue* and Richards in 'Vaughan Williams, the Cinema, and England' make reference to a recording of several of the cues from *The Loves of Joanna Godden*. The record was part of the Columbia Masterworks series (MM 794), and was a collection of music from films: Charles Williams conducting the Queen's Hall Light Orchestra in Allan Gray's Prelude to *Stairway to Heaven* and the same composer's theme for *This Man is Mine*, as well as the theme from the concerto in *Spellbound* (by Miklos Rozsa), and a theme from Mischa Spoliansky's score to *Wanted for Murder*. Ernest Irving conducted the Philharmonia Orchestra in music from *The Loves of Joanna Godden*. My thanks to Robert Fink for facilitating my discovery of this album in a record shop in Kansas City, MO. According to Jon Burlingame, the suite was re-released in 1993 on a disc entitled *Themes by Hollywood's Great Composers* Volume II (Sony AK 57136).

58 Ursula Vaughan Williams, *R.V.W.*, 280.

59 Kennedy, *The Works of Ralph Vaughan Williams*, 299–300.

60 Ursula Vaughan Williams, *R.V.W.*, 280.

61 Ibid., 286. Like his other biographers, Ursula Vaughan Williams prioritises in this statement the film's importance as having given Vaughan Williams the impetus to create a score that would *evolve* into a greater work, rather than attending much at all to the film score itself.

Vaughan Williams Essays

62   Kennedy, *The Works of Ralph Vaughan Williams*, 299–300.
63   Roger Manvell and John Huntley, *The Technique of Film Music*, revised and enlarged by Richard Arnell and Peter Day (London and New York: Focal Press, 1975), 114.
64   Following *Scott*, Vaughan Williams worked on the music for *Bitter Springs*, and was also involved with two shorter documentary-style short films, *Dim Little Island* for the Central Office of Information (COI), and for the British Transport Commission, *The England of Elizabeth*. Vaughan Williams actually collaborated with Ernest Irving on the score for *Bitter Springs*, which was released on 10 July 1950. One can easily discern two different hands in the original manuscript; about halfway through the manuscript Vaughan Williams's music disappears completely, leaving only Irving's hand. This may have to do with the fact that Vaughan Williams's first wife, Adeline, was close to her death when the film was being produced. Kennedy, *The Works of Ralph Vaughan Williams*, 190.
65   Vaughan Williams, 'Composing For the Films', 165.

Selected Bibliography

Aldgate, Anthony and Jeffrey Richards (eds), *Britain Can Take It: The British Cinema in the Second World War*, 2nd edn. Edinburgh: Edinburgh University Press, 1994.
Balcon, Sir Michael, 'The Technical Problems of "Scott of the Antarctic"', *Sight & Sound* 17/68 (Winter 1948–49), 153–6.
Barr, Charles, *Ealing Studios*, 3rd edn. Berkeley: University of California Press, 1998.
Burlingame, Jon, *Sound and Vision: 60 Years of Motion Picture Soundtracks*, New York: Billboard Books, 2000.
Calvocoressi, M.D., 'Ravel's Letters to Calvocoressi', *The Musical Quarterly* XXVII/1 (January 1941), 1–19.
Chapman, James, *The British at War: Cinema, State and Propaganda, 1939–1945,* London: I.B. Tauris Publishers, 1998.
Cherry-Garrard, Apsley, *The Worst Journey in the World: Antarctic 1910–1913*, London: Chatto and Windus, 1965.
Day, James, *The Master Musicians: Vaughan Williams*, Oxford and New York: Oxford University Press, 1998.
Douglas, Roy, *Working with Vaughan Williams: The Correspondence of Ralph Vaughan Williams and Roy Douglas*, London: The British Library, 1988.
Evans, Mark, *Soundtrack: The Music of the Movies*. New York: Da Capo Press, 1979.
Foreman, Lewis, Notes from the compact disc *Marco Polo Film Music Classics: Vaughan Williams*. Marco Polo 223665, 1995.
Foss, Hubert, *Ralph Vaughan Williams, A Study*, London: George G. Harrap & Co. Ltd., 1959.
Frogley, Alain, *Vaughan Williams Studies*. Cambridge: Cambridge University Press, 1996.
Howes, Frank, *The Music of Ralph Vaughan Williams*, London: Oxford University Press, 1954.
Huntley, John, 'British Film Music', *Film Music Notes* III/7 (April 1944).
Huntley, John, *British Film Music*, London: Skelton Robinson, nd [1947].
Huntley, John, 'The Film Music of Ralph Vaughan Williams', in Lewis Foreman, ed., *Vaughan Williams in Perspective*, London: Albion Music, 1998.
Hurd, Michael, *The Great Composers: Vaughan Williams*, New York: Thomas Y. Crowell Company, 1970.
Irving, Ernest, *Cue For Music: An Autobiography*, London: Dennis Dobson, 1959.
Irving, Ernest, 'Music in Films', *Music and Letters* XXIV/4 (1943), 223–35.

James, David, *Scott of the Antarctic: The Film and its Production*, London: Convoy Publications, 1948.

Kennedy, Michael, *A Catalogue of the Works of Ralph Vaughan Williams*, 2nd edn. Oxford and New York: Oxford University Press, 1996.

Kennedy, Michael, Notes from the compact disc *Vaughan Williams: Sinfonia antartica, The Wasps – Aristophanic Suite*, EMI Classics 64020, 1991.

Kennedy, Michael, *The Works of Ralph Vaughan Williams*, 2nd edn. Oxford: Clarendon Press, 1980.

Mathieson, Muir, 'Feature Film Music and the Documentary', *Documentary News Letter* 6// 57 (June/July 1947), 109–11.

Mathieson, Muir, 'Music for Crown', *Hollywood Quarterly* III/3 (Spring, 1948), 323–6.

McConnell, Stanlie, 'Items and Comments', *Film Music Notes* VI/1 (September–October 1946), 5.

Morton, Lawrence, 'Rule, Britannia!', *Hollywood Quarterly* III/2 (Winter, 1947–48), 211–14.

Orenstein, Arbie, *Ravel: Man and Musician*, New York: Dover Publications, Inc., 1975.

Orenstein, Arbie (ed.), *A Ravel Reader: Correspondence, Articles, Interviews*, New York: Columbia University Press, 1990.

Orledge, Robert, *Debussy and the Theatre*, Cambridge: Cambridge University Press, 1982.

Pakenham, Simona, *Ralph Vaughan Williams: A Discovery of his Music*, London: Macmillan and Co. Ltd, 1957.

Pratley, Gerald, 'Ralph Vaughan Williams' *Sinfonia Antartica*: A Radio Program In Two Parts', *Film Music Notes* XIV/2 (November–December 1954), 12–14.

Richards, Jeffrey, *Films and British National Identity: From Dickens to* Dad's Army, Manchester and New York: Manchester University Press, 1997.

Richards, Jeffrey, *Visions of Yesterday*, London: Routledge and Kegan Paul, 1973.

Scott, Capt. Robert F., *Scott's Last Expedition*, Vol. I. New York: Dodd, Mead and Company, 1913.

Steele, Vernon, 'Sound Track: *The Invaders*', *Pacific Coast Musician* (18 April 1942), 9.

Vaughan Williams, Ralph, 'Ernest Irving: 1878–1953', *Music and Letters* XXXV/1 (1953), 17–18.

Vaughan Williams, Ralph, *National Music and Other Essays*, Oxford: Clarendon Press, 1996.

Vaughan Williams, Ursula, *R.V.W.: A Biography of Ralph Vaughan Williams*, London: Oxford University Press, 1964.

Chapter 11

Vaughan Williams and the English Music Festival: 1910

Charles Edward McGuire

At the beginning of the twentieth century, English composers looked toward the provincial music festival as a sure venue for national recognition. While the mainstays of the festival repertory remained the oratorios of George Frederick Handel and Felix Mendelssohn, festival officials sought to enlarge their repertoires by promoting the creation of large-scale choral compositions, steadily commissioning native English composers for this purpose. Due to this enlightened policy, English composers produced a plethora of works for the festivals, and these scores steadily gained sophistication and quality. This improvement was recognized by the critics and audiences of the time, and was later thought to mark the beginning of a fresh compositional era in England – a new (or second) 'English Musical Renaissance'.

Despite the popular demand for oratorios and cantatas, the English music festival at the time was undergoing a profound ideological shift. Throughout the last quarter of the nineteenth century, the festivals moved from choral domination (programming many more choral works than instrumental ones) to an almost even split between choral and instrumental compositions. Perhaps the most visible manifestation of this phenomenon occurred in 1910, when the Leeds Festival and the Three Choirs Festival premièred two compositions by Ralph Vaughan Williams: Leeds heard the first performance of *A Sea Symphony*, a four-movement work for chorus and orchestra, while Gloucester Cathedral presented the *Fantasia on a Theme by Thomas Tallis* for string orchestra. These premières were a coup for the composer. The performances virtually assured Vaughan Williams's reputation at the forefront among composers of the post-Elgar generation.[1]

The *Tallis Fantasia* was hardly a traditional festival composition. While instrumental works were increasingly commissioned by the Three Choirs Festival by the end of the nineteenth century, the *Tallis Fantasia* was one of the first performed within the Cathedral itself. Aspects of *A Sea Symphony* further indicate that Vaughan Williams attempted to distance this work from usual festival fare. Viewed together, both compositions illustrate the expansion of the repertoire of the contemporary English music festival away from the traditional realms of oratorio and cantata toward instrumental music as well as hybrids of vocal and instrumental forms. In the generation after Edward Elgar, composers such as Vaughan Williams ensured that instrumental music in general – and the symphony in particular – would be enshrined as the pinnacle of composition, even in the highly conservative milieu of the English music festival. However, as will be seen through a detailed analysis of both the evolution of instrumental music at English festivals and Vaughan Williams's festival compositions of the first decade of the twentieth century, this change took place over many years, and was based entirely on works such as *Toward the Unknown Region* and *A Sea Symphony* that adapted vocal techniques to a new expressive purpose. This adaptation would in turn further a movement towards instrumental compositions such as the *Tallis Fantasia*.

The festival was both the most important musical institution for the English composer until the beginning of the First World War and the highlight of the local musical season for many communities. Festivals brought professional instrumentalists from London, as well as famous continental composers, singers and soloists to a provincial city. There was also the excitement surrounding the first performances of works especially commissioned for the festival. For the composer whose work was to be premièred, such commissions were extremely valuable, virtually guaranteeing publication of the new score as well as the attendant publicity. Publishers, such as Novello, could count on the ready sale of these compositions to local choral organizations and smaller amateur festivals. Cultivating such a public following was entirely necessary for the composer, because, with the singular exception of Sir Arthur Sullivan, few nineteenth-century British composers had gained lasting fame through any venue other than the festival.[2]

By 1910, Vaughan Williams was thoroughly steeped in the world of the music festival, and choral music in general. As was typical for an English composer of the time, most of his significant published compositions to this point were vocal: solo songs and hymns. His few large-scale works included a mass (his Cambridge doctoral exercise), some chamber music, and a few other instrumental compositions.[3] He had also participated in or conducted a number of smaller choral groups and festivals. While a student at Cambridge, he conducted a small choral society.[4] His principal composition teachers, Hubert Parry and Charles Stanford, were sought after as conductors and composers for most of the major festivals, and Vaughan Williams's training at the Royal College of Music was geared primarily towards the production of cantatas and oratorios. Further, Vaughan Williams's first regular professional musical employment was as the organist and choir director of the St Barnabas Church in London (from 1895 to 1899), where he founded a choral society. In 1905, Vaughan Williams became the music director of the Leith Hill Music Festival, a post he held until 1953. This competition festival included a massed choir concert at the end of the singing classes and contests, featuring a semi-professional orchestra often recruited by Vaughan Williams himself. Somewhat unusual for the time, Vaughan Williams took an active part in planning and encouraging Leith Hill, lobbying the Festival Committee to include more difficult competition music, suggesting potential vocal soloists for the final concerts, and making time to conduct rehearsals of the individual choirs before the massed meeting. In a characteristic demonstration of his generosity, Vaughan Williams refused payment for his services by the Festival.[5]

Through immersing himself in the creation and performance of choral music, Vaughan Williams developed skills that served him well when he received his first festival commission. In 1907, the Leeds Festival premièred a short choral piece entitled *Toward the Unknown Region*, using a poem by Walt Whitman. The composition was enthusiastically received.[6] It was a typical festival composition: a small, orchestrated part-song (less than 13 minutes in length), unified by an introductory set of themes. *Toward the Unknown Region* is solid and technically accomplished, benefiting from the composer's expertise in writing for voices and an eminently perceivable narrative structure audible throughout the composition. It is cast according to the double-expansion model: Vaughan Williams presents Whitman's five verses in two sections. Each of these sections spreads stanzas of Whitman's text over progressively longer musical periods.

Other than the bifurcated formal procedure, there is nothing particularly remarkable about Vaughan Williams's text setting in *Toward the Unknown Region*. He employed a number of techniques that were common to contemporary English choral composers. After an eleven-bar orchestral introduction that states the two primary themes of the composition, Vaughan Williams presents the first three lines of the poem over a scant ten measures. He matches the simplicity of the initial question ('Darest thou, O my soul/To walk with me toward the unknown region,/ where neither ground is for the feet nor any path to follow?') by creating a homorhythmic and hymn-like setting, accompanied by a combination of the first two themes from the instrumental introduction (Example 11.1). The second and third

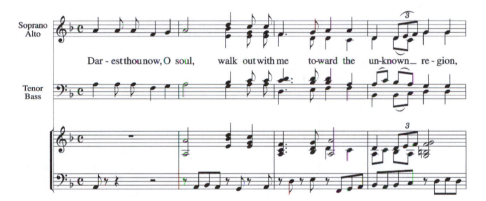

Example 11.1 Vaughan Williams, *Toward the Unknown Region*, measures 12–15 (beginning of first stanza)

stanzas spin out from this forthright initial statement. Vaughan Williams then broadens the vocal gestures so that each segment of a line receives its own texture: the opening chromatic and monophonic segment of the second stanza is matched by a contrapuntal theme for the second line, which in turn is followed by a terse, almost homophonic presentation of the third line. Vaughan Williams uses the same device in the third verse, emphasizing the long expanse of this section with a static, sequential accompaniment that features harp and other sonorous illustrations of the poem's 'heavenly music'. Whereas the composer packed the first stanza into ten measures, the second spreads over 28 and the third over 37.

Vaughan Williams changes his method of presenting Whitman's text at the beginning of the second section, which corresponds to the fourth stanza of the poem.

Much of the musical and textual repetition is lost (each choral voice only repeats one text phrase), so the expansion begins again. Vaughan Williams sets this opening stanza of the section over only 13 measures, moving from an imitative contrapuntal gesture (with the same contour as the middle line of the second stanza) to a final rhythmic unification of the upper three voices in the last few measures. This unification overlaps with the last stanza via an extended B natural held by the bass (m. 112; the only vocal counterpoint in that measure). After this moment of repose on the word 'Then', Vaughan Williams increases tension by having the chorus repeat the first line over an active orchestra, which finally erupts in a peroration that contains elements reminiscent of a march, a hymn and an anthem. This long celebratory flowering unfolds over 89 measures – longer by far than any two other verses of the piece combined, and well over a third of the entire composition.[7]

Besides this dual expansion, a device Vaughan Williams uses continually within *Toward the Unknown Region* is the tension generated through the juxtaposition of duple and triple divisions of the beat. The orchestral introduction and opening stanza stay completely in a duple division (with the exception of a delicious triplet spicing of the word 'unknown' in the soprano at m.15 – see m. 4 of Example 11.1). The first sustained triplet passages in the accompaniment arrive in the middle of the third stanza, and continue to its end, emphasizing the word 'dreams' (and shifting to sextuplets in the process; m. 84). After passing through one vocal triplet and a few accompanimental ones at the beginning of the fourth stanza, Vaughan Williams begins to integrate triplets into the climactic vocal parts of the fifth stanza. This signals the opening of the composition's final transcendent climax, with a semi quaver triplet accompaniment that underlines the words 'O joy!/O fruit of all!' at mm. 180–87. The elaborate rhetorical structure is convincing due to its subtlety, skillfully avoiding the obvious until the climactic moment at the end of the composition.

The confident craftsmanship exhibited in *Toward the Unknown Region* is occasionally marred by a somewhat heavy-handed use of pictorial elements, especially the harp invocation for 'dream' (m. 84 and following) and the repeated half-step descent for the words 'No map there' and 'Or guide', attempting to depict an eerie sense of loss (mm. 25–8). All of these missteps, though, are offset by the oddly optimistic passage of D major counterpoint in the middle of the second stanza where the words detail the lack of human comforts in the unknown region (mm. 30–37). While Vaughan Williams was still occasionally clumsy in his prosody, he was also given to flashes of ironic brilliance.

Toward the Unknown Region is distinguished from the many narrative secular choral compositions premièred at similar festivals throughout the last part of the nineteenth century due to its use of a short, philosophical poem. However, the textures Vaughan Williams used were entirely typical in contemporary choral composition: free counterpoint alternating with poignant homophony and triumphant monophony. Even Whitman's text itself was reminiscent of other choral festival compositions. Settings of Whitman's texts were by that time occurring with regularity. Stanford used Whitman for the text of his 1884 *Elegiac Ode*, and Charles Wood (another of Vaughan Williams's early teachers) set Whitman in the early 1890s. Further, as Byron Adams notes in his article on Vaughan Williams's setting of biblical texts, the Whitman lines used in both this composition and *A Sea Symphony* are strongly reminiscent of the Psalms.[8] Psalm texts were common fodder for festival compositions, usually as simple settings.[9] The subject of *Toward the Unknown Region* is notably psalm-like in its character, as it presents a confident belief in the afterlife and a general tone of moral uplift. Finally, *Toward the Unknown Region* was also short enough and technically undemanding in a way that insured its popularity with amateur choral societies when published after the festival.[10] The piece was precisely the type of work that audiences – and festival committees – expected from an English composer.

Many of these choral techniques reoccur in Vaughan Williams's 1910 Leeds Festival commission, *A Sea Symphony*. The Whitman text is psalm-like in its lines and execution, and the combination of simple polyphony, homophony and monophony mark it as extremely similar to other contemporary choral festival compositions. Yet its inclusion at Leeds was not initially guaranteed. Despite the fact that *Toward the Unknown Region* was successful, the Leeds Festival Committee was wary of offering Vaughan Williams a commission for the next festival. In the Festival Minutes of 1 March 1909, the Committee decided to approach Vaughan Williams for a new choral composition, but included a caveat with its recommendation:

> The names of younger composers have been gone through and it is proposed in the first instance to write Mr Vaughan Williams and Mr Basil Harwood. The Committee are not in favour of including much new music and they desire expecially [sic] to depreciate the introduction of works the nature of which is unknown to the Committee. In the past the time and energies of the Chorus have often been wasted in new works of great difficulty and little merit.[11]

On 22 June, the Programme Committee wrote to Vaughan Williams asking him to send a score of a new work, but would not commit to its acceptance. They sought the view of an outstanding composer well known in Leeds, and consequently sent the score of *A Sea Symphony* to Stanford for 'his opinion and advice'.[12] Only after the Committee received Stanford's favorable review on 13 July did they offer to include Vaughan Williams's work in the Wednesday evening concert, further suggesting an honorarium of 30 guineas for the composition.[13]

Despite its name, there is nothing conventionally 'symphonic' about *A Sea Symphony*. The composition is a multi-movement work that, as Oliver Neighbour and others have suggested, is a hybrid of the secular cantata and some elements of symphonic procedure.[14] Just as the festival secular cantata of the period would either be a narrative tale or a multi-sectioned rendition of one or more texts on a cohesive subject, *A Sea Symphony* includes a loosely integrated text, with all four movements drawn from Whitman's poems. Each selection of poetry is about some aspect of the sea, either the real sea and its relationship to humanity or the sea as a metaphor for the journey of mankind. The text itself is optimistic and idealistic. The first two movements present lofty and grand celebrations of the sea and those who tame it (the sailors and captains) and the technology which allows for mastery over the waves (the ships themselves), sentiments entirely expected by English festival audiences in the years preceding the First World War. Vaughan Williams instilled some contrast within the last two movements, first devising a more contemplative third movement, using the sea as a metaphor for nature, and finally ending the composition in a seemingly triumphant finale which in reality contains many elements.

The subject of the 'sea itself', with its long-standing associations as the source of England's imperial power, would have been inspiring and reassuring for a British audience. Works dealing with the sea frequently appeared at English festivals, including such popular scores as Elgar's *Sea Pictures* and Stanford's *Sea Songs.* Vaughan Williams further imbued *A Sea Symphony* with a certain ready-made familiarity through the use of several seagoing folk-songs, and a number of call-and-response solo and choral passages within the composition.[15]

A final element heartily embraced by the festival audiences was Vaughan Williams's use of processional hymns for perorations, just like the end of *Toward the Unknown Region*. Usually labeled 'Parryesque' by commentators,[16] Vaughan Williams employs this processional style in the repetition of the scherzo of the words 'A motley procession' at Aa. For the first few measures (Example 11.2), the chorus

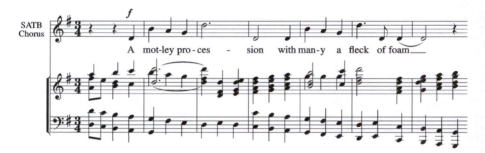

**Example 11.2 Vaughan Williams, *A Sea Symphony*, movement III, cue Aa,
measures 1–6**

sings this line in unison, while the string accompaniment could easily be that of a four-part hymn.[17] The step-wise walking bass is evocative of a processional, as is the straightforward tonality and general rhythmic simplicity. The style of this and other related sections would not have been out of place at a coronation, and the composer emphasizes the connection with Anglican ritual through the use of organ within the texture.[18] Whitman's text may be universal, and Vaughan Williams later certainly subscribed to internationalist political beliefs, but the expression of sentiment occurs throughout the entire composition within the ideology of English nationalism.

While the four movements can be described as having some aspects of symphonic form, including use of sonata form in the first movement, and Vaughan Williams's calling the third movement a 'scherzo', certain fundamental elements of symphonic procedure are conspicuously absent in this composition.[19] First and foremost, the orchestra is never the main musical focus; it performs a secondary role to the chorus and the soloists throughout. While the orchestra unifies all of the movements through a simple system of leitmotifs, it rarely rises above functioning as an accompaniment.[20] The orchestra is given no opportunity for extended development of the compositional material.[21] The few segments where Vaughan Williams uses sequential repetition and fragmentation occur only within transitional sections, and these usually follow a pattern of winding down before the next large choral or solo section begins.[22] A typical example occurs at the beginning of the composition. Following the triumphant choral opening that is introduced by two bars of trumpet fanfare, the first major segment of solely orchestral material (Example 11.3) serves

Example 11.3 Vaughan Williams, *A Sea Symphony*, movement I, cue C, measures 1–8

only to bring the motion of the opening to a halt, so the initial fanfare and vocal exultation might be repeated within a moment of new expansion. Vaughan Williams then has the orchestra blast out a six-note motive that provides a pitch-counterpoint to the vocal line (but not a rhythmic one) for the last three measures of choral exclamation (mm. 1–3 of this example), using the same sequence in each measure. When the voices are removed from the texture, Vaughan Williams begins slightly altering the sequence immediately, creating the orchestral equivalent of a stutter by slightly rearranging the triplets. After two measures of such triplets he abruptly slows to a foursquare duple rhythm (with now four divisions in the bar instead of the six previous ones) and over the next two bars, allows the line to descend to a low B flat (m. 8). This brings rhythmic motion to a halt, and Vaughan Williams uses a timpani roll which decrescendos in the same measure to support the trumpet and choral fanfare that follows, repeating the opening texture, text and choral phrase.

Most of the other major transitions of *A Sea Symphony* work in a similar fashion: a grand shift in rhythm brings about an abrupt structural decrescendo, after which Vaughan Williams begins the next textural section, or recapitulates the previous one.

Since *A Sea Symphony* is driven more by the interplay between chorus and soloists than interaction between the vocalists and orchestra, the lack of cohesive development is an integral part of the composed conception. Symphonic development is much likelier to occur within an entirely instrumental context, relying as it does on such techniques such as repetition, atomization and rearrangement of themes or motives. There are few extended instrumental passages within *A Sea Symphony*, and the most prominent of those appear in contexts of completing the forms of individual movements, such as the brief return to the initial themes at the end of the second movement at P and following (tempered by a brief recapitulation of baritone soloist).

Within a choral context, however, development is much more difficult to sustain because the required repetition and fragmentation is most easily accomplished by using imitative counterpoint. In *A Sea Symphony*, Vaughan Williams's choral style is akin to that of Elgar and Parry: even within the large-scale choruses, relatively little imitative counterpoint occurs. The style of choral texture Vaughan Williams favors is basically homophonic, contrasted with limited sections of free imitation. Such passages, like the choral section in the first movement that supports and eventually completes the soprano soloist's exultation, 'But do you reserve especially for yourself and for the soul of man', include limited amounts of word-repetition, and even a few points of imitation, though the imitation is hardly pervasive. Only two or three of the four vocal parts present this imitation at any given moment, as is the case of the first imitative entrance (Example 11.4). While the tenor and bass chorus parts echo the soprano soloist's initial line, the altos and sopranos present contrasting lines. The imitation is never exact. Immediately after this semi-imitative entrance, Vaughan Williams successively introduces a number of contrasting ideas. He does not single out one particular idea and subject it to developmental procedures. Further, this section is extremely brief: the choral polyphony lasts for only 12 measures before moving to a homophonic conclusion.

Vaughan Williams's decision to avoid textual repetition as much as possible throughout *A Sea Symphony* placed further limits upon the use of developmental procedures. The most extended use of textual repetition within the score appears at times when Vaughan Williams builds tension, usually over a sequential orchestral accompaniment, before launching into a processional hymn. Perhaps the most obvious example of this occurs near the end of the third movement, just before the return of the text and music for 'A motley procession', between Z and Aa. Vaughan Williams repeats the word 'following' six times in several different vocal textures, fragmenting the word and divorcing it briefly from the rest of its line.

All of these techniques were ones familiar to the English festival audience. There are, however, certain aspects of *A Sea Symphony* that depart markedly from what was expected. First, the work's celebration of technological progress, nautical or otherwise, was extremely rare within contemporary English secular cantatas and other choral works. Most secular cantatas, even ones using a new libretto, set historical subjects usually drawn from the Middle Ages or the vague reaches of Antiquity. The cantatas Elgar wrote for 1890s festivals are a case in point: *King Olaf* and *The Black Knight* are both medieval tales, and *Caractacus* takes place during the

Example 11.4 Vaughan Williams, *A Sea Symphony*, movement I, cue U, measures 1–6

Example 11.4   (*continued*)

Roman occupation of ancient Britain.[23] Such compositions often sought to affirm England's imperial destiny. By contrast, *A Sea Symphony* is thoroughly modern. Each of the four movements affirms some aspect of technology, from the opening triumph of the steamships leaving port in the first movement ('See the steamers, coming and going, skimming in our out of port/See, dusky and undulating, see, the long pennants of smoke/Behold the sea itself/And on its limitless, heaving breast, the ships'), to the image of 'the great vessel sailing and tacking' splitting the ocean's surface in the third. When references to the conquest of the sea by human technology occur, the tone is triumphant and processional, often underlined by the organ. Instead of reinforcing the usual elements of history and nature, Vaughan Williams chose Whitman texts for the first three movements of *A Sea Symphony* that affirm the technological progress of the human race.

Finally, despite a triumphant conclusion to the text he sets in the fourth movement, Vaughan Williams concludes *A Sea Symphony* ambiguously. The typical contemporary English choral composition finished in a triumphant blaze of sonority. Even those compositions that end softly, such as Elgar's *The Kingdom,* do so with a sense of victory intact, often substituting a sort of contemplative, quiet transcendance for martial assurance. At the end of *A Sea Symphony*, Vaughan Williams sends the soul forth on a journey of discovery that is full of 'daring Joy, safe' as it sets out on 'all the seas of God'. The words seem a fitting end to a movement that has treated the sea as a metaphor for an inner pilgrimage. But the approach to this conclusion and the coda itself are both tainted with a certain unease. Throughout the movement, Vaughan Williams exploits a conflict between E flat (a prominent pitch and the nominal key of both the opening and closing of the movement) and E natural, though its use within the key of G major (an important subsidiary key throughout the composition) in much the same way that Beethoven exploited a tension between B natural and B flat in the Ninth Symphony. While Beethoven resolved the conflict by the close of his symphony, at the end of *A Sea Symphony*, such is not the case: the lack of tonal affirmation undercuts the text.

There are few symbolic associations that can be confidently ascribed to either E flat or E natural in *A Sea Symphony*. The opening choral fantasia of the fourth movement, which contemplates the nature of the infinite, is firmly in E flat. However, the most triumphant section of that movement, when the infinite is personified as God, centers on E natural (R). Vaughan Williams builds to this climax brilliantly; its affirmative mood is breathtaking. This climactic passage succeeds an extended duet between the baritone and the soprano soloists (the first in the work). The segment incorporates a call-and-response pattern between the soloists and the chorus in simple homophonic style over a full-textured orchestral accompaniment that includes prominent use of the organ. The text sung within this section refers to the triumph of Whitman's transcendentalist deity:

O thou transcendent
Nameless, the fibre and the breath,
Light of the light, shedding forth universes, thou centre of them.

But a single key cannot hold any specific symbolic meaning within this structure. In the next section, starting at S, the baritone soloist moves the expressive focus from

---

the grand idea of God to the soul itself. At this point, E naturals are erased, replaced with E flats. This motion is not sustained, however: as soon as the soul is released on its journey in the next segment (starting at eight measures before U), the E naturals return. The succeeding passage, a monophonic choral segment of great force ('Sail forth, steer for the deep waters only') remains steadfastly in the key of G.

The incessant bifurcated alternation between the two pitches is never firmly resolved. The end of the fourth movement is nominally in E flat major, but there is little preparation or cohesive explanation for the abrupt return to this key. And after the chorus and soloists fade out, having completed their paean to the soul's spiritual journey ('O my brave soul! O farther sail!'), which ends firmly on an E flat major chord (Example 11.5, mm. 1–4), the orchestra immediately destabilizes this thought by presenting the last chords within an unsettled first inversion (Example 11.5, mm.

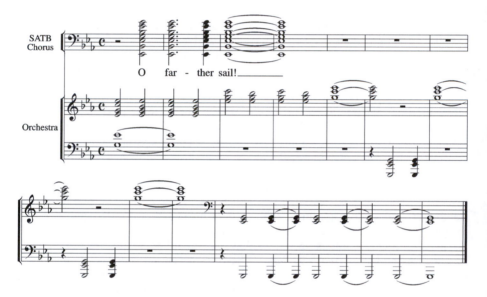

Example 11.5 Vaughan Williams, *A Sea Symphony*, movement IV, from 4 measures before cue Cc to the end of the composition

5 and following). As the confident words evaporate, all that is left is a feeling of unease, because the orchestra has been articulating the pitch G as the basis of its chord instead of the root E flat. Consequently, the transcendent triumph dissolves into an ending at once quiet and ambivalent.

Both *Toward the Unknown Region* and *A Sea Symphony* are works which fulfilled many of the expectations of festival committees and audiences while expanding the formal parameters and expressive means of the 'festival cantata'. While many elements of *A Sea Symphony* were novel, or at least unusual (such as its mysterious ending, its formal title of a symphony, its modern subject, and its embrace of technology), the composition included far more elements that were typical of the

English cantata of the time, including its choral writing, its favoring of vocal over instrumental textures and its lack of cohesive symphonic development. In the history of English festival repertoire, it was a progressive step, yet this score still looked back to an aesthetic predicated on the Handelian and Mendelssohnian oratorio. As choral works, the principle reason both *Toward the Unknown Region* and *A Sea Symphony* stand out from dozens of similar contemporary compositions is because of their force and excellence of their musical material. The *Fantasia on a Theme by Thomas Tallis*, on the other hand, was a highly unusual work to be presented within the context of the Three Choirs Festival. While it celebrated an ancient choral composer whose work had just begun to be performed through Vaughan Williams's own *English Hymnal* and the Tallis edition edited by E.H. Fellowes and R.R. Terry, Vaughan Williams used a choral work as the basis of a purely instrumental composition. And the première of the *Tallis Fantasia* at the Three Choirs Festival was wholly unprecedented in the annals of that organization. Until this point in the history of the music festival, such instrumental compositions were rarely presented in the sacred environs of the Cathedral, and such a work had never before preceded the performance of a revered oratorio.

The eventual inclusion of a piece like the *Tallis Fantasia* at the Three Choirs Festival was the result of an inevitable evolution in the nature of English festivals. Almost two centuries of festival programming before 1910 encompass a fluid continuum of changing concert habits, tastes and acceptance of differing schools of composition.[24] Perhaps the only constant throughout this period was that Handel's *Messiah* would be included in its own concert; by 1850, Mendelssohn's *Elijah* joined it in popularity, and both became the foundation of all festival programmes. Festival audiences expected a performance of both works, and it was long suspected that a festival would fail aesthetically and financially if they were omitted. Once *Messiah* and *Elijah* became staples of the festivals, the programming of other works could become more fluid, depending on the taste of the organizers. The inclusion of a composition like the *Tallis Fantasia* in Gloucester Cathedral at a Three Choirs Festival is a token of both the gradual redefinition of what music was appropriate within a sacred space and a general move in English music to promote 'abstract' instrumental compositions as exemplifying a highly developed musical taste. The shift of sacred music's dominance of an entire festival to the equal inclusion of instrumental music progressed from the liberal idea of holding some sacred compositions apart and mixing others with secular vocal pieces (the eighteenth century) to a more conservative division, holding sacred and secular apart entirely (the first half of the nineteenth century), to a redesignation of sacred music to include certain symphonies, concertos and even excerpts from the music dramas of Richard Wagner (the second half of the nineteenth century).

The evolving definition of what constituted 'sacred' music and what could be appropriately performed within a church or cathedral – and even at a festival itself – is a complex matter for music historians. For instance, the performance of oratorios at the Three Choirs Festival within the Cathedral – the bulwark of the festival in 1910, presented within the understanding that the concerts were in themselves part of a prayer service – did not occur at the first festivals in the eighteenth century. Instead, *Messiah* and other complete Handel oratorios and odes were relegated to secular concerts.[25] These secular concerts were further distinguished from sacred concerts by the fact that the former were held in the evening, and the latter in the morning. Most of the first festivals (such as those in the Three Choirs cities, Salisbury, Oxford, and others) took place in cathedrals or important churches, and included opening prayer services.

Oratorios only entered the churches and cathedrals slowly. Selections from the *Messiah* were heard in Salisbury Cathedral as early as 1752, but the entire oratorio was not performed in a cathedral until 1759 (at the Hereford meeting of the Three Choirs Festival). Even then, performances of the work in any church were sporadic until the late 1760s: inside the Cathedral the oratorio was only heard at the 1761 and 1769 Three Choirs Festivals. The Salisbury Annual Musical Festival did not begin regular performances of *Messiah* until 1768, and in Cambridge, *Messiah* was presented in St Mary's Church starting in 1767. The unbroken Three Choirs tradition of *Messiah* concerts in the Cathedral began in 1769 and lasted until 1960, with omissions only during the two world wars, the 1834 Hereford Festival (where only a selection was played after Mozart's *Requiem*) and the 1875 Worcester Festival (the so-called 'Mock Festival'), which included no music other than a few anthems. Even in these early years of the festival, *Messiah* held a special place. Until 1784, most festivals presented only *Messiah* in cathedrals.

The division between 'sacred' and 'secular' music became increasingly polarized with the introduction of civic festivals like that in Birmingham at the end of the eighteenth century. Instead of being tied to a particular cathedral, civic festivals were initially founded in the northern industrial cities. Like cathedral festivals, these civic ventures originated as charitable functions (for instance, the Birmingham Festival's purpose was to increase the general fund of a local hospital). The civic festivals usually split their performances between a large local church for concerts of sacred music (such as St Philip's in Birmingham) and a hall or theater for secular concerts (St Andrew's Hall in Norwich and the local opera theater in Birmingham). The secular concerts were offered in the evening, and the sacred ones in the morning. Like the cathedral festivals, most of the civic festivals began with an opening service that included antiphons and a sermon.[26]

In the mid-nineteenth century, the civic festivals took the first step in differentiating how sacred space and secular space were perceived. Two important festival municipalities, Birmingham and Leeds, removed festivals from churches by building town halls (in 1834 and 1858, respectively).[27] Town halls changed the nature of civic festivals by directly divorcing them from consecrated space, altering the perception of the oratorio as only one element in the liturgy of a sacred service. For a time, festivals continued to have many quasi-liturgical trappings, since a reverential silence was still expected at any performance of an oratorio or sacred cantata,[28] and the main festival town halls included substantial pipe organs (either temporary or permanent). Further, by strictly adhering to the practice of commissioning only oratorios and sacred cantatas as 'novelties', even the civic festivals preserved the 'sacred' character of the music festival. But as the century advanced, eager municipalities created their own festivals on the Birmingham and Leeds models, eschewing a church or cathedral for concerts presented in a theater or town hall, as was the case in Sheffield.[29]

Once festivals moved morning concerts out of the churches, change was inevitable, if gradual. Opening services disappeared, and the practice of segregating oratorio performances to morning concerts vanished. Festival programmers retained some distinction between sacred and secular concerts, however, as is still apparent from the programme of the 1861 Birmingham Festival (Table 11.1). The two

Table 11.1   Birmingham Festival programme, 1861

Date	Works performed
Aug. 27, morning	Mendelssohn, *Elijah*
Aug. 27, evening	Rossini, overture to *The Siege of Corinth* and 'Sorgete' (aria from *Maometto Secondo*); Donizetti, 'Signorina, in tanta fretta' (duet from *Don Pasquale*), 'Spirito gentil' (aria from *Favorita*) and 'Da quel dì' (duet from *Linda di Chamouni*); Hatton, 'Save Father on the Sea' (song); Curschmann, 'Ti prego, O Madre pia' (trio); Bishop, 'Blow, gentle gales' (glee); Verdi, 'Ah! fors' è lui' (aria from *La Traviata*); Mozart, 'Là ci darem' (duet from *Don Giovanni*) and 'Crudel perchè' (duet from *Le Nozze di Figaro*); Blumenthal, 'The days that are no more' (song); Weber, 'Softly sighs' (scena) and overture to *Der Freyschütz*; Mendelssohn, Piano concerto in G minor; Balfe, 'Fresh as a rose' (ballad); Spohr, 'Night's lingering shades' (trio from *Azor e Zemira*); Auber, 'Isabelle la Cruelle' (air from *La Circassienne*); Bellini, 'Ah, non creda mirarti' (aria from *Sonnambula*); Mercadante, 'Claudio! ritorna' (duet from *Elisa e Claudio*); Meyerbeer, The Shadow Song (scena from *Dinorah*); Martini, 'Vadisi via di quà'
Aug. 28, morning	Handel, *Samson*
Aug. 28, evening	Haydn, *The Creation*
Aug. 29, morning	Handel, *Messiah*
Aug. 29, evening	Auber, overture to *Masaniello*; Mozart, 'Soave sia il vento' (trio from *Così fan Tutte*) and 'Sola, Sola' (sextet from *Don Giovanni*); Adam, 'Ah, vous dirai-je, maman?' (air); Ricci, 'Che l'antipatica vostra figura' (duet from *Chiara di Rosemberg*); Kücken, 'Twilight is darkening' (song); Beethoven, Piano concerto in E flat; Donizetti, 'Ardon gl' incensi' (aria from *Lucia di Lammermoor*); 'Bravo, bravo il mio Belcore' (aria from *L'Elisir d'Amore*), 'Mille volte sul campo d'onor' (aria from *Pia di Tolomei*) and 'Pronta io son' (duet from *Don Pasquale*); Balfe, 'Tu m'ami' (balatta from *La Zingara*); Mendelssohn, grand finale from *Lorilei;* Rossini, overture from *William Tell* and 'Se la vita ancor t' è cara' (duet from *Semiramide*); Spohr, 'Dearest Maiden' (duet from *Jessonda*); Verdi, 'E scherzo od è follia' (quintet from *Un Ballo in Maschera*); Hook, 'Within a mile of Edinboro' (song); Meyerbeer, 'Ah! now I feel' (romance from *Dinorah*)
Aug. 30, morning	Beethoven, Grand Service in D (*Missa Solemnis*); Hummel, 'Alma Virgo' (motet); Handel, *Israel in Egypt* (with additional accompaniments by Costa)
Aug. 30, evening	Handel, *Judas Maccabeus*

Source: 1906 Birmingham Festival Programme, Music Department of the Birmingham
         Public Library.

evening oratorio concerts featured only oratorios, no instrumental selections were heard in the other sacred concerts, and the concerts on the evenings of 27 and 29 August were entirely secular. By the beginning of the twentieth century, the division between 'sacred' and 'secular' had shifted even more, as is clear from the programme of the Birmingham Festival of 1906 (Table 11.2). The first three

Table 11.2   Birmingham Festival programme, 1906

Date	Works Performed
Oct. 2, morning	Mendelssohn, *Elijah*
Oct. 2, evening	Elgar, *The Apostles*
Oct. 3, morning	Elgar, *The Kingdom*; Bach, 'Sing Ye to the Lord'; Brahms, Symphony no. 1
Oct. 3, evening	Josef Holbrooke, *The Bells*; Beethoven, Violin Concerto; Mozart, aria from *Il Seraglio*; Percy Pitt, *Sinfonietta in g minor*; Strauss, *Don Juan*; Berlioz, *Roman Carnival Overture*
Oct. 4, morning	Handel, *Messiah*
Oct. 4, evening	Granville Bantock, *Omar Khayyam*; Strauss, *Tod und Verklärung*; Wagner, overture to *Tannhäuser*
Oct. 5, morning	Wagner, overture to *Die fliegende Höllander*; Weber 'Deceived One' (aria from *Euryanthe*); Stanford, *The Revenge*; Mendelssohn, *Lobegesang*

concerts, including an evening one, featured oratorios. *Elijah* and Elgar's *The Apostles*, both extended oratorios, received their own concerts on the first morning and evening. Elgar's *The Kingdom* was given its première during the morning concert of the second day, together with a number of other works, including a Bach motet and Brahms's First Symphony.

Blurring of performance space is even more apparent in the 1908 Sheffield Festival (Table 11.3), which placed sacred and secular vocal music side by side on the same programmes. All save two of the concerts mixed sacred and secular vocal pieces. The only completely sacred concerts were those devoted to long sacred vocal works, *Elijah* and the *St Matthew Passion*. The most secular of the concerts from this festival occurred on Wednesday evening, when the only representative sacred composition was Walford Davies's *Everyman,* an unusual cantata in that it was based on a fifteenth-century print of an English translation of a Dutch morality play. The other concerts featured programmes almost equally divided between sacred and secular selections. Perhaps the most interesting concert of this series is the last one, on Friday evening, which mixed all types of vocal music (sacred, secular, *a cappella*, chamber and orchestrally accompanied) with instrumental selections, representing a wide swath of compositional schools (High Renaissance and High Baroque vocal polyphony, late nineteenth-century German partsongs, and English characteristic pieces). While such a festival remained rooted in the celebrated continental composers of the late nineteenth century (Bach, Mendelssohn,

Table 11.3   Sheffield Music Festival programme, 1908

Date	Works Performed
5 Oct., evening	God Save the King; Mendelssohn, *Elijah*
6 Oct., morning	Franck, *The Beatitudes*; Tchaikovsky, Concerto for Piano in B-flat; Berlioz, 'Te Deum'
7 Oct., evening	York Bowen, Overture in G major of Orchestra; Walford Davies, *Everyman*; Bach, Concerto in E major #2; Delius, *Sea Drift*; Bach, Chaconne; Strauss, *Till Eulenspiegel's Merry Pranks*
8 Oct., morning	Debussy, *L'Enfant Prodigue*; Mozart, Symphony no. 35; Verdi, 'Manzoni' Requiem; Rimsky-Korsakov, choral suite from the opera *The Eve of Christmas*; Wagner, *Der Meistersinger*, Act III (selections)
9 Oct., morning	Bach, *St Matthew Passion*
9 Oct., evening	Palestrina, 'Lamentation' (for male voices); Verdi, 'Lauda all Vergine Maria–Paradiso;' Cornelius, 'O Death thou art the Tranquil Night;' Strauss, 'Love' and 'Betrothal Dance' for male chorus; Brahms, Four Songs for Female Voices, Horn and Harp; Bach, 'Motet #6–Praise the Lord'; Beethoven, Symphony no. 9

Source: Sheffield Local Studies Department, 'Festival Programmes'.

Beethoven and Wagner – including war-horses like Beethoven's Ninth Symphony, *Elijah* and the *St Matthew Passion*), the festival's programmers were not afraid to experiment with some old and some relatively new music.

As the strictures separating the sacred from the secular began to blur, including the redefinition of the nature of hallowed space, instrumental music was introduced into festival programmes with increasing frequency. The acceptance and incorporation of instrumental music into the festival was most remarkable in the period between 1880 and 1914. The Birmingham Festival is a typical case: during this time, the quantity of instrumental music presented increased vastly. Festival programmers began to supplement the usual symphonies and concertos with other genres, including characteristic pieces (such as Gounod's *Funeral March of a Marionette*, heard in 1876; Stanford's *Orchestral Serenade in G major*, performed in 1882; and Liszt's *Hungarian Rhapsody*, played in 1885), and chamber music. Symphonies could now be novelties. At least two symphonies produced in this period were meant as such: Prout's Third (1885), and Sibelius's Fourth (1912).

But the most important advancement of instrumental music at the century's end, and the best sign of its increasing stature within English musical ideology, was the inclusion by festival programmers of symphonies and instrumental pieces in concerts otherwise devoted to sacred works. The first time sacred and secular music were mixed in the same concert at Birmingham was in 1891, in an evening concert that featured Cherubini's *Anacreon* overture, an 'Offertorium' by Mozart, Schubert's 'Tantum Ergo' and a violin concerto by Joachim. *The Times*'s review of this concert expressed a rather muted critical response:

> The programme of this evening's concert, though by no means unattractive, was a marvel of ineffective arrangement. The old rough-and-ready distinction between sacred and secular music, according to which only compositions of a vocal kind set to words of a definitely sacred character were admitted into the first class without respect to the style of their expression has, of course, disappeared, and it is well away; but to open a concert with Cherubini's *Anacreon* overture, to pass by way of 'Blest Pair of Sirens' to 'Dove Sono' and thence to two Latin hymns and, finally, to sandwich Mozart's 'Ave Verum' between the overture to *Euryanthe* and Schumann's fantasia for violin, shows a plentiful lack of wisdom and disregard of legitimate effect.[30]

The reviewer objected to the jumble of works presented within the concert, but not that such works should rub shoulders in one event. The very mixture of sacred and secular was seen by this reviewer to represent a type of progress: 'the old rough-and-ready distinction ... is well away' – implying both a previous careless disregard to programming concerts which kept sacred and instrumental apart and a certain relief that a new, 'progressive' era of festival performances had begun. The next Birmingham Festival (1894) produced a similar concert, programming Beethoven's *Egmont* overture, the première of a *Stabat Mater* by Henshel, Schubert's 'Unfinished' Symphony and Dvořák's *Husitká* overture together in the same evening.[31] The 1897 festival offered no such mixed concerts, but from 1901 onwards, the festival mixed instrumental and sacred music in both morning and evening performances.

Perhaps as a holdover from the solely sacred morning concerts of the nineteenth century, morning performances in the first few years of the twentieth remained more conservative than evening ones. In Birmingham's concerts, oratorios were coupled with conservative symphonies (usually ones by Beethoven or Schubert). But such reserve was not maintained for long: in 1906, a morning concert included Beethoven's *Mass in D*, Tchaikovsky's *Violin Concerto*, Ritter's motet 'O amantisime sponse Jesu' and the prelude to *Parsifal*. The 1909 festival returned momentarily to the more conservative symphony and oratorio pairing for the morning concerts (presenting *Gerontius* with Mozart's 'Jupiter' Symphony in one morning concert and Schubert's 'Unfinished' Symphony, Cherubini's *Mass in C*, Brahms's 'Song of Destiny' and Beethoven's Third Symphony in another), but the last morning concert at the final festival of 1912 included a truly incongruous selection of music: the Brahms' *Requiem*, Scriabin's *Prometheus*, the closing scene from Strauss's *Salome*, Beethoven's Seventh Symphony and two sacred pieces by Bach. It is important to note that the mixture here of sacred works with others is on a different level than that of performing an oratorio and a symphony in the same concert: the sacred works presented in this final morning of the 1912 festival scarcely articulated a standard Anglican – or even Christian – viewpoint.[32]

A similar evolution of programme philosophy that allowed for an increasing amount of instrumental music is illustrated by the history of the Leeds Festival. As the Leeds Festival became a more permanent institution in the last quarter of the nineteenth century, it began to present instrumental music in varying degrees, depending on the year. Leeds was even more adventurous in its programming than Birmingham, coupling traditional Beethoven, Schumann and Schubert symphonies with a number of non-German continental composers, including Tchaikovsky (Symphonies no. 4 and 5 were heard at Leeds in 1910 and 1913, respectively, and *Francesca da Rimini* was presented in 1901), Rachmaninov (1910), Glazunov (1907), Grieg (1907), Holbrooke (1904), Spohr and Saint-Saëns (1901). Leeds was also active in promoting English instrumental music, featuring compositions by Sullivan (1889), German, Sterndale Bennett, and Elgar (all 1901), Stanford (1904) and Wallace (1910).[33]

Leeds antedated Birmingham in the transgression of boundaries between sacred and secular space. Even the first festival in 1858 included a limited combination of sacred and secular music. That festival's last concert on Saturday evening was a selection of secular choruses, duets, songs and chamber music, which ended with the 'Hallelujah' chorus from *Messiah*. By the turn of the century, at least some of the Leeds Festival morning concerts were adventurously integrated. For example, a morning concert of 1901 featured Verdi's *Requiem*, Bach's *Brandenburg Concerto no. 3*, Stanford's 'Last Post', Palestrina's motet 'Surge Illuminare', and Tchaikovsky's *Francesca da Rimini*.[34] From this date most Leeds Festivals combined both sacred and instrumental music.

The introduction of instrumental music into the repertory of the Three Choirs Festival was similar to the Birmingham and Leeds Festivals, with a few differences. First, the Three Choirs Festival retained its sacred conventions long after the civic festivals began to shed them, and even strengthened them in the late 1860s. While many of the civic festivals at the end of the nineteenth century used the same hall for both sacred and secular concerts, the Three Choirs Festival kept a strict division between sacred concerts, which were always heard within the Cathedral, and secular ones, produced at an outside hall or theater. Second, the Three Choirs Festivals maintained their opening prayer service long after civic festivals shed such rituals. The Three Choirs services were (and still are) strictly religious in character, including anthems and sometimes even a set of responses, complemented by an instrumental prelude and postlude (usually played by the orchestra). A sermon was delivered, often by a noted cleric. Further, oratorio concerts in the Cathedral were considered to be prayer services, and ritualistic orders providing a rite prefacing and concluding each oratorio were used at such concerts until the First World War.[35]

Instrumental music broke into the sacred morning space of the Cathedral at the 1870 Hereford meeting of the festival. The Thursday morning concert included Mendelssohn's 'Reformation' Symphony, the same composer's 42nd Psalm, selections from his *Christus*, a new cantata by Holme entitled *Praise ye the Lord*, and a selection of Handel's sacred songs.[36] Thus, the first symphony heard in the Cathedral at a Three Choirs Festival was one with a sacred Protestant connotation. The *Musical Times* even emphasized the appropriateness of its performance there:

> The performance on Thursday morning commenced with Mendelssohn's 'Reformation Symphony'. Abstractly a symphony in a cathedral might sound somewhat secular; but such a symphony, and upon such a subject, the composition, too, of one of the most deeply religious men who ever glorified his faith by the aid of music, was not only in accordance with the sacred character of the building, but seemed to gain in intensity of expression by the holy nature of the surroundings.[37]

The critic from *The Times* carried this sentiment even further:

> A hearing of the 'Reformation' Symphony under such exceptional circumstances must have brought to many the conviction that if, at any future time, what has been briefly

hinted should be made a rule, and the whole of the Festival performances be held in the Cathedral, there is no reason why the orchestral symphonies of the great masters should be excluded. God made art as God made all things, and the symphonies of Beethoven, as well as many of those composed by Haydn and Mozart, being among the highest manifestation of an art which, worthily employed, has not been inappropriately termed 'divine', would surely not be out of place on such occasions as those referred to. Of course, a severe discretion should be exercised in the choice of the works to be given, and even single movements might be detached from the rest where the character of an entire symphony would appear to be in the slightest degree unsuitable.[38]

The Times's reviewer promoted only certain symphonies as suitable for the Cathedral: all of Beethoven's, and a selection of the works of Haydn and Mozart. Editing was also possible, and the reviewer was open to the possibility that some symphonies or excerpts of them would not be suitable for the sacred space. He promoted symphonies as the pinnacle of artistic achievement, and excused their inclusion within the Cathedral by calling at least a selected few 'divine'.

In this early period of including symphonies within the Cathedral, critics demanded suitable choices that would reflect the solemnity of the sacred space. The next combined concert at a Three Choirs Festival took place at the Hereford meeting of 1873, when a symphony by Spohr was inserted between an oratorio by Ouseley, Spohr's own *A Christian's Prayer* and one of Handel's 'Chandos' anthems. In contrast to Mendelssohn's symphony, the critics lambasted the inclusion of Spohr's composition within the Cathedral, deriding its effect. The critic of *The Musical Times* argued that the work 'scarcely seemed to tone with the character which should distinguish Cathedral performances at a festival'.[39] Even with such admonishments, once symphonies entered the space, they could not easily be dispensed with; by 1881, Hereford and Worcester both programmed at least one symphony in a morning Cathedral concert.[40] From this point forward, criticism of symphonies within the Cathedral was negative only if the work in question was part of a programme that was too long.[41]

As the role of instrumental music at the Three Choirs Festival Cathedral concerts solidified after 1880, several broad rules were usually followed. First, unlike the Birmingham Festival concert of 1891, performances that mixed sacred vocal music with instrumental compositions within the Cathedral could only combine abstract, non-programmatic works with vocal ones. Thus, opera overtures, Richard Strauss's tone poems and symphonies like Beethoven's Sixth were not included in cathedral concerts. Second, when an oratorio was heard in the Cathedral, the only type of composition suitable for performance with it was a symphony. Concertos and other compositions were programmed on cathedral concerts, but only ones that featured a mixture of vocal selections, such as motets, Bach cantatas, and choral psalm settings – never an oratorio. Finally, the symphony became the composition that would serve as an orchestral 'prelude' to an oratorio, much like an Anglican church service of the time would feature an organ prelude before the service itself began.[42]

Table 11.4 presents a typical programme of the time, demonstrating most of these rules. At this festival, seven cathedral concerts were heard, five of which featured instrumental selections. Four of these concerts began with symphonies, including two which preluded oratorios: those on the evening of 10 September and the morning of 12 September. The concert on the morning of 11 September also featured

Table 11.4   Three Choirs Festival programme, Gloucester, 1901

Date and Location	Works Performed
8 Sept., opening (Cathedral)	Schubert, 'Unfinished' Symphony; Selby, *Magnificat and Nunc Dimittis*; West, 'Lord I have loved the habitation of Thine House'; Elgar, 'Angel's Farewell' from *Gerontius*
10 Sept., morning (Cathedral)	Chopin, 'Funeral March'; Mendelssohn, *Elijah*
10 Sept., evening (Cathedral)	Mozart, 'Jupiter' Symphony; C. Lee Williams, 'Harvest Song'; Spohr, *The Last Judgement*
11 Sept., morning (Cathedral)	Brahms, Symphony no. 1 in C minor; Cherubini, *Mass in D minor*; Handel, Second Organ Concerto; Lloyd, 'In piam memoriam Victoria Reginae'; Mackenzie, *Rose of Sharon* (selection)
11 Sept., evening (Hall)	Cowen, *An Orchestral Poem*; Hervey, *A Descriptive Ballad*; Bell, *A Symphonic Prelude*; Bridge, *A Dramatic Scene*; short works by Elgar, Stanford and Parry
12 Sept., morning (Cathedral)	Beethoven, *Symphony no. 3 (Eroica)*; Parry, *Job*; Verdi, *Requiem*
12 Sept., evening (Cathedral)	Brewer, *Emmaus*; a Bach cantata; Mendelssohn, *Hymn of Praise* (Lobegesang)
13 Sept., morning (Cathedral)	Handel, *Messiah*

Source: Williams, et al., *Annals* (Gloucester: 1931), 29–31.

a symphony, but no full oratorio (the sacred vocal works were a mass and a motet, and selections of a sacred cantata); thus this concert included an organ concerto as well. At this festival, one of the rules stated above was slightly bent, as the 'prelude' to the concert of Mendelssohn's *Elijah* on the morning of 10 September was Chopin's 'Funeral March'. This is the only exception from this period, and was considered to be highly proper, as it mourned the death of the late Queen Victoria (this was the first Three Choirs Festival after her death). The festival organizers relegated orchestral compositions with specific programmatic titles or references (such as Cowen's 'An Orchestral Poem', Hervey's 'A Descriptive Ballad' and Bell's 'A Symphonic Prelude') to the evening secular concerts in the Shire Hall. Until 1905, the instrumental compositions heard within the Cathedral were cornerstones of the symphonic canon of the time. Works by Beethoven, Brahms, Mozart and Haydn were most frequently performed within the Cathedral. The first symphony by a composer whose work fell outside the Austro-German tradition was only presented in 1900, at Hereford, when that festival programmed Tchaikovsky's Sixth Symphony. None of these works were novelties; in every case, their premières had long since passed.

Eventually, the performance of symphonies within the Cathedral was viewed as the next step in the development of the festival's prestige. When looking back on one such concert, rather than questioning the inclusion of symphonies within the sacred space, the official Three Choirs Festival history celebrated them as a great musical event for any musician:

> To listen to a Beethoven Symphony in Gloucester Cathedral must surely be one of the most satisfying experiences in the life of a musician, amateur or professional. In the *'Eroica'* not a note seemed out of place in the sacred building, and the orchestra, directed by Mr. Herbert A. Brewer, gave a superb rendering of the immortal strains of the old master.[43]

The author's use of grandiose claims, while typical for English critics addressing the subject of the symphony at the end of the nineteenth century, perhaps intentionally over-emphasized the appropriateness of the inclusion of 'immortal' Beethoven within the Cathedral. All of the language used is highly positive: Beethoven in the Cathedral would be the 'most satisfying' experience for any musician, and the symphony itself was rendered 'perfectly' in that space, making it extremely satisfying to hear – quite an unlikely experience in such a reverberant acoustic.

In 1905, this conservative programming strategy began to change. The first two cathedral concerts of the festival that year were traditional enough. Tuesday opened in the Cathedral with *Gerontius* and Brahms's Fourth Symphony, and the evening cathedral concert included a Bach cantata, the Mozart *Requiem* and Beethoven's Fourth Symphony. The cathedral concert on Wednesday morning began not with a symphony, oratorio or sacred composition, but Strauss's symphonic poem *Tod und Verklärung*, which prefaced a number of miscellaneous sacred compositions. While the programme for the 1906 festival at Hereford was much more conservative (having only one Cathedral concert with an instrumental selection, Brahms's Third Symphony), the festivals from 1907 to 1909 all either included some new genre of composition in the cathedral concerts, or symphonies by composers who were not Austro-German. Gloucester performed Glazunov's Symphony in C, Parry's *Sinfonia Sacra* and Brahms's 'St Anthony' variations in 1907; Worcester presented Beethoven's violin concerto in the Cathedral in 1908; and Hereford programmed Elgar's First Symphony in the venue in 1909. The Three Choirs Cathedral concerts began to open up to different genres of music, drawing compositions from home and an expanded area abroad.

By 1910, then, all of the major English music festivals included a good deal of instrumental music within their programmes. The focus of the festival as an institution was changing. All of the festivals paired symphonies with oratorios, and most even commissioned instrumental works for at least their non-oratorio or secular concerts. Such was the case with the Three Choirs Festival, which began commissioning instrumental compositions for the evening secular concerts by 1895, featuring Rosalind Ellicott's *Fantaisie in A minor for Piano and Orchestra* (1895), Samuel Coleridge-Taylor's *Ballade in A minor* (1898), and Granville Bantock's orchestral poem *The Witch of Atlas* (1902). The Three Choirs Festival had even attempted to commission its own symphony, perhaps following the example of Birmingham, which presented its first novelty symphony in 1895. After the mixed success of his first oratorio, *The Light of Life* (*Lux Christi*) at the Worcester Three Choirs meeting of 1896, Elgar received a commission for the 1899 festival in that city. He proposed a programmatic symphony based on the life of General Charles Gordon, the military hero killed at the battle of Khartoum.[44]

The repertoire shift at the Three Choirs and other English music festivals was a clear indication of the increasing importance of instrumental music in elite English society. But why did this change occur? Most commentators have viewed the educational establishments founded throughout the century as primarily responsible for the change. While the creation of a native school of composition was one of the primary goals of these institutions, concentrated training of instrumentalists flourished in the developing musical schools such as the Royal College of Music, the Royal Academy of Music and others.[45] And while the teachers of composition at these institutions, including Stanford, Parry and Sullivan, were regular festival contributors, either as composers or conductors, each was also extremely close to the German tradition.[46] Studying with these composers meant embracing instrumental music in general – and the symphony in particular – as the pinnacle of musical art. This viewpoint was presented to the English music-loving public virtually daily in the form of newspaper and magazine articles, concert reviews and burgeoning scholarly studies. A typical example of the time even went so far as to promote instrumental music as one of the most significant improvements of the age:

> That grounds for a reasoned optimism [about the state of music in England] exist we are far from denying. Foremost among the improvements of our time are the multiplication of opportunities for hearing great instrumental music at reasonable prices.[47]

This example, typical of criticism of the time, even went so far as to use instrumental music to supplant vocal as the way to moral improvement.[48]

Positioning instrumental music in this way positioned it as a mark of taste and refinement for the middle and upper classes. With the rise of Tonic Sol-fa and other amateur singing methods and organizations in the last half of the nineteenth century, the oratorios and vocal music concerts that had heretofore been the exclusive purview of the middle and upper classes were suddenly legion. The sight-singing methods of John Hullah, Joseph Mainzer and John Curwen first concentrated on teaching the working classes hymn tunes and other simple musical forms, but soon spread to the oratorio choruses of Handel and Mendelssohn. By the late 1870s, the sight-singing movement was so pervasive that oratorios and cantatas were often published in Tonic Sol-fa concurrently with their release in standard notation. Oratorios and cantatas, heretofore heard only in concerts accessible to the middle classes and above, was now opened up entirely to and widely enjoyed by the working class.

Such class sentiments were obvious to the practitioners of sight-singing. Even by 1880, the middle-class leaders of the movement (such as John Spencer Curwen, son of Tonic Sol-fa's propagator), noted the centrality of Handel to the 'improvement' of the working classes, and the replacement of vocal music by German instrumental forms in matters of élite musical taste:

> As our working classes improve in musical skill – as they are rapidly doing, thanks to the Tonic Sol-fa method – Handel will doubtless become more than ever the favourite of the masses of the English people. It has often been said that the spirit of modern music is instrumental, whereas the spirit of the old music was vocal. The improvement of musical instruments and their superiority to voices so far as the development of musical progress goes, have called off the attention of composers, and made them seek new fields of discovery. The art of writing for voices bids fair to be lost, if we are to consider recent

German writers as leading the van of progress. But to appreciate instrumental music requires a long apprenticeship, while vocal music appeals at once to every one. Handel is essentially a writer for voices; he seeks his effects from them, and speaks his greatest thoughts always through the chorus. He may be described as the greatest of vocal writers, and hence he will become more and more the favourite of the people at large.[49]

Curwen noted a hierarchy of taste within music. Handel without question was considered to be 'great and beneficent'. His music (like all vocal music) was immediately understandable, even to the masses. Conversely, Curwen maintained that the composition of instrumental music alienated recent composers from the working classes, because writing it caused composers to lose facility in vocal composition. Moreover, to Curwen, the appreciation of instrumental music took longer to cultivate. Consequently, it was an activity suitable to the leisured classes, who had the time to partake of such requirements. Handel was therefore the perfect central composer for the hard-working people, as he required a much smaller investment of time to comprehend.[50]

Further, the era of the 'disposable' large-scale festival choral composition was drawing to a close. The apogee of the English oratorio occurred in Birmingham in 1903 and 1906, when Elgar's *The Apostles* and *The Kingdom* premièred to enormous public and critical acclaim – generated by the phenomenal success of Elgar's *Gerontius* at the 1901 Lower Rhine Festival in Düsseldorf. Attendance at concerts of each composition at major festivals was greater than the audience size for performances of either *Messiah* and *Elijah* for the entire decade. In 1911, Handel's and Mendelssohn's oratorios regained their former stature, but only until the cessation of all festival activities brought about by the First World War.

Within this context, the performance of Vaughan Williams's *Fantasia on a Theme by Thomas Tallis* in a Three Choirs cathedral concert can be viewed as part of this evolutionary process towards the inclusion of newly composed instrumental music by English composers. Its only unusual aspects were that it was a new, commissioned composition, billed as a novelty, and specifically requested as an instrumental composition by the Festival Committee.[51] As an instrumental composition, it did not fit into the by-then 'traditional' cathedral inclusions of the symphony and concerto, or the more recent incorporation of tone poem. Vaughan Williams's *Tallis Fantasia* was not the first Three Choirs Cathedral instrumental novelty; that honor belongs to Charles Harford Lloyd, whose Concerto in F minor for Organ and Orchestra was heard at the 1895 Gloucester meeting of the Three Choirs.[52] The actual novelty of Lloyd's composition was lessened due to its genre: it was an organ concerto (one of the traditional instrumental compositions in sacred music concerts at most English music festivals), and it was first performed in a mixed programme which included no major oratorio – just a Brahms part-song, a new sacred choral work by Cowen rapidly destined for obscurity, and Beethoven's *Mass in C*. Vaughan Williams's *Tallis Fantasia*, in contrast, was a true sign of the change in both English festival programming and English music in general. It was not presented as part of a mixed cathedral concert at the festival, but as part of an oratorio concert; the only other item on the programme was Elgar's *Gerontius*, by then an established presence at the festivals.

Much has been written about the *Fantasia on a Theme by Thomas Tallis*, including a number of analyses. A particularly successful investigation of the score is Anthony Pople's essay 'Vaughan Williams, Tallis, and the Phantasy Principle', which elucidates the usual methods of characterization of the composition (either as evocative of antiquity, architecture, vocal church music, or a rural voice, among others) and produces a detailed description of Vaughan Williams's original conception of the composition as well as the cuts he made before further performances in 1913 and 1919.[53] For Pople, Vaughan Williams's revisions greatly improved the composition, 'moving the Fantasia away from a pre-war genre favored by dilettante into a piece whose measured traversal of a stylistic network opened up a significant part of the creative space in which the composer accomplished the remainder of his life's work'.[54] Pople relates the *Tallis Fantasia* to contemporary fantasias and similar works, noting especially W.W. Cobbett's contests to revive the Jacobean 'Phantasy' as well as definitions by Fuller Maitland in the second edition of *Grove's Dictionary of Music and Musicians* (1904–10) and Stanford's 1911 *Musical Composition*.[55] Considering the general structural elements of the *Tallis Fantasia*, such comparisons are extremely illuminating: like the expectations of the 'Phantasy', Vaughan Williams's *Tallis Fantasia* is a single-movement work, includes free-form variations and fragmentations of a theme, and contains little traditional development.

As a festival novelty, the *Tallis Fantasia* belongs to a select group of 'prelude' compositions from the last decade of the nineteenth century and the first decade of the twentieth, all save one presented first at the Gloucester Festival, and all newly composed works including within them some sort of sacred reference or connotation. Just as Vaughan Williams understood the general Elizabethan revival context from which he incorporated the word 'Fantasia' into the title of this composition, the self-contained, semi-programmatic, ternary festival prelude composition must also have held a similar contextual resonance.

Aside from the general practice of performing Beethoven and Brahms symphonies as preludes to the opening services and sacred compositions at cathedral concerts, four compositions must be considered: Charles Harford Lloyd's *Festival Overture* (Gloucester, 1898), Samuel Coleridge-Taylor's *Solemn Prelude* (Worcester, 1899), W. Hayes's *Symphonic Variations* (Gloucester, 1904) and Joseph W.G. Hathaway's prelude *In Te, Domine, Speravi* (Gloucester, 1907). Like Vaughan Williams's *Tallis Fantasia*, each of the new works included some interior reference to the solemnity of the occasion of presentation within the Cathedral. Based on the last line of the 'Te Deum', the religious meaning of Hathaway's *In Te, Domine, Speravi* ('In you, O Lord, I have trusted') is obvious. Colderidge-Taylor's composition was called 'Solemn', and its opening B minor theme, starting with a bell-tolling pattern on an F sharp was said by the *Musical Times* critic to 'justify the title of the prelude'.[56] A similar sentiment greeted Lloyd's *Festival Overture:*

> Dr. Harford Lloyd's 'Festival Overture' hardly ranks, perhaps, as a strong piece, and there is little of the conventionally festive, as expressed by the pomp and circumstance of sound. I take this as a result of the restraint invited by a work destined for use in a religious service. The slow introduction is quite tender in feeling, and not less beautiful in effect, while in the *Allegro* many passages show the earnest endeavour of a capable man to be impressive and even exciting without stepping over the bounds of propriety as we understand that term in the church.[57]

In other words, a restraint of feeling and expression within the music added to the appropriateness of the composition. Finally, the very basis of W. Hayes's *Variations* was predicated on associations of the sacred space itself, as it included a reference to a well-known chime melody of Gloucester Cathedral.[58] All of these works were used either as a prelude to the opening prayer service, or as a prelude to a mixed concert that did not feature an oratorio.

The *Tallis Fantasia* included within it an association much like this peal of bells, and also maintained a reserve that was deemed appropriate to its content: when reviewed by the *Musical Times* critic, the composition was thought to portray a sort of serious, contemplative charm.[59] As is well-known, Vaughan Williams based his composition on a theme from a hymn by Tallis, initially included in a 1567 set of metrical psalms published by John Day. Vaughan Williams was familiar with the tune because he had included a setting of it (with an eighteenth-century text) in the 1906 *English Hymnal*.[60] In his discussion of the *Tallis Fantasia*, Wilfrid Mellers makes much of the struggle of Anglicanism versus Catholicism within Tallis's music, calling him a 'double man' – an ascription he also gives to Vaughan Williams for his production of the *Tallis Fantasia*). Ultimately, though, Mellers sees the use of the simple psalm setting as inherently Anglican in its outlook, because it is based in homophony rather than monophony or polyphony. He transfers this interpretation from Tallis's hymn to Vaughan Williams's fantasia.[61] It is strange that he does not carry this problematic but interesting description to its logical conclusion, since the score that the *Tallis Fantasia* 'preluded' was none other than Elgar's consummately Catholic *Dream of Gerontius*, which was being presented in Gloucester Cathedral for the first time.

By 1910, *Gerontius* was the most popular oratorio by an English composer in the festival repertory. *Gerontius* itself, the story of a Soul's journey from earthly death to judgment in heaven, included many strongly Catholic elements: a litany of saints, references to the Virgin Mary, and even Purgatory. At the Hereford and Worcester Three Choirs Festivals, *Gerontius* began appearing in 1902, albeit in a bowdlerized, 'anglicanised' form (omitting parts of the litany of the saints, and some references to the Virgin Mary).[62] At the Gloucester Three Choirs meetings, the cathedral clergy prevented the oratorio's performance because it was considered to be 'inappropriate' within the Cathedral.[63] Although this decree was initially promulgated in 1903, the Gloucester clergy persevered in excluding the composition until 1910.

It is possible, therefore, to interpret the *Tallis Fantasia* as a composition designed in part to give an Anglican balance to Elgar's Catholic *Gerontius* – a composition that might, through aesthetic means, 'sanitize' the space through the sound of the orchestra itself, and place *Gerontius* within an Anglican context. While the text Vaughan Williams set to the hymn in 1906 was the relatively calm 'I heard the voice of Jesus say', the hymn's original text, 'Why fumeth in fight' concerned heretical Catholics. Vaughan Williams's own inclusion of a Tallis composition within the *English Hymnal* strongly indicates that the Tudor composer (who was in fact, a recusant Catholic) was considered as an Anglican by the Established Church, and by extension, the festival audience. Moreover, Vaughan Williams's own use of the very same tune to represent Protestantism in his early Bunyan settings, as demonstrated elsewhere in this volume by Nathaniel Lew (chapter 9), suggests that Vaughan Williams not only saw Tallis's composition as representing Protestantism, but also emphasizing a particularly good and noble aspect of it.

The festival premières of *Toward the Unknown Region, A Sea Symphony* and the *Fantasia on a Theme by Thomas Tallis* were only the beginning of Vaughan Williams's long relationship with the English music festival. For the rest of his long career, his contacts with festivals of all sorts grew. He remained the conductor of the Leith Hill Festival until 1953, and retained an active presence there by conducting the annual concert of J.S. Bach's *St Matthew Passion* for some years after that.[64] He was a member of the board of various other amateur festivals, such as the one at Petersfield.[65] His association with the great charity festivals also expanded over the course of his career. The Three Choirs Festivals premièred two additional Vaughan Williams compositions before the beginning of the First World War: *Five Mystical Songs* at the 1911 Worcester meeting and his *Fantasia on Christmas Carols* at the 1912 Hereford meeting. During the interwar period, Vaughan Williams's compositions appeared regularly at the surviving festivals, either as premières, or at early performances. Vaughan Williams premières during this period included *Job* at the Norwich Festival of 1930, and *Two Hymn Tune Preludes* at the 1936 Hereford Three Choirs Festival. Most years of the Three Choirs included at least one representative composition, and the meetings of the Norwich Festival during the 1920s always featured one.

The compositions by Vaughan Williams included at these festivals are nothing like the typical festival fare before 1910. In the years between 1920 and 1938, the major English festivals presented 19 scores by Vaughan Williams. If oratorios and cantatas were the typical English offering to the festival before 1910, Vaughan Williams's own compositional trends following the First World War weakened that tradition. The only oratorio included was the highly concentrated and concise *Sancta Civitas*, performed at the Worcester Three Choirs Festival of 1932. Several of Vaughan Williams's compositions on sacred texts were performed in the Cathedral as well, including *Four Hymns* at the 1920 festival in Worcester, the *Magnificat* for Contralto, Chorus and Orchestra at the 1932 Worcester meeting, *Two Hymn Tune Preludes* at Hereford in 1936, and two performances of the *Dona Nobis Pacem* just before the Second World War, in 1937 and 1938 at Gloucester and Hereford, respectively. These eight performances make up barely a third of the compositions by Vaughan Williams heard at these festivals. The remainder included compositions from a variety of genres: six performances of three different symphonies (the *London*, the *Pastoral* and *A Sea Symphony*); *The Shepherds of the Delectable Mountains* and excerpts from *The Poisoned Kiss*; as well as such works as *Job*, *Five Tudor Portraits*, and the Viola Suite. The 1910 première of the *Fantasia on a Theme by Thomas Tallis* was a harbinger of things to come.

But as a token of his festival success, the year 1910 stands unequaled in Vaughan Williams's career. In that year, he had two compositions premièred by major festivals, an occurrence that was not repeated for the rest of his life. After that year, Vaughan Williams had only four more festival première years, each presenting only a single new work. Further, in only five of the 22 years with festivals between 1911 and 1938 were there performances of more than one Vaughan Williams composition at the major festivals. And, surprisingly, Vaughan Williams was never commissioned by the nineteenth century's most prestigious festival, Birmingham.

The compositions by Vaughan Williams heard at English festivals were mostly ones premièred at other venues. Even *Sancta Civitas*, Vaughan Williams's ideosyncratic contribution to the genre of the English oratorio, was heard first at Oxford instead of one of the traditional festivals. As the trajectory of Vaughan Williams's own career demonstrates, the success and fame that a festival première brought a composer at the end of the nineteenth century was not nearly as important after the first quarter of the twentieth.

Vaughan Williams's own compositions for the 1910 Leeds and Three Choirs Festivals are the first major signs of the shift in this festival aesthetic. Both *A Sea Symphony* and the *Fantasia on a Theme by Thomas Tallis* moved away from the traditional choral genres so long celebrated at English musical festivals. In these works, Vaughan Williams responded to the critical pressure for British composers to turn from the familiar rut of producing disposable choral scores – a practice castigated as insular and derivative – to cultivate the more cosmopolitan instrumental genres. This process began with the gradual loosening of the definition of the kind of space in which instrumental music was presented at the festivals: first, breaking into the traditional morning sacred concerts at civic festivals; and, slightly later, breaking into the cathedral concerts at the Three Choirs Festivals. Commissioning of instrumental music, like Vaughan Williams's *Tallis Fantasia*, soon followed. The fundamental changes in music festivals after the First World War (the tragic decimation of male choristers as well as the eventual switch of active leisure-time musical activities such as singing to passive listening to radio) made this change more permanent and, ultimately, more devastating to the prestige and cultural value of English choral music than Vaughan Williams – or anyone else – could possibly have forseen in 1910.

Notes

1   In her biography of her husband, Ursula Vaughan Williams remarked on the importance of this year, noting especially that the commission of the *Tallis Fantasia* by the Three Choirs Festival admitted Vaughan Williams into 'a very special world of music'. See Ursula Vaughan Williams, *R.V.W.: A Biography of Ralph Vaughan Williams* (London, 1964), 88.

2   Edward Elgar is a case in point. Throughout the 1890s, Elgar produced a number of festival compositions, including an overture and four major vocal works (*Lux Christi*, *Scenes from the Saga of King Olaf*, *The Black Knight* and *Caractacus*), each of which built his reputation in amateur musical societies. Even after the opus 36 orchestral *Variations on an Original Theme (Enigma)* appeared in 1899 to great critical and public acclaim, Elgar still relied on the festival to promote his next three major compositions, oratorios that solidified his national and international fame. It was only after he achieved this level of notoriety (and he had created a repertoire that could be continually recycled at the festivals) that Elgar began producing his major body of instrumental work. The festival was also considered the most legitimate venue for the English composer. While Sullivan was initially famous for the light operettas written with W.S. Gilbert, he spent a great deal of time and effort in the last decades of his life presenting his oratorios and cantatas at festivals and conducting the Leeds Festival.

3   For a detailed description of Vaughan Williams's early instrumental works, see Michael Villancourt's 'Coming of Age: the Earliest Orchestral Music of Ralph Vaughan Williams', in *Vaughan Williams Studies* ed. Alain Frogley (Cambridge, 1996), 23–46.

4   Ursula Vaughan Williams, *R.V.W.*, 42.
5   In the first year of the Leith Hill competition, the Festival Committee, which included his sister Margaret, did try to pay Vaughan Williams five guineas for his services, but the composer refused even this sum: 'The Honorable Treasurer stated that in accordance with the resolution passed at the last meeting he had forwarded a cheque for £5.5.0 to Dr Vaughan Williams, who in reply, had written, sending a message to the Committee as follows – He was very grateful to them for their kind thought, but if they would allow him, he would ask a still greater favour – i.e. to be considered as part of the organization, in which case he could not receive a present, as it would be like giving a present to himself. He therefore returned the cheque, but was none the less grateful to them for the kind thought which prompted them to send it to him. It was always a great pleasure to him to do what he could for the [Leith Hill Musical Competition].' Leith Hill Musical Competition Minute-Book, Vol. I, p. 54 (minutes from the meeting held on 24 September 1906).
6   The review in the *Musical Times* noted that the première of *Toward the Unknown Region* 'establishes a high reputation for its young composer. It exhibits power to maintain due perspective on a large canvas, and to invest musical ideas with deep and impressive significance'. *Musical Times* (1 November 1907), 737.
7   Vaughan Williams was heavily indebted to his former teacher Parry for this compositional model. Parry used a similar device in his *Blest Pair of Sirens*. See Jeremy Dibble's *C. Hubert H. Parry: His Life and Music* (Oxford, 1992), esp. 255–8.
8   Byron Adams, 'Scripture, Church, and Culture: Biblical Texts in the Works of Ralph Vaughan Williams', in Frogley, ed., *Vaughan Williams Studies*, 103–4.
9   Following the continued success of the production of Mendelssohn's setting of the 42nd Psalm at English festivals, a number of psalm settings were either specifically commissioned or performed at festivals in the last few decades of the nineteenth century, including those of the 137th Psalm by Goetz and Oliver A. King (1882 and 1888, respectively); Ebenezer Prout's Psalm 126 (1891); E.H. Thorne's Psalm 57 (1887); and John E. West's Psalm 130 (1891). Foreign composers were also well represented in this sub-genre. Louis Spohr's 84th Psalm, first heard in England in 1847, was performed frequently at music festivals throughout the rest of the century.
10 Such was probably the object of the publishers. Breitkopf and Härtel issued a piano vocal score and a Tonic Sol-fa edition of *Toward the Unknown Region* in 1907. See Michael Kennedy's *A Catalogue of the Works of Ralph Vaughan Williams* 2nd edn (Oxford, 1996), 37.
11 Minute Book of the Managing Committee of the Leeds Festival, 1908–14, f. 16 (1 March 1909).
12 Ibid., f. 135 (22 June 1909).
13 Ibid., f. 138 (13 July 1909). In contrast, at the same festival Elgar received 100 guineas for conducting his first symphony, a composition premièred in 1908, and Rachmaninov was given 100 guineas to perform as a piano soloist. But this offer did in fact reflect that Leeds held Vaughan Williams in somewhat higher esteem, as he had only received 10 guineas for *Toward the Unknown Region* in 1907. Showing his usual generosity, Vaughan Williams eventually asked for only 20 guineas (ibid., f. 37 (19 July 1909) and 44 (28 July 1909)).
14 See Oliver Neighbour's 'The Place of the Eighth among Vaughan Williams's Symphonies' in Frogley, ed., *Vaughan Williams Studies*, esp. 214. Frank Howes attempts to make the case that despite the fact that the chorus is the work's underlying force, the composition is still symphonic because of the forms it uses throughout (see Howes, *The Music of Ralph Vaughan Williams* (Oxford, 1954), p. 3). Howes, like many analysts, relies on topicality only; he does not or cannot explain the lack of satisfying development

or the terse returns that occur throughout the composition. Calling the work a symphony is problematic. Even the critic from the *Musical Times*, when reviewing the first performance, felt it necessary to explain Vaughan Williams's chosen appellation: 'The Symphony deserves its title, because in the general form and relation of its four movements it has some relation to the classic symphonic plan' (*Musical Times*, 1 November 1910, 720). Note that both Howes and the early critics' descriptions rely only on general tenets. There is no detailed level of analysis or underlying philosophy within them. Further, there is some evidence that Vaughan Williams did not originally conceive of the work as a symphony *per se*. Ursula Vaughan Williams notes that an early title of the work was *The Ocean,* with no reference to the name 'symphony' whatsoever. The name was changed to *A Sea Symphony* by 1909, several years into its composition (Ursula Vaughan Williams, *R.V.W.*, 87–8).

15   Such passages appear in the first, second and fourth movements. In the first movement, examples may be heard between the baritone soloist and chorus to the words 'Of dashing spray' at H and further to 'And out of these a chant for the sailors of all' from 12 measures before M to U. Most of the second movement is call and response between the baritone soloist and the chorus, and selections of the fourth movement, from 'O thou transcendent' (R and following) include large passages of this texture between both soprano and baritone soloists and the chorus.

16   See, for instance, James Day's *Vaughan Williams*, 3rd edn. (Oxford, 1998), 36.

17   This was a typical device in festival choral compositions of the time, but one that Vaughan Williams was particularly suited to employ himself: the years he worked on *A Sea Symphony* overlapped with his editing of the *English Hymnal*. See Day, *Vaughan Williams*, 30–31.

18   Another interesting use of the organ to evoke the church occurs in the fourth movement, when the text turns to describe the individual who is the 'true son of God': the poet (cue H and following). Here, the chorus does not break into a marching hymn, but does pull into occasional homophony, and the organ's emphasis is extremely audible.

19   Like Howes, Elliot Schwartz unsuccessfully attempts to force *A Sea Symphony* into a rigid mold, calling the third movement a 'sonatine'. See his *The Symphonies of Ralph Vaughan Williams* (Amherst, 1964), 29.

20   Schwartz identifies three separate leitmotives used for this purpose. See his narrative description of the symphony, ibid., 21.

21   This was probably a conscious design on Vaughan Williams's part. During the work's long gestation, Vaughan Williams studied with Ravel, and embraced the idea that 'one should only develop for the sake of arriving at something better'. See Vaughan Williams's 'A Musical Autobiography' in *National Music and Other Essays*, ed. Michael Kennedy (Oxford, 1996), 191.

22   A similar compositional contour may be witnessed in Elgar's *Gerontius,* where the orchestra is given a much greater role in the composition, but the larger segments and even the smaller leitmotives all tend to spin down to slower rhythms before the next section ensues. See the present author's 'Epic Narration: the Oratorios of Edward Elgar', PhD thesis, Harvard University, 1998, esp. 159–73.

23   Other examples of cantatas with medieval subjects include Ethel Mary Boyce's *Young Lochivar* (1890) and *The Lay of the Brown Rosary* (1891) and the pseudo-Wagnerian *Sigurd* by Charles Brown (1890). The same is true for contemporary English oratorios not based on biblical excerpts: the most common subjects were either antique and medieval saints' lives, such as Frederick Hymen Cowen's *St Ursula* (1881); Alfred R. Gaul's *Joan of Arc* (1887); Frederick Arthur Gore Ouseley's *St Polycarp* (1854); and Joseph Smith's *St Kevin* (1885); or stylized tales, like Elgar's *Gerontius* and Walford Davies's *Everyman* that are understood to occur in a far-off, mythical time.

24   For a discussion of the evolution of festival programming, see McGuire, 'Epic Narration', 9–19.

25   See Daniel Lysons, John Amott, C. Lee Williams and H. Godwin Chance, *Origin and Progress of the Three Choirs of Gloucester, Worcester and Hereford, and of the Charity Connected with It* (Gloucester, 1895), 36 and 62 and Douglas J. Reid and Brian Pritchard's 'Some Festival Programmes of the Eighteenth and Nineteenth Centuries: 1. Salisbury and Winchester', *Royal Music Association Research Chronicle (RMARC)*, no. 5 (1965), esp. 57–61.

26   Adoption of the opening service occurred at different times at different festivals, as Pritchard noted in 'Some Festival Programmes of the Eighteenth and Nineteenth Century: 3. Liverpool and Manchester', *RMARC* no. 7 (1969), 1.

27   Birmingham had the only lasting civic festival with a town hall constructed after the festival's origin. City officials in Leeds founded its festival after the local town hall was built. In both cases, though, permanent interior renovations occurred to make festivals more convenient. Both had their seating plans redesigned, and permanent organs installed.

28   See for instance, Hugh Reginald Haweis's description of listening to oratorios in his memoir, *My Musical Memories* (New York, 1884), 211. When silence was not observed at an oratorio, it was thought to be a sign of poor breeding and irreverence. At a Glasgow concert of *Elijah* in 1865, an individual condemned applause at the oratorio as close to heresy: 'Conduct of this description shows a depraved taste, and a low appreciation of the nature of an Oratorio, which ought to minister to the highest and the holiest purposes, as that of Friday night was admirably adapted to, had it not been depraved of all the solemnity which belonged to it by the plaudits of a thoughtless multitude ... I, for one, must in future deny myself the pleasure of attending an Oratorio, so long as its solemn music and the sacred language of Holy Writ are converted, by a Glasgow audience, into a mere vulgar, not to say profane, entertainment.' *The Tonic Sol-fa Reporter*, January 1865, 4.

29   Sheffield's festival, founded in 1896 and proceeding triennially from 1896, was first held in the Sheffield Albert Hall, and moved to the City Hall following the First World War.

30   *The Times*, 9 October 1891, 3.

31   At this concert, there was no critical outcry in the main national or musical press.

32   Birmingham was a typical model of the incorporation of instrumental music at the English festivals of the eighteenth and nineteenth centuries. Other festivals, not having the permanency of the Three Choirs or Birmingham, can only provide glimpses of the varying tastes for instrumental music instead of a picture of its evolution within the festival. Most others began producing instrumental music in strictly secular concerts at around the same time and in the same manner: for instance, the Cambridge Festivals held in 1811 and 1812 included symphonies by Haydn and Gluck, the Oxford Festival of 1827 included a Symphony by Rombergand, an evening concert in the theater at the Manchester Festival of 1828 opened with a symphony by Beethoven (not identified) and began its second half with Weber's overture to *Der Freischütz*. Symphonies by Beethoven, Mozart, and the overture to Mendelssohn's *Midsummer Night's Dream* appear in concerts of the York Festival between 1823 and 1835. See Douglas J. Reid's 'Some Festival Programmes of the Eighteenth and Nineteenth Centuries: 2. Cambridge and Oxford', *RMARC* no. 6 (1966), 9–10, 21; Brian Pritchard's 'Some Festival Programmes of the Eighteenth and Nineteenth Centuries: 3. Liverpool and Manchester', *RMARC* no. 7 (1969), 19; and Pritchard and Reid's 'Some Festival Programmes of the Eighteenth and Nineteenth Century: 4. Birmingham, Derby, Newcastle Upon Tyne and York', *RMARC* no. 8 (1970), 20–22. Unfortunately, the listings in both of these articles are terse, and do not often give complete accounts of the miscellaneous programmes. The

authors do not state if this is the fault of the sources or an editorial decision on the part of the compilers.

33   Leeds was at the forefront of promoting a good deal of instrumental music to English audiences. At the 1895 Festival (Sullivan's penultimate one as its Music Director), Leeds presented symphonies by Mozart, Mendelssohn and Schumann; a symphonic poem by Massenet; an orchestral suite by German; overtures by Rossini and Mozart and Chopin's *Piano Concerto in E minor*.

34   J. Sprittles, 'Leeds Musical Festivals', in *Publications of the Thoresby Society: Miscellany*, vol. 13, part 2, no. 108 (1960), 226. Though it must be noted that only the Bach concerto may be considered a wholly secular work. Stanford's 'Last Post', a choral work setting W.E. Henley's poem dwells at length on God's acceptance of England's war-dead. Tchaikovsky's *Francesca da Rimini* was inspired by an episode in Dante's *Inferno*, providing at the very least an object lesson on avoiding the sin of lasciviousness.

35   For an example of a prayer service constructed around an oratorio, see McGuire, 'Epic Narration', 24–6. Nearly identical rites of service also exist for the Canterbury Cathedral Special Oratorio Services. Canterbury Cathedral Archives, UC 100/1/17A and 25.

36   Lysons et al., *Origin and Progress*, 276.

37   *Musical Times*, 1 September 1870, 587.

38   *The Times*, 26 August 1870.

39   *Musical Times*, 1 October 1873, 241. The critic of *The Times* expressed a similar sentiment, stating that Spohr's composition was 'more in place at a concert room than in a church' (*The Times*, 12 September 1873).

40   In 1881, Hereford presented Beethoven's Fourth symphony in the Cathedral. The *Musical Times*'s review of the concert noted that the work 'created an impression which we trust will lead to the performance of other purely instrumental works at future cathedral festivals' (*Musical Times*, 1 November no. 465, vol. 22, p. 511). The place of the symphony in the Cathedral was by no means assured at this point, but it was closer to acceptance.

41   For instance, the *Musical Times* review of Beethoven's Fourth Symphony at the 1882 meeting admonished the festival programmers for not placing the symphony in one of the evening secular concerts because of the Cathedral programme's length. See *Musical Times*, 1 October 1882, 539.

42   A similar practice existed at Canterbury Cathedral. From before 1899 to the beginning of the First World War, the Cathedral conducted a series of periodic 'Special Oratorio Services'. Between 1899 and 1901, only oratorios and orchestrally accompanied vocal works were presented (and the compositions included were rather conservative: Mendelssohn's *Lobegesang*, Stainer's *Crucifixion,* Handel's *Messiah*, Spohr's *The Last Judgment*, Gounod's *Redemption*, and Sullivan's *The Light of the World*). However, by January of 1901, movements from symphonies, performed by full orchestra, were used as 'voluntaries' before and after the services. For instance, a special oratorio service on 5 December 1901 ended with the fourth movement of Beethoven's Fifth Symphony. By 1903, the services presented symphonies whole: for instance, Brahms's Second Symphony was heard on 28 May of that year. Later, the cathedral authorities allowed works as diverse as Saint-Saëns's *Cello Concerto* to grace the services (27 February 1907). Canterbury Cathedral Archives, UC 100/1/17A–29.

43   C. Lee Williams, Godwin Chance and T. Hannam-Clark, *Annals to the Three Choirs of Gloucester, Hereford and Worcester: Continuation of History and Progress from 1895 to 1930* (Gloucester: Minchin and Gibbs, 1931), 23. The concert in question occurred at the 1898 Gloucester meeting.

44   Elgar did not complete this commission, and the 1899 Worcester Festival programmed another performance of *Lux Christi* instead. In a letter dated 11 November 1898 to his

friend August Jaeger, Elgar himself acknowledged the problem that such a symphony would have at the Three Choirs Festival: he anticipated reticence from the Dean and Chapter. See Jerrold Northrup Moore's *Edward Elgar: A Creative Life* (Oxford, 1985), esp. 256–7.

45 See, for instance, Frank Howes's *The English Musical Renaissance* (New York, 1966), esp. 129–62.

46 Both Sullivan and Stanford studied at the Leipzig Conservatory, and Stanford pursued further private studies with Freiderich Keil in Berlin. While Parry did not study abroad, he did take formal composition lessons with Edward Danreuther (after failing to garner tuition from Brahms).

47 Charles L. Graves, 'Musical England', in *Post-Victorian Music, with Other Studies and Sketches* (London, 1911; reprint, Port Washington and London, 1970), 364.

48 For a discussion of the perceived role of vocal music as a moral influence in Victorian society, see the present author's 'Music and Morality: John Curwen, Tonic Sol-fa and the Temperance Movement', in *Choruses and Choral Communities*, ed. Karen Ahlquist (forthcoming).

49 John Spencer Curwen, 'The Influence of Handel', from *The Tonic Sol-fa Reporter*, August 1880, 277.

50 At least some individuals publicly agreed with these sentiments. In an attempt to place the symphony above all other musical genres, Elgar stated that 'I hold that the Symphony without a programme is the highest development of art. *Views to the contrary are, we shall often find,* held by those to whom the joy of music come late in life to who would deny to musicians that peculiar gift, which is their own, a musical ear, or an *ear for music. I use,* as you notice, a very old-fashioned expression *but we all know what* it conveys: a love of music for its own sake.' Edward Elgar, *A Future for English Music*, ed. Percy Young (London, 1968), 207. Emphasis by Young and Elgar. At first glance, Elgar seems to be making a similar sort of hierarchical division between those who could appreciate instrumental music (trained musicians with definite skills) and a group of 'other' music appreciators who only discover music at a later time, and who used it for extra-musical purposes. This positioned instrumental music and those who value it over the vocal music practiced by many for the purpose of moral improvement, including many adherents of Tonic Sol-fa.

51 Ursula Vaughan Williams, *R.V.W.*, 88.

52 Lloyd was a 'favourite son' composer at the Three Choirs Festivals. He was the organist of Gloucester Cathedral from 1876 to 1882, and, as was tradition at the time, he conducted the Gloucester meetings in 1887 and 1880. Thereafter he took on a number of prestigious posts, including organist of Christ Church Cathedral in Oxford, as well as teaching organ and composition at the Royal College of Music. The Three Choirs Festivals premièred a significant number of his major compositions, including a *Festival Overture*, heard at the opening cathedral service at the 1898 Gloucester meeting.

53 Anthony Pople, 'Vaughan Williams, Tallis, and the Phantasy Principle', in *Vaughan Williams Studies*, ed. Frogley, 47–80. For the list of frequent characterizations of the composition, see esp. 50–56.

54 Ibid., 80.

55 Ibid., 48–9.

56 *Musical Times*, 1 October 1899, 669.

57 *Musical Times*, 1 October 1898, 660.

58 Williams et al., *Annals to the Three Choirs*, op. cit., pp. 33–4.

59 *Musical Times* (1 October 1910), 650.

60 Mellers, 49–50.

61 Ibid., 47.

62   For a description of the changes, see Moore (note 44), 374–5.
63   *The Yorkshire Post*, 20 November 1903.
64   See *And Choirs Singing: an Account of the Leith Hill Musical Festival, 1905–1985*, ed. Brian Tucker (Dorking, 1985), esp. 45–52.
65   See Marjorie Hunt and Mary Ray's *Petersfield Music Makers, Petersfield Monograph no. 3* (Horndean, 1986), 4.

Contributors

Byron Adams (b. 1955) earned a Bachelor of Music degree, magna cum laude, from Jacksonville University; he received a Master of Music degree from the University of Southern California; he received his doctoral degree from Cornell University, studying musicology with William Austin and composition with Karel Husa. Byron Adams's scholarly work was recognized when he was awarded the first Ralph Vaughan Williams Research Fellowship in 1985. He has published widely on the subject of twentieth-century English music, giving lectures and interviews on this topic over the BBC and at the 1995 National Meeting of the American Musicological Society. Articles and reviews by Professor Adams have appeared in *19th Century Music, Music and Letters, MLA Notes, Current Musicology* and *The Musical Quarterly*, as well as in *Vaughan Williams Studies* (1996), published by Cambridge University Press. Professor Adams has contributed four entries to the revised edition of the *New Grove Dictionary of Music and Musicians*, including those on Husa and Walton. In 2000, the Lesbian and Gay Study Group of the American Musicological Society bestowed the Philip Brett Award on Professor Adams for two essays dealing with the intersection of nationalism and homoeroticism in twentieth-century English music. Byron Adams is presently Professor of Composition and Musicology at the University of California, Riverside.

Renée Chérie Clark is a musicologist and Instructor of Music History at Western Kentucky University. Currently she is PhD-A.B.D. at the University of Illinois at Urbana-Champaign and is working toward completing her dissertation, *The Art Songs of Ralph Vaughan Williams: Musical Readings and National Identity*. In 1996 Ms Clark received the Ralph Vaughan Williams Fellowship and in 1998–9 she returned to England as a Rotary International Ambassadorial Scholar.

Walter Aaron Clark is an Associate Professor of Musicology at the University of Kansas. He is the author of *Isaac Albéniz: Portrait of a Romantic* (Oxford) and *Isaac Albéniz: A Guide to Research* (Garland), and he has edited a collection of essays entitled *From Tejano to Tango: Latin American Popular Music* (Routledge). He is currently writing a biography of Enrique Granados (Oxford).

Murray Dineen is an Associate Professor of Music Theory at the University of Ottawa. His research interests lie in the aesthetics and philosophy of music, in Schoenberg and the study of harmony, in cultural policy, and in the performance of music.

Daniel Goldmark is an Assistant Professor of Musicology at the University of Alabama in Tuscaloosa. He is currently at work on two books concerning the history and reception of music in Hollywood animated cartoons. He also spent five years as an editor and producer at Rhino Entertainment in Los Angeles.

Rufus Hallmark, Chair of the Department of Music, Mason Gross School of the Arts, Rutgers University, has written a number of detailed source-critical and analytical studies of the *lieder* of Schubert and Schumann and is the editor of *The German Lied in the Nineteenth Century* (Schirmer, 1996). Also active as a singer, Hallmark has performed many of the songs he has written about, including the *Songs of Travel*. He was awarded the Ralph Vaughan Williams Fellowship in 1995.

Nathaniel G. Lew received his PhD in the History and Literature of Music from the University of California, Berkeley. His scholarship examines the role of opera in twentieth-century British culture and the development of nineteenth-century Russian musical style. He is presently an Assistant Professor of Music at St. Michael's College, Colchester, Vermont.

Alison Sanders McFarland is an Assistant Professor of Musicology at Louisiana State University. She is the recipient of grants and fellowships, including the Fulbright fellowship and the Gladys Krieble Delmas fellowship, and she was the fifth Ralph Vaughan Williams Research Fellow. Her publications include articles and reviews in *Studi musicali*, *The International Journal of Musicology*, *Music and Letters*, and in *Early Music*.

Charles Edward McGuire is a scholar whose areas of expertise include music of Edward Elgar, Tonic Sol-fa and other Victorian sight-singing methods, the music festival, and the oratorio in the nineteenth and twentieth centuries. He is the author of *Elgar's Oratories: The Creation of an Epic Narrative* (Ashgate, 2002) and has published articles in *19th Century Music* and *The Elgar Society Journal*; and has given papers before the American Musicological Society, the Conference on Music in Nineteenth-Century Britain, and the Midwest Victorian Studies Association. He is currently Assistant Professor of Musicology at Oberlin Conservatory of Music.

Julian Onderdonk is a music historian specializing in twentieth-century British music and society. His PhD dissertation on Vaughan Williams's folk-song collecting was completed in 1998. He has taught at New York University, the Pennsylvania State University, Williams College, and now teaches in the Music History Department at West Chester University.

Stephen Town, Professor of Music at Northwest Missouri State University, Maryville, Missouri, was educated at the University of North Texas (B.M., M.M.) and Indiana University (D.M.). He has published research and reviews in the leading music journals of America encompassing eighteenth-, nineteenth- and twentieth-century music.

Robin Wells studied at the Royal College of Music, at Reading University and in Paris with Marcel Dupré. In 1965 he joined the music department at Charterhouse where he has taught the piano, the organ, keyboard skills, music history, analysis and composition. In 1987 he succeeded William Llewellyn as Director of Music at Charterhouse where in 2000 he was responsible for organizing with Byron Adams the week-long symposium 'RVW 2000'. One of his particular interests is the music of Herbert Howells, about whom he has written and lectured; in 1986 Wells was invited by Novello and Co. to edit the posthumous organ works of Howells. In addition to his position at Charterhouse, Wells has served on many local and regional committees and is known as a teacher, organist, conductor, examiner and composer.

Index

Note: Works by Vaughan Williams are indexed under their title. Other works are indexed under their composer. Abbreviation VW = Vaughan Williams.